BOOKS BY JAN KOTT

Shakespeare Our Contemporary

Theatre Notebook

The Eating of the Gods

THE EATING OF THE GODS

THE EATING
OF THE GODS

An Interpretation
of Greek Tragedy

JAN KOTT

Random House
New York

Translated by Boleslaw Taborski
and Edward J. Czerwinski

"The Vertical Axis," "Ajax Thrice Deceived," "The Veiled Alcestis," "The Bacchae," "Medea at Pescara" and "Orestes, Electra, Hamlet" were all translated by Boleslaw Taborski. "But Where Now Is Famous Heracles?" was translated by Edward J. Czerwinski. Portions of this book were first published in *Mosaic (Literature and Ideas)*, *Performance*, and *Theatre Quarterly*.

LIBRARY OF CONGRESS CATALOGING IN PUBLICATION DATA

Kott, Jan.
   The eating of the gods.

   Includes bibliographical references.
   1. Greek drama (Tragedy)—History and criticism.
I. Title.
PA3131.K613   882'.01   72–10585
ISBN 0–394–48119–4

Manufactured in the United States of America
First Edition

GRATEFUL ACKNOWLEDGMENT IS MADE FOR PERMISSION TO REPRINT LINES FROM THE FOLLOWING WORKS:

The Drama Review: "I Can't Get No Satisfaction," by Jan Kott, in *The Drama Review*, Vol. XIII, No. 1 (T-41), Fall 1968. Copyright © 1968 by The Drama Review. All rights reserved.

Alfred A. Knopf, Inc.: *The Myth of Sisyphus*, by Albert Camus, translated by Justin O'Brien. Copyright © 1955 by Alfred A. Knopf, Inc.

Methuen & Company Ltd.: "Ajax," translated by H. D. F. Kitto, from *Form and Meaning in Drama*, London 1956.

Penguin Books Ltd.: *The Iliad* by Homer, translated by E. V. Rieu. Copyright © 1966 by E. V. Rieu. *The Odyssey* by Homer, translated by E. V. Rieu. Copyright 1946 by E. V. Rieu.

Prentice-Hall, Inc.: *The Bacchae by Euripides: A Translation with Commentary*, by Geoffrey S. Kirk. Copyright © 1970 by Prentice-Hall, Inc.

University of Chicago Press: Pindar, *Nemean VI*, translated by Richmond Lattimore, 1947. *The Iliad of Homer*, translated by Richmond Lattimore, 1951. *The Complete Greek Tragedies, Euripides I; Alcestis*, translated by Richmond Lattimore, 1955. *The Complete Greek Tragedies, Sophocles I; Electra*, translated by David Grene, 1954. *The Complete Greek Tragedies, Aeschylus II; Prometheus Bound*, translated by David Grene, 1960. *The Complete Greek Tragedies, Sophocles II; The Women of Trachis*, translated by Michael Jameson, 1957; *Ajax*, translated by John Moore, 1957; *Philoctetes*, translated by David Grene, 1957. *The Complete Greek Tragedies, Euripides V; Electra*, translated by Emily Townsend Vermeule, 1959; *The Bacchae*, translated by William Arrowsmith, 1959. *The Complete Greek Tragedies, Euripides II; Heracles*, translated by William Arrowsmith, 1956.

University of Michigan Press: "Works and Days" and "Theogony" from *Hesiod*, translated by Richmond Lattimore. Copyright © 1959 by The University of Michigan.

JERZY STEMPOWSKI
In Memoriam

Preface

I started writing this book in Warsaw in 1966; I continued writing it at Yale and Berkeley, and completed it in Stony Brook. I discussed it in seminars and owe a great deal to the inspiration and criticism of my students. I am even more indebted to my colleagues and friends, who never spared either their harsh comments or their warm encouragement. The late Irving Ribner, a dear and close friend, always put his infallible scholarship at my disposal. For me his loss is irreparable. I spent many mornings and evenings with Ruby Cohn and Rose Zimbardo talking about written and unwritten chapters of this book. Kenneth Cavander and Leif Sjöberg looked over my manuscript, and I thank them for helping me to avoid numerous errors in my reading of Greek texts. But most of all I wish to express my appreciation for the inexhaustible kindness of Bernard M. W. Knox, who looked through a large part of this book, spared me lapses and mistakes, and whose suggestions and advice were of inestimable help.

From the very first plan of this book, Anne Freedgood looked after it warmly and solicitously, and with patience waited for its completion; thanks to her editorial efforts, *The Eating of the Gods* reached this final form.

The first and most faithful reader of this book, from the first to the last chapter, was my son-in-law, Karol Berger: I found in him a friend who helped to formulate my ideas and make them sharper and more precise.

I wish to express my gratitude to the Council and the Committee of the Research Foundation of the State University of New York for support which helped me in writing a part of this book during the summer of 1970.

I wrote this book in Polish, but it is hard to say when and where it will appear in my own language. The English text is the first and authorized edition.

J.K.
Stony Brook, June 1972

Contents

PREFACE   ix

The Vertical Axis, or The Ambiguities of Prometheus   *3*

Ajax Thrice Deceived, or The Heroism of the Absurd   *43*

The Veiled Alcestis   *78*

"But Where Now Is Famous Heracles?"   *109*

     I.   *The Faces of Heracles*   *109*

     II.   *Black Sophocles, or The Circulation of Poisons*   *124*

     III.   *"Oh to Be a Stone!"*   *147*

     IV.   Philoctetes, *or The Refusal*   *162*

The Eating of the Gods, or The Bacchae   *186*

APPENDICES   *231*

Medea *at Pescara*   *233*

Orestes, Electra, Hamlet   *240*

Lucian in Cymbeline   *268*

NOTES   *275*

INDEX   *325*

THE EATING OF THE GODS

The Vertical Axis, or The Ambiguities of Prometheus

I.

Gods are above, men are below. In his trilogy, Aeschylus placed Prometheus' agony upon one of the roofs of the world, a lone and empty peak in the mountains of the Caucasus. Prometheus was chained to a rock, then thrust to the bottom of Tartarus, the abyss below Hades. Prometheus' fall was physical and spectacular amid roars of thunder and flashes of lightning.[1] Performances began early at dawn and the spectators must have been shivering with cold in their seats when, in the first episode, the god Hephaestus announced that every night for ten thousand years Prometheus would wait for the morning sun to melt the frost on his body.

In Aeschylus' drama the entire cosmos takes part: the gods, men and the elements. This cosmos has a vertical structure: above, the seat of the gods and power; below, the place of exile and punishment. In the middle is the flat circle of the earth and the flat dish of the *orchestra* around it where the action unfolds. The vertical structure of the world with its definite functions, symbols and destiny, the above and the below, is one of the most universal and most perennial archetypes. "Hell, the center of the earth, and the 'gate' of the sky are then situated on the same axis, and it is along this axis that passage from one cosmic region to another was effected," writes Eliade in *Cosmos and History*.[2]

Genesis opens with the division into the above and the below: "In the beginning God created the heavens and the earth" (Gen. i.1). The Old Testament God speaks to prophets from above and prefers to summon them to the top of the mountain when demanding a sacrifice from them or announcing His will to them. "After these things God tested Abraham, and said to him, 'Abraham!' And he said, 'Here am I' " (Gen. xxii.1). The Ten Commandments are given to Moses by God at the top of a mountain. "And the Lord came down upon Mount Sinai, to the top of the mountain; and the Lord called Moses to the top of the mountain, and Moses went up" (Ex. xix.20).

This cosmic pillar, *axis mundi*, can most clearly be seen in Jacob's vision:

And he dreamed that there was a ladder set up on the earth, and the top of it reached to heaven; and behold, the angels of God were ascending and descending on it! And behold, the Lord stood above it and said, "I am the Lord . . ."

(Gen. xxix.12–13)

The succeeding chapters of cosmic drama in the Judaeo-Christian tradition are played out on the world's vertical axis, from the creation of man and the hurling of the rebellious angels into the abyss to Christ's Ascension and the Virgin's Assumption.[3] The final chapter, involving the rising of the dead and the Last Judgment, will also take place on the same *axis mundi*.

In Greek cosmogonies, too, in the beginning primeval Chaos was split into the above and the below. In the Pelasgian myth the Great Mother of All Things divided the heavens from the waters and hovered naked over the waters like the Spirit of God in Genesis. In Hesiod's *Theogony*, Mother Earth emerged first from Chaos and in sleep gave birth to Heaven:

But Gaia's first born was one who matched her every dimension,
Ouranos, the starry sky, to cover her all over,
to be unshakable standing-place for the blessed immortals.[4]

Olympus and Tartarus, the vertical axis of all myths, reward, punishment, and mediation, existed from the beginning of the world.[5] Zeus warns the gods in the *Iliad* that for disobedience they will be thrown "as far beneath the house of Hades as from earth the sky lies" (Book VIII, 16).[6] And so, the *axis mundi* is divided into three equal sectors, and the distance from earth to the bottom of hell is twice that of the distance from earth to heaven.

The same topocosm, the term introduced by Theodore H. Gaster in *Thespis* and used by Northrop Frye for his analysis of archetypal space structures in poetry,[7] is present in the ending of Plato's *Republic*, in the *Aeneid*, in *The Divine Comedy* and in *Paradise Lost*. But it appears in its purest form in painting. From the late Middle Ages to the end of the Baroque period, God is invariably placed at the top of the picture. Below are the Holy Family and descending choirs of seraphim and archangels. The angels in the middle part of the picture open the tombs and help those who are saved to climb upward. Devils push the damned downward, and the last of the nine circles of hell is at the very bottom of the picture.

The opposition of above and below has passed from cosmology and metaphysics[8] into the language of sociology and political rhetoric (upper, middle and lower class), and into psychology and psychoanalysis (superego, ego and id). The fall has two meanings, a literal and a symbolic one. Both occur in the Biblical account of the fall of the proud angels as well as in *The Fall* by Camus. The archetype is durable, but the values of the sign (positive—belonging to the "above," and negative —to the "below") can be reversed. Freud gave his *Interpretation of Dreams* this motto from Virgil: *Flectere si nequeo superos, Acheronta movebo.* The struggle of the below with the above is an image of rebellion.

Marx saw in the Paris Commune the "storming of the heavens." Revolutionary justice often employs the spatial image of "leveling," and it was not by chance that the Bible-educated Puritans of Cromwell, who wanted to introduce justice swiftly and thoroughly, called themselves "levelers."

Prometheus is crucified by the emissaries of the gods who have come from above to punish him for his excessive love for men who are below. Zeus is not seen, but it is to him that Prometheus directs his reproaches and threats—to him, and to men who are the audience. God and man are both parties in the drama. Prometheus is the accused; but the accused turns into the accuser, whereas in the *Oedipus* of Sophocles, it is the accuser who becomes the accused. Above, a political drama is being performed, and the rulers change. Below, men have emerged from their primeval animal condition. Men change; so do the forces of nature and the gods. The entire cosmos moves in time but still preserves its vertical structure, with Olympus, Tartarus and earth's flat (*orchestra*-like) circle in between. A topocosm moves in time, but a time that runs at different speeds for gods and for men. Gods are immortal, men mortal—*brotoi* who die but once. Emissaries of the gods derisively call them "ephemerids": for an ephemerid, a damselfly, one day is *all* time.

II.

Prometheus twice declares that his torture will last ten thousand years. The real time of the performance, from Prometheus' transfixion on the rocks of the Caucasus to his being hurled into the abyss, probably did not exceed an hour. The present—ten thousand years for Prometheus and one hour for the audience—is contained between the past and the future. The past at the gods' level began with the cosmos being split into the above and the below, whereas at men's level it was anthropology and the history of civilization. The present in *Prometheus* is the third chapter of the theogony, the beginning of the reign of Zeus:

> have I not seen two tyrants thrown? the third,
> who now is king, I shall yet live to see him
> fall.
>
> (*Prom.* 957–59)[9]

The two former tyrants are Uranus and Cronos. Cronos had castrated his father Uranus and was himself thrust into Tartarus by his son Zeus. Hesiod's and Aeschylus' theogonies seem not unlike an Elizabethan royal tragedy. Northrop Frye calls it the tragedy of the fall of the Prince or the tragedy of order. It has three actors: the King and Father, the Usurper who kills him, and the Revenger who performs the function of Fate.

The nemesis-figure is partly a revenger and partly an avenger. He is primarily obsessed with killing the rebel-figure, but he has a secondary function of restoring something of the previous order.[10]

Analogies are, however, fallacious. The notion of the primeval order and harmony of nature, whose images in the Middle Ages and the Renaissance were the heavenly firmament and the music of the spheres, does not exist in Aeschylus' theogony. Here the crucible changes at the same time as its contents. Theogony is also cosmogony. The *data* of nature and the *facta* of fortune, in Frye's juxtapositions, are one and the same. The cosmos is not yet set, not ready; the forces of nature are the progeny of the first gods and take part in their struggles. In divine genealogy Prometheus was the son of Gaea and one of the Titans. From Mother Earth he had received the gift of forecasting the future. In Zeus's conflict with Cronos, Prometheus first sided with the older generation of the gods. But his mother told him that the time when one could win by force was over, that the future belonged to those who would learn to use cunning:

> not by strength nor overmastering force
> the fates allowed the conquerors to conquer
> but by guile only.
>
> (*Prom.* 215–17)

Aeschylus' theogony is at the same time a somewhat bitter story of power. The cosmos is perfected by succeeding catastrophes, but tyrants go on ruling. Cronos had been too stupid to follow Prometheus' advice; Zeus realized "historical necessity," but as soon as he gained power he ruled even more cruelly. Might and Violence, Zeus's emissaries—the ironical high functionary of security organs and the silent guard—are watching the craftsman Hephaestus carefully perform his task of chaining Prometheus to the rock. The heavenly throne has been occupied by the third tyrant.

If the pattern of order lost and restored does not fit here, perhaps we can apply its opposite, called by Frye the tragedy of the sick society. The principal parts are allotted to the same actors, only the functions they perform are different. King the Father is Father the Tyrant. The two most frequent descriptions of Zeus in *Prometheus Bound* are Father and Tyrant.

There is no order-figure: the head of the state is as bad as everyone else, and the only action we feel much in sympathy with is that of revenge—revenge on him, usually. In a society that is evil, cruel, sick or repressive, the hero is likely to be crushed simply because he is a hero. In the tragedies of order the action focusses on a rebel whose fortune is too big for nature. In tragedies of a sick society the central figure is often a victim, and the victim's nature is too big for his fortune.

The rebel is at the same time a victim; he dies in order to make room for an avenger who executes the will of destiny. But destiny mocks: Frye calls it "a nemesis of misrule."[11]

The "pure" structures of the tragedy of order and the tragedy of corruption are in essence one and the same. The use of one or the other scheme seems, even in the case of Shakespeare, to depend only on interpretation. In order to become king one must kill the king, or at any rate the pretenders to the throne. But to kill the king or the pretenders to the throne means, in turn, to be killed by their sons or friends. In *King John, Richard II* and *Richard III* the behavior and fate of the legal rulers are not very different from what befalls the usurpers. Their successors—Henry III, Henry IV, even Richmond, later Henry VII—are no less ironic instruments of "fate" than Marlowe's fearful Edward II. The wheel of fortune is turned by the wind of civil war. If the royal roundabout is turned by nature, it is only the nature of power and force. Sometimes the use of the model of the tragedy of order, or again the tragedy of anarchy, depends on the choice of the initial moment. *Hamlet* is a tragedy of order —if we regard the poisoning of King Hamlet by Claudius as the first link in the chain of events. Old Hamlet will then be the good king and father, Claudius the usurper, Prince Hamlet the instrument of fate. But if the first link in the chain is seen as the duel of old Hamlet and old Fortinbras, then the original order never existed. Claudius is then the lord "of misrule," Hamlet the rebel and victim, young Fortinbras the figure of nemesis. To Ophelia and Laertes, Hamlet is the killer of their father; to Fortinbras, he is the son of his father's killer. We know next to nothing about Fortinbras. Nemesis walks over corpses, is ambiguous and jeering.

Zeus is a tyrant, Prometheus a rebel and victim, while Zeus's as yet unborn son is the figure of fate. The future is foretold—but there are two contradictory forecasts. There is talk about not one but two as yet unborn sons of Zeus. The first of them is the Nemesis of restored order, the other the Nemesis of revenge. In the first episode, Hephaestus tells Prometheus: "Always the grievous burden of your torture will be there to wear you down, for he who shall cause it to cease has yet to be born" (25–27). The liberator-son will restore the broken alliance between Zeus and Prometheus; his coming will be the end of the era of terror. The tyrant will become father again,

> hastily he'll come
> to meet my haste, to join in amity
> and union with me—one day he shall come.
>
> (*Prom.* 193–95)

The first prediction foretells the solution of the conflict; the other foretells the repetition of a cycle which
had begun with the overthrow of Uranus by his son
Cronos. In union with a woman, Zeus will beget a "son
stronger than father." The wheel of power will turn yet
again. Zeus will be thrust into Tartarus by his son, like
his father and his father's father. The tyrant will come to
know the difference between power and slavery.

> CHORUS:
> You voice your wishes for the God's destruction.
>
> PROMETHEUS:
> They are my wishes, yet shall come to pass.
>
> CHORUS:
> Must we expect someone to conquer Zeus?
>
> PROMETHEUS:
> Yes; he shall suffer worse than I do now.
>
> (*Prom.* 928–31)

But the future of the cosmos continues to be unresolved.
The dramatic action consists in Prometheus' refusal to
reveal to Zeus the secret of the future by naming the
woman who will bear him the avenger-son. Aeschylus'
cosmogony is highly dramatic, as theatre and as philosophy. Zeus is all-powerful, Prometheus knows the future.
On the prisoner depends the future of the tyrant. This
opposition sets the cosmos in action. Force is limited by
lack of knowledge; knowledge is limited by force.[12]

Who is free? Only he who has no one else above him,
says Might, the high police official who assists at Prome-

theus' torture: "There is nothing without discomfort except the overlordship of the Gods. For only Zeus is free"
(49 ff.). But Zeus has no power over the future. Necessity
is stronger than the strongest. "Against necessity,
against its strength, no one can fight and win" (103).
Necessity is stronger than he who suppresses the rebellion and stronger than he who rebels. "Craft is far
weaker than necessity," Prometheus confesses with bitterness (513). *Techne* is both art and technique, practical
activity, an imprint of mind on matter, and so the changing of the world. Necessity is stronger than both the man
who changes the world and the one who resists change,
stronger than the changer and the matter being changed.
What, then, is Aeschylean necessity?

CHORUS:
Who then is the steersman of necessity?

PROMETHEUS:
The triple-formed Fates and the remembering Furies.

CHORUS:
Is Zeus weaker than these?

PROMETHEUS:
Yes, for he, too, cannot escape what is fated.

'(*Prom.* 515–18)

The three Moiras and the Furies seem here to be more
than mere traditional mythological figures. In the Aeschylean cosmos, split into the above and the below, a
cosmos in constant flux, even destiny is antithetic.
Moiras weave the thread of time; Furies are memory,
relentless and inflexible. In the Greek topocosm, Moiras
were placed at the very pinnacle of the heavenly structure; the Furies were the deities of the underground.
Moiras and Furies seem to be images of two different
"necessities." The Furies were deities of revenge, of pay-

ing for blood with blood, for death with death, and so they saw to it that the cycle was repeated. The white Moiras are measures of time—*moira* means a share or a phase. Moiras are bound neither by memory nor by the duty of revenge. They are of necessity free from repeating the past. "Time in its aging course teaches all things," Prometheus says (981). But it seems that Moiras and Furies depict, as it were, two different notions of time: historic time, which is unidirectional, and mythic time, which is cyclic. In the *Prometheus* of Aeschylus we have both times.[13]

In this realistic cosmogony, fate is, as it were, built in. Within the structure, movement results from the cosmos having been split into the above and the below. Necessity is not above Zeus and Prometheus, rather—as Hegel would have said—it is in their opposition. This necessity is paradoxical in that one of its components is awareness. The awareness of necessity changes necessity. The choice of necessity depends on Prometheus, and is his tragic choice.

Earthly time and time for the gods are of different kinds and run at different speeds. But when a god unites in an embrace with a woman and begets a son by her, both times cross each other in close-up as on a television screen. The liberator-son is to be born of Zeus's union with a woman, of Io's progeny in the thirteenth generation. The thirteen generations are measured in human time. But before the son is born, divine time and human time will cross each other once more.

Prometheus tells Oceanus about Zeus's cruel revenge over the vanquished Titans. Atlas had been condemned to support the firmament of heaven on his shoulders. The giant Typhoeus of a hundred heads from which he had emitted fire and stones had been crushed by the slopes of Etna. The undaunted Titan will rebel once more, and in anger at Zeus will emit streams of lava.

Commentators on the whole have taken the view that the story of Typhoeus is an unnecessary show of poetic virtuosity and a mythological interpolation. It seems, however, that Aeschylus deliberately wanted to mingle earthly time with that of the gods. The famous eruption of Etna took place in 479 B.C., a year after the battle of Salamis and less than twenty-five years before *Prometheus* was staged. Aeschylus brought cosmic time nearer to the present of the audience.

The Promethean cycle, like Aeschylus' *Oresteia,* comes to its close on the threshold of Athenian history. In the *Eumenides,* the last part of the *Oresteia,* all conflicts are resolved: between the gods of the sky and the gods of the underground, between patriarchate and matriarchate, between law and revenge, between *polis* and family bonds. The *Oresteia* ends with the calling of the tribunal at the Areopagus, and taken as a whole, it is an "optimistic tragedy." But in the final part of the *Eumenides* there is no longer any human drama; discussion is carried on by ideas dressed in costume. This may be the reason why Hegel liked the play so much. The Promethean trilogy probably ended with the reconciliation of the protagonists and the establishment of the cult of Prometheus and Heracles in Athens. But the first and the third parts of the trilogy are lost. The present of Prometheus' torture is still our time. The future continues to be two-horned, like the Turkish moon. Above, the time of unlimited terror goes on; below, still "craft is far weaker than necessity."

III.

There is no paradise lost on any level of the Aeschylean topocosm, nor in either of its times. Prometheus was motivated by pity for the misery of mankind whom he compared to ants crawling in the crevices of the earth. When Zeus came to power he did nothing for men; he even contemplated their extinction and substitution by a new race of beings. It was then that Prometheus stole the fire from the gods, carrying off hot ash in a hollow stalk of fennel in order not to scorch his hands. In the Greek islands peasants even today carry fire in the pith of a giant fennel. One thing is worth noticing in this rough anthropology of progress: the emergence from the natural state begins by arousing the capacity for rational thinking. "I found them witless and gave them the use of their wits and made them masters of their mind" (442 ff.). Or in a more precise rendering, "I made them into rational beings," distinguishing *ennous* (in control of one's faculties) from *eike* (referring to precivilized chaos). Before, "they handled all things in bewilderment and confusion," "all their doings were indeed without intelligent calculation" (447, 453).[14]

Civilization has its origins in the analysis of perceptions, in the discovery of a visual and aural code. "For men at first had eyes but saw to no purpose; they had ears but did not hear" (445). Only now are they for the first time capable of foretelling and discovering the time of the stars. "For them there was no secure token by which to tell winter nor the flowering spring nor the summer with its crops; . . . until I showed them the rising of the stars, and the settings, hard to observe" (451 ff.). Astronomy is the first awareness of topocosm in cyclic movement.

But more astonishing is the next step in man's education. Prometheus taught men figures and letters.[15]

Καὶ μὴν ἀρχϑμόν, ἔξοχον σοφισμάτων,
ἐξηῦρον αὐτοῖς, γραμμάτων τε συνϑέσεις,
μνήμην ἁπάντων, μουσομήτορ ἐργάνην.

(*Prom.* 459–61)

(Literally: And moreover number I discovered, outstanding among clever inventions, and the arrangements of letters, the remembering of all things, the tool of the creative mind.)

What is striking here is the very clear awareness of the instrumental, operative function of numerals and letters.[16] *Sophismata* are means and instruments, clever tricks and devices; *grammaton de suntheseis* indicates a kind of theory of combinations, arranging words from individual letters. Prometheus invented the symbolic sign, that is to say he distinguished between that which signifies and that which is signified. The number system and symbolic alphabet are *mnemen hapanton,* the remembering of all things, which enable one to repeat the world and set it in order intellectually. Prometheus' discourse on the origins of civilization seems amazingly close to Jean-Jacques Rousseau's *Discours sur l'origine et les fondements de l'inégalité parmi les hommes* (1776), published twenty-two centuries later and called by Lévi-Strauss "without doubt the first anthropological treatise in French literature."[17] For Rousseau, as for Aeschylus, the transition from nature to culture, from the animal to the human state, is the birth of intellect. The state of society is the "state of reasoning." In his celebrated *Discours* he writes:

This repeated attention of various beings to themselves and to each other must naturally have engendered in man's mind the perception of certain relations. The relations which we express by the words big and little, strong and weak, fast and slow, bold and fearful, and other such ideas which we compared as occasion demands and almost without thinking about them, eventually produced in man a kind of reflection, or rather an automatic prudence which indicated the precautions most necessary to his safety.

In the anthropology of Aeschylus' Prometheus, observation of the stars has preceded the invention of the system of natural numbers and the alphabet. Only later come practical skills and the beginnings of the history of material culture: the breeding and training of beasts of burden like the yoke oxen, harnessing horses to a cart, launching ships to sail the sea. Carts had to be preceded by the invention of the wheel, sailing by an analysis of direction; so of necessity the elements of astronomy and geometry originated earlier than the cart and the vessel.

In the next chapter of the history of civilization, medicine was to be combined with the art of divination. The Aeschylean Prometheus teaches men to prepare medicines which cure all diseases "by the blendings of mild simples" and to divine the future from the color of the intestines of slaughtered animals. "It was I who set in the order the omens of the highway and the flight of crooked-taloned birds, which of them were propitious or lucky by nature, and what manner of life each led, and what were their mutual hates, loves and companionships" (488 ff.). Divination was practical knowledge, systematics based on experience, a kind of prescientific natural history. Prometheus (whose name literally means "he who knows in advance," "forethought") taught people to foresee things. Medicine and divination were the same art of foreseeing, almost in the sense of meteorological forecasts.[18] The history of progress is completed with the discovery of the technology of metals, the working of copper, iron, silver and gold: "all arts that mortals have come from Prometheus" (506). But the origin of all was fire, "the teacher of each craft to men" (111).[19]

One question that comes to mind is why Aeschylus, in this exposition of anthropology, did not mention the fact that Prometheus had to teach men cooking also? Before the discovery of fire, men had known only raw food.

After Lévi-Strauss's great cultural mythology, *Le Cru et le Cuit (The Raw and the Cooked)*, one must be struck by the similarity of the Promethean myth to the culinary myths preserved by "savage thought." *"D'une certaine manière, les mythes se pensent entre eux"* (The thinking processes were taking place in the myths in their reflections upon themselves and their interrelation), writes Lévi-Strauss in his "Ouverture."[20] In the myths on food preparation of South American Indians, particularly the *gé* and *bororo* myths, the jaguar appears, as the brother-in-law and friend of man, to whom he has brought fire. Fire here, as in the Promethean myth, is connected with passing from nature to culture. Like Prometheus, the jaguar is the "giver of the arts of civilization." In mythological consciousness, preparing dishes is a "mediation" activity. In its literal sense, cooking requires the mediation of water and utensil; to cure food in smoke requires the mediation of air. In its symbolic sense, preparing dishes is a "mediation activity between heaven and earth, life and death, nature and society." Death means decay; the mediation of fire preserves food from decay. The South American culinary myths *gé* and *sherenté* are really cosmological myths. This meta-myth says: if the sun goes too far away from earth the whole world will decay; if the sun comes too near the world will burn. The culinary myth about the jaguar, the giver of fire, turns out to be a myth about relations between the above and the below in the topocosm.

"Les mythes se pensent entre eux." It may well be that Prometheus' mysterious words, "I hunted out the secret spring of fire" (109), recall a fragment of a lost layer of the myth—in the retrieval of which we may be helped by man's good brother-in-law, the jaguar from South America. In Hesiod's *Theogony* there is one link of the Promethean myth which Aeschylus rejected. There Prometheus is punished not for having stolen fire and given it to the

human race, but for another insult to Zeus. When it came to offering sacrifices, he slaughtered an ox and divided it into two parts. He put the bones together and covered them carefully with a layer of white suet. He then separated the best parts of the meat and covered them with stomach membrane. He left the choice to Zeus. The lord of heaven cheated himself: attracted by the fat, he got the bones. "Ever since that time the races of mortal men on earth have burned/the white bones to the immortals on the smoky altars" (556–57). The angry Zeus took fire away from men. "Let them eat their flesh raw!" shouts Zeus in the ironic *Dialogues of the Gods*.[21] Perhaps Lucian was right in his interpretation of the culinary sense of this myth. If Zeus punished men by making them eat raw meat, they must previously have roasted or smoked it.

This part of the myth apparently seemed unnecessary, or even unintelligible, to Aeschylus. Only a trace of it remains. In the speech about medicine and divination Prometheus adds that he taught men how to recognize the colors of intestines that would please the gods, "and the dappled beauty of the gall and lobe" (494). The Prometheus of Aeschylus not only taught men how to offer sacrifices to the gods but introduced animal sacrifices. In later versions of the myth, this tradition persists very clearly: *"Prometheus bovem primus occidit,"* writes Pliny in *Natural History* (VII, 209). Prometheus, who first slaughtered the ox, taught men to eat meat.[22] To eat it, and therefore to prepare it too.

Like the jaguar in the *gé* and *bororo* myths, Prometheus becomes involved in culinary operations. And, just as in the mythology of South American Indians, three elements intermingle: the gift of fire, the mediation between men and gods, the offering of sacrifices and cooking of food. It is possible that in a lost version of the myth there were also the oppositions between raw and cooked, roasting and smoking, which are essential to Lévi-

Strauss. Prometheus burned the bones as a sacrifice to the gods—but what did he do with the meat he gave to men? The jaguar taught men to smoke meat as well. When he himself was burned later in the fire, tobacco leaves were dried in the smoke.

In Hesiod's *Works and Days,* men had fire at the beginning, but Zeus took it away from them, in order to force them to work (42 ff.). In the beginning was Paradise. Paradise is a full larder.[23] In this realistic poem on the life and occupations of the farmer and cattle-breeder, a poem abounding in sober and practical instructions which do not leave much room for the imagination, there is the odd image of an oar hung over the smoking fireplace. In the *Odyssey,* guests are first offered a jug of water and a basin, then bread, smoked sheep cheeses and dishes full of meat, all brought from the pantry. The meat goes bad quickly, and in order to preserve it the intervention of fire is essential. The meat is smoked, hanging on long rods over the fireplace. It would seem that in *Works and Days* yet another fragment survives of the original culinary myth of Prometheus, who, like the South American jaguar, taught men to smoke meat.

> Soon you could have hung up your steering oar
>   in the smoke of the fireplace,
> and the work the oxen and patient mules do
>   would be abolished.

> (*Works and Days,* 45–46)

"*Les mythes se pensent* entre eux." "Therefore the Lord God sent him forth from the garden of Eden, to till the ground from which he was taken. He drove out the man; and at the east of the garden of Eden he placed the cherubim, and a flaming sword which turned every way, to guard the way to the tree of life" (Gen. iii.23–24). The expulsion from Paradise means taking away the fire which prevents food from going bad. In *Works and Days,* Prometheus takes the fire away from Zeus and gives it back to men again. But as in the Bible, so in Hesiod, Paradise has already been lost, and forever. Hesiod's version of the Promethean myth seems, at least on the surface, contradictory to that of Aeschylus. In *Works and Days,* the taking away of fire is the origin of the labors of men, who ever after shall till the soil in the sweat of their brow. In *Prometheus* all inventions and the progress of civilization begin with the gift of fire. As Lévi-Strauss points out, even when mutually contradictory, myths nevertheless explain and complement one another; they are the same basic human experience told in different ways, transmitted on different levels of historic consciousness. In Hesiod as in Aeschylus, the myth of stolen or given fire is connected with the end of the state of nature and the beginning of culture. And only now can one ask the most important question: What manner of civilization do myths describe?

Anthropology distinguishes between "cold" and "hot" civilizations. The "cold" civilizations have no history, or as Lévi-Strauss writes, "are history without history." Resisting all changes, time in them is cyclic, measured by the succession of night and day, the seasons and the movements of the stars. The constellation of Pleiades in Hesiod, as in the myths of South American Indians, forecasts the coming of drought.[24] "Hot" civilizations are antagonistic, divided into the rulers and the ruled; events that occur in them are irreversible; time is unidirectional "piling up the discoveries and inventions to build great civilizations."[25] Myths operate, as it were, on the vertical axis of topocosm; they are a cyclic mediation between the above and the below, between heaven and earth. Aeschylus' topocosm has its above and its below, but these function in unidirectional time. The original myth of the thief and giver of fire continues to function on the vertical axis of topocosm, but at the same time this myth fulfills a new function and is immersed in "hot" history. Aeschylus' *Prometheus* is *still* a myth, but *already* a tragedy.

"In Greek tragedy," writes Northrop Frye, "the gods have the function of enforcing what we have called the primary contract of man and nature. The gods are to human society what the warrior aristocracy is to the workers within human society itself." Gods are above, men are below. But, at the same time, in the topocosm of *Prometheus,* above is the order of power, below the order of civilization. Above, sons deprive fathers of their thrones and new tyrants continually change places. Below, invention follows invention and the progress of civilization is constant, uninterrupted. It is a sober and realistic point of view: *techne,* the development of human skills, is cumulative, unidirectional and evolutionary. All rulers are alike and every authority contains the potential danger of tyranny. Progress exists below, but does not exist above. In Aeschylus' anthropology, a particularly interesting phenomenon is the characteristic acceleration (or rather approximation) of time on both levels, above and below, to the present time of the audience witnessing the tragedy. Mythological time becomes historic time.

In the history of civilization, as told by Prometheus to the chorus, special emphasis is put on "intelligent calculation" which is generally recognized as the particular attribute of the Athenians. Γνώμη, the intelligent capacity for making distinctions and choices, was generally considered by Greek philosophers to be the quality that distinguished men from the animals. "They did everything without intelligence" (ἄτερ γνώμης) (456), says Prometheus about the human ants before the discovery of fire. It is possible that Aristotle had Prometheus in mind when he proposed as the definition of man "the creature which knows how to count."[26] Prometheus in Aeschylus has the sting and intellectual perversity of the new generation of philosophers. No wonder that toward the end of the play Hermes reproaches him for being a sophist: "You, *subtle-spirit*, you/bitterly overbitter, you that sinned/against the immortals" (944–46).

The "above" was even nearer to Greek present time. The memory of past tyrants must have been even fresher than in the times of Euripides, and the fear of tyranny's return never left Athens. Aeschylus himself, for that matter, knew tyranny from his own experience, having spent fifteen years in Syracuse at the court of the Sicilian tyrant.

> For new are the steersmen that rule Olympus:
> and new are the customs by which Zeus rules,
> customs that have no law to them,
> but what was great before he brings to nothingness.
>
> (*Prom.* 148–51)

In the now classic study of *Prometheus* by Thomson, and in the more recent one by Podlecki, it has been shown with precision to what extent Aeschylus' Olympus was presented in the categories and terms of fifth-century political thought.[27] "Violence and pride," says the Chorus in *Oedipus Rex*, "engender the 'tyrannos.' " *Kratos* and *Bia*, the Controller and the Executive, as Havelock calls them,[28] assist in the crucifying of Prometheus. "Might and Violence, in you," Hephaestus tells them, "the command of Zeus has its perfect fulfilment." The authority of Zeus is new—he has only just captured Cronos' throne. And Hephaestus adds, "Every ruler is harsh whose rule is new" (35). Aeschylus believed that time blunts the severity of the tyrant. Our own experiences are more sobering: we know well that in his old age the tyrant becomes even more suspicious and cruel. Zeus was cruel and suspicious from the moment he assumed power. He behaved in accordance with the advice Machiavelli would give the Prince almost twenty centuries later. Zeus first wiped out his enemies, then he turned against the friends who had helped him to bring down his predecessor.

> This is a sickness rooted and inherent
> in the nature of a tyranny:
> that he that holds it does not trust his friends.
>
> (*Prom.* 224–26)

The tyrant stands above the law and time-honored customs. Zeus ruled by decrees issued ad hoc, decrees which Aeschylus called "private law." The Chorus speaks like Herodotus, when he accused the tyrants:

> This is a tyrant's deed; this is unlovely,
> a thing done by a tyrant's private laws,
> and with this thing Zeus shows his haughtiness
> of temper toward the Gods that were of old.
>
> (*Prom.* 402–5)

Below are the people; above at the tyrant's court, in the celestial fortress ("the tower in which you live," 956),[29] everybody is related to everyone else by blood or marriage. There relationships are half family, half feudal. There is the king the father, his sons and bastards, the princes. Oceanus is Prometheus' father-in-law, Hephaestus his cousin. "Our kinship," he explains to Might, "has strange power; that, and our life together" (39). In this "sociological" reading, Prometheus is a rebellious representative of the old aristocracy, and as such is extinguished by the new ruler. The aristocracy of the Greek *polis* represented the staunchest opposition to the tyrants, and the aristocrats were their first victims.

The strength of Aeschylus lies in the incomparably concrete manner in which he represents tyranny. The atmosphere on that desolate, wind-swept rock in the Caucasus is as stuffy as in a dungeon. And I am not surprised that Jonathan Miller, when producing *Prometheus,* in Robert Lowell's adaptation at Yale, set the scene in the courtyard of a Renaissance palace, a courtyard deep as a well. The palace walls enclosed the scene at the rear, high at the top of which was a portico full of statues of the gods. In this kingdom of terror fear paralyzes everyone—except Prometheus and the Chorus. Fear disrupts bonds of blood and friendship. Young princes, like Hermes, are errand boys and flunkeys of the ruler. Old princes, like Oceanus, have long ago given up all resistance; they delude themselves into believing that although they have lost all remnants of dignity, they have at least kept their wits; like discredited politicians, they believe in compromise but are afraid of everything and are ready to do anything that would please the ruler. It is not enough to obey the ruler; one must love him, even when one is in prison. Might, the high police official, explains this in a matter-of-fact way. Prometheus must "learn," he says, "to endure and like the sovereignty of Zeus" (10). Nor is it enough merely to punish the ruler's enemies; one must also hate whomsoever the ruler hates. This time it is a lesson for Hephaestus: "Why is it that you do not hate a God whom the Gods hate most of all?" (36). And again, a little later: "But to turn a deaf ear to the Father's words—how can that be?" (40). The police officials like best of all to call the tyrant "Father."

Number One is not seen, but his physical presence can be felt from the opening scene to the last. Every word spoken on the lonely rock is reported back to the father, every word is listened to. Above, successive tyrants assume power in their turn, and the time "of unlimited torture" continues uninterrupted. Below, the ants have learned to cook, write and count, build houses, send ships out on the water, melt metals. In this rough anthropology, politics and *techne*—the history of power and the history of material culture—are rigidly separated from each other. Progress is irrevocable, but force also is unalterable. Myth functions on the vertical axis of topocosm. Myth is the mediation between heaven and earth. In *Prometheus Bound,* mediation will not take place. The play ends with an earthquake.

IV.

Men obtained fire from Prometheus. In the first *stasimon* of the Chorus in *Antigone,* men have learned everything themselves. "Speech, and thought swift as the wind, and a temper that enables him to live in communities, all these he has taught himself."[30] Gods receive no mention, with the exception of Earth, Mother of All. But earth is tilled here, year after year, by man who harnessed horses to a plow. "And earth, oldest of the gods, indestructible, inexhaustible, he wears down as his plows move back and forth year after year, turning the soil with the breed of horses" (335 ff.).

Hesiod's and Aeschylus' theogonies have often been seen as opposed to the anthropocentric quality of man's apologia in Sophocles. Man is here alone, there are no gods, and he is indebted to himself for everything. "He snares the tribe of light-witted birds, the nations of wild beasts, the salt life of the sea, takes them in his net-woven meshes, man the intelligent" (342 ff.). But it is not the anthropocentric quality that seems most important here. In this Chorus, which precedes the bringing in of Antigone after she has tossed a handful of earth on her brother's naked body, the praise of human greatness is combined with anxiety: "Many are the wonders and terrors, and nothing more wonderful and terrible than man" (332 ff.). *Deina* is a wonderful and terrible phenomenon ("miracle" and "wonder" have both these meanings); man is *deinotaton*, the stranger, the alien and the alienated. Strongest and most ingenious of creatures, he is "alienated" from the nature he has harnessed; he can also be alienated from the city he has built, he can even be alienated from himself. *Hypsipolis* and *apolis* (370), "high in his city" and "stateless." His fatherland is a no man's land. His rapacity is boundless; he can change the future. Only for death has he found no remedy (see 358 ff.). Martin Heidegger was the first to analyze this anxiety of human existence in the Chorus of *Antigone* as being part of man's condition:

> Everywhere journeying, inexperienced and without issue, he comes to nothingness.
> Through no flight can he resist
> the one assault of death,
> even if he has succeeded in cleverly evading
> painful sickness.[31]

How close this is to Hamlet's soliloquy:

> What a piece of work is man! How noble in reason! how infinite in faculties! in form and moving, how express and admirable! in action how like an angel! in apprehension, how like a god! the beauty of the world! the paragon of animals! And yet, to me, what is this quintessence of dust? Man delights not me—
>
> (II, ii, 299–304)

If awareness is a "hole in being" in the Sophoclean theatre of cruelty, the hole destroys both being and itself. There is much that is strange, but nothing is stranger than man.

The realistic and historical anthropology of material culture and the rule of force in *Prometheus* seem utterly remote from the existentialist vision of the human condition in the first *stasimon* of *Antigone.* Yet fire was but the second gift of Prometheus to men—the first was far more mysterious.

PROMETHEUS:
I caused mortals to cease foreseeing doom.

CHORUS:
What cure did you provide them with against that sickness?

PROMETHEUS:
I placed in them blind hopes.

CHORUS:
That was a great gift you gave to men.

(*Prom.* 250–53)

In the preface to his translation of *Prometheus Bound,* David Grene connects these "blind hopes" with the myth quoted by Plato in the *Gorgias.* In the early days of Zeus's rule, men knew in advance the day of their death and were still alive when they stood before their judges, fully clothed and with all their possessions. Since this led to many abuses, Zeus abolished the custom. Aeschylus used this myth for his own ends. Animals know the hour of their death. Prometheus brought men out of the animal state; he took from them mere animal reason and gave them human reason. He freed them from fear and gave them "blind hopes."

The uncertainty of death is better than its certainty. This is understood by all those who have been told they have a terminal illness. Grene's interpretation is humane and subtle; but the Aeschylean Prometheus, the "one who looks ahead," was the one who knew and wanted to know.

> I have known all before,
> all that shall be, and clearly known.
>
> (*Prom.* 100–1)

He taught men not to fear, but not at the price of ignorance. When Io came to him, the only mortal among the characters in the tragedy, he revealed everything that was to befall her until the very end of her earthly wanderings. When he hesitated for a moment because his knowledge seemed to him too cruel, the Chorus interjects: "Speak, tell us to the end. For sufferers it is sweet to know beforehand clearly the pain that still remains for them" (699 ff.). And Prometheus went on to complete his story of Io's future torments. Io is, after Prometheus, the most important character in the tragedy. The episode with her occupies the central place, and "blind hope" seems particularly applicable to her fate.

Io was the daughter of Inachos, a stony brook near Argos. Such gods of the rivers were the progeny of Oceanus. Thus Io was Oceanus' granddaughter, and Prometheus tells the Chorus this. It could have been important in the original myth: water is the archetype of birth and sex. On another plane, Io was the moon.[32] The new moon was connected with the rise of the waters and all fluids. Io became the lover of Zeus. But when Hera found out, she turned the lovely girl into a cow and told Argus, the hundred-eyed monster, to guard her. Zeus then sent Hermes to lull the monster to sleep with his flute and kill him, so Io was freed. But then Hera sent a malicious

gadfly to chase her and sting her till she bled. Io's wanderings ended in Egypt, where Zeus restored her human
form and where she bore him a son.

Aeschylus purified the old moon myth and local legend, discarding its anecdotal color. In his version Argus
is barely mentioned during the course of Io's deliriums.
She is persecuted by Hera, and also by a divine relent-
lessness which she does not understand. But it was not
Hera who changed her into a cow; Zeus himself did. In
no other Greek tragedy until Euripides' *Bacchae* were lust
and the blind force of instinct shown so violently and
brutally. Io tells how every night, in her chaste bedroom,
she dreamed about union with the god:

> There were always
> night visions that kept haunting me and coming
> into my maiden chamber and exhorting
> with winning words, "O maiden greatly blessed,
> why are you still a maiden, you who might
> make marriage with the greatest? Zeus is stricken
> with lust for you; he is afire to try
> the bed of love with you: do not disdain him.
> Go, child, to Lerna's meadow, deep in grass,
> to where your father's flock and cattle stand
> that Zeus's eye may cease from longing for you."
> With such dreams I was cruelly beset
> night after night.
>
> (*Prom.* 645–57)

Io felt the god's will. She had been touched with the
finger, or rather member, of the god. But she was not
united to Zeus. The holy heifer, the horned maiden, was
chased by the invisible gadfly, from whose sting her head
spun. She runs onto the stage mooing and wailing. In the
Prometheus staged at Yale, Irene Worth did not wear a
mask with cow's horns. Sometimes she would make a

gesture of driving away the invisible gadfly with her left
hand, as if wagging a tail. She would shift her weight
impatiently from foot to foot; a couple of times she
kicked her foot against the floor. Her costume was not
stylized, she wore only a long dress. But her eyes were
the big, still eyes of a cow. I had seen such eyes once
before, in China, some thousand miles from the Tibetan
border. In the mountains a young girl was caught who
came from the aboriginal tribes which were said to be
ignorant of the use of metals. She was brought to the
school. I will never forget the eyes of that girl. There was
no fright in them. There was nothing. The eyes were
dark-blue, moist, at the same time quite transparent.
Like two lakes. Eyes uncorrupted by thought. She had
the eyes of a sacred cow. Prometheus is all awareness, all
intelligence; chained to a rock, he remains immobile
from the first scene to the last. Io is all body; chased and
bleeding from the sting of the invisible gadfly, she cannot stand still for a moment. Already in her wanderings
she has run through one fourth of the then known world.

Prometheus has been criticized as being an intellectual
drama, without movement or action. But Aeschylus is
always the most spectacular of the Greek tragedians.
"My heart is a dance of fear," says the Chorus in *The
Libation-bearers.* And it dances its dance of fear. The
"nonverbal," such as the red carpet on which Agamemnon walks to his doom, is an inseparable part of this
theatre and almost invariably assumes the character of a
symbolic sign or an archetypal image. The flat dish of the
orchestra depicted the circle of the earth surrounded by
the ocean. Here "the cow-horned maid" went on her
voyage. "When you shall cross the channel that divides
Europe from Asia, turn to the rising sun, to the burnt
plains, sun-scorched; cross by the edge of the foaming
sea till you come to Gorgona" (791 ff.). In the anthropology of civilization and tyranny the mythological time of

Prometheus turns into historic time. Now the mythological topocosm becomes in its turn the geographic chart of the world. Io's wanderings, writes Havelock, seem some fragment of a fifth-century Greek Baedeker.

Io's route is based upon the original circular map of the world, divided by a horizontal water diameter into two equal continents and split vertically by a meridian which coincides with the Nile and its presumed southern extension. The Aegean Sea forms roughly the centre of the wheel; the circumference is formed by the stream of the Homeric Okeanos, which is connected with the internal water system. This stream conveys Io from India to the mouth of the "Ethiop" river to the far south of Africa. . . . She then accomplishes the circuit of the southeastern quadrant and ends up on the meridian again, which she then traces by the water route back to the Nile delta just opposite the place from where she started.[33]

Io, "the unlucky, wandering maid," probably ran around the eastern semicircle of the *orchestra*. In the next part of the trilogy the scenic arrangement was the same, and in the same spot Prometheus stood chained to the rock awaiting his rescuer. Heracles, if one is to trust Thomson's reconstruction, was to tell Prometheus about his journey to the western limits of the world, when he was returning to Europe from Africa through the Pillars of Hercules at Gibraltar. The flat dish of the *orchestra-*earth, with its eastern and western perimeters, illustrated his dramatic wanderings, just as it had those of the pursued Io.

Io leaves the stage as she had entered, wailing and crying. The invisible gadfly stings her more and more painfully, her wits are clouded, she is now only a suffering animal—like men before they received the gift of fire. "Like the shapes of the dreams," Prometheus described them, "they dragged through long lives and handled all things in bewilderment and confusion" (446 ff.). Io does not see anything any more, she hears nothing, she runs forward pursued by the invisible gadfly, a sheer body being stung to bleeding:

> my tongue ungoverned
> babbles, the words in a muddy flow strike
> on the waves of the mischief I hate, strike wild
> without aim or sense.
>
> (*Prom.* 884–87)

Io's sufferings are unmerited. Like Pasiphaë, in a lost tragedy of which only a fragment has survived, she can say: "God visited me with madness, so though I suffer, my sin was not freely willed . . . What could I see in a bull, to would my heart with such distress, so shameful?" Io "the cow-horned maiden" was *thrust,* as Camus would say, into the world in which the body desires and is desired. She cannot distinguish any more between herself and desire. God covets her cow-flesh, or her cow-flesh covets god. But not she herself. The human cow feels only disgust, revulsion, Sartrean *nausée* toward herself, her body and the world; she is terrified by the invisible gadfly. The defenseless Io, the stung heifer, is the perfect image of Schopenhauer's blind cosmic will. Eros and Thanatos, procreation and death, are not our choices: they are thrust upon us. Chased by blind instinct through seas and continents, Io represents the black Eros of desire. "Wings, and no eyes, figure unheedy haste," Helena in *A Midsummer Night's Dream* is stung by the same invisible gadfly.

But it was to men, with their blind will, that Prometheus offered "blind hopes." Aeschylus is the only one of the great tragic playwrights who can reconcile the rationale of the myth with its universality; its earthly sense and its irrational cosmic hope. At the end of her wanderings Io is to unite with Zeus and bear him a son. The myth functions on the vertical axis of the cosmos as mediation between heaven and earth. Io has been chosen by god; the invisible gadfly who will not let her rest is "the god-sent scourge." In both the realistic and surrealistic imagination of the Greeks, intercourse with god is always bodily. In order to unite with god, one has first to be an animal. *"Abêtissez-vous,"* wrote Pascal. To become like animals was one of the earliest, and remained one of the most permanent, mystic experiences. "The cow-horned maiden" is god's mystic bride. From Zeus's union with Io, a woman is to be born in the thirteenth generation with whom Zeus will again be united. She will bear him a son, the archetype of reconciliation.

This son, not called by name in *Prometheus Bound,* is Heracles. At the end of the trilogy he will shoot down with an arrow from his bow the eagle which, when Prometheus is put to torture once more, will have eaten his regenerating liver every morning. Heracles, the expected One, is the figure of reconciliation in the Promethean trilogy. But the price of reconciliation has been fixed from the outset. It is forecast to Prometheus by Zeus's emissary, Hermes:

> Look for no ending to this agony
> until a god will freely suffer for you,
> will take on him your pain, and in your stead
> descend to where the sun is turned to darkenss,
> to black depths of death.
>
> (1026 ff., Hamilton's translation)[34]

This god, also unnamed, is Chiron, the centaur, one of the most mysterious figures in Greek mythology. He belonged to the oldest generation of the gods and was, perhaps, a son of Cronos. He was a sage, teacher and the first physician. He taught the art of medicine to Asclepius, raised Achilles, and was a friend of Heracles'. By chance he was wounded in the leg with his poisoned arrow. He was able to cure everybody, treating the most severe wounds, but could not heal himself. Tired of unending suffering, he agreed to die for Prometheus.[35]

Sons of the gods come down to earth, suffer, die, descend to hell, but are later resurrected. Chiron is the only god in Greek mythology, possibly in any mythology, who descended to hell voluntarily and forever. The reconciliation, and the price paid for it, happens in the same vertical axis of topocosm. God the tyrant will now become god the father. Zeus the avenger will turn into Zeus the just. But the price of the New Covenant is the death of another god. The "blind hope" is theophany, the ultimate reconciliation between the "above" and the "below," but Cosmos remains split forever into Olympus and Tartarus. In the divine economy, the sum of the world's sufferings remains constant, and Chiron's incurable wound is a symbol of the suffering that has no end and will never be rewarded.

V.

Marx called Prometheus "the loftiest saint and martyr in the philosophical calendar."[36] "The patron saint of the proletariat" is a contemporary view of Prometheus, quoted by Thomson.[37] In no other Greek tragedy has "the above," in its double sense and symbolic meaning of the gods and naked force, been attacked so ferociously. "I am the enemy of all the gods that gave me ill for good" (975). Io the poor heifer hates her persecutor with all her bleeding body. To her both predictions are directed; but her only hope is he who will topple Zeus off his throne: of the Son as Redeemer for her is the Son as Revenger.

IO:

Can Zeus ever fall from power?

PROMETHEUS:

You would be glad to see that catastrophe, I think.

IO:

Surely, since Zeus is my persecutor.

PROMETHEUS:

Then know that this shall be.

(*Prom.* 775–78)

Everyone hates Zeus: Prometheus, Io and the abused forces of nature. Everyone except police officials, the political intriguer Oceanus and the messenger boy Hermes. In Aeschylus the Chorus is never only a witness and commentator on events, and *Prometheus Bound* is the only tragedy in which the Chorus perishes with the hero. The Chorus of sea nymphs, representing the elements of water and air, have come to express their compassion for Prometheus. The Chorus, terrified at first at the openness of the rebellion, gradually learns the bitter history of the world. Prometheus, who taught men courage, now does so again through this assembly of girls and birds. He has revolutionized the Chorus.

HERMES:

You,
you, who are so sympathetic with his troubles,
away with you from here, quickly away!
lest you should find your wits stunned by the thunder
and its hard deafening roar.

CHORUS:

. . . How dare you bid us practise baseness? We
will bear along with him what we must bear.
I have learnt to hate all traitors.

(*Prom.* 1058 ff.)

In the cosmic perspective there is a choice between two as yet unborn sons of Zeus: the son of the New Covenant and the son "stronger than the father." In the dramatic perspective of *Prometheus Bound* the choice is between loyalty to oneself and betrayal, courage and cowardice, inflexible determination and resignation. In political categories it is a choice between a revolutionary program and compromise.[38] "There is significance in rebelling," Mao writes in his *Red Book*. The choices open to Prometheus are the options of a prisoner. "Such is the reward," Hephaestus tells him, "you reap of your man-loving disposition. For you, a God, feared not the anger of the Gods, but gave honors to mortals beyond what was just" (28 ff.). But what is the scale that enables us to define what is "just" and what is an abuse of the just; what is "due" and what is more than due in relations between guard and prisoner, between the above and the below? Prometheus, wrote Marx, did not want to be "the tyrant's slave and the executioner's henchman." In the same introduction to his doctoral dissertation, dated "March 1841," he goes on to say:

Prometheus' confession: "I am the enemy of all the gods," is a confession of faith in philosophy, its notion directed against all gods of heaven and earth, who do not recognize human consciousness as the highest deity. This deity will not suffer any rivals.

This Marxian manifesto of Prometheanism seems far closer to the unbound and romantic Prometheus figures of Goethe and Shelley than to the severe and realistic anthropology of Aeschylus.[39] In the real world, split into the above and the below, Aeschylus says that the only choice is between reconciliation and a new tyranny, between compromise and a new son "stronger than the father." And yet "every ruler is harsh whose rule is new."

Aeschylus, it seems, knew very well that heaven is never empty for long and that a new god occupies the place of every fallen one.

Goethe's, Byron's and Shelley's Prometheus figures were brothers of Satan.[40] But angels had fallen from heaven because of the sin of pride. Lucifer is the Prince of Reason. The last deity of all, the one that "will not suffer rivals," one that seems even more cruel than the former, is the arrogance of reason. This deity considers itself to have mastered destiny, to be able to change and direct it. "Freedom is the recognition of necessity," Marx wrote. The Hegelian realization of the realm of reason and Marxian "historic necessity" are among those "blind hopes" Prometheus offered to men.[41]

"What is a man's freedom," says a tortured prisoner in Malraux's *Times of Contempt,* "if not consciousness and organization of his destinies?" "I liberated the mortals," says Prometheus at the opening of the tragedy, "from going shattered to death" (235). And just before the end, a moment before being thrown into Tartarus, he exclaims defiantly: "Why should I fear, since death is not my fate?" (933). Martyrs of all faiths have said they were immortal; revolutionaries have gone to their deaths declaring that theirs was the victory beyond the grave. In nineteenth-century interpretations, Prometheus was Saint Satan, Saint Carbonarius, Saint Proletarian. He liberated the spirit, or humanity. Fate, destiny, historic necessity—all in their different ways contributed to the passage of time, the working-out of morality, rationality, meaning. Theogony changes into theodicy. The capture of heaven, or of history, was to be the recompense for all sufferings. But what if the hope of Io stung by the invisible gadfly and the hope of Prometheus thrown down into Tartarus were blind too?

CHORUS:
What is fated for Zeus besides eternal sovereignty?

PROMETHEUS:
Inquire of this no further, do not entreat me.

CHORUS:
This is some solemn secret, I suppose, that you are hiding.

(*Prom.* 519–21)

Shortly before the end, Prometheus says, "Time in its aging course teaches all things" (981). The sacred Iranian book *Bundahisn* says something very similar: "Time is more powerful than the two Creations."[42] But what is it exactly that time teaches? The ambiguity of the Aeschylean *Prometheus* consists in the coexistence of two kinds of time. There is the didactic time of theophany, in which the end of cosmogony and history will be Athens and the Great Conciliation, just as it was to be the Prussian state for Hegel; and there is time without hope, in which Prometheus is thrown, once and for all, into Tartarus to the accompaniment of heavenly fireworks. For the optimistic nineteenth-century poets and philosophers, Prometheus was *ultimately* to triumph, and suffering was the price of progress. The tragedy of Prometheus was that he had come *too early*. But closer to our experience is Camus' bitter interpretation: Prometheus' greatness is his revolt without hope:

". . . A revolution is always accomplished against the gods, beginning with the revolution of Prometheus, the first of modern conquerors. It is man's demands made against his fate; the demands of the poor are but a pretext. . . .
"Yes, man is his own end. And he is his only end. If he aims to be something, it is in this life. . . . Conquerors sometimes talk of vanquishing and overcoming. But it is always 'overcom-

ing oneself' that they mean. . . . Every man has felt himself to
be the equal of a god at certain moments. At least, this is the
way it is expressed. But this comes from the fact that in a flash
he felt the amazing grandeur of the human mind. The conquerors are merely those among men who are conscious
enough of their strength to be sure of living constantly on
those heights and fully aware of that grandeur. . . .

"There they find the creature mutilated, but they also encounter there the only values they like and admire, man and
his silence. . . ."[43]

One can express this in yet another way. The greatness
of Prometheus is hopeful despair or desperate hope.
"Being deprived of hope," Camus concludes, "is not
despairing."[44] But this is still not the bitterest interpretation of Prometheus' fate.

In Cicero's treatise, which contains one of the few
fragments preserved of the two lost parts of the trilogy,
Prometheus is depicted as unable to bear his endless
torture any longer, so that he wishes only for human
death: *"amore mortis terminum anquirens mali"* ("yearning
for death as end to misery").[45]

This is also a conclusion of the tragedy of "the absurd
rebel." There are two other forms of time. The time of
one human life's duration is a time of suffering. In one
of Pindar's odes, which is perhaps connected with the
end of Prometheus' tragedy, the eagle who guards Zeus's
thunder once fell asleep as the Muses sang to the accompaniment of Apollo's lyre. It was the eagle that every
morning flew to the rocks of the Caucasus to feed on
Prometheus' liver.[46]

> On the sceptre of Zeus the eagle sleeps,
> Drooping his swift wings on either side.[47]

The eagle fell asleep to the sweet sounds of music, and
anger departed from among the Olympians. This is the

fourth and last form of time, that of forgetfulness and the passing into nothingness.

Kafka must have known Cicero's treatise and Pindar's ode because in his notebook he set down the four legends[48] of Prometheus:

According to the first, because he had betrayed the gods to men he was chained to a rock in the Caucasus and the gods sent eagles that devoured his liver, which always grew again.

According to the second, Prometheus in his agony, as the beaks hacked into him, pressed deeper and deeper into his rock until he became one with it.

According to the third, in the course of thousands of years his treachery was forgotten, the gods forgot, the eagles forgot, he himself forgot.

According to the fourth, everyone grew weary of what had become meaningless. The gods grew weary, the eagles grew weary, the wound closed wearily.

What remained was the inexplicable range of mountains. Legend tries to explain the inexplicable. Since it arises out of a foundation of truth, it must end in the realm of the inexplicable.

Kafka, with his incomparable intelligence, realized that when topocosm has lost its meaning, all that can be left of it are the desolate mountains between heaven and earth. But this is not the end of the Prometheus myth. In the entire history of drama there are only two works in which the hero cannot leave his place from the beginning to the end of the play.[49] The first is *Prometheus Bound.* In the other, the heroine is buried in the earth, first up to her waist, then up to her neck. There is no chorus. There is only a paralyzed man who cannot approach her. All that is left of the external world of objects is a parasol and a big black handbag containing toilet articles and a revolver. The woman kisses the revolver and puts it aside; soon it is too late—she is buried up to her neck, with her hands in the earth. She has to live until she dies. Time is measured with bells. The below and the above continue to exist; but the earth is merely a heap of sand, and the sky is empty without a single cloud. The only action is being buried in the earth, deeper and deeper. This is the fifth form of time: sinking into the earth, which means no more than sinking into the earth.

There is no need for Zeus any more. Beckett's *Happy Days* is the final version of the Prometheus myth.

Ajax Thrice Deceived, or The Heroism of the Absurd

MI.

y name is Ajax: agony is its meaning."[1] In all the tragedies of Sophocles, except the last, where old Oedipus chooses the place of his death, heroes are plunged to the rock bottom of the human condition; we observe them at a point when they have become alien to men and alien to the world. The last *agon* is the hero's agony. After the murder of the mother and her lover, no Furies will come, no judgment or purification will follow. The Chorus will speak its trite moral and disperse. Orestes and Electra remain alone with their crime. They are superfluous to the gods, alien in their city, alien even to each other. No word will be uttered between them. They lived to avenge their father. Duty and hate are two corpses. As the blood flows slowly from the bodies of Clytemnestra and Aegisthus, Orestes and Electra lose their raisons d'être.

In the plays of Sophocles, his art serves to prepare this all-important moment in which the protagonist finally realizes that the ground is being cut from under his feet, and the gods are silent. Only then, in full awareness of the human condition, is a heroic choice possible: to commit suicide or to go on living, and like Oedipus with eyes gouged out by his own hand, defy the absurd of the world through continuing in life. In the seven extant tragedies of Sophocles, there are six suicides, one attempted suicide and two calls for death to be hastened.[2] But only in *Ajax* does the protagonist commit suicide in full view of the spectators, in the high-noon sun. And only in *Ajax* does the corpse remain on the stage throughout the lengthy second part of the performance, until the end of the tragedy.

Black blood flows from Ajax's nostrils, and the captive princess Tecmessa covers the body with a shawl. But Teucer, Ajax's half brother, will soon uncover the corpse. And the corpse will remain to the end the most important character in the tragedy. Dead, Ajax still hates and is hated. After Achilles' death, when Achilles' armor was to be given to the bravest of the Greeks, Ajax was deceived. The voting was faked, or the judges were venal, and the armor, which had been forged by the blacksmith god Hephaestus, was allotted to Odysseus. The next day, at dawn, Ajax set out from his tent to murder the Greek generals. He was deceived again. Athene blinded his eyes with a bloody mist,[3] and instead of the sons of Atreus and Odysseus, he chopped up oxen and rams. He could not survive his shame.

After Ajax's suicide, the tragedy should have ended. Ajax killed himself, but the world did not cease to exist. What is the world that Ajax had come to hate? Ajax's suicide can be measured only by the standard of the real world. But the real world can also be measured by the standard of Ajax's suicide.

The second part of the tragedy is a judgment on Ajax. In this judgment, the corpse is also the accuser.[4] The cruel reckoning with the world of the first half ends on a political settling of accounts and on abuse. The corpse is still too large. Compared to the corpse, all of them, friend and foe alike, even Odysseus, thanks to whom Ajax will ultimately be buried, are small and insipid.

Ajax is generally regarded as the most Homeric of Sophocles' tragedies; but in the inexorable confrontation of Homeric legend with an unheroic world, the heroes of the *Iliad* are even more cruelly degraded than in Euripides. Ajax must first be despoiled of greatness and heroism before Sophocles will give him a moment of cold clear-sightedness and restore to him a gloomy greatness, so different from the Homeric, and another, much more bitter kind of heroism.

The immense corpse still lies on the stage. Menelaus, Agamemnon and Odysseus have departed. Sailors and Teucer pay their last respects to Ajax. The corpse is ceremoniously carried off the stage in a funeral procession. But which Ajax did they bury in Sophocles' tragedy?

II.

Achilles raged with fury when he heard at the council of war that Agamemnon had resolved to take his captive Briseis away from him. He drew his sword halfway out of its sheath and was about to assault the king when Athene suddenly stood behind him "and seized him by his golden locks. No one but Achilles was aware of her; the rest saw nothing. He swung around in amazement, recognized Pallas Athene at once—so terrible was the brilliance of her eyes—and spoke out to her boldly: 'And why have you come here, Daughter of aegis-bearing Zeus? Is it to witness the arrogance of my lord Agamemnon? I tell you bluntly—and I make no idle threats—that he stands to pay for this outrage with his life.' 'I came from heaven,' replied Athene of the Flashing Eyes, 'in the hope of bringing you to your senses . . . Come now, give up this strife and take your hand from your sword. Sting him with words instead . . .' " (*Iliad*, I, 197 ff.).[5]

When Achilles' armor was given to Odysseus, the enraged Ajax set out at night for the tents of the sons of Atreus. Athene stood behind him, as in the *Iliad*. But Athene took away his reason and confused his senses. With his sword Ajax attacked a herd of oxen and rams instead of the generals.

Briseis was "bright-cheeked," and Achilles slept with her every night. Achilles' armor had been forged by Hephaestus. Both Briseis and the armor are symbols. Briseis was Achilles' war booty; after his death the armor was to be given to the bravest of the Greeks. Both are trophies, tokens of bravery, of a hero's status.

"The wrath of Achilles, sing, o Goddess . . ." "The wrath of Achilles is my theme . . ." Homer's Achilles and Sophocles' Ajax are placed in the same kind of situation.[7] The heroic order is threatened. Achilles returns to his ship and waits. But after his friend Patroclus' death he rejoins the fight and kills Hector, prince of Troy. His choice was glory, or long life. He chose glory. The heroic order was saved. In *Ajax* it is totally destroyed. "Of the men, Telamonian Aias [Ajax] was by far the best, but only while Achilles was in dudgeon . . ." (*Iliad,* II, 768). "I will dip them all in shit," wrote Flaubert of his characters. Sophocles dips the bravest of the Greeks, next to Achilles, in the blood of slaughtered animals. "His head is moist with sweat, his murderous hands are moistened too . . ." (*Ajax,* 9). In the *Iliad,* Ajax also sweated profusely: "He was panting hard, and the sweat streamed from all his limbs" (XVI, 108). But that was in battle, when he pushed the Trojans off the Greek ships. In Sophocles, Ajax appears like a sweating butcher. Athene calls him onstage to exhibit him to a frightened Odysseus.

ATHENE:
Tell me, please, what happened to Laertes' son?
He didn't escape you?

AJAX:
Oho, that villainous sneak! You want to know where *he* is?

ATHENE:
Yes. Your adversary, you know. Odysseus.

AJAX:
He's sitting there inside, my sweetest prisoner.
I don't intend for him to die just yet.

ATHENE:
What are you going to do first?

AJAX:
First bind him to the pole that props my barrack.

ATHENE:
Poor miserable man! What treatment will you give him?

AJAX:
Crimson his back with this whip first, then kill him.

(101 ff.)

Athene tormented Ajax, whom she had driven to madness, just as Ajax tormented the white ram whose feet he had bound with a rope. Until quite recently, classical philologists regarded Sophocles' work as statuesque, noble and pious theatre. In the true Sophocles, Heracles howls with pain while being burned alive, Philoctetes howls with the pain of his festering wound, and Ajax howls.[8] Ajax howls the loudest. The prologue of *Ajax,* with Athene egging the hero on, with the frightened Odysseus and the giant slaughtering rams, reminds one of satyr drama[9] or Aristophanes' parodies; the modern spectator is also reminded of Brecht. The unobvious becomes obvious; the obvious becomes unobvious. To murder one's enemies is heroic; to torture animals instead of men is unheroic.

> . . . some he slew on the tent's floor
> Cleanly with a neck-cut; others he hacked asunder
> With slashes on their ribs. But two special
> White-footed rams he lifted up, shore off
> One's head and the tip of its tongue, and cast them from
> him;
> The other he bound upright against a pillar,
> Seized a stout length of harness, made from it
> A singing whip, two-thonged, to lash him with,
> And, mid the blows, poured forth such awful curses
> As no man, but some demon, must have taught him.
>
> (234 ff.)

Odysseus speaks about the murder of shepherds guarding the army's herds; Athene tells about the slaughter of the sheep and cattle; Ajax's captive, Tecmessa, tells how he slashed the bulls' throats and broke the sheepdogs' backs. This wearying and sadistic description of the torture of animals occupies the entire prologue and half of the first episode. During this long scene, while Tecmessa gives her account of Ajax's madness and his screams are heard from the tent, the Chorus depicts "non-verbally" through gestures and body movements, his madness, humiliation and torment. "If we are clearly so incapable today of giving an idea of Aeschylus, Sophocles, Shakespeare that is worthy of them," wrote Artaud, "it is probably because we have lost the sense of their theater's physics."[10] If, instead of a stylized dance of the Chorus dressed in chitons, we imagine actors trained as in Grotowski's theatre, we will certainly be closer to the cruel theatre of Sophocles.

The flaps of his tent are now open, Ajax sits there on a heap of slaughtered animals, like a butcher in his stall. Sophocles, like Shakespeare and the Elizabethans after him, was not afraid of the sight of blood and chopped-off heads. What was essential for him was the hero's degradation, physical and spectacular. Athene made Ajax an object lesson onstage.[11] "I shall show you his madness in plain view," she says to Odysseus. "Take note of it; then you can publish it to all the Greeks." (66 f.).

The Greeks in the *Iliad* are cruel and their hate knows no bounds. Agamemnon warns that no Trojan will be left alive and even unborn babies will be torn from their mothers' wombs; Achilles drags Hector's corpse with horses and kills twelve Trojan prisoners in front of Patroclus' funeral pyre. But torture does not exist in Homer's world. Killing is a serious action, described objectively, dryly, with precision, like a difficult surgical operation: ". . . he struck Aeneas on the hip, where the thigh turns in the hip-joint—the cup-bone as they call it. He crushed the cup-bone, and he broke both sinews too —the skin was lacerated by the jagged boulder. The noble Aeneas sank to his knees and supported himself with one great hand on the ground; but the world went black as night before his eyes" (*Iliad*, V, 30). To kill requires a knowledge of the human body; to describe killing is to transmit this knowledge. "Meriones . . . caught him with his lance half-way between the navel and the privy parts, the most painful spot in which a wretched soldier can be struck" (XIII, 567).

The narrator is always impartial and maintains proper respect for both the one who kills and the one who is killed. "Achilles saw that Hector's body was completely covered by the fine bronze armour he had taken from the great Patroclus when he killed him, except for an opening at the gullet where the collar bones lead over from the shoulders to the neck, the easiest place to kill a man. As Hector charged him, Prince Achilles drove at this spot with his lance; and the point went right through the tender flesh of Hector's neck, though the heavy bronze head did not cut his windpipe, and left him able to address his conqueror" (XXII, 321).

Homer always lets his heroes die with dignity. Death is part of the heroic order. ". . . if after living through this war we could be sure of ageless immortality, I should neither take my place in the front line nor send you out to win honour in the field. But things are not like that" (XII, 322 ff.).

Since one has to die in any case, it is better to be a hero. He who wins and he who loses both know they will die.[12] Perhaps that is why Homer was more interested in the technical description of the blow than in the feelings of his heroes. "Meges the mighty spearman caught up this man and struck him with his sharp lance on the nape of the neck. The point came through between his jaws and severed his tongue at the root. He fell down in the dust and bit the cold bronze with his teeth" (V, 72).

Man is not divided into body and soul,[13] nor is there a division into the lofty and the vulgar. Death belongs to the same natural order as the hearty breakfast before the battle and the captive girl waiting in the tent after the battle. Even the relentless sting of a stubborn fly is prop-

erly appraised in this heroic world. "Athene of the Flashing Eyes was delighted to note that Menelaus had prayed
to her before all other gods. She strengthened his shoulders and his knees and implanted in his breast the daring
of a fly, which is so fond of human blood that it returns
to the attack however often a man may brush it from his
face" (XVII, 567). In Book XII, Athene and Apollo take
the shape of vultures and enjoy the view of battle from
the top of an oak tree.[14]

Death looms at every turn, and so do the gods. A god
can deflect the arrow shot by the best of archers so that
it hits the spot where thick leather belts cross and does
not pierce the body. The Homeric gods are chance, the
good or bad luck that makes a sword slip down the armor, or a foot slip in a pool of slimy blood. "In a moment, the god can make a brave man run away and lose
a battle, and the next day he will spur him on to fight"
(XVI, 689). Sometimes gods, like Ate, are red blood,
which streams over the eyes in anger. Like the spleen and
liver, gods are on occasion only a name, a seat and source
of passions.

Gods are near, involved in human affairs, but among
gods, as among men, there are those who are weaker and
those who are stronger. When Iris came to Achilles, the
prudent Greek first asked her which of the gods had sent
her with a message. Gods are involved in human affairs,
and for this very reason they take sides. Athene warns
Diomedes not to count on her help too much: "There
are other gods, and they might wake the Trojans up" (X,
579).

Homer's gods seldom pity men, but they never treat
them with contempt. They are immortal, and from that
viewpoint they compare men to leaves which a strong
wind can shake off the tree in an instant. It is hard to be
jealous of leaves tossed by the wind, and there is no
reason to despise or degrade them. Sophocles' Athene

in *Ajax* belongs to a world which is different from Homer's. She occasionally reminds one of an old and envious camp follower who loiters around the camp and has at last found an occasion to bellow, "I can darken even the most brilliant vision" (85). She hisses for joy that she can humble and denigrate Ajax: "Is not laughter at one's enemies the kind that gives most pleasure?" (78 f.)[15]

Homer's gods do not give men lessons in morality. Sophocles' Athene is part of another kind of culture, one in which man's greatness, or even success, is suspect in the eyes of the gods.

> For time approaching, and time hereafter,
> And time forgotten, one rule stands:
> That greatness never
> Shall touch the life of man without destruction.
>
> (*Antigone*, 603 ff.)[16]

Ajax's humiliation by Athene is a particularly cruel, almost grotesque lesson of the new divine didactics:

> Do you see, Odysseus, how great the gods' power is?
> Who was more full of foresight than this man,
> Or abler, do you think, to act with judgment?
>
> (118 ff.)

The gods in Homer scrupulously saw to it that men offered them their due sacrifices. But Sophocles' Athene does not care for offerings any more. When she calls him, Ajax remembers, even in his madness, to assure her that he will offer her gifts of pure gold on the altar. But this Athene is interested not in offers, but in principles. Athene tormenting Ajax is a goddess of theology.

> And when once Athena stood
> Beside him in the fight, urging him on

To strike the enemy with his deadly hand,
He answered then, that second time, with words
To shudder at, not speak: "Goddess," he said,
"Go stand beside the other Greeks; help them.
For where I bide, no enemy will break through."

(774 ff.)

Homer compares Ajax to a stubborn donkey. Sophocles' Ajax is no less stubborn. To his father, who tells him always to call the gods for help, he replies "Father, with God's help even a worthless man could triumph. I propose, without that help, to win my prize of fame" (767 ff.).

It is significant that of all the heroes in the *Iliad*, it was to Ajax that Sophocles gave metaphysical doubts. On an Attic vase of the second half of the sixth century B.C., Ajax playing dice with Achilles is twice as broad in his shoulders and considerably taller.[17] This Homeric giant, "taller than all the rest by a head and shoulders" (III, 226), who hurled Trojans off a ship by "swinging a huge pole twenty-two cubits long" (XV, 677), did not seem prone to intellectual reflection. Ajax knew his strength and wanted to be strong not only "in himself" but "for himself," not only *in se*, but also *per se*. That giant, who suddenly wants to be responsible for his own life from the beginning to the end and combat the world on his own behalf, seems to be the first modern hero of Greek tragedy. This is the Ajax Sophocles found in the *Iliad*, but as always, he read Homer virulently and dramatically, with absolute consistency, one might say.

When, fighting for the body of Patroclus, the Greeks could not contain the attacking Trojans, "the great Telamonian Aias turned with an exclamation of disgust to Menelaus. 'Any fool,' he said, 'can see that Father Zeus himself is helping the Trojans. Every spear they cast goes home. Whether it comes from a bungler's or a marksman's hand, Zeus sees it to its target, while ours fall gently to the ground and do no harm at all. Well, we must contrive without him . . .' " (XVII, 469 ff.).

Ajax is not arrogant; athletes seldom are. Ajax does not slight the gods. It is simply that he can do without their help. He has in him "the silent strength of earth,"[18] as J. H. Finley will say of him.

Homer's gods respected the sullen fierceness of Ajax. Humility was no part of the heroic code of either gods or men. It was only Sophocles' Athene who demanded humility of mortals. The goddess went into a rage be-cause—the Messenger repeats the words of Calchas the soothsayer—Ajax's thoughts were "too great for a man." It was the same Calchas who had ordered Iphigenia to be slaughtered on the altar of Artemis and who in all post-Homeric tradition represents the new "guilt-culture," as Dodds called it, the dark envy of the gods.[19]

All the basic opposites are already present in the pro-logue. "I see you," Athene says to Odysseus in the first line of *Ajax,* "always hunting for some occasion against your enemies."[20] The animal has been hunted down; in a little while the goddess will show the mad Ajax to Odysseus. Athene is pitiless; Odysseus pities Ajax. But Odysseus' pity does not evoke Athene's anger. It is a pious pity: "I know that a god's contriving may do any-thing" (86). The pious politician knows that, gods will-ing, one can do anything to man. He knows and accepts this.

> For I see the true state of all us that live—
> We are dim shapes, no more, and weightless shadow.
>
> (125 ff.)[21]

The pious politician knows that man is nothing; a handful of dust in the hands of those who are stronger;

dust that can be wiped away. The pious politician obeys the gods. For the pious politician the gods always arrive in time.²² Odysseus says to Athene:

> You come just as I need you. Now and always,
> As heretofore, your hand shall be my guide.
>
> (34 f.)

Of all those who have written about *Ajax*, C. Whitman must have been the only one to realize that Athene and Odysseus represent the same policy and morality. Athene, he wrote, "stands for a vision of life which Odysseus accepts, but which Ajax has always rejected and still rejects."²³ Heroic Ajax, mad Ajax, humiliated Ajax did not want to admit that man was but shadow.

> Man's life is a day. What is he?
> What is he not? A shadow in a dream
> Is man: but when God sheds a brightness,
> Shining life is on earth
> And life is sweet as honey.
>
> (*Pythian* VIII).²⁴

Sophocles was only one generation older than Pindar, but when a god appears in his tragedies, no brightness is shed and life does not become sweet as honey. When a god appears, man is hunted to death. Having emerged from his madness, Ajax cries, "But the martial goddess, daughter of Zeus, cruelly works my ruin" (401).

III.

"You darkness, my sole light!" (394). Like Oedipus when he has gouged out his eyes, Ajax, on emerging from his madness, sees for the first time the real world

and himself in it. He has been caught in a double trap.
To the Greeks he is the Ajax who wanted to assassinate
the leaders of the expedition. To himself, he is the Ajax
who has lost the status of a hero. In the unheroic world
he will die by being stoned as a traitor. In the heroic
world he has been made ridiculous forever.

> Here I am, the bold, the valiant,
> Unflinching in the shock of war,
> A terrible threat to unsuspecting beasts.
> Oh! what a mockery I have come to! What indignity!
>
> (364 ff.)

Ajax has been hurled down to the lowest depths, ultimately brought to the situation which, for Sophocles, is
the only true human condition. Ajax, deceived by the
gods and by men, is an alien in the world; he is alien even
to himself, because the Ajax who has ceased to be a hero
is a different Ajax. This new Ajax is *deinotaton*, the
stranger, the alien and the alienated.

> And now, Ajax—what is to be done now?
> I am hated by the gods, that's plain; the Greek camp
>   hates me:
> Troy and the ground I stand upon detest me.
>
> (457 ff.)

From the moment of his emergence from madness to
his suicidal death, the entire action will be, as in Racine's
tragedies, no more than the hero growing equal to the
ultimate decision. This last reckoning with the world
must take place in full awareness. Death seems unavoida-
ble. But there are different kinds of death. Ajax desperately searches for a heroic death. There is no room for
it any more. The world is not divided any more into
Greeks and Trojans.

Shall I make a rush against the walls of Troy,
Join with them all in single combat, do
Some notable exploit, and find my death in it?
But that might give some comfort to the sons of Atreus.
No.

(466 ff.)

Offended by Agamemnon, Achilles returned to his
ship and played his lyre, looking at Patroclus. He waited.
He even announced that he would set sail and return to
his native Phthia. But Achilles had not been put to ridicule. Ajax has nowhere to go. Wherever he goes he will
be Ajax who has slaughtered animals. The heroic world
is like a trap: there is no escape from it. He will be naked
as a worm everywhere, because he has lost his honor.

What countenance can I show my father Telamon?
How will he ever stand the sight of me
If I come before him naked, armed with no glory . . .?

(463 ff.)

If it is not possible to die like a hero, and there is
nowhere one can escape to, one is left with suicide.
"Ajax' attempt to formulate the alternative to heroic suicide," writes Knox, "convinces him of its impossibility."
But "heroic" suicide is not part of the heroic code. "Heroic" suicide was discovered in unheroic periods. The
world of the *Iliad* had not known suicide. The heroes
could choose between cowardice and courage, and
someone else's sword was always at hand. Ajax's suicide
appeared only in the post-Homeric Epic Cycle. A one-
verse scholium, which has been preserved, runs: "The
author of *Aethiopis* says that Aias killed himself about
dawn."[25] Sophocles' Ajax considers the reasons for suicide in a world whose system of values has suddenly
ceased to exist. There are many ways of dying. Also,

suicide can be easy or hard. A man can throw himself on his sword, still deluding himself that the heroic world of values is being saved.

> Let a man nobly live or nobly die
> If he *is* a nobleman . . .
>
> (479 f.)

Ajax had been ready for heroic death from the outset. Until this scene, the world with which he was struggling and in which he suddenly found himself a stranger, the world of the revengeful goddess, the sly Odysseus and the hateful sons of Atreus, was the world of those who kill. But next to it was another world, of those who are killed.

> Ajax, my master, life knows no harder thing
> Than to be at the mercy of compelling fortune.
> I, for example, was born of a free father;
> If any man in Phrygia was lordly and prosperous, he was.
> Now I'm a slave.
>
> (485 ff.)

Tecmessa was Ajax's captive and the mother of his son. "Let a man nobly live or nobly die" means something altogether different for the victors and for the defeated. Ajax's heroic defeat suddenly seems a proud and cruel delusion when set against true human suffering.

> My country was destroyed
> Utterly by your spear, and another fate
> Brought down my mother and my father too,
> To dwell in death with Hades. Then what fatherland
> Shall I ever have but you? Or what prosperity?

You are my only safety. O my lord,
Remember even me.

(515 ff.)

Tecmessa repeats the words of Hector's wife, Andromache, spoken when she bade him farewell: " '. . . So you, Hector, are father and mother and brother to me, as well as my beloved husband. Have pity on me now; stay here on the tower; and do not make your boy an orphan and your wife a widow' " (*Iliad*, VI, 429 ff.). But again Sophocles reads Homer bitterly and dramatically.[26] Andromache's father and seven brothers had been murdered. But she became the wife of Hector, a son of the king of Troy. Tecmessa was only a captive, acquired as booty. ". . . the day you die and by your death desert me, that same day will see me outraged too, forcibly dragged by the Greeks, together with your boy, to lead a slave's life" (496 ff.).

The heroic world stands out like an island in the sea of human suffering. In no other tragedy by Sophocles are the opposites of human and inhuman so sharply contrasted. When Ajax stops howling, his first human words on coming to his senses are, "My son! Where is my son?" Tecmessa brings the boy to him. Ajax has been through the experience of the offended Achilles, now he will, like Hector, bid farewell to his son. Heroism was Achilles' nature; for Hector heroism was a self-imposed duty. It was as if Hector was enforcing a heroic attitude on himself, while trying to escape from it. Hector will know fear and the loneliness of dying: when, fleeing from Achilles, he will run four times around the stone walls of Troy before halting to accept the combat. But the Hector who bid farewell to Astyanax was still a Hector *before* the final test.

"Zeus, and you other immortals, grant that this boy, who is my
    son,
may be as I am, pre-eminent among the Trojans,
great in strength, as I am, and rule strongly over Ilion;
and some day let them say of him: 'He is better by far than his
    father'. . ."

(Iliad, VI, 476 ff.)[27]

Sophocles' Ajax has been through the test; has gone
through humiliation; has reached the bottom. He knows
that childhood is lack of awareness, maturity—only despair. He wants his son to be like him, hate like him, but
be happier than himself. Ajax still wants the impossible.
But happiness is not a heroic precept any more.

> . . . I somewhat envy you:
> You have no sense of all this misery.
> Not knowing anything's the sweetest life
> Ignorance is an evil free from pain—
> Till the time comes when you learn of joy and grief.
> And when you come to that,
> Then you must show your father's enemies
> What sort of a man you are, and what man's son.

(552 ff.)

In the celebrated first chapter of *Mimesis*, Auerbach
contrasts the Homeric world, basking in an even light,
with the stories of the Old Testament, where the spheres
of light and shadow are sharply divided. Homer's world
is like a bas relief where every detail has been treated
with equal attention, respect and care; a bas relief has no
depth. The characters are invariably presented at the
foreground and bring with themselves their own "independent and exclusive present." Always the same, they
"wake every morning as if it were the first day of their

lives." Odysseus returns to Ithaca after two score years as if he had left it for one night. Homer's epic and Genesis represent for Auerbach two different visions of the world and of man. "In Homer the complexity of the psychological life is shown only in the succession and alternation of emotions; whereas the Jewish writers are able to express the simultaneous existence of various layers of consciousness and the conflict between them." Abraham, Isaac and Jacob emerge for a little while from the shadows, "time and place are undefined and call for interpretation; thoughts and feeling remain unexpressed, are only suggested by the silence and the fragmentary speeches; the whole . . . remains mysterious and 'fraught with background.' "[28]

Perhaps a similar trail of shadow follows Achilles or even more Hector. But not until Sophocles do the world and the people emerge from the darkness and inevitably return to it.

> All things doth long, innumerable time
> Bring forth to light, and hide again in darkness . . .
>
> (646–48, Kitto's translation)[29]

Ajax returns to the stage. He has brought a sword out of the tent. This is Ajax who has seen the world rent by an earthquake. He had once taken an oath of loyalty. What is now left of it?

> Nothing is firm; the strongest oath is broken,
> The stubborn purpose fails. For I was hard
> As tempered steel; but now Tecmessa's words
> Have softened me, and I have lost my edge.
> I pity her, to leave her as a widow
> Among my foes, to leave my son an orphan.
>
> (*Ibid.*, 650 ff.)

The heroic world has toppled. Ajax has realized at last that he will not be able either to live or to die heroically. Should he then come to terms with the world? But what kind of world is it in which a hero can become a butcher? "All things long uncounted time brings forth from obscurity and buries once they have appeared. And nothing is beyond expectations" (646–48, Knox's translation). One is not safe from anything; instability is the nature of things, and one can expect anything from the world. To live means to accept the fact that there is nothing stable. "There must be something certain, there must!" exclaimed the terrorist Chen in Malraux's *Man's Fate* who killed from a crazed need for certainty and self-assertion. But if there is nothing one can catch hold of, there is always the earth; one can at least leave a hole in the ground.

> . . . Then I will go
> And find a spot far from the ways of men;
> There will I dig the earth, and hide my sword,
> My hateful sword, where never mortal eye
> Shall look on it again; but Night and Hades
> Shall keep it in their darkness evermore.
>
> (660 ff., Kitto's translation)

Above the heads of the stunned Chorus, which does not understand anything any more, Ajax continues his staggering monologue about the conditions of the Great Surrender.[30]

> From now on this will be my rule: Give way
> To Heaven, and bow before the sons of Atreus.
> They are our rulers . . .
>
> (665 ff.)

The scholiast was astonished at this unexpected stylistic inversion. In Knox's version it sounds even stronger:

"I shall in future know how to give in to the gods and show reverence for the sons of Atreus." Ajax has understood at last that the general surrender has always to be made to the gods. In this monologue the theme of Athene, who made Ajax a laughingstock, returns as an echo. "You see," she told Odysseus, "the gods can do everything to man." What matters in the end is a trifle: the acceptance of power, of all powers—those of the gods, of the rulers and of nature. *They* are stronger, but the acceptance has to be enforced:

> . . . They must be obeyed.
> I must give way, as all dread things give way,
> In turn and deference. Winter's hard-packed snow
> Cedes to the fruitful summer; stubborn night
> At last removes, for day's white steeds to shine.
> The dread blast of the gale slackens and gives
> Peace to the sounding sea; and Sleep, strong jailer,
> In time yields up his captive. Shall I not
> Learn place and wisdom?
>
> (668 ff.)[31]

Time, "the great devourer," crumbles everything great, and its changes are limited to the one relentless opposition between strength and weakness. The hard snows of winter must give way to fruitful summer; the stubborn night is followed by the bright day, and so on. The mountains have been eroded, the world has become flat. How can one live in a flat world? "I must give way, as all dread things give way . . ."

When he emerged from his madness, Ajax roared like a wounded bull. The bull was led into a flat arena. "Shall I not learn place and wisdom?" Knox's version is more tragic and closer to the original: "How shall I not be forced to learn to my sorrow?" Ajax did not want to learn the wisdom of the flat world. The accounts had been settled in full. He had made his decision.

> Now I am going where my way must go;
> Do as I bid you, and you yet may hear
> That I, though wretched now, have found my safety.
>
> (690 ff.)

Ajax and Tecmessa have departed, only the Chorus remains. The soft boots beat faster and faster on the ground, the Chorus runs round the *orchestra*. "I would dance, I am bent upon dancing!" (698). Ajax's tragedy is happening in an unheroic world. The most loyal of friends—the sailors of Salamis—jump for joy between the scene of Ajax's final reckoning with the world and that of his suicide. The frenetic dance of the Chorus, full of mirth and joyous shouts, is not only amazingly theatrical, it has in it a sudden whiff of the absurd. "I would dance, I am bent upon dancing!"[32]

The *orchestra* is empty at last. For the first time Ajax is alone. He has thrust his sword deeply into the ground, blade upward. "The steady immovable sword," as Knox puts it, "on which he kills himself is the one fixed point in a world of which change and movement are the only modes of existence." The ground on which Ajax's big body will fall is Trojan; the sword on which he will fall was a gift of Hector.

> He's firm in the ground, my Slayer. And his cut
> (If I have time even for this reflection)
> Should now be deadliest. For, first, the sword
> Was Hector's gift, a token of guest-friendship,
> And he of all guest-friends my bitterest foe;
> Here, too, it stands, lodged in the hostile ground
> Of Troy . . .
>
> (815 ff.)

Ajax twice mentions the sword he had received from Hector; and over Ajax's body, Teucer relates the story of this sword. After an indecisive duel, Ajax and Hector had exchanged gifts:

"With the very girdle that had been given to him by Ajax, Hector was gripped to the chariot-rail and mangled till he gave up the ghost. It was from Hector that Ajax had this gift, and by this he had perished in his deadly fall. Was it not the Fury who forged this blade, was not that girdle wrought by Hades, the grim artificer? I at least would deem that these things, and all things ever, are planned by gods for men . . ."

(1029 ff., Jebb's translation)³³

In the *Iliad,* Hector must have been dragged by the same girdle which he had received from Ajax in Book VII, but Homer apparently did not consider this a detail worthy of attention, since he did not mention it. Homer's world was not Manichean; there were in it neither curses passing to the tenth generation, nor crimson carpets to tread on which were sufficient to draw anger of the jealous gods. The world had not yet assumed the likeness of a giant mousetrap, set for men from the outset. Gods, if they interfered in human affairs at all, did so haphazardly. Zeus put fates in the balance, or threw them, without even looking, into two urns containing good and evil. Hector's sword and Ajax's girdle, bringing bad luck to their wearers, which recall Aeschylus' dark symbolism, are one of the more striking examples of post-Homeric "guilt-culture." But in Sophocles' *Ajax,* the fatal gift of the sword seems to perform yet another function. In the world described by Homer, the exchange of gifts accompanied the promise and conclusion of marriage, the election of the leader of a common war expedition, and the ceremonious conclusion of peace. Often it took the form of an exchange of metal; exchange, for heroes did not trade. "Guest-friendship" was a system of social bonds, which meant a basis of support in the ever uncertain travels beyond the frontiers of *oikos,* one's family and clan.[34] In Ajax's world, the exchange of gifts was ominous and carried death with it. The heroic world had toppled, and all its institutions suddenly became absurd.

"In Sophocles' *Ajax,*" Arrowsmith observes, "we are meant to see . . . a symbol of the old aristocratic ethos; caught in new and anti-heroic circumstances which degrade him and make him ludicrous, Ajax consistently prefers suicide to a life of absurdity in an alien time."[35] Prometheus was the one who "looked forward"; Ajax was rather like his mythical brother, who "looked back." Prometheus came too early; Ajax, like an antediluvian animal strayed into an alien world, came too late. Both were crushed by a time which was alien to them.

But what is one to do if time is always "alien"? A historical interpretation does not seem satisfactory for the ultimate understanding of Ajax's dismal greatness. "The absurd," wrote Camus in *The Myth of Sisyphus,* "depends as much on man as on the world." And again: "The absurd is essentially a divorce. It lies in neither of the elements compared, it is born of their confrontation."[36] "One can live in the absurd," says Garin in Malraux's *The Conquerors,* "but one cannot live accepting the absurd." Ajax did not want to accept the absurd.

What was there left to him but hate? Ajax *was* a hero. Ajax made ridiculous is not Ajax. In order to regain his heroic status he has to die.

> Let a man nobly live or nobly die
> If he *is* a nobleman.

But heroic decorum is no more, and there is no return to the Homeric world. The sword is Hector's, the ground is Trojan. In the absurd world suicide is a mockery. Nothing can be saved any more. "In the absurd world," wrote Camus, "the value of a notion or of a life is measured by its sterility." The stage is empty, and the world has become desperately void. Only hate remains.

> Dread Furies—
> You who are ever maidens and do watch
> Above all fates and sufferings of men—
> Come with long strides, my helpers; mark my end . . .
> Go, swift and punishing Erinyes,
> Taste the whole army's blood, and spare them nothing.
>
> (834 ff.)

In *Sickness unto Death,* Kierkegaard distinguishes between two kinds of despair. The first, which he calls womanly, or earthly, is a despair over oneself, over the fact that one cannot accept oneself, that one is "alien" to oneself. It is the despair over the fact that one cannot be *different;* for Kierkegaard it is the result of weakness. There is another kind of despair, which Kierkegaard calls manly. It is despair over the fact that one cannot become *oneself.* This is the despair that Camus learned from Kierkegaard. The world wants me to be different, and so, to remain myself, I have to reject the world. I live in a destructive time, and so, to remain myself, I have to assume that time does not exist. It is a despair without hope, in total loneliness, a despair for which there is no cure: ". . . rather than seek help he would prefer to be himself—with all the tortures of hell, if so it must be."[37] The great haters in Malraux know that despair well. "He who kills himself," he wrote in *The Royal Way,* "chases an idealized image formed of himself; one commits suicide only in order to exist."

Ajax passed through the first despair and reached the

other. He realized then that the final reckoning was between his own self and the world. He had by now accepted all the Ajaxes: Ajax the hero; Ajax the tormenter;
Ajax made ridiculous; Ajax for whom there is no heroic
death, who will not have time to take his revenge; Ajax
who will make his son an orphan; Ajax who will leave
Tecmessa as a whore for the Greek generals. Kierkegaard wrote: "... now he would rage against every thing,
he, the one man in the whole existence who is the most
unjustly treated, to whom it is especially important to
have his torment at hand, important that no one should
take it from him—for thus he can convince himself that
he is in the right ... He wills to be himself, himself with
his torment, in order with this torment to protest against
the whole of existence."[38]

Kierkegaard knew that suicide is not only despair but
also rebellion. "Do you not know that I no longer owe
any service to the gods" (589, Jebb's translation). Ajax
is finished with the gods, because it is *their* world, *their*
order, *they* want men to be their shadows. This ultimate
revolt has eternity as its only witness; the unalterable.
The "above" and the "below," Zeus and Hades, are
unalterable.

> I call, first, Zeus, on you.
> (825)

In *Ajax*, as in every true tragedy, myth and archetypes
are still alive. "Darkness is my light!" The great-grandfa-
ther of the mythical Ajax was Zeus, and his grandfather
was Aeacus, one of the three judges of the nether world
with Radamanthos and Minos. Like Racine's Phèdre,[39]
"la fille de Minos et de Pasiphaé," torn between darkness
and light (*"Soleil, je te viens voir pour la dernière fois"* [I, iii,
172]), Ajax bids farewell to light.[40]

>   . . . I greet you
> For this last time and never any more.
> O radiance . . .
>
>   (857 ff.)

He killed himself at high noon, when the shadow of the sword driven into the ground was the shortest.[41] He emerged from darkness and returned to darkness. "All else I have to say, I shall say to those below, in Hades" (865, Knox's translation). He remained unyielding to the end, just like his infernal grandfather. "Why do we loathe Hades more than any god, if not because he is so adamantine and unyielding" (*Iliad*, IX, 165).

In the absurd world, the only heroism left is the refusal to accept it. Ajax refuses to accept the world in which everything goes to waste.

IV.

Malraux's famous line, "Death changes life into destiny," can be read either as a philosophical creed, or as a rule of poetics. Existence becomes essence: Ajax does not exist "for himself" any more; Ajax who could judge Ajax has ceased to exist. Ajax now exists only "for others," has become an object; and an object can be made into anything. In its aesthetic interpretation, Malraux's formula seems close to Aristotle: the hero's death is the end of tragedy. When viewed from the perspective of the past, life and death assume the marks of necessity. A tragic death always occurs *for something;* it means a choice and a reassertion of the order of values. The death of Hector and Achilles' choosing a short life confirm the heroic order. But the death of Ajax does not save anything. It is a heroic gesture in a void, as barren as Camus' description. Ajax committed suicide because he did not want to accept a world in which everything went to waste; but in the world in which everything went to waste, the Ajax who committed suicide had also gone to waste. The second part of the tragedy is a judgment on the corpse.

Everyone, from the first scholiast to the writers of the last decade, has considered the second part of *Ajax* a bore, tasteless, or at any rate an artistic blunder. This stubborn refusal to acknowledge Sophocles' role as innovator is due not only to an aesthetic bias toward the unities in tragedy. The pious philologists were afraid of the black Sophocles, just as Shakespearean scholars for a long time could not accept a Shakespeare without hope, where Cordelia's death and the torments of Lear bring no reward at all. Corneille, one of the few to have understood *Ajax* completely, wrote in his *Discours sur le Poème Dramatique* (1660): ". . . *quelle grâce a eu chez les Athéniens la contestation de Ménélas et de Teucer pour la sépulture d'Ajax, que Sophocle fait mourir au quatrième acte.*" Corneille did not have "Classicist" tastes and he knew what the struggle for power meant. He saw with his own eyes the end of a heroic era.

Into a tragedy ending with Ajax's suicide one could still read hubris and *diké*. In the bickerings over the corpse, the gods do not take part, and there is no pity or fear. The bickerings bring no catharsis. It is not by chance that the bitterness of *Ajax* has been understood in times when people have come to know from their own experience about corpses thrown into a rubbish heap, hasty exhumations and invariably belated rehabilitations, connected with the cult of new leaders.

This argument about the burial of a corpse is one of the most intriguing of Sophocles' dramatic innovations. Teucer and the sailors of Salamis want to pay Ajax the last honors due to a chief. Menelaus and Agamemnon want to throw the body of the traitor to be devoured by dogs and ravens. Unable to avenge themselves on Ajax, they want to take revenge on his corpse. The conceited, proud and cowardly generals hurl abuses at Teucer, a simple archer and the son of a slave woman.

> Why, as it is, being
> Nothing yourself, you have risen up to protect
> That man who now is nothing . . .
>
> (1231 ff.)

There is no agreement as to the date when *Ajax* was written, and one can interpret the climate of the second half in a number of ways. But its topical up-to-dateness is beyond doubt. The anachronisms are there by design, and their tone is Euripidean.[42] Agamemnon and Menelaus probably personify not only the ruthlessness of the Spartan autocrats and their cult of discipline ("Laws will never be rightly kept in a city that knows no fear or reverence," 1073), but also the pride and arrogance of Athens, which graciously allowed her allies to choose between extermination and total submission. This is Menelaus standing over the body of Ajax:

> Listen, then.
> When we brought Ajax here from Greece,
> We thought he would be our ally and our friend:
> On trial we've found him worse than any Trojan—
>
> (1052 ff.)

The Trojan War has been, from Homer to Giraudoux, the most durable literary archetype of war, any war. In *Ajax,* the war is in its tenth year. The word "Trojan" is uttered by Menelaus for the first time when he says that Ajax is more dangerous than the enemy. At headquarters, the intrigues and ambitions of generals and admirals are more important than the fate of the expedition. The full price of the war is being paid only by the soldiers, herded from all over Greece to the close, damp marshes by the Asian shores. In the last song of the Chorus, a Euripidean lament again resounds. The sailors of Salamis have no illusions:

> They bring upon me a ceaseless curse of spear-sped
> Trouble over the length and breadth of Troy,
> A grief and a shame to all Greek men.

> Whoever it was that first revealed to Hellas
> Their common scourge, detested arms and war,
> I curse him. . . .

> . . . None cares
> That my locks are damp with the thick continual dew
> Which is all my thought of Troy.

> (1189 ff.)

The second part of *Ajax* is suddenly projected into modern times. It becomes contemporary to the audience. To all audiences, not only Greek. It is contemporary to a nonheroic world. Its positive hero is Odysseus. In the prologue he chased Ajax like an animal. Now he has rushed onto the stage, indefatigable and at just the right time, as usual. Even from a distance he shouts:

> What is this, gentlemen? For quite some distance
> I could hear the sons of Atreus raising their voices
> Over this valiant corpse.

> (1316 ff.)

In the *Iliad*, the "gigantic" Ajax, "big, sturdy and redoubtable, with a smile on his grim face," was opposed to Odysseus, who had "the quickest brain of any man" and "whose thoughts were like the thoughts of Zeus."

Heraclitus wrote that character means destiny. But character can also mean ideology. To award the armor of
Achilles to Odysseus, Knox shrewdly noted, meant the
end of the heroic era; as strength went down in price,
cunning went up.[43]

> Often the heart of the human herd is blind.
> If it could see the truth,
> Aias would not, in wrath about armour,
> Have driven a smooth sword through his breast.
>
> (*Nemean*, VII, 24–27)[44]

Pindar's noble and silent Ajax falls victim to the mob's
blindness. The signs are reversed: Ajax is associated with
light; the award of the armor to Odysseus is accompanied by the darkness of a new age. Pindar extolled the
aristocratic virtues, and his Odysseus was a *homo novus* of
Athenian democracy, in which only cunning assured success. "Envy attacks the good; fights not the base. It tore
even Telamon's son, throwing him on his sword. In the
grim acrimony, silence checks the tongueless men,
though brave, and the chief prize rewards the shifty liar"
(*Nemean*, VIII, 22–29).[45]

In the second half of the fifth century, Odysseus had
become almost exclusively the image of a practical politician, for whom the end justified the means and who was
devoid of scruples. Such an Odysseus was shown by
Sophocles in *Philoctetes.* Such is Odysseus in the eyes of
Ajax, "the tool of every mischief, filthiest scoundrel of all
the army," "that devious, hateful rogue"; such is Odysseus as seen by the Chorus, "that waiting, labouring
man, how he insults in his black heart"; even for Agamemnon he is "selfish, changeable and unsteady." But
the Odysseus of the prologue and the epilogue is a different, much more deeply delineated character. Sophocles
preserved all existing opposites: the physical opposites

of heaviness and agility; the moral ones, of strength and cunning; those of character, inflexibility and versatility; the historic ones, of the heroic era and unheroic time; but he showed them in the perspective of a tragic opposition between one who rejects the absurdity of the human condition, and one who accepts it. "We are dim shapes, no more than weightless shadow." Odysseus knows this. But for him it is not a reason for despair, only for prudence.

> AGAMEMNON:
> You want me, then, to let this corpse be buried?
>
> ODYSSEUS:
> Yes. For I too shall come to that necessity.
>
> (1364 ff.)

For Teucer, Menelaus and Agamemnon, the corpse of Ajax is still the living Ajax. Only Odysseus realizes that Ajax is no more. Ajax *was.*

> Thersites' body is as good as Ajax',
> When neither are alive.
>
> (*Cymbeline,* IV, ii, 252–53)[46]

The corpse of a heroic fool defying the establishment, and the corpse of a cynical fool jeering against establishment, are no different from each other. Shakespeare also saw the world from the perspective of Odysseus.

Corpses should be buried. All corpses. The bigger a corpse is, the faster this ought to take place. There is always trouble with unburied corpses. The sailors of Salamis have already surrounded Ajax's body in a narrow circle. More of them are arriving. A pious politician knows that unburied corpses are an insult to the gods; a practical politician knows that unburied corpses bring the plague; a far-sighted politician knows that unburied corpses provoke people to evil thoughts. Corpses must be given all their due; even honors. "It's a foul thing to hurt a valiant man in death, though he *was* your enemy" (1344).[47]

Throughout this play, Sophocles remains closest to Homer. Once before, the living Odysseus had met the dead Ajax. When Odysseus descended into Hades, he was surrounded by the shades of heroes, eager for earthly news. "The only soul that stood aloof," Odysseus recollects, "was that of Aias, son of Telamon. . . . I called him now, using his own and his royal father's names, and sought to placate him . . ." Odysseus is even willing to give Achilles' armor to the ghost; he knows full well that only *he*, Odysseus, is alive and only *he* will leave Hades.[48]

"'So not even death itself, Aias, could make you forget your anger with me on account of those accursed arms! . . . No one else is to blame but Zeus, that bitter foe of the Danaan army, who brought you to your doom. Draw near, my prince, and hear me tell our story. . . .' But Aias gave me not a word in answer and went off into Erebus . . ."

(*Odyssey*, XI, 543 ff.)

". . . went off into darkness"—that is how Lattimore renders it. Ajax killed himself because he did not want to be a living ghost and a shadow of Ajax. Now he is only a ghost, but he goes on hating. Stubborn as a donkey, Ajax remains *himself.*

That man is dead, now—just a shadow . . .
(1257)

Sophocles' Ajax is lying on the bier.[49] Maybe Agamemnon was right, after all. This giant of a corpse, this weighty shadow still reeks of hate. But he must be

buried. Odysseus is in a hurry, as ever. He wants to dig
Ajax's grave with his own hands.

> . . . I should like to join
> In the burial of your dead—doing with you
> That labor . . .

> (1377)

Ajax is buried thanks to Odysseus' mercy. He has been
deceived for the third time. He, who has realized at last
that in the absurd world, heroism is absurd too, has been
declared a hero and his grave has become a shrine. He
could not know that only in unheroic times are monu-
ments for hero worship built.

In the last book of *The Republic,* Plato quotes the story
of Er, son of Armenius, about the mysterious and secluded spot on the confines of the earth where souls of
the dead come from heaven and from the underworld to
meet and begin "a new cycle of life and mortality." Every
soul draws a lot and "the life which he chooses shall be
his destiny." There were, Er went on, "many more lives
than the souls present, and they were of all sorts. There
were lives of every animal and of man in every condition." The choices of the souls were often unexpected.
"Many of the souls exchanged a good destiny for an evil
or an evil for a good . . . for the choice of the souls was
in most cases based on their experience of a previous
life." Among the souls who made the choice of a future
life were Ajax and Odysseus.

The soul which obtained the twentieth lot chose the life of a
lion, and this was the soul of Ajax the son of Telamon, who
would not be a man, remembering the injustice which was
done him in the judgement about the arms . . . He hated
human nature by reason of his sufferings . . . There came also
the soul of Odysseus having yet to make a choice, and his lot

happened to be the last of them all. Now the recollection of former toils had disenchanted him of ambition, and he went about for a considerable time in search of the life of a private man who had no cares; he had some difficulty in finding this, which was lying about and had been neglected by everybody else; and when he saw it, he said that he would have done the same had his lot been first instead of last, and that he was delighted to have it.[50]

This is the shrewdest judgment ever made about Ajax and Odysseus. In today's Valley of Transformation, what forms would Ajax and Odysseus choose?[51]

The Veiled Alcestis

You could say that she was living
and you could say that she was dead.

(Alcestis, 141)

I.

Alcestis died for Admetus. Apollo, who had done a year's hard labor tending the sheep of Admetus, king of Thessaly, secured for him an exceptional privilege, in gratitude for the good treatment he had received. This was that Admetus would be spared in the hour of death, provided he found someone to agree to die for him. Friends, father and mother all refused. Only his wife agreed. Before her death she demanded one thing only; Admetus had to swear solemnly he would never marry again.

Her corpse had not yet been buried when Heracles visited Admetus. The latter, famous all over Greece for his hospitality, kept his wife's death secret from his friend, for fear Heracles would not want to stay in a house of mourning. The guest was taken to his quarters, Admetus went to the funeral. Heracles got drunk and began to sing gaily. An old servant of Admetus, indignant at this, told the guest the sad truth. The good-natured Heracles, ashamed at his improper behavior, decided to restore Alcestis to Admetus. The host had hardly returned from the funeral when Heracles was back, accompanied by a silent veiled woman. He told Admetus that he had won her as a prize in an athletic contest and had brought her to console him. The new widower was most reluctant to admit a young woman into his home. But Heracles, adamant, referred to the laws of hospitality. The hospitable Admetus gave way. In the mute stranger Admetus recognized the dead Alcestis. "I was lucky. That I cannot deny" (1158).[1] These are his last words in the play. Admetus was lucky indeed. For three days Alcestis would not be allowed to speak; first she had to perform the rites of purification. And there would be no explanations.

A strange play. It seems self-destructive. Everything in it—the sequence of events, the delineation of characters, the dialogue, the myths evoked, and above all the stage effects—is used in such a way as to make a cruel mockery of Alcestis' resurrection. If it is a tragedy, it consumes itself. There are only two possibilities: either to regard *Alcestis* as a failure, or to consider it as a shocking drama, with an unusual degree of venom and perfidy. *Alcestis* was performed at the Dionysia as a fourth play, which was usually a satyr play. But it differs strikingly from other extant satyr plays.

In the prologue, Apollo wrangles with death; in the

epilogue the beautiful Stranger, veiled and silent, turns
out to be Alcestis, miraculously brought out of her tomb.
But in between, we have a play of an amazingly realistic
texture. Alcestis dies onstage, and it has long been noted
that it is the only natural death in all of Greek drama. She
is not killed, does not commit suicide; she prepares herself for death carefully, quietly and systematically.

> For when she understood the fatal day
> was come, she bathed her white body with water drawn
> from running streams, then opened the cedar chest and took
> her clothes out . . .
>
> (158 ff.)

"Cedar wood," comments A. M. Dale in her critical
edition of *Alcestis*, "protected clothes from damp and
moth."[2] It is a typically female comment, but no doubt
accurate. Alcestis was above all a good housewife. When
Admetus returns home from the funeral, he is shocked
not so much by the empty nuptial bed, but first of all by
the "floor all covered with dust" (946–47).[3] Floors in
Greek tragedies are often stained with blood, but never
before were they "unwashed and dirty."

The realism of *Alcestis* is not only psychological but
impregnated with mundane details. Perhaps the best
thing to call it is "domestic" realism. This term, coined
by Bernard Knox, fits *Alcestis* even better than the prologue to Euripides' *Electra*.[4] The action takes place, of
course, *in front* of Admetus' palace in accordance with
convention, but in no other Greek play up to Menander
do we have such a strong impression of being *inside* the
house. We almost know its arrangement:

> . . . open the guest rooms which are across the court
> from the house, and tell the people who are there to provide

plenty to eat, and make sure that you close the doors
facing the inside court.

(546 ff.)

Admetus tells the servants to conduct Heracles to the
guest rooms, and this is one of the most frequently
quoted proofs that in the front wall of the *skene,* apart
from the middle opening, there were two smaller ones,
to the right and to the left. The essential action of the
play, however, takes place in the bedroom. In the house
of Alcestis and Admetus, and in the drama of Alcestis
and Admetus, the bed is the main piece of furniture.

> O marriage bed,
> it was here that I undressed my maidenhood and gave
> myself up to this husband for whose sake I die. . . .

(176 ff.)

Alcestis is not yet onstage. The Chorus of elders has
come from the city to find out if the queen is already
dead. In this domestic drama, the maid replaces the messenger of tragedy. She tells the Chorus about the day's
events, starting with the morning.

> She fell on the bed and kissed it. All the coverings
> were drenched in the unchecked outpouring of her tears;
> but after much crying, when all her tears were shed,
> she rolled from the couch and walked away with eyes cast
>   down,
> began to leave the room, but turned and turned again
> to fling herself once more upon the bed.

(183 ff.)

At last the palace door is thrown open, and Alcestis is
carried out in a litter. She bids her last farewell to her

husband and children. In this long farewell scene no one mentions Alcestis' heroic decision and the unusual bargain with death. If the story is to be taken at face value, this must have happened very recently, since Apollo has only just left the house of Admetus after a year's service.[5]

In the whole drama, Alcestis' decision is the only tragic choice. But Euripides did not need the scene where a wife sacrificed herself for her husband. He was writing a different play. The bargain with death had taken place *in the past,* so long ago that Admetus has forgotten it. Alcestis even has to remind him in her last moments that she is dying for him.

ADMETUS:
Oh, take me with you, for God's love, take me there too.

ALCESTIS:
No, I am dying in your place. That is enough.

(382 ff.)

Euripides is merciless; a heroic death is transformed into an ordinary death; a deliberately chosen death looks like a natural one. Poor Alcestis has to convince her husband that she is really dying, here and now. "I must die. Not tomorrow. Not on the third day of the month. But in one moment they will be saying I am dead" (320 ff.).[6] Admetus prefers to the end not to believe in Alcestis' death. Even at the last moment he asks: "Are you really leaving us?" (391). Critics and scholars are very harsh with regard to Admetus; almost without exception they think he has behaved like a coward.[7] There are good reasons for it. Everything Admetus says is untimely, either a note too high or too low. But the irony of Euripides is in fact far more pitiless. After all, everything we say to a dying person is untimely. To die now and to have to die in the future are different. One can survive only someone else's death, not one's own.

The death of Alcestis has to be as *real* as possible, so that her resurrection may be as *unreal* as possible. In the entire *Alcestis* play, this is the only opera-seria scene, whereas all other scenes have an opera-buffa tone. Death, with his big sword, arguing with Apollo in the prologue, is a grotesque figure, but Alcestis sees before her another Death, one who does not want to wait. "He frowns from under dark brows. He has wings. It is Death" (261). The word Hades is uttered, always spoken with fear. Only Racine was able to render the cold poetry of those lines:

> Je vois déjà la rame et la barque fatale;
> J'entends le vieux nocher sur la rive infernale.
> Impatient, il crie: "On t'attend ici-bas;
> "Tout est prêt, descends, viens, ne me retarde pas." [8]

Alcestis is a heroine of tragedy, but has a husband taken from comedy. Medea is in a similar position, and in both plays the same kind of dissonance results from a mixture of "merry and tragical, tedious and brief." Even before husband and wife appear on the stage, the Maid expresses quite clearly all the ambiguity of the relationship between the husband and his dying wife: "He is weeping and holding his wife in his hands and begging her not to betray him . . ." (201).[9] Admetus implores Alcestis not to betray him. Betray him with whom? With death? "Raise yourself, my Alcestis, do not betray me now" (250). Admetus makes constant slips of the tongue and is already thinking of betrayal. "The idea of betrayal, and the question of what is betrayal," Wesley D. Smith rightly observes, "are made into a theme in the play, and finally are the subject of the final scene."[10] The mystery of Alcestis' sacrifice, death and miraculous resurrection turns into a comedy of the loyal wife and unfaithful husband. Alcestis, who received a solemn promise that her husband would not marry again, has few illusions.

> I die. Some other woman will possess you now.
> She will not be better, but she might be happier.
>
> (181 f.)

And again, a while before her death, replying to vows of faith:

> Time will soften it. The dead count for nothing at all.
>
> (381)

Up to now they all were amazingly discreet. Alcestis' death seemed natural. Her sacrifice did not cause surprise or admiration; it was regarded as a matter-of-course occurrence by the Chorus, by herself, and obviously, by Admetus. To the Maid alone Alcestis seemed heroic. In his laments Admetus begged Alcestis to wait for him, but it did not even occur to him that he himself could wait for her in his grave.

And now, when the body of Alcestis has been carried away, the husband who agreed that his wife should die for him, meets the father who did not want to die for his son. From Plautus to commedia dell'arte and Molière, in the best tradition of comedy, whenever father confronts son it is the father who is put to shame and ridicule. He is unmasked and punished for having courted a young girl, or for having forbidden the son what he has himself indulged in. Euripides is much more perverse.

> PHERES:
> I should have made a mistake if I had died for you.

ADMETUS:

Is it the same thing to die old and to die young?

PHERES:

Yes. We have only one life and not two to live.

(710 ff.)

It is the son who is derided. This unexpected reversal looks like a Brechtian device: the son is as cowardly and as selfish as the father; neither of them wants to die. "Alcestis' death is sandwiched," wrote Kitto, "between a flippant treatment of the grim figure of Death, and a scene between Admetus and Pheres which is never far from comedy or satire."[11] The bargain with death suddenly sounds modern and irreverent. At once everything is turned upside down. Alcestis' sacrifice seemed heroic and natural; now it is unnatural and foolish. Old Pheres does not mince words, yet we must admit he is right: "She's pure and blameless, yes; but does she have sense?" (728).[12]

The conversation ends with abuse and this scene is, Aristophanes apart, the most brutal and harsh in all Greek drama. The comic pattern is reversed: instead of the father dispossessing a prodigal son, it is the son who renounces his father and mother, and announces that he will not even give them funerals. But before the end of the scene, old Pheres has his say: "Go on, and court more women, so they all can die" (721).

The dead go fast. Alcestis has hardly closed her eyes when Admetus repudiates her. In a sophistical and evasive way he tells Heracles, in a half-truth, that the dead woman was "not of his blood." And when Heracles still has some doubt, he adds brutally and offhandedly: "The dead are dead. Go on in" (541).

Before the night falls and before the play is over, all

oaths of loyalty have to be broken. Instead of restoring Alcestis from her grave to his best friend, Heracles plays a practical joke on him. The good-natured giant behaves in the epilogue like an *agent provocateur* and puts Admetus to the test:

HERACLES:
You have lost a fine wife. Who will say you have not?

ADMETUS:
So fine that I, whom you see, never shall be happy again.

HERACLES:
Time will soften it. The evil still is young and strong.

(1083 ff.)

Heracles, as if he were present at Alcestis' last conversation with Admetus, repeats her words: "Time will soften it. The dead count for nothing at all" (381). Admetus has to be utterly compromised. Again it is the bed that is the main piece of furniture:

HERACLES:
What? You will not remarry but keep an empty bed?

ADMETUS:
No woman ever shall sleep in my arms again.

HERACLES:
Praiseworthy, yes, praiseworthy. And yet foolish, too.

(1089 ff.)

Nothing is left unsaid in this perverse scene. The woman, her face hidden under a thick veil, is standing between Heracles and Admetus in front of the house, waiting. Admetus notices at once that she is young, and her curves remind him of Alcestis. He explains to Heracles that he cannot put her in the men's quarters, as she would be in danger there; only one thing remains: to take her to Alcestis' empty bed. But then

> I fear blame from two quarters, from my countrymen
> who might accuse me of betraying her who helped
> me most, by running to the bed of another girl,
> and from the dead herself. . . .
> I must be very careful.
>
> (1057 ff.)

The Chorus of elders, who at noon, when Alcestis died, had threatened Admetus with eternal damnation, "should he now take a new wife to his bed, he will win my horror and hatred" (464), toward evening become much more philosophical. God has taken away, god has given:

> I cannot put a good name to your fortune; yet
> whoever you are, you must endure what the god gives.
>
> (1070 f.)

Alcestis can be interpreted as a play in praise of hospitality. As a reward for hospitality, the grateful Apollo obtained from the Fates a safe-conduct for Admetus in his hour of death. Because he was hospitable, he made Heracles stay with him on the day Alcestis died. Because he was very hospitable, he took into his house the mute and veiled stranger, and as a result regained his wife. Admetus' hospitality is like the "humor" of the heroes of Plautus and Molière. Admetus is hospitable, just as Harpagon is a miser, Arnolf is jealous and Argan a hypochondriac. But in the comedy of "humors," maniacs are always punished in the end. Admetus has been rewarded for his hospitality. Alcestis demanded marital loyalty for her sacrifice; Admetus regained her by being unfaithful.[13]

Tragic heroes are given in the moment of their ultimate choice an absolute clarity of vision. Heroes of the
comedy of "humors" not only are punished, but sometimes cured, or—like Argan—come to their senses, if
only for a short while. But is Admetus cured? "I see it
now" (940), he says on his return to the empty house
after the funeral. But what has Admetus understood?
That the house is dirty, that children are crying, that he
cannot marry again and that everybody regards him as a
coward.

> What I have gained by living, friends,
> when reputation, life, and action all are bad?
>
> (960 ff.)

The Stranger turns out to be Alcestis. Admetus has
regained his wife. But he is neither cured nor morally
reborn. *Alcestis* reminds one of a prologue to one of G.B.
Shaw's "unpleasant plays": the comedy will begin when
Alcestis regains her speech after three days.

Only the miracle causes difficulties. In the comedy of
"humors" and characters, in comedies of manners and
in psychological comedies, we are not used to miracles.
Maybe the miracle did not happen? Arthur W. Verrall, a
rationalist and positivist brought up on naturalistic
theatre and Victorian melodrama, took the view that
Euripides had written his plays in two ways: with tongue
in cheek for his sophist friends, and pretending to believe in the gods and miracles for the benefit of the
Athenian populace.[14] Alcestis did not *really* die; Heracles
woke her up from lethargy. Arrowsmith was right in saying that one must not ignore Verrall.[15] The resurrection
of Alcestis is full of ambiguity: there is a miracle and
there is none.

But is there still a third possibility? Heracles is a good
friend; too good a friend maybe. He tried hard to con-

sole Admetus in his misery. When the veil is lifted, the beautiful Stranger is not Admetus' wife. What can this pitiful husband do now? He has been cornered, caught in his own trap. He had sworn to the dying Alcestis that very morning: "I will keep my promise to the end" (374). Only a little while before, he declared to the Chorus of citizens of Pherae: "Let me die if I betray her, though she is gone" (1096). But he has already taken the Stranger by the hand, offering to take her into the house. The woman is young and beautiful: ". . . all your body is like hers" (1063). Hospitable Admetus cannot but agree with Heracles that this *is* Alcestis. Second wives, though usually younger, often resemble the first.

> Oh, eyes
> and body of my dearest wife, I have you now
> beyond all hope. I never thought to see you again.
>
> (1132 ff.)

The beautiful Stranger is silent and will remain silent for at least three days. Or forever. *Alcestis* is a play full of puzzles that does not want to unveil its secret. It has been called a romantic comedy and a melodrama, a tragicomedy and the bastard offspring of satyr drama and tragedy, a romance, a grotesque, a burlesque. The Chorus of citizens knew from the start that all was in doubt.

> So sure? I know nothing. Why are you certain?
>
> (95)

II.

Alcestis' youth is connected with the history of Jason and Medea. She was "the beauty among women, Alkestis, loveliest of all the daughters of Pelias" (*Iliad*, II, 714 f., Lattimore translation). The perfidious Medea decided to kill Pelias in a most cruel manner. She promised to restore his youth if he agreed to be cut to pieces by his own daughters and thrown into a cauldron in which she would boil magic herbs. Accordingly, two daughters cut up their father while he was asleep, but Alcestis refused; she had been pious from childhood. But her piety is not as important as the fact that one of her earliest experiences is of a crime instead of a resurrection.

In another, probably much earlier set of myths, Admetus, king of Pherae, was related to Apollo, who had served him for a year as a cattle shepherd as punishment for having killed the Cyclops; Apollo had taken his revenge on the Cyclops because they had forged the thunderbolts with which Zeus killed his son, Asclepius. Asclepius had been a miraculous healer who restored life to the dead. And for this Zeus turned him to ashes.

Concerning Asclepius, Hesiod says: "And the father of men and gods was wrath, and from Olympus he smote the son of Leto with a lurid thunderbolt and killed him, arousing the anger of Phoebus."[16]

The Chorus in *Alcestis* tells the story of Asclepius' punishment and ends with a hopeless coda:

> Where is there any hope for life
> left for me any longer?
>
> (130 f.)

So, in this other account of Alcestis' and Admetus' early history, all attempts to restore life to the dead are punished outright. The mystical Alcestis returned from Hades only once in the *Symposium*. For Plato she was a model of sacrifice. Only lovers, he writes, are able to die for one another. "So noble did this action of hers appear to the gods, as well as to men, that among the many who have done virtuously she is one of the very few to whom, in admiration of her noble action, they have granted the privilege of returning alive to earth; such exceeding honor is paid by the gods to the devotion and virtue of the love."[17]

For Apollodorus, unlike Plato, the moral of this story is totally antisentimental; the gods were not at all happy about Alcestis' action. Persephone decided that a wife should not die for her husband; Alcestis did wrong, her example could be harmful, so she was sent back to earth.[18] Kitto is quite right when he says that Alcestis in Euripides "derives individuality from her evident mistrust of her husband."[19] Alcestis' sacrifice became revolting with the introduction of the disloyal Admetus, her resurrection grotesque with the substitution of the drunken Heracles for the gods of the underworld.

In *Alcestis,* Heracles comes to stay at Admetus' house while on a horse-stealing expedition. On orders from Eurystheus of Tiryns, whom he served, he was to steal the famous mares belonging to Diomedes, king of Thrace. It was the eighth Herculean labor. His descent into Hades and snatching Cerberus by the neck was to be his twelfth labor, and in no canonical version of the myth was it connected with the deliverance of Alcestis. Diomedes' mares were said to spit fire and eat human flesh. Horse thieves rarely believe in miracles; rather, their profession demands skill and cunning.

CHORUS:
It is not easy to put a bridle on their jaws.

HERACLES:
Easy enough, unless their nostrils are snorting fire.

CHORUS:

Not that, but they have teeth that tear a man apart.

HERACLES:

Oh no! Mountain beasts, not horses, feed like that.

(492 ff.)

Admetus' old servant had not seen such a boor in the royal palace before. The guest was not satisfied with what he had been given but asked for more food and drink. And when he became quite drunk, he began to sing and jump about. Such a drunken Heracles is represented in a bronze statuette from Smyrna, now at the New York Metropolitan Museum. Heracles has put his right leg forward, leaning backward, with his arms akimbo. He is looking down, does not seem to see anyone. But this folk Heracles was even fonder of food than of drink. His favorite dish—a liking he shared with all soldiers—was pea soup. But as a Doric hero he also liked "barley-cakes, of which he ate sufficient . . . to have made a hired laborer grunt 'enough!' "[20] Heracles always behaves like a soldier on bivouac. Today is what matters, who knows what tomorrow will bring; so let us eat, drink and be merry.

> Fortune is dark; she moves, but we cannot see the way
> nor can we pin her down by science and study her.
> There, I have told you. Now you can understand. Go on,
> enjoy yourself, drink, call the life you live today
> your own, but only that, the rest belongs to chance.
> Then, beyond all gods, pay your best attentions to
> the Cyprian, man's sweetest. There's a god who's kind.

(785 ff.)

This country Heracles, prancing gaily (often represented in sculpture, particularly the so-called "Farnese

type," with flattened ears, swollen at the tips, ears characteristic of athletes), whom the Servant calls "this ruf-
fian thief, this highwayman" (766), is taken from satyr
drama, and his precepts are very much like Silenus'
speeches to Odysseus in *Cyclops*.[22] *Carpe diem* and "tomorrow we die" represent the same kind of philosophy,
put in another way. Folk heroes, soldiers and thieves
know very well that no one will escape death and that one
can only die once.

> Death is an obligation which we all must pay.
> There is not one man living who can truly say
> if he will be alive or dead on the next day. . . .
>
> . . .
>
> . . . if I am any judge,
> life is not really life but a catastrophe.
>
> (782–84, 801–2)

There is nothing that would terrify Heracles; the horse
thief is a good friend and is ready even to follow Alcestis
down to Hades in order to restore her to Admetus. Being
fond of drink himself, he assumes that Death must be
drunk and will not go far, "drinking the blood of slaughtered beasts beside the grave" (845). In this drunken
mythology Apollo plied even the relentless Fates with
drink, "by a shabby wrestler's trick" (34), in order to
redeem Admetus from death. The story was common
knowledge. Already in Aeschylus' *Eumenides* the Furies
reproached Apollo:

Such was your action in the house of Pheres. Then
you beguiled the Fates to let mortals go free from death.[23]

Miracles in *Alcestis* happen in a drunken stupor. Even
when Euripides renounces the buffo tone for a while, his

references to the myth are ironical. In a most solemn moment, just before Alcestis' death, Admetus assures her that if he had the voice and lyre of Orpheus he would not hesitate to descend after her to the underworld:

> . . . and not the hound
> of Pluto could have stayed me, not the ferryman
> of ghosts, Charon at his oar. I would have brought you
> back to life.
>
> (360 ff.)

Even the most ignorant spectator of *Alcestis* must have known that Orpheus did not succeed in leading Euridice out of the underworld. Hades agreed to let her go on condition that Orpheus not look at his wife until he saw the light of the sun. At the last moment, when they were about to leave the lower regions, Orpheus looked behind at Euridice; he was not sure the gods had not deceived him, and for this he lost her. In the *Symposium*, Plato tells how Alcestis was set free from the kingdom of the dead as a reward for her sacrifice, and about the failure of Orpheus, whom the gods punished for his pusillanimity.

But Orpheus, the son of Oeagrus, the harper, they sent empty away, and presented to him an apparition only of her whom he sought, but herself they would not give up, because he showed no spirit; he was only a harp-player, and did not dare, like Alcestis, to die for love, but was contriving how he might enter Hades alive . . .

The selfish love of Orpheus, just a musician concerned with saving his own skin on this dangerous expedition, is contrasted with the heroic love of Queen Alcestis; we do not know if this didactic version of the myth was Plato's invention or existed before. If it did, then Euripides was exceptionally perverse. Admetus, who wanted to be like Orpheus, not only forgot that the Thracian singer had not succeeded in his wife-recovery expedition; he did not pause even for a moment to think that he was like Orpheus only in his cowardice.[24]

Myths in *Alcestis* are self-destructive, or self-mocking. In Greek catalogues of the dead who returned from Hades, Protesilaus is always mentioned next to Alcestis.[25] He was the first Greek to die on Trojan soil. His wife, Laodamia, in her sorrow put her husband's image —made of bronze, or according to some, of wax—on her bed. Admetus wants to behave like Laodamia. He promises the dying Alcestis that he will order a painted figure of her from the most skillful artisans:

> . . . to set in my room,
> pay my devotions to it, hold it in my arms
> and speak your name, and clasp it close against my heart,
> and think I hold my wife again, though I do not,
> cold consolation, I know it . . .

> (349 ff.)

Euripides' play about Protesilaus and Laodamia has not been preserved, and we cannot even tell if it was a tragedy, or one of those innovatory "semicomedies," which cause classical scholars so much trouble. Only a few fragments are extant of *Protesilaus;* in their tone and atmosphere they seem fairly close to *Alcestis.* "I cannot betray whom I love, even though he is dead" (fragment 657). Another fragment says that the dead do not return: "His fate is the same as awaits you; you and all people" (fragment 651). The third fragment is the most astonishing of all: "Relations with women should be in common" (fragment 655).[26]

We know the story of Protesilaus and Laodamia from numerous sources. Lucian, a great mocker of myths, included Protesilaus' bargain with Pluto in his *Dialogues of the Dead.* This account is most interesting, because it testifies not only to his thorough knowledge of *Alcestis,* but to his having interpreted it as a comedy. Protesilaus argues with Pluto, like Apollo with Death, and suggests reasonable conditions of his release from Hades in a very similar way.

PROTESILAUS:
I think to win her to come with me, and bring two dead for one.

PLUTO:
It may not be, it never has been.

PROTESILAUS:
Bethink thee, Pluto. 'Twas for this same cause that ye gave Orpheus his Euridice; and Heracles had interest enough to be granted Alcestis; she was of my kin.[27]

Protesilaus was freed from Hades for three hours. He appeared in Laodamia's bedroom and spoke through the lips of the statue. When the allotted time was over, Laodamia stabbed herself and joined her husband. In another version Laodamia spent night after night with the statue. Her enthusiasm must have been greater than that of Admetus, who promised himself only "a frigid delight" from Alcestis' image. On one occasion, early in the morning, a servant saw Laodamia in bed and, convinced that she was hiding a lover, told her father. The father found the statue next to her in bed and ordered that it be burned. Laodamia threw herself into the flames and perished.

The latter version seems more modern to us, and if it had not been written down by Hyginus, it could have easily been attributed to Giraudoux. The first version, however, is more dramatic, and as a model of theatrical resurrection it was later to be repeated many times. In

the Baroque theatre, which digested the ancient traditions independently and thoroughly, the dead returned
and statues talked. In *Don Juan*, the statue of the Com-
mander foretold divine punishment to the traitor. In *The
Winter's Tale*, after sixteen years Hermione appeared as
a statue to the husband, who had accused her of unfaithfulness and sentenced her to death. Time did not touch
the statue's beauty.

It is hard to say what results from placing an image of
the dead Alcestis in the bedroom. Euripides probably
did not want to repeat *Protesilaus*. The abandoned idea,
however, was a proof of his searchings for a *theatrical*
solution to Alcestis' return from the grave. As Kitto observed: "The simple restoration of Alcestis by Heracles
. . . would obviously be flat, and (because out of keeping)
uncomfortable too. Shakespeare, in similar circumstances, would keep up the atmosphere of tragi-comedy
by pretending that his restored heroine was a statue.
Euripides is cleverer. Alcestis is veiled, and by a conventional cause (1144 ff.) keeps silent. This enables Euripides to present one of his few triangular scenes . . ."[28]

The Chorus of citizens, in their last ode, just before
the climax, once again recalls that even Asclepius did not
cure people of death, and that followers of Orphism—
faced with it—were powerless. There is no cure for
death; he is the only deity who has no altars and cannot
be placated by any sacrifice or bribe. The Chorus in
Alcestis, like Megara in Euripides' *Heracles*, repeats: "We
have to die . . . Who of all the dead comes home from
Hades?" (*Heracles*, 284, 296).

Exactly at this point, when the Chorus ends its final
ode on the inevitability of death, Heracles appears with
the veiled strange woman. He knows very well they think
him a thief, and he begins by saying that he did not steal
this woman: "It cost me hard work to bring her here"
(1035–36). Only at the very end does he say that he

managed to be on time and caught up with Death: "Beside the tomb itself. I sprang and caught him in my hands" (1141–42). This Death, so heavy he could not run far from the tomb, we know from the prologue. Apollo crossed his path when he came to the house of Admetus looking for his victim.

"Death is a character in his own right," writes W. D. Smith, "a nervous bully who is afraid of a fight, a grotesque bogey out of a fairy-tale."[29] Death's dialogue with Apollo in *Alcestis* is unique in the entire body of Greek drama, and many scholars take the view that its origins were in the folk-tale tradition. The theme of a bond in order to postpone death, of clashes with death and attempts to deceive death is common in folk tales of many countries, but death is unyielding and always wins in the end.[30] Analogies do not take us very far. Much more striking is the amazing similarity of this first Death as a character in drama to all its later doubles in medieval theatre and the comedies of early Renaissance.

Death has been represented as a skeleton with a sickle, or most often with a scythe. The sickle, or scythe, later occasionally also an hourglass, were given to medieval Death as part of a classical inheritance from Saturn.[31] In the prologue to *Alcestis,* death is holding a sword, but he uses it for the same purpose as medieval Deaths used their scythe. "I go to take her now, and dedicate her with my sword . . ." (73–74). Jan Kochanowski, in the first translation of *Alcestis* in the vernacular, done in the middle of the sixteenth century, substituted the scythe for the sword, of course, and beautifully combined the ancient and the Christian traditions.

> And that woman shall now go under ground.
> And I go to her to cross her with my scythe.
> For how I can cut the hair of her head
> To the gods of the earth now dedicated.[32]

In the Sicilian Opera dei Puppi, which has preserved the oldest tradition among puppet theatres and even now performs chivalrous romances closely resembling the medieval *Mélusine*, Death is still a wooden skeleton with a scythe. He spends a great deal of time and care cutting off the heads of sinners; then a head falls off the stage with much noise and rolls into the first row of seats in the auditorium. In a Polish Nativity play, Death laughs at King Herod's appeals for mercy and cuts his head off. The head is made of a turnip, and Death cuts it off with a real scythe, like a ripe ear of corn in the field.[33]

Death is self-confident and impudent only to those weaker than himself. In the prologue to *Alcestis* he is arrogant at first but soon changes his tune when Apollo, who treats him with contempt throughout, aims his bow at him in jest.

APOLLO:
Never fear, I have nothing but justice and fair words for you.

DEATH:
If you mean fairly, what are you doing with a bow?

(38 ff.)

Death in *Alcestis*, as in the medieval Dance of Death and later in morality plays, is egalitarian. He has no regard for youth, personal merit, riches or social status.

DEATH:
My privilege means more to me when they die young.

APOLLO:
If she dies old, she will have a lavish burial.

DEATH:
What you propose, Phoebus, is to favor the rich.

(55 ff.)

Death in *Everyman* behaves in pretty much the same way. He is an equally staunch adherent of egalitarianism. When Everyman tries to bribe him, he is indignant:

> Everyman, it may not be, by no way!
> I set not by gold, silver, nor riches,
> Nor by pope, emperor, king, duke, nor princes.
> For, and I would receive gifts great,
> All the world I might get;
> But my custom is clean contrary.
>
> (124 ff.)

Death in *Alcestis*, as in all later European drama, is relentless and ungrateful, totally devoid of *charis* (70). All medieval texts mention his "ugliness." Death is masterful but sluggish and ludicrous; he assumes the air of superiority but is vulgar and not very clever. Apollo mocks him to his face: "What is this? Have you unrecognized talents for debate?" (58). Kitto rendered this amusingly: "What, you among the intelligentsia."[34]

Most important, in this first stage Death is a comic character. Many scholars simply did not notice it. Alexander J. Tate wrote, with deep respect for the Victorian establishment (after all, Death-Thanatos was a god), but with total disregard for *Alcestis'* theatrical style: "One cannot help a feeling of regret that two such dignified characters should descend to such paltry quibbles and sophistries as Euripides here treats us to."[35]

Apollo prophesies to Death that once again he will encounter someone stronger, will be forced to give back his spoils and go away as he came, "hateful to mankind, loathed by the gods." (62). But the prologue not only forecasts the resolution; in the faultlessly constructed *Alcestis*, the style and theatrical form of the prologue are repeated in the epilogue. *Alcestis* began with a big laugh. The little scene in which Apollo pretends to aim his bow at Death arrogantly waving his big sword is close, in its coarse humor and in the caricature of its gestures, to Aristophanes and to the interludes. In Greek dramatic texts there are no stage directions, but two lines in the epilogue almost sound like notes on a director's copy of the play.

HERACLES:
Be brave. Reach out your hand and take the stranger's.

ADMETUS:
Here is my hand; I feel like Perseus killing the Gorgon.

(1117 ff.)

This gesture must have been widely known, since it has been preserved even on Greek vases.[36] Gorgons killed with their eyes, so Perseus turned his head away and raised his shield; on it he saw Medusa's reflection, and then he struck the blow with his sword. Admetus' gestures at this particular moment are quite out of place, as if they were taken from a different play. *Alcestis* ends as it began: with a big laugh. But when Admetus recognizes his wife in the Stranger, the laughter stops. Laughter is now just as improper as Admetus' gestures were a while earlier. Everything is equally wrong, for that matter. We do not experience fear because we cannot believe in the miracle, and there is no one to feel pity for.

The ending is scathing on three counts: Alcestis' sacrifice, Admetus' hospitality and the miracle which has occurred have all been derided. Kurt von Fritz called it "bitter-sweet"; John R. Wilson defined it most crisply: "Admetus and the others can have their cake and eat it too."[37]

The manner in which classical scholars discuss the puzzle of *Alcestis* closely recalls Heracles' persistent questions and Admetus' evasive replies when the guest arrives at his home at a most inopportune moment.

HERACLES:
Surely you have not lost your wife, Alcestis.

ADMETUS:
Yes and no. There are two ways that I could answer that.

HERACLES:
Did you say that she is dead or that she is still alive?

ADMETUS:
She is, but she is gone away. It troubles me.
. . .

HERACLES:
Being and nonbeing are considered different things.

(518 ff.; 528)

The demigod is undoubtedly right. One must ultimately give an answer to the embarrassing question of whether Alcestis has really died and has really returned. But what does "really" mean?

III.

Molière's *Don Juan*, too, surpassed the bounds of classical divisions, and attempts were made to call it a tragicomedy. In the epilogue the unbeliever is struck by thunder from a blue sky, and the earth opens under him. The sinner is punished by God, but the miracle is a stage miracle: the thunder rolls off a machine, and Don Juan does not sink under the earth but goes slowly down the stage trap. *Alcestis*, like *Don Juan*, is amazingly modern in its mixing of styles. On occasion it seems so modern that one is tempted to call it an anti-tragedy. But it is the anti-tragedy devised for instruments that Greek theatre had at its disposal, and only within the conventions of that theatre can one understand and appreciate what an innovator Euripides was.

Alcestis—constructed like a satyr drama—consists of six agones. To perform it, only two actors were required. The first actor, it is clear from the composition of the scenes, played in turn Apollo, Admetus and the Servant; the second actor performed Death, the Maid, Alcestis, Pheres and Heracles. In the epilogue, Admetus and Heracles are onstage at the same time. Who, then, took the part of the beautiful Stranger?

In the Greek theatre the persona and the mask are one and the same. The theatrical identification or sign of dramatis personae is the mask and the costume. When the veil is lifted, Admetus sees the mask of Alcestis. But the mask has been put on in the epilogue by a walk-on. A persona's theatrical sign is also the voice, though articulation in the Greek theatre was probably as artificial and guttural as in the Japanese Nō drama and the Chinese opera. The beautiful Stranger is mute to the end.

Except for the epilogue of *Alcestis* there is no instance in Greek drama, at any rate where the principal parts are concerned, that the mask of one character is put on by another actor.[38] The Stranger *is* Alcestis because she has her mask, but it is Alcestis in another body. The ambiguity of the icon of this second mute Alcestis is another of the play's puzzles.

It does not seem possible to render the ambiguity of Euripides' *Alcestis* in modern theatre. If in the epilogue the same actress appears who played the first Alcestis, the ending will be unambiguous. If the second Alcestis is played by another actress, the disturbing ambiguity of a resurrected wife will cease to exist; the play may seem to be more modern, but also more flat. Performed in the Greek manner, by two actors in masks, *Alcestis* can only

be a reconstruction, and like all archaeological reconstructions, dead. But in our contemporary theatre, since
Meyerhold, Antonin Artaud and Brecht, the mask has
again become a semantic sign. Let the Stranger brought
by the demigod be played by a beautiful young girl, and
let her later reveal a white mask with Alcestis' features.

Alcestis returned and did not return, the beautiful
Stranger is and is not Alcestis. The Maid said about
Alcestis at the very opening of the play: "You could say
that she was living and you could say that she was dead"
(141).[39] Ambiguity is the principle of *Alcestis:* both the
linguistic pattern and the theatrical matter are subject to
it; the action is ambiguous, and myths which deny resurrection are ironically recalled. But what does ambiguity
mean?

In the relation between the significant and the signified, the surface of the sign itself—its "icon," shape,
form; or its meaning, significance, substance—can be
ambiguous. The mask of Alcestis is ambiguous when put
on by an actor different from the one who wore it first;
or, as in commedia dell'arte and in Shakespeare's comedies, a boy who acts a girl who disguises herself as a boy.
Ambiguous in a different way—at the level of significance—is the red carpet on which Agamemnon walks in
the *Oresteia.* This red carpet is a real carpet, woven from
sheep's wool and dyed with purple shell, and at the same
time it is the sign of the blood Agamemnon has spilt, and
which he will now have to shed himself. The passing over
the red carpet is a blasphemous sacrifice which offends
the gods, and at the same time a real sacrifice ceremony
as the executioner turns into the victim. Agamemnon's
red carpet is the most vivid and most ambiguous theatrical sign.

Euripides' *Alcestis* seems to contain both types of ambiguity. Sometimes it appears to be the only masterpiece
of mannerism in the history of drama. It is like the paint-

ings of an Italian master where the portrait of a knight or a lady, when one approaches the canvas, turns suddenly into an odd cluster of apples, pears and grapes, or into just as clustered but precisely drawn ships with spread sails, cannon and mortar.

Tragedy and comedy are significant structures. A tragedy that could at the same time be interpreted and performed as a comedy, and a comedy that could be interpreted and performed tragically, have both this internal ambiguity as a structure. In the prologue to Plautus' *Amphitryon,* Mercury addresses the audience:

> What? Frowning because I said it's tragedy! I'm a god. I'll change it for you: transform this selfsame play from tragedy to comedy and never blot a line. . . . We'll have a mixture: tragicomedy.
>
> (52 ff.)[40]

In this, the earliest known use of the term "tragicomedy," there are two different definitions. The first is that tragedy can be turned into comedy without one word being changed. Mercury was a god, the god of industry to boot, so he, of course, knew structural operations; it was enough to change the code to attribute a different "signified" to the "significant" (icon). In the second definition, *"Faciam ut conmista sit tragicomoedia,"* what is essential is the mixing and joining of gods, royalty and slaves in one story.

Perhaps we should follow Mercury and his amazing first definition and attempt a final reading of *Alcestis,* seeing it first as a tragedy and then as a comedy. Apart from *The Bacchae* (and there is a marked, though not easily pinpointed kinship between Euripides' first and last masterpieces), *Alcestis* is the only Greek drama in which one can find the structure of ritual which, according to the Cambridge school of anthropology (Jane Harrison and Gilbert Murray), is also the "deep form" of tragedy.[41] The six agones of *Alcestis* correspond almost exactly to the six successive elements of this "meta-form": first, a *contest* between a god and his adversary—Apollo and Death in the prologue; second, *pathos,* or suffering—Alcestis' farewell to her marriage bed, children and Admetus, and her terror when she hears Hades calling her; third, a *messenger* announcing death—the old servant, who gives the sad tidings to Heracles; fourth, *threnos*—Admetus' lament on his return from the burial; fifth, *anagnorisis,* or reversal—the recognition of Alcestis in the strange woman; and sixth, the final *theophany*—the return of the resurrected wife to the house. This is how T. S. Eliot, influenced perhaps by the Cambridge anthropologists, interpreted *Alcestis* in *The Cocktail Party:*

> It is a serious matter
> To bring someone from the dead . . .
> Ah, but we die to each other daily.[42]

But in Euripides' *Alcestis,* only one of the six elements of "ritual form"—the suffering and death of the heroine —retains its tragic *serio.* Admetus' lament is treated ironically, and two elements—Apollo's agon with Death and the sobering of the drunken demigod—are clearly farcical. The price of recognition is betrayal, and the epilogue is only a mock theophany. Tragedy turns into comedy, and the last scene has the tone and gestures of satyr drama again. Maurice Regnault's paradox applies to *Alcestis* as to no other play: "Comedy is born from the absence of tragedy in a tragic world."

Mercury has already changed *Alcestis.* So let us now read it as comedy. Following Northrop Frye, one can demonstrate its model as the succession of three periods: the time of mourning and parting; the time of general confusion and temporary loss of identity "usually portrayed by the stock device of impenetrable disguise";[43] and finally, the time of recognition in which the heroes find themselves and their new place in the reborn community. "As the hero gets closer to the heroine and opposition is overcome," Frye writes in "The Argument of Comedy," "all the right-thinking people come over to his side. Thus a new social unit is formed on the stage, and the moment that this social unit crystallizes is the moment of comic resolution."[44]

In the first phase, which corresponds liturgically to the season of Lent, the lovers are separated and the hero or heroine undergoes a "ritual" death. This phase is often dominated by cruel laws, such as the inhuman condition that Admetus has to find a substitute who will agree to die for him. In the second phase, that of lost identity, it is not only Alcestis who has assumed the "impenetrable disguise"; Admetus, too, on his return to the empty house from the burial, has lost his social place and thereby lost himself. The third phase, of reconciliation and renewal, consists, in comedy, of the lovers' finding each other, and ends with the wedding.

In the Greek marriage ceremony, the most solemn moment was the lifting of the veil by the bride in the presence of her future husband and the wedding guests. This moment, the *anakalypteria*, is represented most expressively in the metope sculptures at Selinunte: the bride unveils herself with a ceremonious gesture.

In the epilogue of *Alcestis*, Heracles brings a veiled woman. The veil is later lifted. But who has lifted it? At this point Admetus is holding the Stranger by the hand, his head turned away, as if from the sight of some horrible Gorgon. It is hardly likely that he would dare to unveil her. It has been most often assumed that the veil is lifted by Heracles. But if this scene is to be a repetition of the *anakalypteria* ceremony, the beautiful Stranger has to lift the veil herself.[45] In this way Alcestis marries Admetus again, but does so as his *second* wife.

Error in persona, in which the wife replaces the mistress, will later turn out to be a stock comedy situation. Admetus' mistake will be repeated by Count Almaviva in *The Marriage of Figaro.* But in *Alcestis* this comedy situation has an air of terror about it. It is the moment when laughter dies on one's lips. Neither reconciliation nor renewal follows. The marriage is poisoned. Read as a comedy, *anagnorisis,* the recognition, is almost tragic in *Alcestis.* In the prologue Death comes for Alcestis; in the epilogue Alcestis, raised from her grave, comes for Admetus. In *Alcestis* the theme of Protesilaus returning for Laodamia recurs again. The mute veiled woman is the image of Death. Only now can we understand why Admetus was terrified when he took the Stranger by the hand. Her hand was icy.[46]

Read as a tragedy, *Alcestis* ends with a mock resurrection; read as a comedy, *Alcestis* ends with a deathly marriage. "I have never understood the difference people make between the comic and the tragic," Ionesco wrote in *Expérience du Théâtre.* "The 'comic' . . . seems to me more hopeless than the 'tragic.' The 'comic' offers no escape . . ."

The unveiling is an allegory of Truth. "Time unveiling Truth" was, following the ancient pattern, a frequent theme in the sculpture and painting of the Renaissance and the Baroque, as well as a rhetorical adage. ". . . to unmask falsehood and bring truth to light," Shakespeare wrote in *The Rape of Lucrece* (940). The lifting of the veil in *Alcestis* is the moment of truth. But this final gesture is ambiguous. The Stranger has unveiled herself, but *Alcestis* has remained veiled.

"But Where Now Is Famous Heracles?"

I. THE FACES OF HERACLES

In Book XI of the *Odyssey,* the first voyage in literature to the land of the dead, the most astonishing episode is the encounter between Odysseus and Heracles. All the dead—ordinary mortals like Odysseus' mother and heroes like Achilles and Ajax, murderers and their victims, hoodlums and earthly lovers of Zeus himself are shades and in Hades forever. Only Heracles is set apart, residing at the same time at the summit and at the very bottom of the Greek cosmos, an immortal in the company of the gods on Olympus and a phantom in Hades.

Odysseus, seeing him, does not hide his amazement: ". . . I observed the mighty Heracles—his wraith, that is to say, since he himself banquets at ease with immortal gods and has for consort Hebe of the slim ankles, the Daughter of almighty Zeus and golden-sandalled Here" (*Odyssey*, 681 ff.).[1]

Heracles alone among men has become immortal, but his deification during Homeric times was hard to accept. Even if the strange theology of the divided Heracles in the *Odyssey* is a later interpolation, it is significant that for Homer, the earthly life of Heracles ended in desolation. The Homeric hell is similar in one respect to all later hells: there is no time at all or only one time—*plusquam perfectum.* For the living, the dead are set and immobile, like an imprint in a calcified shell of an antediluvian insect. But for the dead in Homer's Hades, their entire past is their present; they live in *stasis,* simultaneously within themselves and out of themselves: they can watch their lives. In the frozen past of Hades; all honors and glory on earth are vain. Achilles, comforted by Odysseus with the thought that all Greece venerates him as a god, replies:

> O shining Odysseus, never try to console me for dying,
> I would rather follow the plow as thrall to another
> man, one with no land allotted him and not much to live on,
> than be a king over all perished dead.
>
> (*Odyssey*, XI, 487 ff.)[2]

The dead in Homer's Hades have preserved their bodies, the implements they used, the suits and armor they wore. Like figures in a wax museum, they are replicas of themselves. In this Homeric cemetery of heroes, Heracles is an image of useless and wasted power. He wanders through Hades like a madman in an asylum, overcome with a passion to commit murder. He carries

his bow, drawing the string, looking for someone to kill.
But it is impossible to kill the dead.

All around him was a clamor of the dead as of birds scattering
scared in every direction; but he came on, like dark night,
holding his bow bare with an arrow laid in the bowstring,
and forever looking, as one who shot, with terrible glances.

(*Ibid.*, 605 ff.)

In the brief meeting with Odysseus, Heracles recalls
the hardest of his labors, pulling Cerberus out of Hades.
But now both tamer and watchdog are in Hades forever.
The Greek word *ponos* has two meanings: "labor" and
"pain."[3] The descent into hell during life, if one later has
to die, is useless pain: "I was made bondman to one who
was far worse than I, and he loaded my difficult labors on
me. One time he sent me here to fetch the dog back, and
thought there could be no other labor to be devised
more difficult than that one, but I brought the dog up
and led him free the realm of Hades, and Hermes saw me
on my way, with Pallas Athene" (*ibid.*, 621 ff.).
Heracles' moments of failure interest Homer: "The
tasks of Eurystheus were too much for his strength"
(*Iliad*, VIII, 363).[4] Heracles at the gates of hell yells at the
top of his voice, and Zeus must hurriedly send Athene to
help him. Zeus sends Heracles aid for the second time on
the island of Kos. The godlike Heracles is "weariless
agony" (*ibid.*, XV, 24) to Zeus. The divine plans become
thwarted; Zeus was deceived and must look on while his
beloved son, instead of ruling "over all his neighbours,"
completes "the sordid tasks that were set him by Eurystheus" (*Iliad*, XIX, 133).
To Homer, Heracles is an unsuccessful hero; his
power was either too weak or too strong: "Brute, heavy-
handed, who thought nothing of the bad he was doing . . ." (*Iliad*, V, 403, Lattimore's translation). Homer

found this grim Heracles, hero of "the dirty work,"[5] destroying everything around him and destroyed by his own strength, a tragic figure. It is not accidental that Achilles refers to the example of Heracles at the moment of his ultimate choice, when Thetis tries to dissuade him from returning to the Trojan War and predicts that glory will be repaid by death: "I will accept my own death, at whatever time Zeus wishes to bring it about, and the other immortals. For not even the strength of Heracles fled away from destruction, although he was dearest of all to lord Zeus, son of Kronos, but his fate beat him under . . ." (*ibid.*, XVIII, 115 ff.). Heracles, the strongest among men, also had to die. Heracles was the beloved son of god, and this did not save him from destruction: "I had an endless spell of misery," he says to Odysseus in Hades (*Odyssey*, XI, 620, Lattimore's translation).

In Hesiod's *Theogony*, Heracles cleans the earth of monsters. The enumeration is monotonous: he slew the three-headed giant Geryon (289); he slew the Hydra of Lerna "with the unpitying sword" (317); and slew the "long-winged" eagle, who ate Prometheus' "immortal liver" (523). *Theogony* ends, however, with a universal apotheosis, the concord of heaven and earth, and a long list of loving embraces of gods and goddesses with their earthly lovers. The sons of Zeus climb to Olympus, and Heracles too becomes deified: "Happy he. For he has finished his great work and lives amongst the undying gods, untroubled and unaging all his days" (*Theogony*, 953 ff.). But the image of Heracles is filled with contradictions: In *Catalogues* he appears again as a murderer: "[He] slew the noblest sons of steadfast Neleus, eleven of them." His life ends in disaster: "She [Deianira] did a fearful thing . . . the poisoned robe that held black doom . . ."[6] Here the recovered manuscript ends abruptly.

The dramatic opposition between destruction and

apotheosis, between life, in which suffering and atroci-
ties dominate, and eternal happiness in heaven, is most
apparent in the Homeric Hymn "To Heracles the Lion-
Hearted":

I will sing of Heracles, the son of Zeus and much the mightiest
of men of earth. Alcmena bare him in Thebes, the city of lovely
dances, when the dark-clouded Son of Cronos had lain with
her. Once he used to wander over unmeasured tracts of land
and sea at the bidding of King Eurystheus, and himself did
many deeds of violence and endured many, but now he lives
happily in the glorious home of snowy Olympus, and has neat-
ankled Heby for his wife.

Hail, lord, son of Zeus! Give me success and prosperity.

The myth of Heracles remained broken up until the
end of the classical period and was never put together
into a complete whole. The late Middle Ages and the
Renaissance rediscovered the various faces of Heracles.
A thousand years later the Hercules on the Roman re-
liefs, conquering a wild boar or a hydra, became a model
for St. Michael or St. George slaying the dragon.[7] Heracles the savior, who cleanses the earth of brooding monsters from the underworld during the first days of
creation, bears a striking resemblance to the archangels
storming the gates of hell. The Heraclean myths were
early incorporated into Biblical history; the allegorical
Heracles represented David and Samson. Toward the
end of the Renaissance, when under the influence of
Neo-Platonism Greek myths were endowed with Christian symbolism, Heracles, who went into Hades and returned from there alive, became a Christ figure. Christ
is even called "the Christian Hercules." In paintings,
Hercules was represented not unlike Christopher, the
giant who carried the infant Christ across the water. He
was philosophically Christianized as well. Among the

Neo-Platonists in the circle of Marsilio Ficino and Pico della Mirandola, he was the personification of *virtus heroica*, the power of the spirit, which conquers the bestiality of nature, subdues the passions and renounces pleasure. Even Hercules' club became an emblem of reason and moderation, as in *Iconology* of Cesar Ripa (1593).[8] It was, after all, made of wood from the olive tree.

In the republic of Florence, Hercules conquered not only monsters but also tyrants. And after the Renaissance, the early Romantics took over this Hercules. The hero who shot the eagle feeding on Prometheus' liver now himself became Promethean. Adam Mickiewicz in his *Ode to Youth* (1820), written in the spirit of Schiller, wrote:

> As an infant in his crib cut off the Hydra's head,
> This youth will strangle Centaurs,
> Wrench victims from hell,
> Go to heaven for laurels![9]

The romantic Hercules leads not the jailer but the prisoners out from hell and storms heaven. But even in the postclassical tradition, the dark Hercules, at the same time both executioner and victim, was never forgotten. This hero of the destructive power was Hercules *furens*. Hippocrates, who in *De Morbis Mulierum* was the first to describe in detail the precise symptoms of epilepsy, called it "the Herculean disease." The term later appeared in Renaissance dictionaries and encyclopedias and became proverbial: "Why is it that all men who are outstanding in philosophy, poetry, or the arts are melancholic, and some to such extent that they are infected by the diseases arising from black bile, as the story of Heracles among the heroes tells? For Heracles seems to have been of this character, so the ancients called the disease of epilepsy the 'sacred disease' after him."[10]

In the Middle Ages, epilepsy was looked upon as both a stigma and a prophetic gift. It was a sign of those chosen by the devil or by God. During the Renaissance, when the meaning of "holy madness" was close to that of the Neo-Platonists, it was the physical symptoms of epilepsy that awoke the greatest interest. Melancholic was one of the four humors. The "ecstatic melancholic," in whom black bile burned, became the hero of Elizabethan revenge tragedy. This black avenger often compared himself to Hercules.[11]

In Shakespeare's magnificent syncretism, all the faces of Hercules were represented. When Quince in *A Midsummer Night's Dream* gathers together his troupe of rustics and begins to assign parts, Bottom wishes most of all to play the comic tyrant who smashes and destroys everything around him: ". . . yet my chief humour is for a tyrant. I could play Ercles rarely, or a part to tear a cat in, to make all split" (I, i, 22 ff.).[12] In *The Merchant of Venice*, Portia compares Bassanio, who is to choose the right casket in order to win her hand, to Hercules the rescuer, who liberates innocent victims from the power of monsters:

> Now he goes,
> With no less presence, but with much more love,
> Than young Alcides when he did redeem
> The virgin tribute paid by howling Troy
> To the sea-monster. I stand for sacrifice;
> The rest aloof are the Dardanian wives,
> With bleared visages come forth to view
> The issue of th' exploit. Go, Hercules!
> Live thou, I live.
>
> (III, ii, 52 ff.)

Shakespeare's Antony, a lion's skin slung over his armor, considered himself a descendant of Hercules, to whom he was matched in valor and strength. The night before the battle which ended with his defeat, the soldiers see him as Hercules walking through the camp:

> *3 Sold.*   Peace, I say!
> What should this mean?
>   *2 Sold.* 'Tis the god Hercules, whom Antony lov'd,
> Now leaves him.
>
> (Antony and Cleopatra, IV, iii, 14 ff.)

Antony found his self-image in Hercules the conqueror. But in the moment of despair, when Cleopatra forsakes him and he comes close to defeat, he compares himself to another Hercules, perhaps the most striking of all the images of Hercules in Shakespeare. Hercules now becomes an example of self-destruction which at the same time destroys the world, or at least as much of it as is capable of being destroyed. Antony wishes to end as Hercules *furens:*

> The shirt of Nessus is upon me; teach me,
> Alcides, thou mine ancestor, thy rage;
> Let me lodge Lichas on the horns o' th' moon
> And with those hands that grasp'd the heaviest club
> Subdue my worthiest self.
>
> (Ibid., xii, 43 ff.)

Thomas Heywood, a contemporary of Shakespeare, traced Julius Caesar's genealogy through Hercules. Theseus imitated Hercules; Achilles, Theseus; Alexander, Achilles; Julius Caesar, Alexander: "To see as I have seene, *Hercules* in his owne shape hunting the Boare, knocking downe the Bull, taming the Hart, fighting with Hydra, murdering *Gerion*, slaughtering *Diomed*, wound-

ing the *Stimphalides,* killing the Centaurs, pashing the
Lion, squeezing the Dragon, dragging Cerberus in
Chaynes, and lastly, on his high Pyramides writing *Nil
ultra,* Oh these were sights to make an *Alexander.*"[13]
But even this Herculean model possessed two oppo-
site signs: greatness and weakness. Shakespeare's
Julius Caesar, who moments before his murder com-
pared himself to unshakable Olympus and the Polar
Star, suffered from "falling sickness," that is to say,
he was *Herculanus morbus.*

The Renaissance rediscovered this Hercules in
Seneca. In both Seneca's tragedies, *Furens* and *Oetaeus,*
Hercules is above all a tyrant whose misdeeds, poses and
rhetoric seem to awaken the dramatist's particular interest. The murderer's attacks of madness are portrayed
with a profound knowledge, as if Seneca knew the model
from an autopsy. In *Furens,* Hercules rolls his eyes and
dances like a hysteric; in *Oetaeus* "with dreadful cries he
filled the air" (797).[14] In the eyes of Deianira he is a
rapist whose amorous appetite knows neither measure
nor limits: "His quest is ever love, the maiden's couch."
Hercules boasts that he has freed the human race from
fear, but he sows seeds of fear around him. The murderer of his own wife and sons blames the gods for his
crimes. Deianira has few delusions: "Such his cruel
method of divorce, but he cannot be held the guilty one!
For he contrives to make the world believe that Juno is
the cause of his crimes!" (432 ff.).

Octavia, one of the most curious plays of antiquity and
the first historical tragedy, is at times surprisingly similar
to Shakespeare's Histories. Seneca and Nero are the
main characters. The philosopher, who was Nero's tutor,
warns him of the wrath of the gods should he kill the
senators who oppose his new marriage. Nero's answer is
simple:

NERO:

I, who make gods, would be a fool to fear them.

SENECA:

The more your power, greater your fear should be.

NERO:

I, thanks to Fortune, may do anything.

(450 ff.)[15]

Octavia, for a long time attributed to Seneca, was evidently written after both actors of the drama were dead. What is most interesting is the striking resemblance of Nero in this play to Seneca's mythological Hercules. In the prologue to *Oetaeus,* Hercules, who has not found anyone on earth equal to himself, asks Jupiter for one of the constellations: "Why, o Father, why do you deny the stars to me? . . . Every monstrous shape which has its source in earth or sea or air or hell itself, has yielded to my arms" (12 ff.). This Hercules, like the Roman Caesars, is prepared to deify himself and force himself into Olympus: "Consider me a giant storming heaven. Yea, heaven I might have stormed in very truth" (1303).

Almost all scholars make the point that in Seneca, rhetoric replaced tragic action. But to call oneself a god is always a rhetorical act, quite terrifying rhetoric, but nonetheless traditional. When Philip waged war with the Persians, Isocrates wrote to him: "When you force the barbarians to serve Greece . . . and demand the king of kings to fulfill your orders, nothing else will remain but to become a god." Among the Greeks, the first to become a god was Alexander, Philip's son. The resistance to the deification of a sovereign in the Hellenistic world can best be seen in Plutarch, who quoted the answer the oracle gave when Alexander turned to her for the highest consecration: "Since Alexander wants to be a god, the oracle answers, let him be a god." Alexander thus became a god on request. In Rome, the first Augustus was counted among the gods by resolution of the senate. *"Deus nobis haec etia fecit,"* Virgil wrote (*Eclogue* I, 6); Augustus, who secured peace, was thereby deified.[15] Augustus' canonization came after his death. But later Caesars demanded deification during their lifetimes. Domitian required that he be called *Dominus ac Deus noster* —"Our Lord and God."

The rhetoric of Seneca's Hercules is the rhetoric of the Caesars; the historical Nero not only identified himself with gods and demigods, he even enacted them in the theatre. "And he did actually appear in operatic tragedies," writes Suetonius, "taking the parts of heroes and gods, sometimes even of heroines and goddesses, wearing masks either modelled on his own face or on the face of whatever woman happened to be his current mistress. Among his performances were *Canace in Childbirth, Orestes the Matricide, Oedipus Blinded,* and *Distraught Hercules.*" Hercules was apparently Nero's favorite part, since Suetonius once again refers to it: "Because of his singing and chariot-driving he had a lion so carefully trained that he could safely face it naked before the entire amphitheatre; and then either kill it with his club or else strangle it."[17]

Hercules Oetaeus, unlike Sophocles, ends with an apotheosis. As in the *Odyssey,* Hercules becomes divided after his death. But the oppositions are quite different. In the epilogue his mother appears pressing an urn with the hero's ashes to her breast. Her epitaph for him will be repeated almost verbatim by Shakespeare:

> How small a space Alcides' ashes fill!
> To this small compass this giant come!
> O shining sun, how great a man has gone
> To nothingness.

> (1777 ff.)

At this moment Hercules' voice answers from heaven, or if the tragedy was performed, his shadow appears *in machina:* "The mortal part of me, the part thou savest, was by the overmastering flames consumed; thy part to fire, my father's part to heaven has been consigned" (1966 ff.). Alcmene, who gave birth to Jupiter's son, is the prefiguration of Pietà, the Mother of the Son who ascended to heaven. The imagery and poetics are like a Christian mystery: the ashes remain in the earth and the immortal soul returns to the Father, but the true opposition is still Stoical: emptiness and fame.

> But when life's days are all consumed,
> And comes the final hour, for them
> A pathway to the gods is spread
> By glory.
>
> (1487 ff.).

Hercules' epiphany is profane. Alcmene acts like Caesar's mother: "What sepulcher, o son, what tomb for thee is great enough? Naught save the world itself . . ." (1826).

The posthumous split of Heracles in the *Odyssey* could not, of course, escape the derision of Lucian. Diogenes in *The Dialogues of the Dead* was quite amazed to meet Heracles in Hades: "The bow, the club, the lion's skin, the giant frame; 'tis Heracles complete. Yet how should this be?—a son of Zeus, and mortal? I say, Mighty Conqueror, are you dead? I used to sacrifice to you in the other world; I understood you were a god!"[18]

In vain Heracles attempts to convince Diogenes that he is only a shadow and that the real Heracles rejoices in eternal happiness on Olympus. The relentless Diogenes feels that the reverse can be equally true: "Why, we may find it's the other way round, that you are Heracles and the phantom is in Heaven, married to Hebe!" Lucian's Heracles was finally divided into three after his death:

DIOGENES:
You see you are a phantom. You have no body. At this rate we shall get three Heracleses.

HERACLES:
Three?

DIOGENES:
Yes; look here. One in Heaven: one in Hades, that's you, the phantom: and lastly the body, which by this time has returned to dust. That makes three. Can you think of a good father for number Three?

In the cold pathos of Senecan tragedy and the scoffing intellectual cabaret of Lucian, the myth of Heracles is finally completely split. Two dissimilar halves remain; two different Heracleses instead of one Heracles with two faces. The myth was split from the beginning; but its most striking aspect is the split itself, the plexus of contrasts: an agony in his labors and a failure in his victory. He has two fathers, god and man; he is light and dark; tyrant and slave; filicide and redeemer, the most exalted and most degraded of all heroes.

In the mystical speculation of gnostics, when Greek tradition mixes with the Jewish, Oriental, and early Christian, three great prophets are mentioned: Moses, Hercules and Jesus. But Hercules is an incomplete prophet who thwarts God's plan. He kills the rebelling angels, but finally he is himself defeated because he exchanges his robe with the woman-serpent. The monsters who hatched from the union of Gaea and Uranus were transformed into the rebelling angels. Omphale became the Biblical serpent. But even the cabalistic Hercules is a hero of defeat.[19] With the cosmos torn apart from above and below, Hercules was sent to repair the first Genesis, but he failed to accomplish his mission. The monsters proved stronger, and mediation did not come about.

In the mystical image of Heracles, all the archetypal signs of the mediator between heaven and hell are repeated. Heracles is the son of God the Father and a mortal woman; he descends into hell and after death enters heaven. "The tragic hero," Northrop Frye writes, "is typically on top of the wheel of fortune, halfway between human society on the ground and the something greater in the sky. Prometheus, Adam, and Christ hang between heaven and earth, between a world of paradisal freedom and a world of bondage. Tragic heroes are so much the highest point in their human landscape that they seem the inevitable conductors of the power about them, great trees more likely to be struck by lightning than a clump of grass."[20]

Frye does not mention Heracles, perhaps because in the Greek theatre he was above all the favorite hero of satyr plays and comedy. The Doric Heracles was rude, but in Thessalian legends he appears as a folk hero. To seduce Alcmene, Heracles' mother, Zeus assumes the shape of her husband, Amphitryon, whom he has purposely sent to war. In order to enjoy her in bed, he disturbs the entire order of nature, holding back the sun and making the night three times as long as usual. Everyone in this story is mocked: Zeus, Amphitryon and even the faithful and pious Alcmene; and from Plautus to Giraudoux[21] the conception of Heracles has been one of the most durable themes of comedy. Even Kleist in his *Amphitryon* did not succeed in endowing the play with a tragic stamp. The birth of Heracles in Thessalian legends, and even in Homer, was an endless comedy of errors. The midwife sent by Hera squats cross-legged before Alcmene's house, her clothing tied into knots, in order to delay the arrival on earth of Zeus's son. The Heracles of the twelve labors belongs almost entirely to comedy, from Aristophanes and Plautus[22] to Dürrenmatt's *Heracles and the Aegean Stable.*

Heracles' last labors were the expeditions to paradise and to hell. The tree bearing golden fruit was the wedding present of Mother Earth to Hera, who planted it in her heavenly orchard on the west side of the world, where night meets day and Atlas carries the heavenly dome on his shoulders. Across Mount Atlas ran a vertical axis of the cosmos. The journey to the summit of the earth was a prefiguration of the ascension. But Heracles appeared in paradise to steal the golden apples, just as later he entered hell to snatch Cerberus. The hero of both expeditions, in which Atlas was deceived and Hades wounded, was the Heracles of the satyr plays and the pictures on vases, a giant with a black beard, wildly shaking his club. Aristophanes in *The Frogs* recalls the great cry, which shook all of Hades: "I, Heracles the strong!" Satyr plays and Aristophanic comedy derided the gods, and perhaps for this very reason the comic Heracles appears in the archetypal situations of the son of god— from his delayed birth and the signs of his divine origins to his journey to the height and summit of earth and his descent into hell.

The tragic Heracles appears on Greek stage after he has performed all twelve labors, at the end of his life, and at the very bottom of the human condition. In Sophocles' *Women of Trachis* he burns alive; in Euripides' *Heracles* he wakes up among the bodies of his wife and his sons. Mediation ends in a total destruction. In Sophocles, there is not one word that foreshadows his posthumous apotheosis. In Euripides, Heracles throws off his role as mediator and renounces his divine father. The world is torn asunder from top to bottom, but the sky is not the "paradisal kingdom of freedom," about which Frye writes; and there is hope neither on earth nor in heaven. The human world is submerged in impenetrable cruelty, which can be called gods, Ether or emptiness.[23]

In *Philoctetes*, Heracles appears *ex machina* for the last time to persuade the stubborn Philoctetes to leave for Troy. In this tragedy of the refusal, Heracles of "immortal glory" is already a tool of history which must be fulfilled. But the real human history revealed and foretold in *Philoctetes* is sinister and dreadful.

"Through tragedy the myth attains its most profound content," Nietzsche wrote in *The Birth of Tragedy*, "its most expressive form; it rises once more like a wounded hero, and its whole excess of strength, together with the philosophic calm of the dying, burns in its eyes with a last powerful gleam."[24] The two-sided myth of Heracles became for Sophocles and Euripides a tragedy of a world with no hope for mediation.[25]

II. BLACK SOPHOCLES, OR THE CIRCULATION OF POISONS

1.

Sophocles' tragedy of *The Women of Trachis* takes place on a long day at the end of the last fifteen-month absence of Heracles from his home during his twelve-year journey; the time when dark prophecies foretold the turn in his fate. At dawn Deianira sends her son to learn what happened to his father. Late in the morning the herald leads in the women taken in captivity by Heracles from conquered Oechalia. Deianira learns that among the captive women is Iole, a new consort of her husband's; Heracles sacked the city and slaughtered all the men when her father refused to let Iole share his bed. Late in the afternoon Deianira sends her husband by the same herald a robe dipped in the blood of the centaur Nessus. Early in the evening the son returns and curses his mother. The love potion has proved fatal. Heracles is dying, the robe wrapped around him pouring venom into his bowels. He is still alive but in agony. Late at night the attendants bring Heracles back to Trachis.

The night seems to belong to another time, another day, to a Holy Week when the Son of God is dying on earth. In unbearable pain the son of Zeus lies on the stretcher. The Chorus of women cries in terror: "He is approaching the house in torments from which there is not deliverance, a wonder of unutterable woe" (953 ff.).[1]

When Heracles revives, his first words are directed to his father: "O Zeus! Torture, torture is all you give me!" (966).[2] In this Heraclean *"Eli, Eli, lama sabachthani,"* complaint and reproach are even more bitter: "I wish I had never seen you with these poor eyes that must face now this inexorable flowering of madness" (996 ff.).

The poison has already entered his bowels and eaten into the bone. The son of Zeus screams with pain, and this is one of the most frightful cries in all of Greek tragedy. Only Sophocles' Philoctetes will cry longer and more terribly. Heracles calls on Zeus to shorten his suffering with bolts of lightning, and on Hades to lull him to eternal sleep. His body, swollen with pain and eaten by inner fire, is now his greatest enemy. In this theatre of cruelty, Heracles, after calling upon the gods, now turns to men to beg them to cut his head off from his tormented body. His pleas are in vain. The savior who redeemed the world dies in the dreadful silence of the heavens, alone among men!

O most ungrateful of the Greeks, where are all of you
for whom I destroyed myself purging so many beasts

from all the seas and woods? Now *I* am sick,
will no one turn the beneficial fire, the sword on me?

(1011 ff.)

Not one of the twelve labors of Heracles has been
mentioned up to this time. Sophocles knew Homer by
heart, but as in *Ajax*, he interpreted him in a dark light.
Odysseus remembered well the golden baldric worn by
Heracles in Hades, "depicting with grim artistry the
forms of bears, wild boars, and glaring lions, with scenes
of conflict and of battle, of bloodshed and the massacre
of men" (*Odyssey*, XI, 609 ff., Rieu's translation). Every
time his actions are described in the drama, the "famous" Heracles, "noblest among men," has murdered,
raped, or followed a scorched-earth policy. Servant of
horrible masters, he executed for them even more horrible duties. King Eurystheus called him "a broken thing"
and "a free man's slave," when Heracles dared to propose an archery contest to his sons. Later he derided
him, got drunk and threw him out of his palace. In revenge Heracles lured his son away and "hurled him from
the top of that bastion" in cold blood (273). As penance
Heracles was sold to the Lydian Queen Omphale and
performed such infamous services for her that the herald
in his conversation with Deianira passes over them in
silence.[3]

This same herald, who unaware brought him a gift
from Deianira, is later murdered by Heracles in a most
horrible way. He grabs him "by the foot where the ankle
turns"—Sophocles is always accurate in anatomical descriptions; only here could he get impetus—"and threw
him against a wave-beaten rock that juts from the sea.
. . . skull and blood mixed and spread. All the people
there cried out in horror for the one man in his suffering,
the other dead" (779 ff.).

The famous labors are recalled only now, when Heracles lies on a stretcher screaming in pain as the Hydra's venom is circulating in his veins. The monsters he killed have entered his body. They already *are* his body: great arms, hard neck, huge chest, stomach with knots of muscles. "He who fights against dragons," Nietzsche wrote, "becomes a dragon himself." The descent into hell and his journey to the end of the earth are now only arms, which snatched up the dog and tamed the monster: "O my hands, my hands, O my back, my chest, O my poor arms, see what has become of you from what you once were. You tamed the Lernaean Hydra, and that monstrous host of double form, man joined to steed, a race with whom none may commune, violent, lawless, of surpassing might; you tamed the Erymanthian beast, and the three-headed whelp of Hades underground, a resistless terror, offspring of the dread Echidna; you tamed the dragon that guarded the golden fruit in the utmost places of the earth" (1089 ff., Jebb's translation).

The mediator and savior is now reduced to flesh, at once monstrous and powerless. Like Shakespeare's Lear, the beloved son of Zeus is now "a ruin'd piece of Nature": "Now look at me, torn to shreds, my limbs unhinged, a miserable ruin sacked by invisible disaster . . ." (1103 f.). He is "this broken thing": "I am nothing," but in this "nothing, nothing that can even crawl"[4] (1107), there still remains hatred. By the end of the tragedy one can say of Heracles as of Macbeth: ". . . all that is within him does condemn itself for being there" (V, ii, 24–25). He calls his son to bring forth his mother; he wants him to *look on* as he tortures her. The mediator poisoned with venom wants to see with his own eyes whether the suffering of his father or the screams of his tortured mother will affect his son more. He wants to put him to a test. But Deianira has already killed herself by her own hand.

2.

In this tragedy, Heracles and Deianira never met. It seems that they cannot meet; they belong to two different times and two different worlds. Heracles is mythical and archaic; Deianira is contemporary to the audience and similar to all the women of Trachis, who at daybreak came from the village to hear her lament. Heracles measures the earth from one end to the other; Deianira is one who always waits, whom one takes and leaves.

> We have had children now, whom he sees at times,
> like a farmer working an outlying field,
> who sees it only when he sows and when he reaps.
>
> (31 ff.)

In this first long monologue of Deianira's, dread, fear and terror return incessantly. The earliest that she remembered was "an agonizing fear of marriage"[7] when the first suitors came to her father's house. Later there was fear of her husband and fear about her husband, fear when he was present and fear when he was absent. Dread about her home, dread before the exiles, dread about her children and what would become of them when they were left alone. "We are only safe if he can save himself. His ruin is ours" (85).

When Heracles is absent, Deianira's fate is bitter, but all of her fears and dreads appear to be ordinary and commonplace. She is a daughter of royalty, but complains of her fate like a village girl. Her litany of sorrows is not unlike those found in folk songs of all nations:

> . . . May you never learn
> by your own suffering how my heart is torn.
> You do not know now. So the young thing
> grows in her own places; the heat of the sun-god

does not confound her, nor does the rain, nor any wind.
Pleasurably she enjoys an untroubled life
until the time she is no longer called a maiden
but woman, and takes her share of worry in the night . . .

(142 ff.)

Deianira's nights are long and full of fears, "some each
night dispels—each night brings others on" (30). Her
nights are empty. In the first song the women of Trachis
talk about her sleepless nights and her empty bed:
". . . she pines on her anxious, widowed couch, miserable
in her foreboding of mischance" (104 ff., Jebb's translation). The love story develops slowly. Heracles was not
faithful; Deianira has known this for a long time. "One
man and many women—Heracles has had other women
before" (459). But now for the first time, in the light of
day, he has sent his new bride home. "And now, as you
see, he is coming home and has sent her here," the
Messenger unmercifully admits, "not without a reason,
lady, and not to be a slave" (365 ff.).

The girl, whom she had led under her own roof and
who never answered any questions, is young and pretty.
". . . her youth is coming to full bloom while mine is
fading. The eyes of men love to pluck the blossoms
. . ." (547 f.). Deianira has no illusions; she knows what
she is waiting for. "So now the two of us lie under the
one sheet waiting for his embrace" (539). The shameless
violence of this image only Euripides' Clytemnestra will
repeat when Agamemnon returns from Troy: ". . . he
came home to me with a mad, god-filled girl and introduced her to our bed. So there we were, two brides being
stables in a single stall" (*Electra*, 1032 ff.).[5] The bed will
no longer be empty, but from now on there will be two
women and one man in it: ". . . he may be called my
husband but be the younger woman's man" (550 f.).

A husband, an aging wife, a young girl—Deianira's

drama is ordinary and commonplace. "You can see Heracles and Deianira most Monday mornings in some police court or other," Gilbert Murray wrote in his *Greek Studies,* "as you can see in Broadmoor asylum Medeas who have murdered their children."[6] A disciple of Verrall raised on the naturalistic theatre, Murray came across many instances of Medeas, Heracleses and Deianiras in news items. A mother threw her children into a fire; a love brew concocted by a gypsy proved to be poison; a wife poured acid over her faithless husband— time, after all, is not "out of joint."

Heracles is approaching. He is offering Zeus the first fruit of the earth on the ruins of the destroyed city. But cruelty is still within measure. The Messenger had already told Deianira everything—then why is she questioning him? "Tell me the whole truth" (453). What is it that she still wants to know? "The only thing that could hurt would be not to know. Where is the danger in knowing?" (458). Deianira is from the same race as Oedipus, whose destruction began when he solved the riddle of the Sphinx and who also desperately wanted to know. Deianira's tragedy begins with her recognition of the nature of poison. "Are you afraid of hurting me? You are wrong" (457). Racine, in the margins of Sophocles' Latin edition, wrote in this place: *"Admirable discours d'une jalouse qui veut apprendre son malheur."* [7] The poisons slowly accumulating in the heart are no less lethal than the dried blood of the centaur preserved in a brass urn. Deianira has already made her choice, but she herself is still unaware of it.

For the first time the stage is empty. Only the Chorus remains on the *orchestra.* The women of Trachis, who have listened in silence, now begin their dance and song about monsters: the River-God and the son of Zeus fight over the girl. Deianira's first lament began with her hor-

ror of her monstrous suitor. On the Greek islands and in
Italy, south of Rome, village wells have even to this day
heads of tritons, lions or old men; the water spurts from
black depths between thick lips and flows along a lewd
tongue onto a thick shaggy beard and stone torso.

> . . . my suitor was the river Acheloüs,
> who used to come to ask my father for my hand,
> taking three forms—first, clearly a bull, and then
> a serpent with shimmering coils, then a man's body
> but a bull's face . . .
>
> (9 ff.)

In the erotic dreams of girls, men are wet and from their
monstrous heads water spurts out:

> . . . then a man's body
> but a bull's face, and from his clump of beard
> whole torrents of water splashed like a fountain.
>
> (12 ff.)

Monsters are always born out of traumas, but now they
are being enacted on the stage as if they had become
flesh and blood. The frenetic dance of the Chorus, as in
Chinese opera, turns suddenly into pantomime.[8] Two
monsters fight with each other. They have fourteen
heads, fourteen protruding bellies, fourteen pairs of
arms thrown violently into the air, fourteen pairs of en-
tangled legs. The beat grows more and more violent.
"Then was there clatter of fists and clang of bow, and the
noise of a bull's horns therewith; then were there close-
locked grapplings and deadly blows from the forehead
and loud deep cries from both" (517 ff., Jebb's translation). One of the girls has left the Chorus. She has
stopped dancing. The beat suddenly dies. The Chorus
now sings of her: "But the tender girl with the lovely eyes

sat far from them on a hillside, waiting for the one who would be her husband" (523).

Deianira, who was then waiting for her future husband, is now moistening his robe in the dark blood of the monster. She holds it in her hands. She tells the women of her encounter with this third monster. When Heracles took her "like a heifer taken from its mother," the river stood in their way.[9] Symbols in tragedy are always primeval: light, darkness, fire and water. Nessus, the centaur-ferryman, offered to carry Deianira in his arms to the other side. In the middle of the river he touched her with lust. Heracles heard a cry and shot an arrow, which he had poisoned by dipping it in the Hydra's blood, through the monster's chest. Before dying, the centaur had just time to tell Deianira to take blood from his wound: ". . . you will have a charm over the heart of Heracles . . ." (575).

Deianira hands the robe to the herald, who departs with it hidden away at the very bottom of a trunk, so that light will not touch it for even a moment. Heracles is again approaching. He is now in Cenaeum, at the temple of Zeus, preparing the solemn hecatomb to honor his father. He will slaughter twelve young bulls and a hundred other sacrificial animals in the rays of the evening sun. Outwardly the world is as ordinary as before. From the ashes of the decimated cities, from animal blood offered to an archaic god, from monster-ferrymen who rape women, from poisons in hearts and urns, from love, which is the same as hate—from all these one can still withdraw into the smooth material surface of the world, which seems safe and rational in its immutability. A ball of wool is forever a ball of wool. What can be threatening in a ball of wool?

"The piece has disappeared, devoured by nothing in the house but destroyed by itself, eaten away and crumbled completely to dust" (676 ff.). Deianira tells the village women of the disappearance of the ball of wool as if she were describing a chemical reaction. The ball of wool was consumed by light. The world was injured in its very fabric: ". . . I see something unspeakable, incomprehensible to human reason" (693).

In *Macbeth*, the bloodstains that cannot be washed away are more frightening than the midnight murder of the king. The essence of history is not the procession of kings, but a half-naked, bloodstained unknown soldier ("What bloody man is that?" *Macbeth*, I, ii, 1), who appears for only a moment, and like the Greek herald, reports from the field of battle. Food and sleep are equally poisoned. Things of the earth are viscous, clammy and incoherent, as in a dream:

> . . . what seem'd corporal melted
> As breath into the wind.
>
> (*Macbeth*, I, iii, 81–82)

In this nightmare the true nature of the world is revealed: "But from the earth on which it rests, clotted foam boils up like the rich liquid of the blue-green fruit from the vines of Dionysus, poured on the earth" (701 ff.).[10]

The Weird Sisters and the infernal Porter, who at dawn opens the gates of the castle, are creatures of substance in *Macbeth*, as are the monsters and the Hydra's venom in *The Women of Trachis*. The world in *Macbeth* is contaminated with blood, as in *The Women of Trachis* it is poisoned by venom:

> If you take in your hands this blood, clotted in
> my wounds, wherever it is black with the bile
> of the Hydra, the monstrous serpent of Lerna, in which
> he dipped his arrows . . .
>
> (572 ff.)

The contagion is transitive; the infected is the infecting one. In *The Women of Trachis,* contagion is the structure of the tragedy and its theology. Heracles the savior rescued Deianira from the assault of the beast, but his arrows were poisoned with venom. The mediator, the son of Zeus, saved the world from the monsters. But he kills the monsters with the venom of a monster. Mediation is the renewed infection of the world. The carrier of infection becomes infected: ". . . the Hydra, horrible and monstrous, has soaked in" (836).

In this cosmic bacteriology, the primeval venom of the chthonic Hydra is transmitted by its blood, like the spirochetes of syphilis. Magic is the transposition of the properties of a deity, person or object into a different object, person or deity. Magic operations require a symbolic likeness or physical contact: either indentification or temporal and spatial contiguity. These two magic operations correspond, as Roman Jakobson once pointed out, to the principle of metaphor or metonymy in linguistics. The transposition can be performed on a puppet simulating a person or deity, or by the enactment of the person or the deity. Frazer called this first magic "imitative" and the second "contactual." All the objects with which the body has come in contact—clothing, hair or blood—are part of it. The magic operation is a contagion. "So let him come, the all-desired one, melted under the persuasion of the stratagem from the beast" (680 ff.).[12]

In *The Women of Trachis,* all the operations of "contactual" magic are presented. The blood of the centaur was collected by Deianira in the place of the infection, "wherever it is black with the bile of the Hydra"; the tunic is dipped in it; the herald brings it; Heracles puts it on his bare skin. In each of these operations the basic structure of the contagion is the same: the infected becomes the infector. The circumference is closed, and all the carriers of infection in turn yield to destruction: Nessus, Deianira, the herald, and in the end, Heracles himself.

But in *The Women of Trachis* there is still another conduit through which poisons are circulating. Iole, destroyed by Heracles and destroying everyone around her, is a mute carrier of this second poison: ". . . against her will, this unfortunate girl has sacked and enslaved the land of her fathers" (465). The pregnant girl silently enters Deianira's home like a messenger of misfortune. The women of Trachis already know everything: "That bride, newly come, has borne, has borne a mighty Fury for this house" (893 ff.).

This "realistic" conduit, through which the poison of passion circulates, is parallel to and symmetrical with the mythic, in which Hydra's venom passes through the blood. The circulation of poisons in *The Women of Trachis* can be shown in a square figure (with a vertical line drawn lengthwise) whose four vertexes will represent, in turn, Heracles, the centaur Nessus, Deianira and Iole:

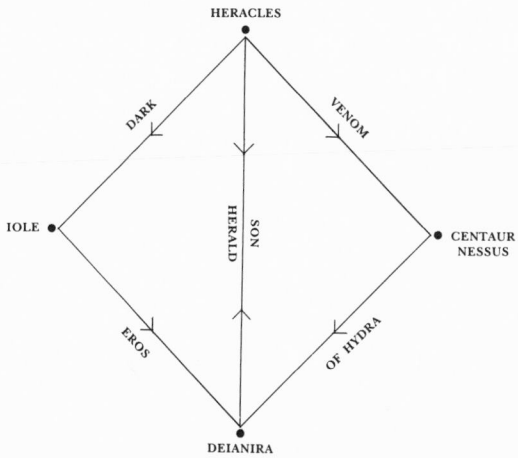

Hydra's venom passes from Heracles through Nessus to Deianira. Dark Eros poisons her from Heracles through Iole. Heracles and Deianira communicate only through the herald and their son. The herald has brought Iole and takes the fatal potion of love with him. "It would not be right to leave empty-handed when you came so well provided" (495 f.). The son brings his mother the news of his father's agony, and his father the news of his mother's suicide. The poison of love and the contaminated blood of the centaur, structurally and theologically, are one and the same venom:

> *J'ai revu l'ennemi que j'avais éloigné:*
> *Ma blessure trop vive aussitôt a saigné.*
> *Ce n'est plus une ardeur dans mes veines cachée:*
> *C'est Venus tout entière a sa proie attachée.*
>
> (*Phèdre*, I, iii)[13]

Racine was the first to see the unity of poisons in *The Women of Trachis;* his Phaedra is destroyed by implacable Venus-Aphrodite, and the venom of the Hydra flows in her veins.[14]

Aphrodite first appears in *The Women of Trachis* when as "the sole umpire of their strife," she observes the battle of the monsters. She appears for the second time when the poisoned robe sticks to Heracles' flesh and she ministers to him in silence, like an executioner's assistant: "Cyprian Aphrodite is revealed; it is her work" (859 ff.).

Both poisons are hidden for a long time. "[I am] a miserable ruin sacked by invisible disaster," Heracles says (1104). "I have welcomed a secret enemy under my roof," Deianira says (375). As in *Phaedra*, the tragedy begins when poisons are brought from darkness to light and called by name: "I want to tell you the work my hands have done" (533). Deianira's hands did not make a mistake. They chose what she wanted to choose. When the son returns with the fatal news, Deianira exits without a word. Everything has already been said.

There are six suicides in the seven extant tragedies of Sophocles, but only two of them, Ajax's and Deianira's, are described in great detail, factually, as in court records. We know only that Antigone hanged herself with a belt in the darkness of a cave; that Haemon threw himself on a sword; that Eurydice also killed herself with a sword; and that Jocasta hanged herself. Ajax threw himself on a sword at high noon in the brilliance of the sun, in view of the spectators. He killed himself out of contempt for the world, which was not worth living in. Deianira, crushed by the world, commits suicide in the dark of the house, offstage. But her nurse follows her step by step, like a movie camera: ". . . secretly, from the shadows, I keep watch over her" (914). "Falling before the altar, she sobbed aloud that she would now be left alone; she wept as she touched each household piece she had ever used . . ." (904 ff., Musurillo's translation).

Deianira, like Euripides' Alcestis, bids farewell to the bed she shared with her husband. The bed is an altar upon which she will sacrifice her own flesh: "she began to spread the bed-clothes on the couch. And when she had done, she climbed on top and sat upon the middle of the bed . . ." (*ibid.*, 914 ff.).

The bed linen, in which all Greek women took such pride, Deianira places in the middle of the bed and kneels on the pile, as on a pyre. She unpins her gold brooch, which was fastened to her peplos, letting the cloth fall from her left arm, uncovering her breast and stomach. Sophocles' knowledge of wounds is as accurate as Homer's: Deianira holds the blade in her right hand and cuts open her stomach, beginning the stroke from the left side. "She has cut her side to the liver and the seat of life with a double-bladed sword" (930 f.).

Deianira cuts open her stomach sitting on the linen with her legs crossed (otherwise it is impossible to slit across one's stomach), according to the rules of hara-kiri. The sword is double-edged; for the fatal seppuku, two diagonal cuts are necessary, from left to right and back down and to the left. Suicide, which is a sacrifice, must be carried out like a ritual.

The tragedy is now coming to a close. On the shore, before Deianira's house, where the herald brought Iole and the captive women, Heracles lies on a stretcher and cries in agony. His son, Hyllus, comes from the house; once again he is a messenger of misfortune between his mother and father.

HYLLUS:
She is dead by her own hand and by no other.

HERACLES:
Ah! She is dead too soon. She should have died by mine.

(1132 f.)

Heracles has thrown off the sheets that covered him. He wants to show his body which is being consumed by poison.

. . . look well at my misfortune, see what I suffer.
I shall take off the coverings and show you. Look,
all of you, do you behold this poor body?

(1077 ff.)

The naked Deianira, stomach slit, lies on the nuptial bed in the house. Heracles is also naked.

3.

When it seems for a moment in *Oedipus Rex* that the prophecies could be wrong and the gods' curses would not be fulfilled, the Chorus rebels and no longer wants to assist in the ceremony: "Why should I take part in the sacred dance?" The Chorus in *Oedipus* understood the essence of tragedy. If patricide and incest are not announced in advance, if they do not constitute the unknown metaphysical order of the universe, if they are not components of divine justice, then they are nothing but chance, one of many casualties in the annals of common events. Camus wrote in *The Myth of Sisyphus:*

In a tragic work fate always makes itself felt better in the guise of logic and naturalness. . . . The drama's whole effort is to show the logical system which, from deduction to deduction, will crown the hero's misfortune. Merely to announce to us that uncommon fate is scarcely horrible, because it is improbable. But if its necessity is demonstrated to us in the framework of everyday life, society, state, familiar emotion, then the horror is hallowed. In that revolt that shakes man and makes him say: "That is not possible," there is an element of desperate certainty that "that" can be.[15]

Perhaps Camus is not right. Perhaps accidental cruelty is absurd. But cruelty endowed with the divine rigor of inevitability is unbearable.

In *The Women of Trachis* there are three prophecies about the fate of Heracles. The first two are like gypsy fortunetelling: "He will return or not return"; "All will be well or worse." Such auguries always prove true, but in *The Women of Trachis* they set the time: "after twelve years," "after fifteen months." The tragedy must be enacted during a set time. The third prophecy, however, has an intended malignity in it. As in *Macbeth,* it seems to announce the impossible.[16] "Long ago my father revealed to me that I should die by nothing that draws breath but by someone dead . . ." (1159).

Such a world, in which the strongest of men and the hero of all Greece dies because of a woman, is stupid. The world in which the son of god dies poisoned by a

monster which he had killed is absurd. But if it was ordained in advance the mediation and mediator would be
contaminated, cruelty is the law of the cosmos, and the
absurd suddenly regains its own shocking logic. Heracles
stops screaming in pain. The prophecies have been
fulfilled.

> . . . what
>
> SPLENDOUR,
>   IT ALL COHERES.
>
> (1174 f.)[17]

In the symbolic space of *The Women of Trachis,* above
the theatre and above the world, rises sacred Mount
Oeta, whose slopes a plow never furrowed and on whose
crags lightning strikes. Ajax, whose gloomy obstinacy
and brutal force are similar to Heracles', disdained the
world, which crumbles like a mountain, and the gods,
who also crumble. In *The Women of Trachis,* Mount Oeta
remains unshaken, and Heracles accepts the immutable
cruelty of the world. The time of mediation is over, and
there will be no new labors of Heracles: "For the dead
there are no more toils" (1173). The Hydra was killed,
but its appalling shape holds Heracles in its grip. The
black shadow of the Hydra falls on the theatre, which is
the whole world.

God is a silent mountain, but the prophecies are coming true. Contaminated by venom, the son of Zeus is
ready to accept the "theology of fraud, malice, and sinister joy."[18] ". . . what splendour, it all coheres." The
prophecies are coming true; therefore one can find right
and reason in open injustice and in the absurdity of the
cosmos. "What constitutes the voluptuousness of
tragedy is cruelty," Nietzsche wrote in *Beyond Good and*

Evil.[18] Heracles now discovers the sinister fascination of cruelty.

If one cannot be the human son of god, one can always be a superman. If mediation does not, never did and never will exist, if cruelty is the rule of the universe, one can confirm it even with one's own agony. If god is nothing but a mute mountain, it seems only fair to kindle a pyre on its peak and there burn alive. But destruction must be carried to the very end. As in *Macbeth:* "Whiles I see lives, the gashes do better upon them" (V, viii, 2–3). Heracles demands that his son carry him up to the rocky peak of Mount Oeta, set up a pyre and kindle it with his own hands:

HYLLUS:
Father, Father, how can you? You are asking me
to be your murderer, polluted with your blood.

HERACLES:
No, I am not. I ask you to be my healer,
the only physician who can cure my suffering.

(1206 ff.)

In the logic of the absurd, all values are overturned: death is a cure and murder is a healing. Miasma was the most horrible of Greek fears: those infected were banished from the community of the living. But now all divine and human laws must be broken.

Only the most archaic of duties—blind devotion to one's father—is not shaken. In the plans of the divine father, as the prophecies attest, was the contamination of the son; now, therefore, Heracles must infect his own son in turn. Hyllus swore by the gods that he was willing to do anything his father commanded, except to touch the pyre with his own hands. But Heracles insists on "this

one small favor" (1217). In these words, "small favor,"
there is divine "malice and sinister joy." Hyllus must take
Iole as his wife. Heracles, of his own free will and without
resorting to the dark prophecies, burdens his son with
Oedipus' crimes: patricide and incest.[20] Incest is not only
formal—Heracles sent Iole home as his bride—and not
only symbolic—Iole's son by Heracles will be, as in
Oedipus, at the same time a son and a brother to Hyllus.
Only these two will remain alive: Hyllus and Iole; they
must both be ruined.

The stretcher on which Heracles lies is raised; in a
moment the procession will move up the mountain:

> In bliss most beautiful
> The Undying Ones have honoured him
> As one whom they love, and Youth is his bride;
> He dwells, a Prince, in golden halls,
> And Hera is his wife's mother.
>
> (Pindar, *Isthmians* III-IV, 65 ff.)[21]

In *The Women of Trachis* there is no ascension, and there
will be no theophany. Sophocles' Heracles offered sacrifices to Zeus on the ruins of sacked cities; now he has
to sacrifice himself. But to whom? Sacrifice means mediation: the repetition of the martyrdom of the sons of god,
tormented to death on earth, or the plea for their new
descent to earth; the sacrifice is an appeasement or
thanksgiving; a payment or a bribe, but always someone
or something must be on the other side. In Sophocles'
tragedies, except for the last, *Oedipus at Colonus,* there is
no mediation: god is not inhuman, god is beyond the
human, like the unharvested mountain belonging to
Zeus.

The sacrifice is offered to the silent mountain. Heracles remains mute to the very end. "O my stubborn soul,
give me a curb as of steel on lips set like stone and let

no cry escape then" (1259 ff., Jebb's translation). Heracles' final sacrifice is only self-destruction. As a stone is only a stone, the signifying and the signified do not differ. Ritual is only form. But this form is empty. When a rite has to endure as pure form, all the rigors must be fulfilled. The holocaust will take place on the rocky cliff of a mountain; the pyre will be made of wood consecrated to Zeus: oak and wild olive; the fire will be ignited by night. As in Deianira's suicide, rigor is cruelty transformed into ceremony.

Fire is not a purification. In the rigid symbolism of tragedy, it means only destruction. When the fire of the venom burned the ball of wool, from the dust which fell to the ground only dirty foam remained, like discarded must.

They take Heracles away. At the end of the tragedy, gods are finally judged by men. The son formulates the message:

> You see how little compassion the Gods
> have shown in all that's happened; they
> who are called our fathers, who begot us,
> can look upon such suffering.
> No one can foresee what is .to come.
> What is here now is pitiful for us
> and shameful for the Gods . . .
>
> (1266 ff.)

Of all Sophocles' tragedies, *The Women of Trachis* contains the most desperate reading of whatever possible understanding of human fate there is. Heracles, who rescued Deianira, was destroyed by her. But Heracles was also destroyed by Iole, who was the first cause of all the misfortunes. Heracles perished from the venom hidden in the blood of the centaur, but the venom was the Hydra's venom. The Hydra killed Heracles, who had killed the Hydra. Eros is venom, and the love charm is poison. The flesh of men and the gods themselves are infected by Eros and venom. Hera, from her own breast, fed the mythological Hydra, who was Cerberus' sister and aunt of the Sphinx, born of the incestuous union of mother and son; Heracles' arrows, soaked in her venom, inflicted an incurable wound on Hera. ". . . and there is nothing here which is not Zeus" (1278).

From afar, only the spasm of the bodies in their lust and agony, poisoned by Eros and venom, can be seen. All the bodies are alike; Deianira's body arouses the lust of monsters, and that is her destiny. Iole's body arouses Heracles' lust, and that is also her fate. "My beauty should somehow bring me pain" (25), Deianira says at the very beginning. "Her own beauty has destroyed her life" (464), she says later of Iole. The body of Heracles, the strongest among men, becomes weak: "Now in my misery I am discovered a woman" (1075).[22]

The same actor played Heracles and Deianira. The mask in Greek theatre represented the person, but in the maze of symbols and permutations in *The Women of Trachis*, it seems as if the entrusting of two roles, Deianira and Heracles, to one actor, to the same body, was an intended sign.[23] "And there is nothing here which is not Zeus."

Above the *orchestra* and above Mount Oeta, the Great Bear circles round and round, bringing happiness and anxiety in turn. This oblique wheel of the Great Bear, which in its yearly cycle rises and falls over the earth, is compared to a wheel of fortune, in which the zenith announces the nadir—the new beginning.[24] But in *The Women of Trachis* the wheel of fortune is rather like the "Wheel of Fire," on which King Lear was broken.

Heracles calls the gift of Deianira "a net filled by the Erinyes" (1052). The Chorus compares Iole, who enters Deianira's house carrying a child fathered by Heracles, to a Fury. The image and style are from Aeschylus. But in the *Oresteia,* the Furies, hungering for blood and relentlessly pursuing murderers, change into watchdogs protecting the City. From Mycenae and Thebes, tortured for three generations, from matri-, patri-, fractri-cides, at the end Athens rose up in an alliance with Zeus's daughter. But in Sophocles there is no mediation between human and superhuman nor between the cruelty of chance and divine necessity. Human life is lived once, and redemption is nonexistent.

Sophocles' theology, in which the gods remain mute and prophecies come true, seems amazingly (and distressingly) similar to the game of chance and necessity, which the most brilliant of contemporary biologists have recently described. Out of the billions of turns of the cosmic roulette wheel, life once emerged, of which we are a part. The magnetic or thermal fields changed, and from a new biochemical situation, mutation occurred, and a drop of life, which has always to repeat itself, will repeat the same change to infinity until a new mutation occurs. Within the cosmos there is no intention. Out of the billions of mutations unpredictably emerged the strange spiral DNA, which might be compared to the ancient Hydra of a thousand heads[25] and which is the code of a human gene. The gene repeats itself, and from the billion blind turns of the roulette wheel, monsters are regenerated according to the law of probability. All prophecies that come true come from DNA. A long time ago, the macrocosmos became "eternal silence of infinite spaces beyond the human." The new microcosmos of biology is also beyond the human. Mutations in the particles of life are undirected and aimless. Thus spoke Zarathustra:

"By chance"—that is the most ancient nobility of the world, and this I restored to all things: I delivered them from their bondage under Purpose. This freedom and heavenly cheer I have placed over all things like an azure hell when I taught that over them and through them "no eternal will" wills. This prankish folly I have put in the place of that will when I taught: "In everything one thing is impossible: rationality."[26]

This strange spiral bristling with nodules is the only one in the whole microcosm and macrocosm which has full awareness of its own existence and full knowledge of suffering.

> Maiden, come from the house with us.
> You have seen a terrible death
> and agonies, many and strange, and there is
> nothing here which is not Zeus.
>
> (1275 ff.)[27]

The procession follows the stretcher. Iole has come from the house and joined the Chorus. Heracles murdered her father and brothers, left her pregnant, and told his son to take her as a wife. She has not said a word throughout the tragedy.[28] We know nothing of her. We do not even know whether she began to hate or love Heracles when he took her in his tent an hour after leveling the city. Iole crosses the stage only twice. The first time she breaks away from the group of captive women and Deianira sees that she is different from her companions. Iole alone bears her fate with dignity. Iole meets human and suprahuman cruelty with silence. This is the only heroic choice left her: she is the most Sophoclean of all the characters in *The Women of Trachis*.

> *L'étoile a pleuré rose au coeur de tes oreilles,*
> *L'infini roulé blanc de ta nuque à tes reins;*
> *La mer a perlé rousse à tes mammes vermeilles,*
> *Et l'Homme saigné noir à ton flanc souverain.*
>
> (Rimbaud, *Quatrain*)

The star wept rose-colored in the heart of your ears,
The infinite rolled white from your nape to your loins;
The sea turned ruddy at your vermilion nipples,
And Man bled black on your sovereign flank.[29]

III. "OH TO BE A STONE!"

Like lambs being led to slaughter, the children wear wreaths on their shoulders; Megara has dressed them in shrouds. In a few moments the tyrant's henchmen will drag her, the sons of Heracles, and old Amphitryon to the place of execution. Amphitryon has already thrown up both hands to the heavens and called to Zeus for immediate help. But he tells Megara to direct her prayers not "above" but "below"—down to Hades. Heracles has descended there. But now he is back.

In Euripides' *Heracles* the hero twice returns from the darkness and greets the bright light: "How gladly I behold the light once more . . ." (524).[1] And after his second return: "I see: heaven and earth the gleaming shafts of the sun . . ." (1089 f.). The first return is from Hades; the second, from another hell and another darkness. During his first return he rescued his sons, his wife, Megara, and his father from imminent death. The second is a return from madness, in which he murdered his wife and sons. On his first return he carries his mythological gear: bow, quiver and club. When he appears a second time he is half naked, tied with ropes to a ruined column of the palace.

In this extraordinary drama, seemingly both comedy and tragedy, the two returns of Heracles have different meanings and different dramatic styles and intensity. Most scholars find the first part flat, conventional, tedious and uneven; the second part is regarded with equal unanimity as a masterpiece.[2] But if the drama seems to break in two, it is because the myth was broken. With stubborn awareness, Euripides presents both halves of the myth with a common human experience, using all the tools of the Greek theatre. Heracles of the twelve labors, savior and mediator, returns from Hades in the middle of the Peloponnesian War. Heracles, son of Zeus and Amphitryon, persecuted by Hera, a demigod and martyr, brought down by misery, accepts his human condition and of his two fathers chooses the mortal.

Heracles is a morality play in two "acts." The first act is derisive and didactic. Two times are mixed together: mythical and historic. The mythical past is now the present. From this diachrony we have a sudden jump into a synchrony.

> What mortal lives who has not heard this name—
> Amphitryon of Argos, who shared his wife
> with Zeus? I am he . . .
>
> (1 ff.)

Amphitryon, expelled from Argos for the murder of his father-in-law, found refuge in Thebes. To ransom Amphitryon so that he could return to Argos, Heracles hired himself out to Eurystheus. His task was to civilize the world. But a revolution broke out in Thebes, and later a civil war. Creon, ruler of Thebes, who descended from the generation of men who sprang up where the dragon's teeth were sowed, was murdered the night before the play begins. Amphitryon, who once shared his wife with Zeus, was thrown out of his bed by the new tyrant before daybreak. Heracles' family escaped in panic from the royal palace and found shelter before the altar of Zeus. As the play begins, everyone is sitting together, Amphitryon, Megara and the children, "in utter destruction, lacking food, water, and clothing; having no beds . . ." (51 f.).

The upheaval, which took place in mythical Thebes during the course of one night, is stunningly close to the revolution and riots of the Peloponnesian War. Often in the course of one night the democratic governments in the Greek colonies were struck down, as the Spartan army was advancing, or the oligarchic governments were destroyed as the Athenian fleet approached. The massacre on Corcyra happened at least three years before the earliest possible date of *Heracles*.[3] Thucydides describes it in his factual style, but in full consciousness that it foretold the end of the Hellenic civilization:

During seven days that Eurymedon [commander of the Athenian navy] stayed with his sixty ships, the Corcyraeans were engaged in butchering those of their fellow-citizens whom they regarded as their enemies: and although the crime imputed was that of attempting to put down the democracy, some were slain also for private hatred, others by their debtors because of the monies owed to them. Death thus raged in every shape; and, as usually happens at such times, there was no length to which violence did not go; sons were killed by their fathers, and suppliants dragged from the altar or slain upon it; while some were even walled up in the temple of Dionysus and died there.

(III, x, 81)[4]

The action in the first "act" of *Heracles* is sketched in broad strokes. At the appropriate moment the tyrant jumps up like a jack-in-the-box, but the simplicity and schematism are purposeful, and the mythical parable, as in Brecht and Dürrenmatt, is clearly rooted in fact. All the details are typical. Lycus the foreigner profits from the disorders in Thebes; he tames the mob, sides with the ruined aristocrats, murders Creon, and declares himself king. He also decides to murder Megara, Amphitryon and the young sons of Heracles. He is afraid that when they grow up, they will avenge the death of their grandfather. Besides, it is always safer to kill everyone at once. However, he respects tradition and does not wish to drag the refugees away from Zeus's altar. He orders the soldiers to bring wood and build pyres. Unless the exiles voluntarily leave the sacred asylum, he will burn them alive: ". . .you are only slaves; I am the master" (252).

Heracles is still in Hades. But there are two different Hades in this drama, just as there are two different times, mythical and historical. One is the Hades from which no mortal returns. "Who of all the dead comes home from Hades?" Megara asks (297). The second Hades is the place to which Heracles descended to capture the three-headed dog. The arguments of Verrall and the rationalists are amazingly close to those of the tyrant Lycus, who asks Megara: ". . . do you think the father of these boys who lies dead with Hades will still come back?" (145 f.). Even the senile and gullible Amphitryon has serious doubts and advises Megara to calm the boys by telling them fables. "Console them with stories, those sweet thieves of wretched make-believe" (99 f.). The sons of Heracles will not believe that their father went to Hades for a dog. And even after Heracles returns, Amphitryon wants to make sure once again:

AMPHITRYON:
Did you really descend to Hades, son?

HERACLES:
Yes; I brought back the triple-headed dog.

AMPHITRYON:
You subdued him? Or was he the goddess' gift?

HERACLES:
Subdued him. Luck was mine . . .

(610 ff.)

This short exchange foreshadows Lucian's subversive dialogue of the gods. The irony is not only verbal. Euripides' dramas must be looked upon as theatre. This is a morality play with songs, dances and pantomime. And as in Brecht, all the theatrical tools are controlled by the dramatist's intellect and used as arguments for a thesis. The old men of Thebes are the Chorus. Only the old men remained faithful to Heracles when the tyrant seized power. Now they climb the stairs leading to Zeus's altar:

> Do not falter. Drag your weary feet
> onward like the colt that, yoked and slow,
> tugs uphill, on rock, the heavy wain.
>   If any man should fall,
>   support him with your hands . . .
>
> (119 ff.)

The first ode of the Chorus on the inefficiency of old age is full of stage directions. The old men fall over, extending hands to pull each other up the stairs. The Chorus of women of Trachis dance the battle of two monstrous suitors over the young Deianira. Heracles' twelve labors are danced by the Chorus of old men. The quaking old men with long white beards lean on canes, because it is difficult for them to walk. But they run like Heracles after the fast hind, break the neck of a lion, cut the heads of the Hydra, and pursue the mares that fed on human flesh. The most derisive pantomime is the lifting of the celestial vault by Heracles.[5] The old men raise their quivering hands, spread out their stiff fingers, and tense their shoulders.

Heracles wanted to civilize the world. He fought with dragons. "He passed below the sea," the Chorus sings, "and set a calmness in the lives of men whose living is

the oar" (401). The monsters have long ago disappeared. "I am the power here," the tyrant Lycus says
(142) and laughs at Heracles' legendary labors. Like our
contemporary leaders, Lycus has contempt for heroism.
Heracles' great labors are ridiculous, like the old men's
ballet. The Heracles who returns to contemporary
Thebes after his descent to Hades is both tragic and
comic. His antediluvian heroism is useless in this brave
new world. "What should I defend if not my wife and
sons and my old father? Farewell, my labors!" (574 f.).

Euripides' Heracles suddenly becomes surprisingly
like a Renaissance mercenary who once and for all bids
farewell to the world of romance and chivalry:

> Farewell the plumed troop, and the big wars
> That make ambition virtue! O, farewell!
> Farewell the neighing steed and the shrill trump,
> The spirit-stirring drum, th' ear-piercing fife,
> The royal banner, and all quality,
> Pride, pomp, and circumstance of glorious war!
> And O ye mortal engines whose rude throats
> Th' immortal Jove's dread clamours counterfeit,
> Farewell! Othello's occupation's gone.
>
> (*Othello*, III, iii, 353–61)

The boys run up to their father, cling to his legs and
grab at his lion skin. The hero holds his sons; he has set
aside his bow, quiver and club; his mythological gear lies
on the ground.

> . . . is this bravery,
> to do Eurystheus' orders and contend
> with lions and hydras, and not to struggle
> for my children's lives? From this time forth
> call me no more "Heracles the victor."
>
> (578 ff.)

The first part of *Heracles* could be called "The Return of the Father." The Doric Heracles who cleansed the earth of monsters, the Thessalian folk giant and relentless traveler, turns into a loving son, faithful husband and concerned father. The change takes place on the linguistic level as well: Amphitryon is now called a father; Megara, a wife; Heracles, a son, husband, and father. The mythical parable ends as a domestic tragicomedy; Heracles returns from Hades to the embraces of his family: "All mankind loves its children" (636).

The tyrant reappears, only to be killed; his last cry for help comes from offstage. The first act ends. At this moment a chariot bearing Iris and Madness, who have been sent by Hera, descends onto the roof of the palace. The second act begins with Heracles' slaying his wife and sons.

The murder is performed offstage. The dark powers of tragedy, Hegel wrote, attack from ambush. The unknown is the enemy, and for this reason is terrifying. The enemy is in us and outside us at the same time. In Euripides' theatre there are two times, two Hades and two madnesses. The first madness is a woman in a Gorgon's mask with serpents in her hair, holding a whip in her hand. The second is in Heracles himself.

It may at first glance appear that Euripides used Homer's method of double motivation. Behind the hero stands a god who directs the arrow to the target or deflects the flying spear from its course. Ate covers the hero's eyes with a bloody mist; Apollo fortifies his languid limbs; Athene restores the clarity of his vision. But the two heavenly emissaries who arrive in a black chariot have a different function in Euripides: Iris and Madness carry on an intellectual discussion between themselves, in which the theology of a jealous god, "of swindling, malice, and ominous joy," is formulated. Iris says: "Let him learn what Hera's anger is, and what is mine. For the gods are nothing, and men prevail, if this one man escape" (840 ff.).

The roles of Hera's divine emissaries are strictly divided, like those of the officers of the secret police; Iris is a propagandist and controller, Madness does the dirty work. At times executioners still have scruples. They know that their superiors despise them, and in a special way they love their victims. "My functions make me loathsome to the gods, nor do I gladly visit men I love" (845 f.). Madness wants to save Heracles from what is apparently injustice. Iris calls her to order: "Hera has not sent you down to show your sanity" (857). The irony here is implacable. Madness, the daughter of night, calls upon the Sun: "O Sun, be my witness: I act against my will" (858). Hangmen have scruples but are obedient. Madness has already leapt from the roof onto Heracles.

The goddesses have discussed the theology of madness; now the herald describes its physiology. The accuracy and preciseness of his account have surprised psychiatrists: "Suddenly he changed: his eyes rolled and bulged from their sockets, and the veins stood out, gorged with blood, and froth began to trickle down his bearded chin. Then he spoke, laughing like a maniac" (931 ff.).

Sophocles' "unseen destroyer," who lurks in the darkness and attacks unexpectedly, is within Heracles and at the same time outside him. The "superhuman enemy," wearing a terrifying mask, springs upon men *ex machina* accompanied by wailing flutes. The inner enemy, who, like a sliver deep in the skin, becomes invisible, is described with complete accuracy. Mad Ajax tore apart sheep with his bare hands and tortured the dogs because he took them for Greek commanders. Mad Heracles kills his sons with arrows and smashes their heads with his club because he took them for the children of Eurystheus:

HERACLES:

    . . . Who killed these boys?

AMPHITRYON:

You and your bow and some god are all guilty.

(1134 f.)

For Goethe and Hegel, as for Marx, Nietzsche and Freud, Prometheus and Oedipus were the purest representations of the human condition in Greek tragedy.[6] Euripides' startling modernity is his attempt to confront and re-evaluate the mythic mad Heracles with the situation of Prometheus and Oedipus. He deliberately uses the same theatrical effects. Heracles appears on stage tied with ropes to a column of the palace, like Prometheus bound to the rocks. Madness and Iris, who have descended *ex machina* in a black chariot, are similar to Might, Violence and Hephaestus, who were sent by Zeus to torture Prometheus, and their roles are similarly divided: the blacksmith Hephaestus, a manual laborer, had mercy on the Titan; Might, a high-ranking *apparatchik*, defended Number One. Prometheus was punished for his unrestrained love of humanity. Theseus calls Heracles "Mankind's benefactor, man's greatest friend" (1252). Heracles' great labors are ridiculed in the first part of the drama; they failed to civilize the world. But they aroused the envy of the gods. Heracles, like Prometheus, is a savior by his own will, and against the will of the gods. Heracles exceeded the human, and for this reason he must be humbled. In the final analysis, what the gods demand is contrition.

"I am the enemy of all the Gods that gave me ill for good," Aeschylus' Prometheus says (975 f.). If hell exists, it is reason enough to hate heaven. The Heracles of Euripides, the murderer of his wife and sons, who twice descended into hell, challenges the gods for the second time in Greek tragedy:

THESEUS:
Your wretchedness towers up and touches heaven.

HERACLES:
Then where it touches heaven, I shall strike.

THESEUS:
What do you think the gods care for your threats?

HERACLES:
Heaven is proud. And I am proud to heaven.

(1240 ff.)

In *Heracles* we have a dual criticism of theology, from the point of view of both *pure* and of *practical* reason: ". . . I do not believe the gods commit adultery, or bind each other in chains. I never did believe it; I never shall; nor that one god is tyrant of the rest. If god is truly god, he is perfect, lacking nothing" (1341 ff.). In the light of pure reason, if god exists, he must be perfection.[7] Gods shaped like men are, as Heracles says, the lie of poets. But in the light of practical reason, god, if he exists, is responsible for the evil of the world. A just god is contradictory to all of man's experiences. God, who has poisoned both mediation and mediator, who torments mankind with eternal plagues, is cruel and jealous. "I had an endless spell of misery," Heracles says to Odysseus in Hades. Euripides knew Homer by heart: "Let me show you my life: a life not worth living now, or ever." Heracles is a touchstone of the injustice of the gods and the cruelty of the world. "Take my father first, a man who killed my mother's father and having such a curse, married Alcmene who gave birth to me. . . . Then Zeus—whoever Zeus may be—begot me for Hera's hatred"[8] (1256 ff.).

Fate is the "enemy." Fate is either a necessity or the

unknown. "Mastered by Hera or by necessity," Amphitryon says of Heracles at the beginning of the play. Euripides was not a nominalist. "Hera" and "necessity" are only names for "the invisible enemy." Fate is *non-awareness*. Heracles unknowingly killed his own sons, as Oedipus unknowingly killed his own father. The "enemy" waited a long time, and the trap was set before Oedipus was born. Only once did he stand at the crossroads: chariots were coming from Thebes, he refused to give way, he raised his hand, and killed his father. He was trapped.

The trap is set by the gods, or it is within ourselves. Born of mother and father, we are condemned to desire our mother and dream of the death of our father: "No man alive can budge necessity" (311). Euripides once again repeats the words of Aeschylus' Prometheus: ". . . for I know well against necessity, against its strength, no one can fight and win" (105 ff.). But this same Oedipus, who killed his father and slept with his mother, solved the Sphinx's riddle.[9] Prometheus learned to know the future, Oedipus learned to know his own past. The "enemy" is above or below human consciousness. Prometheus and Oedipus made known the unknown.

In the parable of Er, the son of Armenius, which closes Plato's *Republic,* Lachesis greets the souls of the dead who have descended into the Valley of Transformation to choose a new life: "The responsibility is with the chooser, God is justified." Lachesis, one of the three Fates, is the daughter of Necessity. Freedom of choice is the awareness of necessity.

Sophocles' *Oedipus* takes place at the hour of choice. It was already foretold the Oedipus would kill his father and sleep with his mother. But now he stands before the Chorus, in the city where a devastating plague is raging. Everything has already happened, and now he has only to give the verdict. He is judge, prosecutor and defendant in the trial of his own destiny. The judge gives the sentence, the prosecutor carries it out: Oedipus gouges out his eyes with his own hands.

The ultimate choice of the accused is to plead guilty or not guilty. Oedipus does not plead guilty but accepts responsibility for his *own* fate; he makes the fate, which was imposed upon him, his own. "Fate is like the awareness of one's own self, but of oneself as an enemy," Hegel wrote. The defender now accuses the prosecutor. Oedipus, who gouged out his own eyes, makes his fate visible. "Perhaps good King Oedipus had one eye too many."[10] Oedipus, who did not plead guilty, decides to live to be a witness of the human condition.[11]

"But from the moment he knows," Camus wrote in *The Myth of Sisyphus,* "his tragedy begins. Yet at the same moment, blind and desperate, he realizes that the only bond linking him to the world is the cool hand of a girl."[12] Yes, but this is Oedipus of Colonus, which was not produced until after Euripides' death. King Oedipus flees from Thebes, which he has finally saved from a plague, himself infected. He wanders over roads far from human habitation, as a warning and threat. When Heracles awakens among the murdered corpses of his sons and wife, a friend offers him a hand:

HERACLES:
Take care. I may pollute your clothes with blood.

THESEUS:
Pollute them then. Spare not. I do not care.

(1399 f.)

In the rays of the setting sun which fall on the arena, Theseus tells Heracles to stand erect: "No mortal man can stain what is divine" (1232). Friendship and the light of day are stronger than contamination: "The morning star," Eluard wrote in one of his most beautiful poems, "disperses monsters." Heracles, in *The Women of Trachis*, poisoned by the Hydra's venom, wishes to infect his son and everyone who is still alive. Both Deianira and Heracles are desperately searching for a final gesture which could give some sense to their destruction. This gesture is Deianira's ceremonial suicide and the pyre on Mount Oeta, upon which Heracles wants to burn alive. Ritual is the ultimate mediation between a cruel god and human defeat.

In Euripides' *Heracles*, ritual is repudiated. Heracles' madness began with a ritualistic cleansing of hands after the murder of the tyrant Lycus. This moment must have been especially important for Euripides, since it is mentioned twice—the first time by the Messenger and later when Heracles regains consciousness:

HERACLES:
Where did my madness take me? Where did I die?

AMPHITRYON:
By the altar, as you purified your hands.

(1144 f.)

Ritual for Euripides is, to use Hegel's term once again, an alienation, only a mock solution of the contradiction between nonhuman and human, not-knowing and knowing, object and subject, nature and freedom, the enemy outside of us and the enemy within. The only one real end of madness is to be free of the fear of magical contamination: "Where there is love contagion cannot come" (1234). Heracles returns to the human world, in which, though there is no hope, despair must be controlled by reason.

"A world of such a novel," Malraux wrote in the introduction to *Days of Wrath*, "a world of tragedy, is always an ancient world: man, crowd, elements, woman, destiny. It can be reduced to two active forces: the hero and the meaning which he gives to his life." For Sophocles' characters, life is disaster, and their heroic choice is to give meaning to their own defeat. The Chorus in *Oedipus at Colonus* says: "Nothing surpasses not being born." Antigone, Deianira and Jocasta commit suicide out of despair; Ajax throws himself on the sword out of contempt for the world. But Oedipus chooses to live in order to give meaning to his defeat. In the same way, Theseus says to Heracles: "Hellas will not suffer you to die in your blindness" (1254).[13]

"It is not important," Sartre wrote, "what is done to us; it is only important what we have done with what is done to us." The heroic choices of Heracles and Oedipus were to live after their destruction.[14] "Oh to be a stone!" (1397). Stone is pure essence. But Heracles already knows that it is not given to man to be a stone. He knows that the murderer of sons and wife is the same Heracles who cleansed the earth of monsters. He picks up his club, bow and arrows from the ground again. "But now, I see, I must serve necessity" (1357). But this new "necessity" is different from the dance of the jealous Hera, "pounding with her feet Olympus' gleaming floors" (1304). Heracles accepts himself and his human condition:

THESEUS:
. . . But where now is famous Heracles?

HERACLES:
What were you when you were underground?

THESEUS:
In courage I was the least of men.

(1414 ff.)

In this final dialogue, the underground realm of Hades signifies only "a trail of shadow" through which every man must pass in order to grow. Heracles accepts his human condition with eyes filled with tears. "Even a god would weep, if he knew it," Amphitryon remarks[15] (1115). But Heracles knows that only men, not gods cry. He accepts the human condition with reasonable despair. He knows that even the strongest can be broken, and that madness and shame belong to all mankind.

> Men must endure
> their going hence, even as their coming hither:
> Ripeness is all.
>
> (*King Lear*, V, ii, 9–11)

Heracles will go with Theseus to Athens, where he will await his own death. But to bury loved ones who died before us still belongs to the human condition. "All mankind loves its children." The pyre is waiting. It was prepared by the tyrant's henchmen to burn the sons of Heracles alive. The pyre always waits for its victims and never waits in vain.

HERACLES:
Bury my children.

AMPHITRYON:
Who will bury me?

HERACLES:
I.

AMPHITRYON:
When will you come?

HERACLES:
When you bury them.

(1419 ff.)

In answer to the Sphinx's riddle, Oedipus replied "man." The theme of two fathers comes up six times in *Heracles*.[16] Amphitryon mentions it twice, Lycus once, the Chorus three times. In order to know his fate, Oedipus had to discover who his father was.[17] Heracles at the close of the tragedy deliberately chooses his father: ". . . I count you my father now, not Zeus" (1265). To accept the human condition is to choose a human father. But this choice is at the same time a denial of the heavenly father. Prometheus and Oedipus are finally joined in Euripides' *Heracles.*

IV. *PHILOCTETES,* OR THE REFUSAL

1.

In Sophocles' *Philoctetes,* as in *The Tempest,* the audience is a sea and the stage is an island. Just a few moments before the play begins, Odysseus and Achilles' son Neoptolemus have landed on Lemnos' rocky shore. Odysseus has been on Lemnos once before: ten years earlier when the Greek armada, bound for Troy, cast anchor there, he abandoned Philoctetes on the island, asleep in a cave, because after Philoctetes was bitten by a snake on the island of Chryse, he had been a great nuisance to his shipmates: his wound stank, and he groaned so loudly that he disturbed his companions in their prayers.

Odysseus remembers that the beach leads to a steep, rocky precipice in which there is a cave with two exits. Neoptolemus crosses the flat dish of the *orchestra* and comes to the stairs leading to the *skene:*

NEOPTOLEMUS:
. . . I think I see such a cave.

ODYSSEUS:
Above or below? I cannot see it myself.

NEOPTOLEMUS:
Above here, and no trace of footpath.

ODYSSEUS:
See if he is housed within, asleep.

NEOPTOLEMUS:
I see an empty hut, with no one there.

(27 ff.)[1]

The imaginary scenery is created from the very first lines of the tragedy: the sea, the flat shore, the wall of mountains leading to the beach. This setting exactly fits the architecture of Greek theatre. The cave "with two mouths" (16) is the wood structure of the *skene* with a curtained-off center door and two open side doors: "This, that you see, is his two-fronted house, and he sleeps inside on the rock" (159 ff.). But by the end of the drama both openings of the cave are called simply doors: "Two doors cut in the rock . . ." (952). The island with the cave among the cliffs has already been fixed in the imagination.

"Be not afeard. The isle is full of noises . . ." (*The Tempest*, III, ii, 129). The Chorus of sailors standing on the flat *orchestra*-shore look with fright at the empty cave: ". . . we are strangers, and this land is strange . . ." (136). From the depths of the island, bounced off the cliffs and repeated by echoes, comes a groan. "I hear a voice . . . voice of a man, crawling along the path . . . the voice of a man wounded . . ." (205 ff.). The sailors have good hearing; steps are heard more and more clearly. But they have a strange sound; the walker is dragging one foot. They are the steps of a cripple.

> . . . of their seven ships the leader was Philoktetes
> skilled in bow's work . . .
> Yet he himself lay apart in the island, suffering strong
> pains,
> in Lemnos the sacrosanct, where the sons of the Achaians
> had left him
> in agony from the sore bite of the wicked water snake.
>   . . . yet soon the Argives
> beside their ships were to remember lord Philoktetes.
>
> (*Iliad*, II, 718 f., 721 ff., Lattimore's translation)

All three of the symbolic signs in the later tragedies about Philoctetes are in these seven lines of Homer: the island, the wound and the bow. But only Sophocles among the three Greek tragedians made Lemnos a desert island: ". . . no one sets foot on it, there are no houses" (3). On this desolate island, a chapter from the history of the world will be enacted in which the gods are involved. On Mount Oeta, Philoctetes had set fire to the pyre on which Heracles was burned alive. As a reward he inherited Heracles' bow and arrows. Left on Lemnos, he held on to the bow with tightly clenched fists. From this bow a last arrow will be shot, killing Paris and ending the Trojan War. In the epilogue, Heracles himself will come down *ex machina* to persuade the stubborn Philoctetes to set off for Troy: "It is not down in any map; true places never are."[2]

Lemnos appears on every map, and with a favorable wind is only a day's journey from Scyrus, where Odysseus went to get Neoptolemus. Scholars have even found Philoctetes' cave on the northeastern shore of an island where the cliff rises directly from the rocky shore of Mount Hermaeum, from which the moans of the exile reverberated,[3] and from which later, when Troy is taken, one of the beacons is lit to send the news of victory from Mount Ida to Argos.[4] But Lemnos is also one of the "true places" in which, Melville believed, the mythical history of the world is enacted. Hephaestus was thrown out of Olympus onto Lemnos and set up his forge in the crater of Mosychlus, which now raises its bare slopes on the western shore of Lemnos, south of Mount Hermaeum. Philoctetes, feeling a new attack of unendurable pain, begged Neoptolemus to throw him down into the crater: ". . . take up this body of mine and burn it on what they call the Lemnian fire" (800). When Prometheus stole the fire from Olympus, he brought it to Lemnos, or, in another version of the myth, stole it from Hephaestus' forge on Lemnos.[5] Philoctetes, like the first men taught by Prometheus, strikes fire from stones: "Whenever I had no fire, rubbing stone on stone I would at last produce the spark that kept me still in life" (294 ff.).

On this Lemnos, mythical and real, the first uninhabited island in the history of literature, the exile spent nine years of his life. In the cave, which shielded him from the cold of night and the relentless heat of day, Neoptolemus finds "a pallet bed, stuffed with leaves" (33) and a bucket of cut wood, "a poor workman's contrivance," (35 f.). This first Robinson Crusoe did not begin the cultivation of the land on his desert island, nor did he start breeding cattle. He quenched his thirst from the water in the well, which even today, just as Odysseus remembered then, is at the left of the cave; he appeased his hunger with birds and small game shot with his bow. When Orestes in Sophocles' *Electra* crossed over to Argos at the break of dawn, he heard the song of the birds. On Philoctetes' island, the birds never sang. Neither trees nor flowers gave off a scent. On the island there was only one smell: the stench of his wound. ". . . some rags are drying in the sun full of the oozing matter from a sore" (38 f.).

This nauseating odor of pus, which anyone who has spent even a short time in an army hospital during a war will never forget, accompanies Philoctetes from the first to the last line of the drama. "Lame and foul-smelling," Philoctetes says of himself (1032). The wound, which periodically opens up to ooze blood and pus, is described in all its hideousness: ". . . the raging, bleeding sore, running, in his maggot-rotten foot" (699 f.).

In *Ajax*, blood and foam pour from the nostrils of the corpse. In *Oedipus Rex*, the Messenger tells the Chorus exactly how Oedipus cut the noose on which Jocasta was hanging, and how, when the corpse fell to the ground, he tore off the golden brooches she wore on her peplos and gouged out his eyes with the pins. The Oedipus of *Oedipus at Colonus* is, despite Antigone's loving care, a dirty, sickening old man: "The abominable filth grown old with him, rotting his sides! And on his sightless face the ragged hair streams in the wind. There's the same quality in the food he carries for his thin old belly" (1258 ff.). Sophocles, the most cruel of Greek tragedians, never shrinks from the physical image of agony;[6] his heroes are like statues, but these statues shed real blood and exude black pus besides. "The sweat is soaking all his body over, and a black flux of blood and matter has broken out of his foot" (*Philoctetes*, 823 ff.).

Philoctetes was bitten by a snake on Chryse on his way to Troy. Chryse was a little islet to the west of Lemnos which vanished beneath the sea like Atlantis. "It was swallowed up by the sea," Pausanius writes. The disappearance of Chryse was foretold, if we are to believe Herodotus, by the prophecy of Onomacritus. On Chryse, an island both real and mythical like Lemnos, Jason offered sacrifices when the Argonauts were seeking the golden fleece, as did Heracles when he set out for Troy. Philoctetes passed the holy precinct on Chryse, as did Oedipus, who at Colonus stopped over at the sanctuary dedicated to the underworld gods.

A scene on a vase preserved from the fourth century B.C. depicts Philoctetes bitten by a snake which is the guardian of the shrine. A priestess is throwing up her hands as if she were frightened or as if she were uttering a blessing. On her dress there are two rows of discs, which symbolize stairs; and on her head, a striped hat, *calathos,* in the shape of a small cylinder, which seems to indicate a link with the underworld.[7] Philoctetes, bitten in the foot by the snake, will henceforth shuffle along like a cripple. Oedipus had pierced eye sockets; Laius, his father, had a bad leg; Labdacus, his grandfather, limped. Religious scholars and anthropologists consider a wound in the leg and difficulty in walking signs of relations with chthonic deities.[8]

It is of course easiest for snakes to bite a man in the leg. But the wound that does not heal is a *figura* and a sign. In a different version of the myth, perhaps the earliest, Philoctetes wounds himself with a poisoned arrow which, together with a bow, he had inherited from Heracles. This was his punishment for revealing the secret of Heracles' grave. The arrow leaped from the quiver and pierced his foot.[9] The centaur Chiron was also wounded in the foot by Heracles' arrows dipped in the venom of the Hydra. Chiron, the teacher of Asclepius, who healed both men and gods, could not heal himself. Tormented with insufferable pain, he, although immortal, preferred to die and agreed to go to Tartarus —as ransom for the pardon of Prometheus. As Kerényi put it, "A healer, he crept away with his pain into the darkness of his cave like a sick animal, and longed to die."[10] Kerényi's Chiron is an unintentional image of Sophocles' Philoctetes.

Sophocles refers to Chiron only once in *The Women of Trachis:* "I know that arrow which struck Nessus injured even Chiron, who was a god, and all animals, whatever it touches, it kills" (714 ff.). In *Philoctetes* a miraculous grass which mitigates pain is thrice mentioned. When Neoptolemus finds the cave empty, he supposes that the cripple has gone to find the weed that alleviates pain (44). When Philoctetes is preparing to leave Lemnos, he wishes to take with him only the healing grass "to lull the pain to sleep." (650) The Chorus pities Philoctetes because he has no one "to assuage the burning flux . . . of his envenomed foot with healing herbs gathered from the bounteous earth . . ." (699 ff., Jebb's translation). On the slopes of Mount Pelion, in the Valley of Pelethronion, where Chiron, tormented with pain, took shelter in the cave, an herb grew which healed wounds inflicted by the bite of snakes and poisoned arrows. Plinius named it "kentaureion" or "chironion."[11] Philoctetes on Lemnos applies the herb of Chiron to his wound.

The incurable wound is a sacred wound as well.[12] The serpent is an archetype of the invisible becoming visible. Philoctetes became a leper to people because he was chosen by the gods to fulfill his given role: "These afflictions that have come upon him are the work of Chryse, bitter of heart. As for his present loneliness and suffering, this, too, no doubt is part of the God's plan that he may not bend against Troy the divine invincible bow until the time shall be fulfilled . . ." (193 ff.). The young Neoptolemus has not the least doubt that Philoctetes was bitten by a serpent by special decree of the gods. But the gods did not tell Philoctetes about this. The snake that made him a cripple is for him "my worst enemy" (631). If the gods sent it, they sent it because they despised him. "I am nothing now . . . God-hated wretch" (1030 f.).

Sophocles' Philoctetes, like his Heracles, are tools in the hands of destroying gods. "I have become," Heracles says in *The Women of Trachis*, "a miserable ruin sacked by invisible disaster" (1104). Heracles was burned alive, poisoned by the Hydra's venom, after performing the twelve labors. Long before, the snake bit Philoctetes so that eventually he would go to Troy and fulfill his role. In Sophocles' theology, to be chosen by the gods is mis-

ery; the mediator is an outcast among people. The
stigma is a stinking wound.

Chiron's wound was incurable. "No hope of cure,"
Neoptolemus says of Philoctetes at the end of the human
drama, a moment before the appearance of Heracles *ex
machina*. The tragic world is incurable.[13] Consciousness,
for the existentialists, is a hole in being. Tragic consciousness is like an ulcerating wound which never heals
over. "No hope of cure" sounds like a line from Camus.
The incurable wound is a double sign: of men chosen by
the gods for mediation and of those who refuse to submit
to the gods, history and order. Healing is always payment for submission.

The serpent which bit Philoctetes is the emblem of
Asclepius, whose sons are to heal Philoctetes. The sons
of the god are military doctors in the Greek camp. But
the stubborn Philoctetes is a mediator who refuses to be
cured: "Never, if of my will I must see Troy" (1392).

2.

Philoctetes was excluded from the human community,
abandoned with a heap of rags and a handful of food.
The sailors who during those nine long years landed
on Lemnos left him new heaps of rags and scraps of
provisions. There was only the deserted anchorage,
the empty sea. The screams reverberating from the
rocks reached only the waves hitting against the
empty shore. ". . . neighbor to himself alone, powerless to walk, with no one in the land to be near him
while he suffered" (691 ff., Jebb's translation). Philoctetes is thrown to the very bottom of the human condition, "utterly alone," the Chorus says, ". . . he
makes his bed without neighbors . . . His thoughts are
set continually on pain and hunger" (182 ff.). Like
Beckett's cripples, he has been reduced to hunger,

thirst and agony. "In all I saw before me nothing but pain; but of that a great abundance . . ." (283 f.).

This human rag, this "dead man among the living," is still owner of the invincible bow. Odysseus, who chose the young son of Achilles to help him, must deliver Philoctetes to Troy. Without this bow and without this man, the war cannot be won. Once again he is needed. He must be delivered alive: by ruse, force or persuasion. The outcast must become a savior, a leprous national hero. The gods, the whole assembly of Greeks, and history itself, which must be fulfilled, call for Philoctetes' return. Against this threefold pressure Philoctetes can set only his wound, which is a witness of divine and human injustice. "No one but me could have stood even the sight of what I have suffered" (636 f., Knox's translation). Philoctetes is a wound which has not healed. The wound is his strength.

On the desert island a brutal political drama is now being enacted. Sophocles' *Philoctetes* has a bitter and startling reality for anyone who knows from his own or from others' experience about the breaking down of political prisoners whose names can be exploited anew, or how deportees are handled whose abilities may come in handy again, or forced emigrés who suddenly have become needed by their fatherland.

NEOPTOLEMUS:
What do you bid me do, but to tell lies?

ODYSSEUS:
By craft I bid you take him, Philoctetes.

NEOPTOLEMUS:
And why by craft rather than by persuasion?

ODYSSEUS:
He will not be persuaded; force will fail.

(100 ff.)

The simplest method is deceit. It is an old rule of prosecutors to promise prisoners that they will see their families. Neoptolemus gives his word to Philoctetes that he will take him to his home at Oeta and that he will see his old father. Philoctetes believes him and hands over the bow. Heracles' bow is now in Odysseus' hands. But at this very moment the young son of Achilles, who for the first time in his life has encountered hypocrisy, is shocked by the image of human misfortune. He reveals the truth to Philoctetes: they will take him to the Greek camp. The sailors have already seized him by the arms. But the living corpse prefers to smash himself on the rocks.

> Never! I would rather suffer anything than this.
> There is still my steep and rugged precipice here.
>
> (999 f.)

The sailors have backed away from Philoctetes. Odysseus, the old pragmatist, has felt from the beginning that the unerring bow is more important than its stinking owner, whom suddenly the gods have favored and made the savior of the nation. If he persists, let him remain there—but without the bow. Philoctetes knows what that means. The island is full of birds. "I shall myself in death be a feast for those that fed me" (956 f.). This bitter sarcasm will be repeated by Hamlet when Claudius asks where Polonius is: "At supper. . . . Not where he eats, but where he is eaten" (IV, iii, 18, 20). The image of Philoctetes being eaten by birds will return again:

> What hope shall I find of food to keep my wretched life alive?
> Above me, in the clouds, down the shrill winds
> the birds; no strength in me to stop them.
>
> (1090 ff.)

The sky above is hidden by clouds, below is the empty sea; the cripple will become food for birds, like Prometheus chained to the rock in the Caucasus. Lemnos is the island of all myths.

Deceit and force fail: Neoptolemus returns the bow to Philoctetes. Nothing but persuasion remains. The delegates of authority always begin with the Great Necessity.

NEOPTOLEMUS:
Necessity,
a great necessity compels it. Do not be angry.

PHILOCTETES:
Then I am lost. I am betrayed.

(92 ff.)

If a prisoner believes in the Great Necessity he is lost forever.[14] Philoctetes is fully aware of two different necessities: the necessity of the oppressors and the necessity of the oppressed: "Necessity has taught me, little by little, to suffer and to be patient" (538 f.). This Great Necessity is said to be sent by the gods. But the gods are always on the side of the oppressors. In no other Sophoclean tragedy are the gods mentioned so often. As in *Ajax,* the Odysseus in *Philoctetes* is a pious politician who knows well that god's name is never taken in vain. The gods help those who help the gods. The last year of the Trojan War, which was for Sophocles an image of the Peloponnesian War, has changed his new Odysseus into a cynical politician. Odysseus is now ready to declare even in public that by the laws of nature, gods are always on the side of the strongest.

Melos was a small Greek island colony near the Sea of Crete which tried to preserve its neutrality in the war between Athens and Sparta. Athens demanded the capitulation of the island, which it called an "alliance."

The Melians, as Thucydides relates, called upon the gods: ". . . we trust that the gods may grant us fortune as good as yours, since we are just men fighting against unjust . . ." The Athenians replied: ". . . Of the gods we believe, and of men we know, that by a necessary law of their nature they rule wherever they can. . . . Thus, as far as the gods are concerned, we have no fear and no reason to fear that we shall be at a disadvantage"[15] (V, xvii, 103–4). Thirty-eight ships, their own and their allies', accompanied the Greek envoys, with three thousand heavy infantry and over three hundred archers. The Melians did not yield. The Athenians slaughtered all the grown men on the island and sold the women and children as slaves. This was in the sixteenth year of the Peloponnesian War, and seven years before the production of *Philoctetes* in Athens.

ODYSSEUS:
It is Zeus, I would have you know, Zeus this land's ruler, who has determined. I am only his servant.

PHILOCTETES:
Hateful creature,
what things you can invent! You plead the Gods
to screen your actions and make the Gods out liars.

ODYSSEUS:
They speak the truth. The road must be traveled.

(989 ff.)

Neoptolemus calls on the gods twenty-two times. ". . . I wish that you would trust the gods . . ." (1374 f.). Everything that happens, down to the smallest detail, he claims, is a manifestation of "god's will," "the divine plan," "divine decree"—from Philoctetes' wound to his own expedition to Lemnos and to the sharing of the glory of victory with Philoctetes. Suffering is rewarded, and a theodicy is realized in history, and during one decade at that. Against Odysseus' gods of the establishment and against Neoptolemus' gods of quick justice, Philoctetes can oppose only his own suffering. The gods who taught him are deaf. ". . . shall I praise them when, praising the ways of the gods, I find that the gods are evil?" (451 f., Jebb's translation). For the third time the theme of Prometheus challenging the gods recurs on Lemnos.

> Never, never! That is my fixed purpose.
> Not though the Lord of the Lightning, bearing his fiery bolts,
> come against me, burning me
> with flame and glare.
> Let Ilium go down and all that under its walls
> had the heart to cast me away, crippled!
>
> (1197 ff.)

This is Philoctetes third "no." But his resistance will be broken at the very end of the drama. When arguments about the Great Necessity and Providence do not work, flat practical reason remains. "Your anger has made a savage of you" (1321). Philoctetes is insisting on his own downfall. This obstinacy, to Neoptolemus, exceeds human measure. ". . . learn not to be defiant in misfortune" (1387). But what is human measure? "What is the natural measure of my sorrow?" asks Sophocles' Electra (236). And measure of what—misfortune or obstinacy? ". . . unhappy generations of death-bound men whose lives have known extremes!" says the Chorus (178 f.). The simple sailors know better than Neoptolemus what human and inhuman measure is. ". . . I know of no other," the Chorus repeats, ". . . whose destiny was more his enemy . . ." (680, 682).

Philoctetes' consciousness is his stinking wound. His former friends, as in the tragedy of *Ajax,* turn out to be scoundrels. He stank to them when they were offering their prayers, but now they want him to sit with them while they offer new prayers. They promise him a share in the glory of Troy's defeat and an honored place in the assembly of the Greeks. "Again, again you have touched my old hurt" (1170). To the very end, Neoptolemus does not understand Philoctetes' obstinacy. Philoctetes' wound is his dignity. The only dignity left to him. And now they want him to deny it. "Eyes of mine, that have seen all, can you endure to see my living with my murderers, the sons of Atreus?" (1355). They promise him a cure as a reward. For nine years on his desert island he dreamed of a cure for his wound. But it was a different kind of cure: ". . . if I saw them dead, I could dream that I was free of my sickness" (1043 f.).

Philoctetes' refusal is final, and Neoptolemus has no choice but to keep his pledge and take him home.

NEOPTOLEMUS:
How shall I avoid the blame of the Greeks?

PHILOCTETES:
Give it no thought.

NEOPTOLEMUS:
What if they come and harry my country?

PHILOCTETES:
I shall be there.

NEOPTOLEMUS:
What help will you be able to give me?

PHILOCTETES:
With the bow of Heracles.

(1403 ff.)

Like deserted Lemnos and the incurable wound, the bow, a gift of Apollo, is at once mythical and real. Neoptolemus looks at it with superstitious adoration: "May I see it closer, touch and adore it like a God?" (657 f.). The bow was for him *theos*. In myth, objects bring with them the properties of their owners. With this bow Heracles cleansed the earth and the seas of monsters, but when he dipped the arrows in the Hydra's venom, her poison was spread anew around the world. The centaur Chiron was wounded by a poisoned arrow from this bow. Achilles, foster child of Chiron and father of Neoptolemus, was wounded mortally in the foot by the same bow, which Paris borrowed briefly. Paris will later be hit in the knee by an arrow from Heracles' bow, shot by Philoctetes. In mythical theology it is always the same bow; arrows wound the heroes in the leg, and human history is enacted. It seems that the gods have but one bow to hunt men down.

Philoctetes and Neoptolemus slowly descend the stairs leading from the *skene* to the rocky shore. Philoctetes stops for a moment. He has Heracles' bow in his hands, the bow wrenched from the gods. During this short moment, before Heracles appears *ex machina* on the roof of the cave, the hero chosen by the gods to fulfill a historical mission rises above his fate. But for a brief moment the bow is torn away from its sinister destiny. Troy will not fall.[16]

NEOPTOLEMUS:
Brace yourself, stand firm on your feet.

PHILOCTETES:
To the limit of my strength.

(1403 f.)

3.

In the post-Homeric tradition, it is Diomedes who goes after Philoctetes on Lemnos. In Aeschylus' lost tragedy, it is Odysseus who finally convinces Philoctetes to go to Troy with him. In Euripides' tragedy, to avoid recognition Odysseus disguises himself as a fugitive from Troy and takes Diomedes with him in case force is needed. Against tradition, Sophocles chose Neoptolemus to accompany Odysseus. It may be worth reflecting why. Heroic Achilles and cunning Odysseus are eternal opposites, the exemplifications of two attitudes and two character structures; in fifth-century Athens, torn between two classes and two parties, these Homeric psychological and moral opposites suddenly became actual and political.[17] Achilles' desire for glory at any price and Odysseus' for success at any price began to signify the choice between the callous traditionalism of the aristocratic leaders and the unscrupulous cupidity of the democratic politicians and tradesmen.

Neoptolemus' mission endows the tragedy with intellectual relevance and allows Sophocles to enrich the action by the involvement of Achilles' son in deceit and blackmail and to resolve it by his dramatic defection from Odysseus' politics. To many critics, Neoptolemus is the hero of *Philoctetes* and one of the finest characters in Greek tragedy. As Kitto has pointed out: ". . . the part of Neoptolemus has a much wider range than any other in extant Greek Tragedy. . . . Indeed, the greater part of the play, from the moment when Neoptolemus has committed himself to Odysseus, may be reasonably described as a long and inexorable turning of the screw on him in his false position. If any Greek play can be said to show development of character, it is this one."[18]

But this Neoptolemus, who grows morally and whose character changes, exists only in Kitto's reading of the play. The heroes of Greek tragedy, and especially Sophoclean tragedy, do not change, nor do those in the subplot rise to tragic heights. From the beginning of the drama to the end, Sophocles' Neoptolemus is a young man who is devoured by ambition and whose one unchanging trait is instability. "Character is destiny," Heraclitus wrote. But one can rather say of Sophocles' heroes that destiny is their character. Destiny assigned to Neoptolemus the role of a war criminal in captured Troy. From *The Little Iliad* on, through all the versions of the myth, in epics and in tragedies, it is he who drags Priam by the hair from Zeus's altar and murders him at the entrance of his palace, or in another version, at the base of the altar. Neoptolemus murders Astyanax, the little son of Hector and Andromache; like Hitler's hangmen in the Warsaw Ghetto, he seizes the boy by the legs and throws him against a wall. In another version, he throws him from a tower.[19] In Euripides' *The Trojan Women*, produced in 415 B.C. and therefore six years earlier than *Philoctetes*, Neoptolemus does not even allow Andromache, as the herald Talthybius reports, to perform "the rites of burial to her little child."

Polyxena, the daughter of Hecuba and Priam, was given to the slain Achilles as an offering so that even after death he could partake in the distribution of the captives. "The whole army of the Greeks," the same herald Talthybius relates in Euripides' *Hecuba*, "drawn up in ranks, was present at the execution, waiting and watching while Polyxena was led by Achilles' son slowly through the center of the camp and up the tomb" (521 ff.). "Torn between pity and duty, Achilles' son stood hesitating," the herald continues, (Neoptolemus' hesitancy and indecision, which are permanent aspects of his "character" and which are so clearly outlined in *Philoctetes*, are worth noting here), "and then slashed her throat with the edge of his sword. The blood gushed out . . ." (566 ff.).[20] Neoptolemus' cruelty must have been particularly strongly fixed in tradition, since Priam in Virgil's *Aeneid* "could not refrain from uttering his indignation: 'You are poles apart from Achilles—your father, you lyingly claim.'" And Andromache, whom he has taken as a captive, bitterly "endure[s] the contemptuous treatment of Achilles' insolent son, and bore his children in slavery."[21]

Neoptolemus' end is also inglorious. After returning to Greece, he goes to Delphi to demand satisfaction for the death of his father from Apollo, whose bow he has lent to Paris—or perhaps he impersonated him at the moment of shooting: ". . . no man his conqueror but bested by a god, Phoebus the archer" (*Philoctetes*, 334 f.). Receiving no answer, he burns down the temple in a rage. For this he is severely punished; he dies in Delphi, slain by the priest with a sacred knife. In another version he is murdered by Orestes.[22]

In all great tragedies, but particularly in Sophocles' and Shakespeare's, the characters carry within them their future and their death ("death transforms life into destiny"). "Fate" is included in "character," or in other words, "character" is nothing but biography. Neoptolemus in *Philoctetes* is presented consciously, and with surprising art, in a threefold perspective: he is the son of a great father from a heroic epoch who is eager to remain faithful to his father; he is an immature youth yearning for fame in an epoch that has already become unheroic; and he is the relentless tormentor of Troy.

"I would prefer to fail with honor than win by cheating," Neoptolemus says to Odysseus in the prologue (95), when he hears his plans. But a few seconds later, when Odysseus, the great manipulator, seduces him with the chance to become the conqueror of Troy, the price does not appear too high: "Well, then I will do it, casting aside all shame" (120). To Philoctetes' plea for the return of his bow, which Neoptolemus refuses to give back, he answers: "Justice and interest make me obedient to those in authority" (925 f.). The great Sophoclean irony is to unite in one sentence "duties" and "profits." "I practiced craft and treachery with success," he says to Odysseus after his "change of heart" (1228).

"Bad son of a noble father," Philoctetes calls him (1284), ". . . inspiring confidence, but sly and treacherous" (1272). And near the end of the play, when Neoptolemus promises him a cure in return for a journey to Troy and reconciliation with Agamemnon and Menelaus, he characterizes him even more terribly: "Giver of dread advice" (1380).

The future is foretold three times. Philoctetes says to Neoptolemus, who has already broken his word once: "May you perish—no, not yet, before I learn if you will still change your mind. If not, may you die a miserable death" (961 f., Knox's translation).[23] But the key to Sophocles' theology is the first prophecy when Philoctetes, before he is seized by a new attack of pains, entrusts his bow to Neoptolemus: "Bow in prayer to the gods' envy that the bow may not be to you a sorrow nor as it was to me and its former master" (776 ff.). The bow, a sign of mediation, a gift of the gods, brings suffering and misfortune. It is a bow of destruction. Heracles, who first received it, speaks the third and last prophecy in the epilogue.

Philoctetes and Neoptolemus have already descended from the *skene* onto the flat arena. Philoctetes has laid aside the bow and arrows and kneels to kiss the ground before leaving the island. Suddenly a voice sounds.

> I am the voice of Heracles in your ears;
> I am the shape of Heracles before you.

It is to serve you I come and leave my home among
the dead.

(1410 ff.)

Heracles, who has slowly descended to the roof of the
cave, pronounces a judgment on his own life, which
sounds like an epitaph: "Let me reveal to you my own
story first, let me show the tasks and sufferings that were
mine, and, at the last, the winning of deathless merit"
(1418 ff.). The great labors of Heracles have meant constant suffering.[24] In this speech from the roof of the *skene*,
the word "suffering" is repeated three times. As in *The
Women of Trachis* and in Euripides' *Heracles*, this is the
tragic Heracles who has come from Homer's Hades
where he told Odysseus: "I had an endless spell of misery." In the theology and structure of *Philoctetes*, the
owner of the bow is Heracles' double. In *The Women of
Trachis*, Heracles screamed for death to come quickly
while he was burning alive from the Hydra's venom.
Philoctetes, in unbearable pain, begs Neoptolemus for a
mortal blow, to cut off his foot from his body.

Heracles descends *ex machina* to repeat the will of Zeus
to Philoctetes: "All this must be your suffering too, the
winning of a life to an end in glory, out of this suffering"
(1422 ff.). *Philoctetes* does not end in a joyful epiphany.
Immortal glory but not immortal life is the reward for
agony. "Shall I then yield?" Philoctetes has asked himself only a moment before. "Go with this man to Troy!"
is Heracles' command (1425). Philoctetes is the only one
of Sophocles' tragic heroes who is broken.

Troy has already been conquered, but it must be conquered for a second time. All Troys must be leveled one
by one until the end of the world. Just before Heracles
is carried back into the heavens, he speaks his last
warning:

> . . . But this remember,
> When you shall come to sack that town, keep holy in the sight
>   of god.
> All else our father Zeus thinks of less moment.
> Holiness does not die with the men that die.
> Whether they die or live, it cannot perish.

(1440 ff.)

Sophocles' *Philoctetes* was written in 409 B.C. Four years earlier, in the year 413 and in the nineteenth year of the Peloponnesian War, the expedition of the Athenian fleet against Sicily ended in terrible destruction. Thucidydes' is always factual, but in describing this, he does not try to hide his horror:

The prisoners in the quarries were at first hardly treated by the Syracusans. Crowded in a narrow hole, without any roof to cover them, the heat of the sun and the stifling closeness of the air tormented them during the day, and then the nights, which came on autumnal and chilly, made them ill by the violence of the change; besides, as they had to do everything in the same place for want of room, and the bodies of those who died of their wounds or from the variation in the temperature, or from similar causes, were left heaped together one upon another, intolerable stenches arose; while hunger and thirst never ceased to afflict them, each man during eight months having only half a pint of water and a pint of corn given him daily. In short, no single suffering so apprehended by men thrust into such a place was spared them. For some seventy days they thus lived all together, after which all, except the Athenians and any Siceliots or Italiots who had joined in the expedition, were sold. The total number of prisoners taken it would be difficult to state exactly, but it could not have been less than seven thousand.

This was the greatest Hellenic achievement of any in this war, or, in my opinion, in Hellenic history; at once most glorious to the victors, and most calamitous to the conquered. They were beaten at all points and altogether; all that they suffered was great; they were destroyed, as the saying is, with a total destruction, their fleet, their army—everything was destroyed, and few out of many returned home.

(VII, xxiii, 87)[25]

During World War II, the most popular book in occupied Central Europe was Tolstoy's *War and Peace*. This fatalistic picture of war, as cruel as the Russian winter, opposes the cruelty and stupidity of the commanders to the forces of nature, which are what in the end seem to triumph over the invaders. *War and Peace* teaches patience, but it does not deprive its readers of hope. It seems that in a similar way during the Peloponnesian War, especially in its second and third decades, the picture of the Trojan War in the *Iliad* and the post-Homeric cycles suddenly became close to the common experience. But in the new image that emerged, none of the heroism remained; conquerors and conquered alike destroy each other; victory is destruction; and the main agents of the new "historical necessity" are Odysseus and Neoptolemus.

You have told me the two deaths that most could hurt me.
Alas, what should I look for
when Ajax and Antilochus are dead,
and still Odysseus lives, that in their stead
ought to be counted among the dead?

(426 ff.)

Sophocles' tragedies are not historical parables, but their contemporaneity, although hidden, does not cease to be significant. Like Shakespeare's *Tempest*, *Philoctetes* seems to be a personal confession but the autobiographical touch, which one can hear at times in the bitter confessions and outbursts, is the whole of human experience. Sophocles was eighty-five when he wrote *Philoctetes*.

He outlived Pericles, Nichias and Demosthenes. Ironically, Odysseuses and Thersiteses are still alive.

In the year 420 B.C., when the cult of Asclepius was taken up in Athens, Sophocles kept the holy serpent, which was an image of god, in his own home and perhaps fed it fresh eggs and mice with his own hands every morning.[26] In the year 413, after the destruction of Sicily, he was chosen one of the ten commissioners of the Committee of Public Salvation, and bitterly regretted his participation in it. Apparently he had a perfect awareness of the coming defeat. He died in 406, two years before the fall of Athens.

> I take my last farewell of this island now.
> Farewell to the cave which shared my sleepless nights
> to the nymphs of the meadow's spring . . .
>
> (1452 ff., Knox's translation)[27]

The desert island, on which for nine years only the moans of the exile resounded and on which the stench of his wound was dispersed, is transformed now into an enchanted land inhabited by nymphs. On inhospitable Lemnos, where for nine years Philoctetes suffered from hunger and thirst, the stony brooks now babble with running water and the "homeless cave" is transformed into a shelter. The island was a refuge from cruel history, and Philoctetes kisses its earth twice before departing.

> Farewell, sea-circled island,
> do not begrudge my leaving
> send me a wind
> to where destiny transports me . . .
>
> (1464 ff., Knox's translation)[28]

Philoctetes' farewell to the island has the heartbreaking sadness of the epilogue to *The Tempest,* and the same awareness of the inevitability of human fate. One cannot run away from history; everything must be repeated once again. "And my ending is despair . . ." (*Tempest*, Epilogue, 15).

Of the hundreds of sculptures and images of Heracles on vases—slender youths and muscular athletes in the prime of life, bearded, smooth, bald,[29] almost girlish; drunk; pensive; struggling with monsters; naked; helmeted; covered with a lion skin; suffering and triumphant; with Athene; with Prometheus; with Hephaestus —which of these Heracleses arrived on Philoctetes' desert island? In my imagination it is the Heracles from the metope in the temple of Zeus on Olympus. He carries the heavens, has a naked skull, and one of his arms is crumpled. The pelvis is visible; from the crotch down only traces of his legs remain, but one can still see tension in them. His chest is ripped open, his stomach muscles are strained. He has empty, bloated eye sockets.

The Eating
of the Gods, or
The Bacchae

T

I.

he corpse of Pentheus, torn to pieces on Mount Cithaeron by his mother, Agave, her sisters and the women of Thebes, is gathered together and placed on the stage by his grandfather Cadmus, the former king of Thebes. Only the head is missing. A short while before, Agave had danced with it in her hands. At last the head is put against the body. The *disiecta membra* are joined together. Dionysus, wearing a mask with a fixed smile, is lifted by machine high above the stage roof: "Long ago my father Zeus ordained these things" (1349).[1] Cadmus and Agave go into exile. The bacchants recite the closing moral: "But god has found his way for what no man expected" (1391). They depart without dancing, their heads down. In the empty arena only the corpse remains.

The principal actors in Euripides' tragedy *The Bacchae* are Dionysus and Pentheus, the god and the man, the King and the Stranger.

> I am Dionysus, the son of Zeus,
> come back to Thebes, this land where I was born.
> . . . And here I stand, a god incognito,
> disguised as man . . .
>
> (1–2, 5–6)

In the shape of a youth, and looking like a girl with his long fair hair falling to his shoulders, Dionysus comes to Thebes from Asia with a train of women beating drums, dancing and singing. They wear loosely sewn fawn skins and brandish the sacred thyrsi, long sticks twined with ivy branches and tipped with pine cones. The tomb of Semele, Dionysus' mother, is represented on the stage: in the courtyard in front of the royal palace white smoke rises from it day and night. No one in the royal family believes that Semele was taken by god the father and bore him a child. They suspect her of having an earthly lover. For this, Dionysus has stricken the women of Thebes with madness. They have left the city and fled to the mountains to celebrate the Dionysian ritual—all of them, even Semele's sisters Ino, Autonoë and Agave, Pentheus' mother.

The middle part of the tragedy contains two symmetric agones; twice the King meets the Stranger. Pentheus tells the soldiers to find the disturber of the peace and bring him in chains before him.

PENTHEUS:
> First of all,
> I shall cut off your girlish curls.

DIONYSUS:
> My hair is holy.
> My curls belong to god.

(492)

Pentheus does not know of a god for whom long hair is holy and who orders women to dance in the mountains. There has been no such god in Thebes.

> . . . a foreigner has come to Thebes
> from Lydia, one of those charlatan magicians,
> with long yellow curls smelling of perfumes,
> with flushed cheeks and the spells of Aphrodite
> in his eyes. His days and nights he spends
> with women and girls, dangling before them the joys
> of initiation in his mysteries.

(233 ff.)

Pentheus looks at the Stranger the way a sheriff in Arizona would at a bearded guru who has invaded the town with a gang of tattered girls. He counters the arrogance of mysticism with the arrogance of pragmatic reason, cuts off the Stranger's tresses and orders him to be locked in a stable. The god has been offended. Sacrilege has been committed. The Chorus cries to the heavens for revenge.

No sooner have the Bacchants completed their threnody than the earth shakes, flames burst from Semele's tomb and a wing of the royal palace falls down. The god has emerged from darkness into light. He has returned to his women. They touch his hands from which the fetters have fallen. He is alive.

In the second agon Pentheus has lost all his self-confidence. The Stranger has trapped him even before he leads him to the place of execution. Pentheus wants to see the women on Mount Cithaeron. He, too, has been liberated by Dionysus. "Your mind was once unsound, but now you think as sane men do" (947). Pentheus is now ready for anything.

> DIONYSUS:
>   I shall go inside with you
> and help you dress.
>
> PENTHEUS:
>   Dress? In a *woman's* dress,
> you mean? I would die of shame.
>
>   (827 ff.)

But this shame gives him a strange delight. He puts on a gaudy dress made of fawn skin which comes down to his ankles. On his head he wears a wig of long fair tresses. He sings, dances convulsively and sways his head from side to side. When the Stranger adjusts his wig for him, he shivers with excitement: "Arrange it. I am in your hands completely" (932).

Dionysus leads Pentheus out of Thebes, just as he led out the women. Since Pentheus cannot see the women when they reach the slopes of Cithaeron, he suggests climbing a tree for a better view. Dionysus bends a tall fir tree until its top touches the ground and puts Pentheus on it, then lets it go with Pentheus huddling in the top. The sexual symbolism of this image is striking. But Pentheus will not enjoy the view for long. The frenzied women have already noticed him. He will not be a spectator but the victim of the sacrament. "And let the dance begin" (114). The dance of these women on the mountain clearing, to the ceaseless beat of the drums and the

shrill wailing of the Phrygian pipes, drives them to ecstasy.

> He delights in the raw flesh. . . .
> He is Bromius who leads us!
>
> (139, 141)

The climax of the Dionysian rite in Euripides' *Bacchae*
is the *sparagmos* and the *omophagia*, tearing wild animals
to pieces and consuming their raw flesh, still warm with
blood.[2]

> Unarmed, they swooped down upon the herds of cattle
> grazing there on the green of the meadow. And then
> you could have seen a single woman with bare hands
> tear a fat calf, still bellowing with fright,
> in two, while others clawed the heifers to pieces.
> There were ribs and cloven hooves scattered everywhere,
> and scraps smeared with blood hung from the fir trees.
>
> (735 ff.)

In the dramatic structure of *The Bacchae* this is a forecast, a preparation and a dress rehearsal for the tragic
sparagmos, in which Pentheus himself is the scapegoat.
The women, in their godsent frenzy, take him for an
animal hiding among the pines. They try to get him
down by throwing stones, then uproot the tree, tearing
at the branches. Even when Pentheus takes off his wig of
fair tresses, Agave does not recognize her son. "First his
mother started the slaughter as priestess and falls upon
him . . ." (1114).[3]

This account by the Messenger, who has rushed in
from the mountains, is made visual when Cadmus brings
the torn fragments of Pentheus' body onstage; what follows is the cruelest recognition scene in all Greek drama.
Agave enters the stage with a severed head impaled on

a thyrsus. All the characters are present. On the roof
stands Dionysus—a smiling bull. The Chorus of *The Bacchae,* which a little while before was leaping ecstatically
and wallowing in the *orchestra,* in praise of Dionysus'
victory, is now motionless. Only Agave continues to
dance. The holy trance has not yet left her. She is proud
of her prey. In her blindness she believes she has killed
a lion and brought back its severed head. She wants the
Chorus to fulfill the ritual of *omophagia* and consume the
fresh meat.

AGAVE:
> Then share my glory,
share the feast.

CHORUS:
> Share, unhappy woman?

> (1184 f.)[4]

The ritual has meant filicide. Agave recognizes that the
lion's head is the head of Pentheus. Why lion's? There
were no lions on Mount Cithaeron. To answer this question is to begin the interpretation of both the ritual and
the tragedy. Next to the bull and the snake, the lion was
one of the three emblems of Dionysus. But why, in the
hour of his agony, was Pentheus given an emblem of the
god?

The parallelism of the two agones in *The Bacchae* corresponds to the structural symmetry of the first and second
halves of the play, but it is a peculiar parallelism and a
peculiar symmetry, shaping a central symbolic reversal
of situation, role and sign between the protagonists,
Dionysus and Pentheus.[5]

They are both the same age. Their mothers are sisters.
They have a common grandfather, Cadmus.[6] Before the
youth in armor, proud of his newly acquired manhood,

stands the girl-like Stranger. Dionysus has always been a bisexual deity. In the fragment of a lost tragedy by Aeschylus he causes astonishment by his appearance: "Where do you come from, man-woman, and where is your home? What is the meaning of your dress?" In Ovid, and later in Seneca, he has the face of a virgin. Pentheus calls the visitor an "effeminate stranger," but in the second half he himself puts on the dress of a bacchant. He learns from the Stranger how a woman moves; he wiggles like a female impersonator. In this very moment the Stranger undergoes a change. He is no longer a gentle, defenseless boy-girl.

> PENTHEUS:
> . . . And you—you are a bull
> who walks before me there. Horns have sprouted
> from your head. Have you always been a beast?
> But now I see a bull.
>
> DIONYSUS:
> It is the god you see. . . .
>
> (920 ff.)

Pentheus sees in the Stranger the divine bull. The Chorus, too, observes the metamorphosis: "He dressed in woman's dress . . . led by a bull to Hades" (1156, 1159). The Bacchae now demand an apotheosis. The time of the visible god has come, visible in all his attributes. The epiphany is foretold: "Appear as a bull or a many-headed snake or a fire-blazing lion to behold!" (1016 f., Kirk's translation).

Dionysus comes to Thebes as a stranger; Pentheus leaves Thebes as a stranger. He wanted to be a spectator at a holy orgy, but it is Dionysus who turns out to be the great voyeur. The godlike King had thrown the Stranger into the palace stable; now the Stranger, transformed into a god, looks in his glory from the tall stage roof at the royal body. The persecutor becomes the persecuted, the hunted becomes the executioner, and these switches in roles are parallel. Pentheus sends his soldiers like a pack of hounds to track down the Stranger. "We captured the quarry you sent us out to catch. But our prey here was tame . . ." (435 f.). But it is Pentheus who is hunted down and torn like a beast by a pack of women —"Happy was the hunting" (1171). The hunter has become the beast.

Pentheus is made the scapegoat. The scapegoat is a surrogate who must be made to resemble the One whom he has replaced; in an ancient ritual a ram led to sacrifice had his horns gilded and a wreath hung around his neck. The scapegoat is the image of the One to whom he is sacrificed. The ritual is a repetition of divine sacrifice. Pentheus is torn to pieces because the Other had also been torn to pieces. Pentheus' body is put together from the torn fragments, because the dismembered fragments of the Other had also been joined together. "Long ago my father Zeus ordained these things."

II.

Accounts of Dionysian myths, no matter what their source, character and date of recording, show an amazing similarity. It is as if on every occasion the same event has been described. Only the names of antagonists and places vary.

Zeus, or Persephone at his command, sent the newly born Dionysus to be brought up by Athamas, king of Orchomenus, and his wife Ino, the sister of Semele, Autonoë and Agave. Hera punished the royal couple with madness: they killed their own son, mistaking him for a deer. When Dionysus came to Thrace after a long trip which took him from the mythical mountain Nysa ("tree") through Crete, Egypt and India, King Lycurgus resisted him. Dionysus made him lose his reason: in one version, Lycurgus mistook his own son for a vine bush and cut him down with an ax. For this Lycurgus was taken to the mountains and torn apart by wild horses. Also in Orchomenus, when Dionysus returned, the king's three daughters refused to take part in the mysteries. Dionysus, in the shape of a girl, had invited them himself. Angered, he turned in front of them into a lion, a bull and a panther. The sisters fell into madness: the oldest tore her son to pieces, then all three of them ate him. Toward the end of his trip, in Argos, when the king refused to believe in his divine origin, Dionysus drove all the women in the city to madness: they tore their children to pieces and ate them raw.[7]

If we put these accounts one on top of the other, like cutout drawings, certain common elements in them emerge. These are: madness, the divine frenzy, sent most commonly by Dionysus; the murder of a child, most commonly a son; murder effected by tearing to pieces *(sparagmos);* murder connected with eating of raw flesh ("the joy of eating raw flesh," praised by the Chorus in *The Bacchae* [138]); the son torn apart and eaten by the mother. This pattern in its bare structure is not a myth, nor is it—as has been frequently asserted—grouped legends from the period when the invasion of the Dionysian cult was being resisted. It is an image of the same ritual, a ritual which repeats and commemorates events that happened, in Mircea Eliade's words, "at the beginning of time, *in illo tempore.*" As Dodds has stated: "History no doubt repeats itself; but it is only ritual that repeats itself *exactly.*"[8] The sacral offering is the repetition of the first sacrifice. It is told in the ur-myth, the original Dionysian myth, with which two "indirect" myths are connected:

perhaps they are variations of the basic myth. They will take us a step further in the interpretation of *The Bacchae.*

The first is the story of Actaeon. He had watched Artemis bathing in a mountain brook. The offended goddess turned him into a stag and set his own dogs on him. Actaeon climbed a tree, but the dogs got at him and tore him to pieces. The fifty hounds who—baited by the goddess—failed to recognize their own master are like the mad women of Thebes who tore their king to pieces. Euripides recalls the history of Actaeon three times in *The Bacchae.* The wild dogs, writes G. S. Kirk in his commentary, "are described as 'carnivorous' or 'eaters of raw food,' reminding one of the 'joy of eating raw flesh.' "9 Actaeon was the son of Autonoë, the sister of Semele and Agave, so he was Dionysus' and Pentheus' first cousin. Everything is still happening in the same family; all three were grandsons of Cadmus, and, like Pentheus, Actaeon was a king. Actaeon's slaughter occurred on the same spot, on Mount Cithaeron. Like Pentheus, he was a scapegoat. And in that *sparagmos* too, the ritual victim was a youth and the body was torn by a woman.10

> AGAVE:
>   But where did [Pentheus] die?
> At home? Or whereabouts?
>
> CADMUS:
>   . . . where previously the hounds
> divided out Acteon.
>
> (1290 ff., Kirk's translation)

Orpheus too is recalled in *The Bacchae.* In all the accounts he is connected with Dionysus, as his prophet, originator of the cult, initiator of the mysteries. He is one of the figures of Dionysus and his alter ego, as John the

Baptist is of Christ. "Orpheus," Proclus wrote, "because he was the principal in the Dionysian rites, is said to have suffered the same fate as the god."[11] Orpheus, at Dionysus' instigation, was torn to pieces by the Maenads. The gods saved only his head and his lyre.[12] Thus Orpheus, too, was a scapegoat, the Surrogate made to resemble the One whom he stands for; his *sparagmos*, too, was only a repetition of the first sacrifice, *in illo tempore*. "Later Orphic priests, who wore Egyptian costume," observes Graves, "called the demi-god whose raw bull's flesh they ate 'Dionysus.' " In this cult as well, the ritual communion, the eating of the living god, is connected with *sparagmos*.

The basic Dionysian myth, present most strongly in the Orphic tradition, tells about the passion, death and resurrection of the divine child. The newly born son of Zeus, called Dionysus, or in other records Zagreus, was kidnapped by the Titans. He tried to escape or confuse his captors by taking in turn the shape of a goat, lion, snake, tiger and bull. While he was in this last disguise, the Titans tore him to pieces and consumed his raw flesh. Zeus killed the Titans with a flash of lightning, and of the soot that remained of the fire that had burned them, men were created. Dionysus' head was saved by Athene or Rhea; his dismembered fragments, the *disiecta membra*, were miraculously joined together; Dionysus was resurrected.[13] In a fragment of his lost tragedy, *Cretans*, Euripides writes: "We lead pure lives since we were initiated in the mysteries of Zeus and Ida; we pour libations in honour of Zagreus, who enjoys nocturnal rites, we take part in the feasts of *omophagia* lighting torches in the mountains in homage to the Great Mother" (Nauck, 475).

The Dionysus myth is genetic and cosmic at the same time. The first human beings grew out of the earth, like plants. Titans were the image of subterranean forces *(chthonic).* In the Platonic and Neo-Platonic interpretation, the myth spoke about the double nature of man. Men rose from the Titans' ashes. But Titans had eaten Dionysus before they turned to ashes. Hence the proverbial expressions: "Titans in us," "the Titanic nature of man." The soul imprisoned in the body, in the Orphic doctrine and for the mystically inclined Neo-Platonists, was a Dionysian substance, which survived in the ashes of the Titans.

The resurrected Dionysus descended into Hades in order to free his dead mother, Semele. Then he ascended to Olympus with her and was admitted to the company of the immortal ones. Semele became Persephone, who, at the advent of winter, descends to the underworld, leaving it toward the close of the season to rejoin the spring Dionysus. The dismembering and reunification of Dionysus is the cosmic myth of eternal renewal, death and rebirth, chaos and cosmos. Plutarch, in his famous treatise *De E Delphico,* considers the opposites contained in this myth and their significance, almost like a modern structural anthropologist:

We hear from the mythographers, both prose writers and poets, that the god is by nature indestructible and eternal, but yet, under the impulsion of some predestined plan and purpose, he undergoes transformation in his beings. At one time he sets fire to nature and reduces all things to one likeness; at another, entering upon a state of infinite diversity (such as prevails at present), with varied shapes, sufferings, and powers, he is called Cosmos (to use the name which is best known). The wiser folk, in their secret doctrines which they conceal from the world, call the transformation into fire by the name of Apollo because of the oneness of that state, or by the name of Phoebus because of its purity and lack of defilement. But when the god is changed and distributed into winds, water, earth, stars, plants, and animals, they describe this experience and transformation allegorically by the terms "rending" and "dismemberment." They apply to him the names Dionysus, Zagreus, Nyetelius, Isodaites, and they construct allegorical myths in which the transformations that have been described are represented as death and destruction followed by restoration to life and rebirth.[14]

To Plutarch's list of Dionysian gods we can add many new names today. The myth, in which the beginning of nature's fertility and its annual renewal are connected with the coming of god's son on earth, his murder and resurrection, is one of the most common and persistent; it is present in civilizations as remote from one another as the Mediterranean and the Polynesian, or those of the Mayas and the Uitoto cannibals. "Creation cannot take place except from a *living being who is immolated,*" writes Eliade in a way very similar to Plutarch's. "A single being transforms itself into a Cosmos, or takes multiple rebirth in a whole vegetable species or race of mankind. A living 'whole' bursts into fragments and disperses itself in myriads of animated forms. In other terms, here again we find the well-known cosmogonic pattern of the primordial 'wholeness' broken into fragments by the act of creation."

In the anthropological perspective, especially since the studies of Jensen and Eliade, the structure of this myth and its common elements are very clearly delineated. After the creation, fertility comes only from a new union of heaven and earth. Out of this is born a son or sons of god the father. Mother is either Earth or a mortal woman, who will later become the Great Mother. The son of god is killed, torn to pieces, and his body becomes food. His scattered fragments are reunited and he is resurrected; he visits the realm of the dead and with his mother enters the heavens. The repetition of the passion and sacrifice of the son of god and of the murder, dismembering and eating of the Deputy's body is the guarantee of abundance, fertility and renewal, and in more spiritual religions, a form of participation in the sacred history of the world and a guarantee of salvation.[15]

The edible plant is not given by Nature: it is the product of an assassination, because that is how it was created at the beginning of time . . . Cannibalism is not a "natural" depravity of primitive man . . . but a kind of cultural behaviour based upon a religious vision of life. So that the vegetable world may continue, man must kill and be killed; he must, moreover, assume sexuality, even to its extreme limits—the orgy. An Abyssinian song proclaims this: "She who has not yet given birth, let her give birth; he who has not yet killed, let him kill!" It is a way of saying that the two sexes are condemned each to accept its destiny.[16]

In such myths and *sparagmos* rites, women are the priestesses. They tear bodies to pieces and partake of the raw flesh. The sacrificial victim is always male: a child of the male sex, or a young man, or a ram, he-goat, or bull.

CHORUS:
Who struck the blow?

AGAVE:
Mine was the privilege first.

CHORUS:
Happy Agave . . .

AGAVE:
. . . is what I am called in the sacred bands!

(1179 ff., Kirk's translation)

Sacral cannibalism found in the Dionysian myths its most cruel and dramatic expression. In archaic Greek culture the finality of later tragedy is already present: mother kills, tears apart and consumes her own son; the son's body is the tormented body of a god, earthly nourishment and communion.

Anthropologists and psychoanalysts have not as yet devoted sufficient attention to this darkest of rituals. *Omophagia* of the son by the mother is similar to incest, and at the same time its structural reversal. In an incestuous relationship with the mother, the son is the father's surrogate, thus the sacral killing of king the father is linked with sacral incest. In the symbols of Dionysian rite, it is not god the father who is torn to shreds, but god the son; *genesis* annihilated, moved back to its origins. The eating of the son by the mother is the reversal of giving birth and feeding; the negation of succession, since it is king the son who has been eaten; and the negation of time, because it is a return to the point where it all began. This simultaneous fili- , regi- , and dei-cide is the ultimate completion of the cycle. Cosmos has become chaos again so that everything can begin anew. "The symbolic return to Chaos," writes Eliade, "is indispensable to any new creation."[17] Fertility is mortally wounded in order that it may be renewed.

—Blessèd, blessèd are those who know the mysteries of god.
—Blessèd is he who hallows his life in the worship of god,
   he whom the spirit of god possesseth, who is one
   with those who belong to the holy body of god.

(73 ff.)

III.

The sacral *sparagmos* and agony of Pentheus in *The Bacchae* takes place offstage, and the audience learns about it from messengers. But the Chorus of bacchants is present on the stage from the first to the last scene. The

Chorus, as in Aeschylus, not only witnesses events but participates in them. It is a Chorus of believers, not unlike a congregation assembled to take part in the sacrifice. It is touched by the hand of the living god who in the epiphany will appear in his animal shape. The Chorus calls for his coming, praises his glory, bewails his imprisonment and triumphs when his adversary has been beaten down. The name of the god is repeated until the voices grow hoarse and choke. The chants are religious songs, extraordinarily close in their fervent appeals for the coming of the savior to the prophecies of Isaiah and the medieval hymns sung in Christian churches during Holy Week.

The Chorus sings in the first *stasimon:*

> —O Thebes, nurse of Semele,
> crown your hair with ivy!
> Grow green with bryony!
> Redden with berries! O city,
> with boughs of oak and fir,
> come dance the dance of god!
>
> (105 ff.)

Compare Isaiah (lii.1):

> Awake, awake, put on your strength, O Zion;
> put on your beautiful garments,
>   O Jerusalem, the holy city;
> for there shall no more come into you
>   the uncircumcised and the unclean.

Bacchants:

> —Blessèd are the dancers and those who are purified,
>   who dance on the hill in the holy dance of god.
> —Blessèd are they who keep the rite of Cybele the Mother.

—Blessèd are the thyrsus-bearers, those who wield in
   their hands
the holy wand of god.
Blessèd are those who wear the crown of the ivy of god.
—Blessèd, blessèd are they: Dionysus is their god!

(76 ff.)

The song becomes a dance. "Why should I take part
in the sacred dance?" cries the leader of the Chorus in
Oedipus when it seems for a while that man can be
stronger than the curse of the gods. "My heart is a dance
of fear," sing the women in the *Libation-bearers,* when the
Stranger pours a libation on the tomb of Agamemnon.
"What dance shall I dance for death?" calls the Chorus
of Theban elders when Heracles murders his wife and
sons. Dionysus is a god who enters the body through
dance. "Be favourable, O Insewn, Inspirer of frenzied
woman!" are the words of the Homeric Hymn to
Dionysus. "We singers sing of you as we begin and as we
end a strain, and none forgetting you may call holy song
to mind."[18]

The Chorus of bacchants from Lydia dances the madness sent by Dionysus on the women of Thebes.
Dionysus is a deity to be drunk down.[19] To be possessed
means to be possessed by god. The sacral dance and the
sacred Eros are prayers of the body. "A bacchant,
through his orgiastic rites, imitates the drama of the
suffering Dionysus; an Orphic, through his initiation ceremonial, repeats the original gestures of Orpheus . . . A
dance always imitates an archetypal gesture or commemorates a mythical moment."[20]

In Negro spirituals, God is praised in rhythms that are
the sign and symbol of sex. Singers in colored surplices
praise the Lord with deep voices. They wave their arms,
jump, clap their hands, shout a hundred, a thousand
times, as if they still could not believe that God has been

born, that he will lead the chosen out of captivity, that he is a living God; that he can be touched, that he is food and drink. The joy at the good tidings shakes the body. Legs, hands, belly and breasts all begin to dance. The mysticism of Negro spirituals, like that of the bacchants, is physical. Lucian wrote in *Saltatio:* "whosoever beholds dancing must be able 'to understand the mute and hear the silent.' " Further on, in the same treatise, he tells how a certain barbaric prince, invited to the theatre by Nero, said to the first dancer after the performance: "I did not realise, my friend, that though you have this one body, you have many souls."[21]

The Dionysian rite in *The Bacchae* takes place offstage. The medium is the body of the Chorus. The sacred also has its technology. "Among primitives as well as among the civilized," writes Eliade, "religious life brings about, in one way or another, the religious use of sensibility. Broadly speaking, there can be no religious experience without the intervention of the senses . . ."[22] Artaud transformed Rimbaud's *"long, immense, et raisonné dérèglement de tous le sens"* into a method: "It is through the skin that metaphysics must be made to reenter our minds."

The dance to the beat of drums, punctuated by the wailing of flutes and high tones of pipes, leads into a holy trance. When, at the climax of the tragedy, the Messenger speaks about Pentheus' torn body, the dance becomes a spasm. The dances of the Uitoto tribe, described by Eliade, "consist of repetitions of all the mythical events, including therefore the first assassination, followed by anthropophagy." The Chorus in *The Bacchae,* as in an initiation rite, discovers the *tremendum*—the "almost simultaneous revelation of the sacred, of death and of sexuality."[23]

No other extant Greek tragedy is as permeated by religious imagery as *The Bacchae.* Just before the *sparagmos,* the slopes of Cithaeron flow with milk and wine, water runs from the rocks, streams of honey trickle from laurel-adorned wands. The cult of Dionysus blended with old agrarian rites of the nature deities' death and resurrection. The Roman Bacchus was almost exclusively the god of wine; the Greek Dionysus incarnated all vital fluids; water, milk, wine and sperm. "The wine miracle at Cana was the same as the miracle in the temple of Dionysus, and it is profoundly significant that, on the Damascus Chalice, Christ is enthroned among vine tendrils like Dionysus himself."[24] The Dionysian miracle of Cana on the slopes of Cithaeron occurs offstage, but *The Bacchae* is one of very few tragedies in which a miracle is part of the action onstage. The earth shakes, a wing of the royal palace collapses, shackles fall off Dionysus' hands. Verrall and the rationalists took the view that the miracle is an illusion of the Chorus. Later interpreters thought that the Greek stage had been equipped with theatre machinery which made spectacular effects possible; these "irrationalists," brought up on nineteenth-century naturalistic theatre, believed that a visible and "real" miracle could be made only by such means. It seems that Verrall with all his positivist narrow-mindedness was closer to the truth. On a bare stage, Greek as well as modern, the shaking of the earth is confirmed by the shaking of bodies. The miracles of the mysteries do not need pyrotechnics.[25]

It is not only the mythological apparatus that is put in motion in *The Bacchae*. In no other tragedy, perhaps excepting Aeschylus' *Prometheus,* are the images evoked so close to basic religious archetypes. When Semele was about to go into labor, Zeus visited her in a pillar of fire. Semele was consumed by flames, but Dionysus was saved by Zeus in his thigh. "My mother was Cadmus' daughter, Semele by name, midwived by fire, delivered by the lightning's blast" (3 ff.). In the anthropology of religious signs, to be struck by thunder means to be counted among the chosen ones by the god, through a mystic death and the promise of resurrection.[26] The last supernatural event evoked in *The Bacchae* is the bending of a tall pine tree by Dionysus:

> And now the stranger worked a miracle.
> Reaching for the highest branch of a great fir,
> he bent it down . . .
>   . . . No mortal could have done it.
> Then he seated Pentheus at the highest tip
> and with his hands let the trunk rise straightly up,
> slowly and gently, lest it throw its rider.
> And the tree rose, towering to heaven, with my master
> huddled at the top.
>
>   (1063–65, 1069–74)

Before the ultimate fulfillment of the sacrifice, the solemn liturgical *gestus* of elevation occurs. Pentheus' flight toward the heavens is ecstatic levitation, known from shamans' accounts as well as from the experience of Christian mystics. The imprisonment of Dionysus in the darkness, his symbolic death, is a forecast of Pentheus' real death. Pentheus' flight to heaven in turn prefigures Dionysus' final ascension.

Pentheus' fragmented body is put together, as the members of Dionysus' torn body were reassembled. Agave, the priestess, is still holding the head.

>   I am overjoyed,
>   great things have I achieved,
>   great and manifest for this land.
>
>   (1198 ff., Kirk's translation)

In the Greek theatre, the mask is the person; the ritual emblem denotes the god. Agave rushes onto the stage with a mask impaled on a thyrsus. Experience of Oriental

theatres—the Japanese Nō dramas, the Chinese opera
and the sacred Hindu theatre—may be just as important
for the understanding of Greek theatre as archaeological
records and vase drawings. They are all theatres of symbolic sign.

> bring from the mountains
> a freshly cut tendril to these halls.
>
> (1169 f., Kirk's translation)[27]

Agave has removed the mask from the thyrsus. Still
dazed, she continues to see in it the head of a slaughtered beast. She strokes the crest of the soft hair. What
sort of mask was it? The *tendril,* fastened to the thyrsus,
looking like a curling shot of ivy, is not a lion's head, but
a wig of long tresses.

In the first agon, Pentheus tore a wig from the Stranger's head. When Pentheus is dressed as a bacchant, he
wears the same wig of long fair hair. The Stranger himself adjusts a misplaced lock. When the frenzied Maenads drag him off the tree, he tries in vain to get his
mother to recognize him by taking off the wig. Agave
then enters with his wig attached to the thyrsus instead
of laurel leaves. When god-man is transformed in the
final epiphany into an animal god, his emblem, the "hair
of Dionysus," covers the body of his Surrogate in place
of the head. "My hair is holy. My curls belong to god."
The travels of the wig of long fair tresses must be the
most brilliant use of a stage prop in the entire history of
drama.

In *The Bacchae,* the signs of ritual not only appear in
metaphors and on the verbal level of the drama but are
visible theatrical signs. The myth and the rite in *The
Bacchae* not only are *topos* and plot but reach deep into
the structure of performance. Man and God, King and

Stranger, the Surrogate and the One exchange their parts in turn; as in a pattern of theory of combinations, all signs are reversed one after the other and all permutations are exhausted. The symbolic signs of *The Bacchae* can, however, be understood in two ways, as if they belonged to two different systems, two different languages, two separate codes, and meant something different in each. The ritual icons, the "significant," have two separate "significations," the sacred and the profane. Such signs, which operate on two different levels, are the "divine" wig of fair tresses and the tree with Pentheus on it, which have a double—mystical and sexual—symbolism. In *The Bacchae,* two separate and contradictory structures coexist. The eating of the god, the rite of death and renewal, becomes in the end a cruel killing of son by mother. The ritual turns into a ritual murder. Brecht wrote in his "Little Organon": "Theater may be said to be derived from ritual, but that is only to say that it becomes theater once the two have separated."[28]

IV.

Christian liturgy is a symbolic repetition of the birth, life, passion, death and resurrection of the Son of God. Three kinds of time coexist and intermingle in it; two of them are "earthly," the circular time of the yearly calendar and the linear time of historic events; the third time is cosmic or "divine." The liturgical year arranges events in the life of Christ into a cycle of the solar year. The psalms invoked in the Mass, the fragments of Scripture read in the Lesson, the color of the chasuble the celebrant wears, all change. The liturgy of Advent and Holy Week, particularly in the Catholic and Orthodox Churches, means bringing up to date in the most literal sense the chronology of events from sacred history. On Christmas Eve and on Good Friday, the earthly hours are the annual repetition of the hour of Nativity and the three hours of dying.

The canon of the Mass does not change. It is the repetition, or as theologians say, re-creation of events which occurred in time but are out of time. The Offertory, the Elevation and the Consecration are on every occasion the repetition of the sacrifice of the Son of God, and the transubstantiation of bread and wine into His true Flesh and Blood. "Christ is in agony until the end of the world," wrote Pascal.

In the Mass, Christ is present in time and out of time; He is at the same time the sacrificer and the sacrificed; He speaks the words of transubstantiation Himself, in the first person, through the lips of the priest: *"Hoc est enim corpus meum," "Hic est enim calix sanguinis mei."* This *mysterium fidei* was formulated by Tertullian in his pre-Augustinian *credo quia absurdum:* "And the Son of God is dead, which is to be believed because it is absurd. And buried He rose again, which is certain because it is impossible." Jung, who quotes Tertullian, shows also one of the most universal structures of ritual sacrifice:

The dual aspect of the Mass finds expression not only in the contrast between human and divine action, but also in the dual aspect of God and the God-man, who, although they are by nature a unity, nevertheless represent duality in the ritual drama. Without this "dichotomy of God," if I may use such a term, the whole act of sacrifice would be inconceivable and would lack actuality.[29]

In a ritual, which is a re-creation of the death and resurrection of a god, cosmic time and historic time are identified. The Surrogate and the One who has been substituted, the Sacrificed and the Sacrificer, God-man

and God the Creator, the Son of God and God the Father
are figures, opposites and situations of one Person.

> Believe me that I am in the Father and the Father in me; or else
> believe me for the sake of the works themselves. . . . Yet a little
> while, and the world will see me no more, but you will see me;
> because I live, you will live also.
>
> (John, xiv.11, 19–20)

O. B. Hardison, in his excellent and now classic study
Christian Rite and Christian Drama in the Middle Ages, demonstrates the abstract and rigorous symbolism of liturgy,
which is seen particularly clearly in the Roman Solemn
Mass of the ninth century. The left and right sides of the
altar, the higher and the lower levels, the enclosed and
the open spaces, are symbolic signs. As in paintings of
the Last Judgment (in which angels on God's right descend to meet those saved rising from their graves, and
on the left devils push those who are damned into the
abyss of hell), the right side of the altar is the side of
salvation—of Paradise, Heaven and Grace, the chosen
and the faithful; the left is the side of damnation—of the
temporal world, of God's wrath, of Jews and Hell. In this
"positional symbolism of liturgic space" (as Hardison
calls it), the two separate planes or "stages" are the
presbytery—"the plane of eternity, from which the ascended Christ looks down on suffering humanity"; and
the altar—"the plane or stage of history upon which,
amid the mobs of Jerusalem and the sorrowing disciples,
the incarnate Christ is crucified and dies."

Corresponding to this symbolism of space—structural
in its significant oppositions—is the commutative ("protean," as Hardison calls it) symbolism of persons and
objects, actors and requisites, in the rite of the Roman
Mass. "Christ emerges from the timeless, dies and as-
cends in the figure of the bishop. He reemerges in the

figure of the celebrant. At the end of the Mass, when the bishop rises to give his blessing, the celebrant is again enfolded in the world beyond time. In this interpretation we are close to the great abstractions of Byzantine art. . . ."[30] In addition to the Host, the cross and the altar are Christ's liturgical icons; the altar is both the tomb and the table of the Last Supper.

The passion, death and resurrection of the Son of God is the central event in the closed circle of cosmic time which begins with Genesis and ends with the Last Judgment. In the Mass, prefigurations of Christ's sacrifice are recalled—most clearly the sacrifices of Isaac, the only son of Abraham, and of the lamb in *Exodus*. "In the liturgy of Good Friday," Hardison says, "Christ emerges as the supreme instance of the Divine Victim, the 'lamb' led to the slaughter of the original Passover. The agon of the preceding weeks leads with ritual inevitability to abuse, defilement, torture, and destruction, the Christian embodiment of the *sparagmos* of pagan religion."[31]

In *Exsultet*, perhaps the most dramatic Latin church hymn of the seventh and eighth centuries, still sung during Matins, Christ the Lamb, *sparagmos* and *omophagia*, appear with striking clarity. "For this is the paschal feast, in which the true Lamb was slain, with whose blood the doors of the faithful are consecrated." Cabasilas, the archbishop of Thessalonica in the first half of the fourteenth century, describes the same symbolic rite in the Greek Orthodox Church:

The priest cuts a piece of bread from the loaf, reciting the text: "As a lamb he was led to the slaughter." Laying it on the table he says: "The lamb of God is slain." Then a sign of the cross is imprinted on the bread and a small lance is stabbed into its side, to the text: "and one of the soldiers with a spear pierced his side, and forthwith came there blood and water."

With these words water and wine are mixed in the chalice, which is placed beside the bread.[32]

Saint John Chrysostom, who died A.D. 407, wrote that in the Eucharist, Christ drinks his own blood. The Baroque sixteenth-century theory of mactation spoke of the "mystical slaughter" of Christ on the altar. The Mass is a repetition and renewal of the sacrifice of the Son of God, but the ritual "slaughter of the lamb" is symbolized in the liturgy only by the archetypal gestures of the Offertory. The symbolic sign of Christ's death on the cross is Elevation and Consecration, and according to another interpretation, Fractio, the breaking of the Host in two above the chalice.[33]

Bread and wine, the substances of transubstantiation, also have their archetypal symbolism: they embody the opposites of nature and culture, death and life—and their overcoming. Nature produces corn and vine, but they require cultivation. The kernel and the grape are pure, "natural" substances, but in order to become flour and grape juice they have first to be cut, crushed by human hands and dismembered. Then the flour and the grape juice are subject to fermentation. Fermentation is putrefaction and so—decay and natural death. But fermentation is also a cultivation process; flour and juice—dead matter—come to life, are transformed into food and drink.[34]

The passing from *sacrum* to *profanum* begins with a change of signs and times. The deep symbolism—archetypal and structural, protean and positional—changes to literal and representational signs. Sacral time actualizes into earthly time. In the ceremonies involved in the liturgy of the Holy Week in the eighth and ninth centuries, Hardison points out theatrical qualities in the ritual which preceded the emergence of the first Passion Dia-

logue. The congregation entered the church in procession early on Easter morning; the lights had been
extinguished and the church was in darkness. The dea-
con, out of sight behind the baptistry or altar, lit the first
candle: *Lumen Christi.*[35] As a visible sign of resurrection
he showed the congregation the pall covering the chalice, or the altar cloth, symbolizing the graveclothes that
remained in the empty tomb after Christ had risen. The
celebrants in this ceremony play their individual parts.
Time is earthly: the hour of awe and hope. All that is
needed for drama to be born is a question and a reply.

> *Quem queritis in sepulchro, o Christocolae?*
>
> *Ihesum Nazareneum crucifixum, o celicolae.*
>
> *Non est hic, surrexit sicut ipse dixit; ite nunciate
> quia surrexit.*[36]

From the union of ceremony and trope, the first resurrection play, *Visitatio Sepulchri,* was born; it set the general pattern and form of medieval religious theatre. The
celebrants not only have their given parts but, through
them, are dramatis personae. The clerics in white surplices who sing the first verse, *"Quem queritis . . . ,"* are
angels guarding the tomb; the three clerics who reply are
the three Marys. Of the rite of the Mass, which is a repetition of the sacrifice of the Son of God and the Communion, it is the resurrection that is dramatized. In *Quem
queritis* its earthly and spectacular symbol, the empty
tomb, was found.

The dramatic action of the dialogue is, as Hardison
put it, the visible test. In the earliest preserved record,
from the early ninth century, the three Marys visiting the
tomb are called *Christocolae*—followers of Christ. Two
centuries later, in the text attributed to Aquilea, they are
"tremule mulieres, in hoc tumolo plorantes"—fearful women

weeping at this tomb. In this eleventh-century *Visitatio,* there is psychological motivation; liturgy is brought down to earth, translated into a wholly human situation; the Marys are weeping mothers now.

The medieval resurrection play came into existence as new episodes were added to *Visitatio Sepulchri.* Two apostles, Peter and John, now rushed to the tomb. The three Marys told them the good tidings and produced the graveclothes left behind. The mystery ended with Christ appearing to pilgrims on the road to Emmaus and to Mary Magdalene in the garden. The empty tomb ceased to be a sufficient sign; for the first time the God-man who had risen from the tomb appeared on the stage, represented by an actor.

A new episode introduced in a tenth-century manuscript from Ripoli seems particularly important in the transformation of ritual into theatre. The play begins with the three Marys calling on a spice merchant:

> Let us go buy myrrh
> with perfumed ointment
> that we may anoint
> the body given to burial.

The trader replies:

> Women, listen to me.
> This ointment, if you wish to buy it,
> has a marvellous potency,
> whereby, if you anoint a body with it,
> the body will be unable to decay further,
> nor can worms eat it.
> If you truly want this ointment
> you will give one talent of gold;
> you will not have it otherwise.[37]

The Crucifixion, entombment and appearance of Christ to Mary Magdalene take place simultaneously a thousand years ago in Jerusalem, and *hic et nunc*, in front of the Romanesque basilica at the abbey of St. Gall, on the square in front of the cathedral in Prague, and in the cloisters of the Benedictine abbey at Winchester. The historic time to which the mystery of the death and resurrection of the Son of God has been transferred is also the modern time in which it is enacted. For this anachronistic time, there must be gestures, costumes, props and scenery.

Illuminated medieval manuscripts show the three Marys visiting the market stall where the trader, sitting behind the counter, weighs the spices. In a somewhat later resurrection play, the three Marys haggle with the trader about the price of myrrh, aloe and fragrant oils. The sacred is mixed with the profane. "From a rationalistic point of view," says Hardison, "medieval drama is a tissue of impossibilities strung together on an absurd parody of a plot and staged with a bizarre mixture of improvisation and crude realism."[38]

Visitatio Sepulchri and all passion plays, medieval Nativity cycles, Corpus Christi, mystery and miracle plays modeled on the same pattern, have preserved—as anthropologists would put it—a deep ritual structure. This was formulated from the perspective of Greek tragedy by Gilbert Murray in his famous "Excursus."[39]

The ritual meta-form of tragedy ends with a rebirth of the god-king, a joyous renewal of the alliance between heaven and earth.

Surrexit Dominus de sepulchro.

"The theme of fertility and rebirth," Hardison suggests, "can be treated as analogue, rather than disguised equivalent, of the Christian archetype."[40] In the rite of the Mass, the re-creation of death and resurrection ends with Communion—the eating of the living God, which is spiritual rebirth and promise of salvation.[41] In the three verses of the first text of *Quem queritis,* the same passing from *tristia* to *gaudium* occurs: from the pathos of suffering through the climax of reversal and recognition to the theophany and Good Tidings—"He is not here, he has arisen as he said, go announce that he has arisen." The passion drama ends with a joyous hallelujah.

The naïve, obtrusive and frequently vulgar updating of historic time in medieval religious theatre is strikingly close to the updating of cosmic time in the liturgy. On every Christmas night the Son of God is born. He dies on every Good Friday and rises from the dead every year on Easter. The Easter Matins begin with *Exsultet:*

> This is the night in which Christ snapped the chains
> of death, and rose conqueror from hell,
> a night in which things heavenly are wedded to those
> of earth and divine to human.[42]

The theophany of ritual and of religious drama is one and the same. It is the moment of mediation between heaven and earth in a cosmos torn apart. It is the moment when all figural correspondences become *the* correspondence. It is the reconciliation between god, man and nature.

V.

In his famous introduction, Dodds has called *The Bacchae* a Dionysian passion play. Dionysus' suffering begins with his apprehension by the soldiers of Pentheus, when the first miracle occurs: the chains fall off the prisoner's feet.

PENTHEUS:
>Who is this god whose worship
you have imported into Hellas?

DIONYSUS:
>Dionysus, the son of Zeus.
He initiated me.

>(464 ff.)

The law and order of the state is based on miracles which happened in the past; but miracles which occur in the present are the negation of all order. The coming of the living God is an offense to reason, an offense to the king and a blasphemy.

"If you are the Christ, tell us." But he said to them, "If I tell you, you will not believe; and if I ask you, you will not answer. But from now on the Son of man shall be seated at the right hand of the power of God." And they all said, "Are you the Son of God, then?" And he said to them, "You say that I am."

>(Luke, xxii.67–70)

Ritual dramas repeat themselves. In the first agon of *The Bacchae* the same questions were asked and almost the same answers given.

PENTHEUS:
You say you saw the god. What form did he assume?

DIONYSUS:
Whatever form he wished. The choice was his,
not mine.

. . .

PENTHEUS:
>Where is he?
I cannot see him.

DIONYSUS:
                With me. Your blasphemies
have made you blind.

                         (476 f., 500 f.)

For Pentheus, it is Dionysus who blasphemes. The living god is a public scandal and sacrilege. In order to believe in a god one must see him, but one can only believe in gods whom one cannot see. Dionysus is imprisoned as a blasphemer and depraver. The imprisonment in the dark is a symbolic death. The Chorus now begins its lament. The bacchants of Lydia are standing in front of the royal palace like the three Marys from *Visitatio Sepulchri,* the "fearful women, weeping at this tomb." They call on the god on high to liberate the god imprisoned on earth and punish his oppressor:

> O Dionysus, do you see
> how in shackles we are held
> unbreakably, in the bonds of oppressors?
> Descend from Olympus, lord!

                         (550 ff.)

The symbolic sign of god's resurrection is the same in *The Bacchae* as in all medieval passion plays: emerging from the darkness of the tomb. The ritual death and resurrection of the god is accompanied by the same archetypal signs: earthquake, eclipse and thunder.[43] According to Luke, when Christ was dying, "there was a darkness over the whole land until the ninth hour" (xxiii. 44). According to Matthew, when Christ rose from the dead, "there was a great earthquake; for an angel of the Lord descended from heaven and came and rolled back the stone" (xxviii. 2). In the antiphon of the Good Friday Mass, the Chorus sings: "The veil of the temple was sundered, the tombs were opened, and there was a great earthquake, for the world cried that it could not endure the death of the Son of God.[44]

The Chorus in *The Bacchae* has not yet completed its lament when the stage is shaken by the god's great voice: "Let the earthquake come! Shatter the floor of the world!" (585). And as in medieval resurrection drama when Christ reveals himself to Mary Magdalene and the apostles, so when Dionysus shows himself to the sorrowful women of Lydia, they touch him to convince themselves he is alive: "Were you so overcome with fright you fell to the ground? . . . come, rise. Do not be afraid" (604 ff.).

In the first part of *The Bacchae*, almost exactly halfway through the text,[45] those elements of deep "ritual form" occur which Murray mentions in his "Excursus": the clash between the god and his earthly antagonist, the suffering and symbolic death of the god, the lament, the climactic reversal of the situation, and the joyous theophany. The drama develops from *tristia* to *gaudium* and ends as in a medieval play: "The Lord has arisen from the sepulcher." The bacchants cry the same hallelujah: "The Lord will come upon, will overthrow these halls!" (602). Theophany, which closes the first part of *The Bacchae,* is the same sacred renewal of the alliance between heaven and earth.

CHORUS:
O supreme light of our ecstatic worship
How gladly I gaze on you, I who had desolate loneliness!

(608, Kirk's translation)

The tragedies of Euripides must have been interpreted in the Middle Ages as mystery and miracle plays, since a twelfth-century Latin poet used a fragment of *The Bacchae* to describe the entombment of Christ. The text of *The Bacchae* has reached us via a damaged manuscript, and only thanks to the anonymous poem *Christus Patiens* can we complete a gap in the epilogue of the tragedy:

> Come, old man, the head of the thrice-wretched one
> let us fit on correctly, and reconstruct the whole
> body as harmoniously as we may.
> O dearest face, O youthful cheeks,
> behold, with this covering I hide your head;
> and the bloodstained and furrowed
> limbs . . .[46]

The mangled body to which the medieval poet compared Christ's body was not Dionysus', but the dismembered fragments of Pentheus'. If the second part of the tragedy is a passion drama, it concerns Pentheus, not Dionysus. The death and resurrection of the god are in *The Bacchae* a symbolic sign, but the agony and death of the man are real. The *sparagmos* of animals on the slopes of Cithaeron is described as rite and as liturgy. Bulls humbly bow their heads when the Maenads approach to tear them apart. But Pentheus calls in despair: "Mother! I am Pentheus, your own son!" The passion and death of Pentheus are shown deliberately in all their cruel realism:

> One tore off an arm,
> another a foot still warm in its shoe. His ribs
> were clawed clean of flesh and every hand
> was smeared with blood as they played ball with scraps
> of Pentheus' body.
>
> (1133 ff.)

In a foot torn off with a shoe there is nothing left of sacral offering. Ritual has become slaughter. "Lamb led to slaughter" was a prefiguration of the sacrifice of Christ, but this symbolic lamb is now an agonized man. God himself led the victim to the slaughter place, and with a fixed smile, watched the execution. Euripides, with full artistic consciousness, made use of the "profound form" of ritual, with its protean structural symbolism, only in order to make one aware of it, to expose and destroy it.

In *Iphigenia in Aulis,* another of Euripides' later tragedies, sacral offering is presented as political murder. In *The Bacchae,* the ritual of death and resurrection of the year-god, *eniautos-daimon,* is transformed into a ritual murder. The Substitute—an image and likeness of the Substituted—must die in the same way as he for whom he substitutes. But Pentheus is not transformed symbolically into Dionysus; he has only been mockingly disguised as a bacchant, with Dionysus' wig on his head. Dionysus had been torn to pieces *in illo tempore,* in cosmic time; the dismemberment of Pentheus is carried into historic time, made visible in violent closeup. His fragmented members are put on the stage by Cadmus. The myth has been both tragically and ironically updated.

The signs and structure of ritual have been reversed. The second half of *The Bacchae* develops from *gaudium* to *tristia.* When the Messenger tells about Pentheus' agony, the Chorus is at the climax of joy: the adversary has finally been defeated.

> We dance to the glory of Bacchus!
> We dance to the death of Pentheus,
> the death of the spawn of the dragon!
>
> (1153 ff.)[47]

But this is the last *gaudium* in *The Bacchae.* When Agave enters the stage with the victim's head impaled on the thyrsus, the Chorus is speechless. Agave takes the head off the thyrsus and dances with it like Salome with the head of St. John the Baptist. Then she offers it to the Chorus: "Partake then of the feast!" But the Communion will not happen. The symbolic signs of Lamb and Host are a severed head and fragments of a human body. "What, partake, poor wretch?" (1184 f., Kirk's translation).

The Dionysian spell has been broken. They wake up, as if from a hypnotic dream. The recognition is tragic and double: Agave recognizes the head of Pentheus, and the Dionysian ritual is recognized as murder. The god on the roof is in a hurry to depart. "Why then delay over what is inevitable?" He has just time to condemn Agave and Cadmus to exile. The torn fragments of Pentheus' body are reunited, as Dionysus' *disiecta membra* once were. But there will be no resurrection and no one will sing as in the liturgy of Easter:

> Prepared for the supper of the Lamb,
> Radiant in our white robes,
> Having passed through the Red Sea,
> Let us sing to Christ the Lord.[48]

There is no theophany in the epilogue to *The Bacchae*. Heaven and earth have been decisively separated, and there will be no reconciliation of man, nature and god. Dionysus, smiling and awesome on the stage roof, "the god changing into a dreadful lion" of the Homeric hymns, is above and below the human lot. All signs of the ritual have been finally and ultimately reversed.[49] Dionysus, who came to Thebes as the Stranger, has only now become, in his simultaneous divine and animal epiphany, the estranged god. Cadmus and Agave the filicide are now strangers. The frenzied women of Thebes, who fled to the mountains and tore their own king apart, are also strangers to the city. The bacchants, who came to Thebes with Dionysus from Asiatic Lydia, have already gone away. They were strangers from the outset. But it is the massacred body of Pentheus, covered in mockery with the wig of long blond tresses in which the god entered Thebes—it is this body that is most strange to gods and men.

"Death shall be no more: death, thou shalt die," wrote Donne. Eating of the gods—the Dionysian ritual and the Easter rite—is the victory of life over death, a triumphant feast of rebirth, fertility and abundance. *The Bacchae* ends with the defeat of order and life by sterility, negation and decay. Theophany turns into antitheophany. God has departed. Thebes is empty. All that remains in it is the unburied body of the King.

VI.

Pentheus is the only great unburied corpse in all Greek tragedy. In *The Bacchae*, written toward the close of the greatest dramatic cycle of all time, the principal theme of Greek tragedy—the clash of the profane with the sacred —returns, ready, as it were, for the final solution. Prometheus had taken mankind out of the insect-animal stage by the gift of fire and blind hope. "Only the animal is truly innocent," wrote Hegel at the opening of his *Lectures on the Philosophy of History*. The profane—rebellion and emergence from the innocence of nature—meant a blind, persistent and heroic hope of finding theophany in history. In Aeschylus' dramatic cycles, human time is written into divine time. Walking over the red carpet changes executioner into victim. In this change, in every generation, the divine plan in history is always realized, on the same red carpet. At its end is Athens. "Time in its aging course teaches all things." The sacred has ceased to be blind cruelty; the profane, blind rebellion. *Sacrum* and *profanum* have been reconciled.

Antigone's, Electra's and Oedipus' tragic choices are

made in the confrontation of profane and sacred. The corpse is returned to the family to be buried, but the body still belongs to the state. The corpse was a son, husband and brother, but he was also a defender of or traitor to his native city. The state still wants to preserve its authority over corpses. Hero worship, throwing enemy bodies to the vultures, ceremonious exhumations of ex-traitors returned to grace—all these are among the oldest and most durable privileges of rulers. Power perpetuates itself through the extension of its dominion to the past. Judgment over the dead is the usurpation of the sacred by the profane.

In Hegel's philosophy of history and in his terminology, the Sophoclean *sacrum* and *profanum* are the particular reasons and will of a community torn by contradictions and equiponderant duties toward family and *polis*. The universality of moral duty has ceased to exist. When Antigone is led to the place where she is to die of starvation, the streets of Thebes are empty. Her loyalty to the dead has alienated her from the community of the living. In the epilogue of the tragedy, Creon comes onstage with his son's corpse in his arms. In a moment his wife will commit suicide. The arguments of practical reason have alienated him from all ties of blood. The Thebes of Oedipus' and Creon's offspring is now empty, like the Thebes of King Pentheus at the close of *The Bacchae*. But the sacred and the profane still preserve their validity and greatness.

In a tragedy which develops from dawn to dark, Sophocles' heroes always have an hour of warning, an hour of despair, an hour of self-revelation and an hour of choice. In this insoluble tangle of contradictions, the sacred appears as an inscrutable cosmic plan in which human life is anchored. The profane, however, still retains its power of refusal. Man can refuse to accept the world, which is not worth living in, or looking at. Antigone hangs herself with her girdle; Oedipus—the accused, accuser and judge in the trial brought against the human condition—goes away from Thebes, having gouged out his eyes.

Euripides' heroes, except for Heracles, are not given the four hours of Sophoclean tragedy. They have no choice. In *Hippolytus, Electra, Medea,* the sacred and the profane are equally lethal and mutually destructive. The setting of *Hippolytus* consists of two marble statues—of Artemis and Aphrodite—at both sides of the stage. In the prologue both are garlanded with flowers. But when the marble goddesses change into characters in the play it is clear, as Hegel wrote, "that gods are not to be trifled with; only at Olympus, in the heaven of fantasy and religious imagination do they remain in blissful peace and unity, but now they really enter life, as a definable pattern of human individuality, and through their very definite particularity and mutual antagonism lead to guilt and lawlessness."[50] Medea, sorceress and lover, personification of black Eros, a stranger in Corinth, as the bacchants of Lydia are in Thebes, is raised from the stage roof up into the air, just as Dionysus was. The sacred in *Medea* still has its dismal greatness; the profane is dismally flat.

After the arrival of Dionysus in *The Bacchae,* all women flee from Thebes. In Sophocles, the sacred—the *ethos* of duty and loyalty to the dead—is represented by women. In Euripides, the call of blood, *physis* rising against the bonds of *nomos,* the id revolting against *superego*—is personified by women. Of all Greek plays, *The Bacchae* seems to be most pervaded by eroticism. But men and women have been separated before the tragedy begins. Sex is sterile, just as it was in Oedipus' Thebes after the son's incestuous union with his mother. The arrival of Dionysus, god of fertility, is the destruction of procreation. Eros is perverted in the Thebes of law and order,

as on the green slopes of Mount Cithaeron where
Dionysus rules. Eros suppressed and Eros liberated are
equally barren. In a tyrannical system, Eros is always
suspect. The Puritan tyrant is a voyeur, his *"libidinosa
spectandorum secretorum cupido,"* as a Latin commentator
long ago observed.[51]

All the life forces in Thebes have dried up. Teiresias,
adept in scholastic sophistry[52] contrasts the dry food
Demeter offers with Dionysus' liquid foods. Cadmus and
Teiresias—the *pater familias* and the priest—represent
depraved old age, depraved philosophy and depraved
religion. Two old men, one of whom can hardly walk, the
other blind, clad in long robes of variegated skins, joy-
ously waving fir and laurel branches, swing in a Bacchic
dance. Cadmus, in his vulgar pragmatism, takes the view
that a sufficient proof of Dionysus' divinity is the splen-
dor which will envelop the entire family when his daughter turns out to be the mother of a god. Teiresias, in a
typically Euripidean updating of the action, is an
Athenian sophist, humbling himself before youth, eager
for novelties and metaphysical excitement, endeavoring
to persuade himself and all around him that frenzy is
useful and healthy. The limping old man leads the blind
man to a dance festival.

CADMUS:
. . . I could dance night and day, untiringly
beating the earth with my thyrsus! And how sweet it is
to forget my old age.
TEIRESIAS:
It is the same with me.
I too feel young, young enough to dance.

(187 ff.)

Dionysus promises spontaneity: the Chorus praises
the god, who lets people be themselves, and at the same

time, part of the changing cosmos. Dionysus promises an immediate paradise in which all times—past, present, future—intermingle and in which "I" and "not-I," man, nature and god are one. This apocalypse is one that William Blake knew well:

The apocalypse of the Bible is a world in which all human forces are identified, as Blake says at the end of his *Jerusalem.* That is, all forms are identified as human. Cities and gardens, sun, moon and stars, rivers and stones, trees and human bodies—all are equally alive, equally parts of the same infinite body which is at once the body of God and of risen man. In this world "Each Identity is Eternal," for "In Eternity one Thing never Changes into another Thing."[53]

Most astonishing in *The Bacchae* is the simultaneous presentation of *two* Dionysian apocalypses. The first is a return to the lost paradise, where milk and wine flow from the earth, honey drips from the trees,[54] and all will again be innocent and naked.

> Breasts swollen with milk,
> new mothers who had left their babies behind at home
> nestled gazelles and young wolves in their arms,
> suckling them. Then they crowned their hair with leaves,
> ivy and oak and flowering bryony.

(698 ff.)

The first Dionysian apocalypse is "the green joy of the wide fields" (867). For a little while, Prospero's island in *The Tempest* seemed to Gonzalo a return to the lost paradise: "How lush and lusty the grass looks! how green!" But on the same green grass, a moment later, murder was attempted. The second Dionysian apocalypse is always deadly. The thyrsus, with a pine cone on top, the symbol of fertility and sex, wielded in the ritual dance by the bacchants, "threw inflicted wounds" (762). The green slopes of Mount Cithaeron are stained with blood. Dionysus' second call is the throb of death. Pentheus is defenseless against the temptation of a return to the womb.

> DIONYSUS:
> You will be carried home—
>
> PENTHEUS:
> O luxury!
>
> DIONYSUS:
> cradled in your mother's arms.
>
> (968 ff.)

Nietzsche signed his last legible letters, before he succumbed to incurable madness, "Dionysus" and "The Crucified." In January 1889, when he saw a cabman beating a horse, he threw himself forward and embraced the horse. When later he was sane for a short time, he sent a friend a letter containing just one sentence: "Sing me a new song. The world is transfigured and all the heavens are full of joy."[55] In this desperate cry of Nietzsche's there is a vision of the same apocalypse, which Euripides' Maenads saw on Mount Cithaeron. But after it came the other Dionysian apocalypse—the *omophagia*, first of animals, then of a man.

To become entranced with the absolute is a dangerous experience. Drums keep changing so that the body does not cease its Bacchic dance even for an instant. But the technologies of all mysticisms are always alike; the price of the intensification of all the senses is the loss of control. Both Dionysian calls were well known to Joseph Conrad's heroes: "Follow a dream, and again follow a dream—and so—*ewig—usque ad finem* . . ."; and . . . in the destructive element immerse . . . " The first command, for which Conrad needed words in three languages, was Lord Jim's temptation; the second rings in Kurtz's ears to the very end of *The Heart of Darkness*. Dissolving in the cosmos is a mad affirmation of one's "I." Dionysus promises liberation from alienation and freedom from all ties, but he grants only one ultimate freedom: the freedom to kill. The girls decked with flowers turn into beautiful murderesses.[56]

The Bacchae was first produced in Athens in 406 or 405 B.C., after Euripides' death, at the Dionysian festival. In the center of the first row of seats stood the famous throne of Dionysus, the reserved seat of the god. In other Dionysian theatres, at the Anthesteria and Lenaea festivals, the mask of the god was hung on proscenium columns.[57] Dionysus was a spectator of *The Bacchae*.

Jean Genet requires that there be at least one white spectator, of either sex, at every performance of *The Blacks*. The spectator, dressed "in ceremonial costume," is elaborately greeted and seated "preferably in the front row of the orchestra. The actors will play for him." If there is no white spectator, white masks are to be given to black members of the audience, or a white dummy is seated in the auditorium. In *The Blacks*, as in *The Bacchae*, murder is committed offstage and then performed and danced onstage in masks, ecstatically, in all its cruelty and beauty. In *The Blacks* and in *The Bacchae*, it is a black ritual. "But what exactly is black? First of all, what's his color?"

For directors who, when staging *The Bacchae*, search for existing and nonexistent rituals on the five continents, an examination of Genet's *Blacks* could be beneficial. In the entire history of drama, it is the only other play that has a structure similar to that of *The Bacchae;* the ritual is laid bare and destroyed through its realization on the stage. Directors who think they can forget the discipline of tragedy when staging *The Bacchae* should consider carefully this quotation from *The Blacks:* "Greek tragedy, my dear, decorum. The ultimate gesture is performed offstage."[58]

The ancient cult of Dionysus had turned into popular feasts and state celebrations long before Euripides' time. On faraway islands, a boy was still sometimes flogged on Dionysian holidays to commemorate the old custom; at the Lenaea, amphoras of wine were carried around; in Attica, phallic carnival processions took place. But the cult of Dionysus in Greece had long ago ceased to be a holy orgy. Euripides did not reproach Dionysus—who had long been accepted among the Olympian deities—with his past.

The Bacchae was written in the third decade of the Peloponnesian War; less than two years after its first performance, Athens fell. History, as my old mentor, Jerzy Stempowski, used to say, had been unleashed. Greek civilization was undergoing the greatest of its upheavals, from which it never fully recovered. *The Bacchae* is the tragedy of the madness of Greece, the madness of rulers and of people.[59] "You are mad, grievously mad, beyond the power of any drugs to cure, for you are drugged with madness (326 ff.)." On this occasion, pitiful blind Teiresias has cried out the truth. In *Iphigenia in Aulis,* written in the same period, the same diagnosis is made more brutally:

> MENELAUS:
> Greece is in grief
> and in trouble.
>
> . . .
>
> AGAMEMNON:
> . . . Greece, like yourself,
> some god has driven mad.
>
> (410 f., 412 f.)[60]

In periods of madness, mad gods and their even madder prophets always appear. At the time of the Peloponnesian War, new dark gods came from east, south and north, demanding orgiastic cults and bloody sacrifices: Attis, Sabazius and Adonis, Bendis, Cybele and the Egyptian Isis with cow's horns. For centuries, the mask of Dionysus continued to be hung on the columns of the proscenium. But there came a time, according to Plutarch, when *The Bacchae* was performed before Hyrodes, king of the Parthians, and a real severed head, that of Crassus, was brought into the theatre.

The tables had been taken away and a tragic actor, called Jason of Tralles, was singing the scene . . . just before the entrance of Agave. While he was still being applauded, Sillaces, who stood at the door of the banqueting hall, bowed down low before the King and then threw the head of Crassus into the centre of the company. Clapping their hands and shouting with joy, the Parthians lifted the head up, and, at the King's command, Sillaces was given a seat at the banquet. Then Jason handed to one of the chorus the costume which he had been wearing for the part of Pentheus, seized hold of Crassus' head, and, assuming the part of a woman inspired by Bacchus, sang in a rapturous way the verses: "We bring from the mountain/fresh-cut a shoot to the palace/O happy our hunting!" Everyone was delighted with this. But when he got to the dialogue with the chorus: "Who killed him?" "The honour is mine," Pomaxathres, who happened to be present at the banquet, sprang up and seized hold of the head. "This is for me to say," he said, "and no one else." The King was overjoyed. He gave to Pomaxathres the customary gifts and to Jason he gave a talent. This, they say, was the farce played as an afterpiece to the tragedy of Crassus' expedition.[61]

On this occasion, too, it was history itself that wrote the final interpretation of *The Bacchae*.

APPENDICES

Medea at Pescara

The Greek theatre from the Piraeus had come with *Medea*. I went to see it in Pescara by a roundabout way, through Roccaraso and Palena, by-passing the Maiella ridge—the highest in the Abruzzi—from east and south.

Palena seemed to me the color of roasted coffee beans. The place was empty, as if burned out. Little towns in the Abruzzi look like swallows' nests, or rather wasps' nests. Each is like a honeycomb plastered to a rock. In Umbria and in Provence, too, little towns seem molded together, with their buttresses, steep walls, their churches and castle which give one the impression of being stuck on to one another at the top. But in Umbria, villages and small towns ascend the slopes of gentle hills, sink into the green; hills become vineyards and olive groves. Here little towns are washed by rains and swept by winds. They belong wholly to this desert landscape, and at the same time bring some order into it and provide food for the imagination. Their beauty is austere, they have the protective colors of soil and stone—yellow and gray. Often they melt almost imperceptibly into a large empty rocky wall, or into heaps of yellow sand. It is these stony walls, big heaps of stones and sand, misty mountain tops and vast flat plains, shaped like huge plates, that combine to give the intriguing effect of a waste, a desert landscape. Men and animals are hardly ever seen in it. The little towns seem deserted. Only occasionally will one see donkeys slowly mounting the steep tracks, with their heavy loads of brush. They are led by old women, dressed in black, with cloths arranged flatly on their heads.

The amphitheatre in Pescara is a new one, but it is situated outside the town, and there is nothing in its immediate vicinity. Only the sea is near. The night I was there, a cold wind was blowing from the sea, while hot air still came from the mountains. The stage area consisted of large stone steps. On top of them stood the Doric portico of Medea's house, with a huge closed door. Above the portico the moon was shining, quite low, cut in half. It was covered by clouds in the second half of the performance, almost immediately after Medea said she would murder her children and her rival.

Sometimes natural scenery gives unexpected effects, as when all of sudden the sky or birds start playing their part. Once I saw *Hamlet* performed in the courtyard of Elsinore Castle. During the first great soliloquy some gulls flew just above Hamlet's head, and a couple of them suddenly squatted at his feet.

In the enclosed theatre there is no room for the Chorus, even when the designer extends the forestage halfway through the front rows. The entry of the Chorus is artificial. One does not know whether to keep it there, or to let it come on and off the stage every time. In every performance of Greek tragedies that I had seen, the Chorus had always been a disguised ballet. But the Chorus in Sophocles and Euripides is not a ballet interlude, or an intellectual commentary. It is not external or added on to the tragedy; it does not need any justification. The Chorus is simply the people. Fourteen young women stopped on the stone steps. They had entered the way peasant women do, like the girls in Pescocostanzo when they assemble in the evening by the fountain in the town square. All day long they had pored over the *tombolo,* heavy bags stuffed with hay and sawdust, onto which a newly begun lace is pinned. Lace is made by the arduous and patient manipulation of small wooden bobbins with threads. These bobbins are called *fazzoletti* here. The same kind of lace is made in the same way in Poland, from Żywiec to Zawoja, in all the hungry mountain villages under Babia and Barania Góra.

I do not know what impression *Medea* makes in the marble amphitheatre of Greece. Perhaps it seems monumental and remote. Here in Pescara, from the very first scene, Medea and the Chorus of young women seemed to belong to the soil, the landscape. Medea was in buskins, I suppose because the part was played by a tiny actress. She was an ordinary Medea, humanly unhappy and humanly vindictive; she was like those peasant women, stiff and erect under the fifty-pound loads on their heads, tired but still full of dignity. There was something about her too, of that night, when the sea blew cold wind alternately with the stifling hot wind from the Maiella ridge.

The action of Euripides' *Medea* lasts from the early morning until late in the night. But here the real time and the time of performance were the same. A few hours of such a night were enough to accomplish mad deeds that would seem impossible in the daytime. Daylight would disperse madness like the mists that drowned Pescocostanzo in the mornings.

Not only time was condensed. The unity of place seemed just as natural, there was nothing of contrived poetics about it. I still remember my shock on my first visit to Rome that the Forum Romanum was so small. Just a few hundred steps from the Capitol and the Tarpeian Rock to the Arch to Titus. I went around that arch some distance away from it and spat, like an orthodox Jew. Kings, patricians and plebeians, republicans; all the tribunes and all the consuls, the Ides of March, Nero and Caligula—that square between two hills was enough to provide the setting for almost the entire history of Rome. Just one setting. The Acropolis is even smaller than the Roman Forum. Corinth was certainly no bigger than Pescocostanzo.

On the little square in front of Medea's house one could hear the groans of Glauca being burned alive. In the last scene Jason ran in out of breath; he had run up the hundred steps from the royal palace. Earlier still, Aegeus had appeared: he had come directly from a small harbor where he had left his boat. That fishing harbor could almost be seen from Medea's house. In nearly every tragedy, a ship is waiting in the harbor with sails set. The ship means an escape. But the true heroes are shut in the palace. The palace is both prison and asylum. They cannot go away. If they could go away, there would be no tragedy. Only their confidants are free to go. Of the true tragic heroines, Racine's Bérénice is the only one to depart. But her departure is equivalent to death. We may call it a white death, in a tragedy that is a white tragedy. Bérénice's departure means a delayed death, like a delayed-action mine.

To me, the unity of place in an indoor theatre always seemed artificial. Here, however, everything is close at hand. In the *Medea* at Pescara, night was really night, stone steps were stone steps, the nearby sea was a nearby sea. It was the same with *Hamlet* at Elsinore, which suddenly revealed itself through architecture. *Hamlet* proved itself in Elsinore, not only because Shakespeare placed the action there, but also perhaps because the performance began at dusk; in its second half, the beam from a lighthouse placed in a tower of Elsinore Castle swept the scaffolding erected in the courtyard with its light, yellow and red in turn. Hamlet's father's ghost appeared on real battlements and his voice reached the audience from there.

Medea does not address the gods. They do not exist for her, just as the world does not exist, as her children do not exist. For her, they are Jason's children. More than that, they are Jason himself. She kills them not only to revenge herself on him but because she cannot kill Jason; she kills Jason in them. But actually even Jason does not exist for Medea. Only she exists; she and her defeat. She cannot even for a moment talk or think about anything else. She is locked within herself with her misfortune, as if inside an egg. Medea's mad monomania is undoubtedly a Euripidean discovery. Monomania singles Medea out, separates and cuts her off from the real world. Through her monomania Medea is alone. Heroes of tragedy have to be alone.

But the Chorus of women is of this world. They have come from the village, from the small harbor which is also a village. They have come to commiserate with Medea. She has been deserted by her husband; now they want to take her sons away. In its first odes the Chorus complains of the injustice of the human lot and says that bitter is the life of a girl who remains unmarried, and bitter the life of a woman who marries. The women are on Medea's side and will remain so to the end. But gradually they become more and more terrified, not only by Medea's designs but by the ordeal sent her by the gods. The women's gestures become more and more liturgical. They fall on their knees, begin to beg for mercy and pity, but not for themselves. They beg the god for mercy who takes revenge on Medea, Jason, Creon; who takes vengeance on children for parents' misdeeds, and on grandchildren for those of their grandparents.

It suddenly seemed to me that the women, who went to the top of the stairs to the shut door of Medea's house, began to recite the litany to the Virgin, or to the Heart of Jesus. They were praying, and their prayer was one long moan.

A few days earlier, on the way back from my evening stroll, on the stone steps in front of the collegiate church of Santa Maria del Colle, I had noticed a group of women, dressed in black, reciting a litany. It had been the same kind of moaning that I heard then. The words "have mercy on us" had been shouted almost like a cry of despair. The door of Santa Maria del Colle remained closed. God had literally locked himself in.

The day after the performance of *Medea*, I went to the old fishing harbor in Pescara. In the square, by the entrance to a small house, stood a tall column with the statue of the Virgin. The column and the statue were ugly. They had been erected between the two world wars. On the column was the inscription: "Mary, Queen of Heaven, Mary who rules the thunder, do not kill the sons of Pescara." For the last two weeks it had been raining heavily in Pescocostanzo. The harvest had been soaked; hay could not be brought in. Yesterday, and the

day before, bells rang in all the churches of Pescocostanzo. They rang for two hours, from seven to eight in
the morning and from three to four in the afternoon:
seven bells of the splendidly gilded fourteenth-century
Santa Maria del Colle; two shrill little bells of the new
church on the rock—San Antonio Abate, and—loudest
of all—four bells of the dei Fratri convent, with their
monotonous and ominous sound. They had rung so that
God would take pity and avert the calamity of rain from
Pescocostanzo. Today they rang again; they will ring
tomorrow and the day after tomorrow.

The persistent, mournful, fierce ringing of bells might
end the Greek tragedy with which the Greek theatre from
Piraeus came to Pescara. The bells of Pescocostanzo
have been ringing to appease the same god who punished Medea and the family of Jason. For it is men who
are always guilty; never God. God has not changed here
for three thousand years.

(1962)

Orestes, Electra, Hamlet

O

I.

edipus is a man who was told he had killed his father and married his mother. He has to account for a past which is his own past, though it falls on him like somebody else's. Antigone, in order to throw a handful of earth on her brother's body, has to break the laws of the city-state. She chooses a gesture which by law is punished by death. Orestes, to avenge his father, has to kill his mother and her lover.

Almost all great tragedies can be told in two or three sentences. They are, first and foremost, situations; situations in the exact sense in which the word is used in the theatre. A situation means a relationship between the hero and the world, between the hero and other characters. It always exists in the present.

The tragedy of Oedipus begins at a point when everything has already happened. Oedipus is to learn of his past, then he will decide what he is going to do to himself. The beginning of Antigone's tragedy is her decision to bury her brother. She faces a choice. Orestes' tragedies begin with his arrival at Mycenae. He stands before his deed; before the crime of *others,* which will become his *own* crime. The situation in tragedy is in the present, but it has a past that defines it, and a future that has been forecast. The situation is independent of the hero's character; it is given to him, as it were, from outside. It is the situation that defines the tragedy, and not the character of Antigone, Oedipus or Orestes. The situation is also independent of the dialogue, which only informs us about it. The situation precedes the tragedy; every tragedy seems to be only one of its dramatic realizations.

Tragic situations are in a sense final and exemplary. They can be reduced to a limited and defined number of patterns which can be called basic structures or models. Written tragedies are different realizations of these models.

A myth cannot be comprehended through the linguistic analysis of the records of the story; it cannot be interpreted on the level of phonemes, morphemes or even higher semantic units. It exists outside of them, or rather above them, just as tragedy exists outside of, or above, the dialogue. ". . . a Greek Tragedy without words," Kitto rightly observed, "if the thing were possible, would still be tragic, the 'meaning' is woven into the structure itself."[1] Myths have their historic time and their metahistoric time; the time in which they came into being and their universal validity outside of time. They are intelligible in translation—from language to language, from one civilization to another, from one religious system to another. A tragic situation also has its double time: its historic time and its universal validity. Structural analysis has its discipline: it means economy of interpretation and the abandonment of preliminary metaphysical assumptions. It is an attempt to construct the model and define its variable realizations.

"All that should be, will be." Most writers on the theory of tragedy have used words like "fate," "destiny," "doom." They have spoken of "necessity," which is a constant factor in tragedy. Undoubtedly, in most Greek tragedies, in the tragedies of Shakespeare and Racine, the future, or simply the resolution of action, is always forecast in a certain way, either directly, through the songs of the chorus, auguries, oracles and prophetic dreams, or indirectly, through the very inception of the conflict in such a way as to enable us to foresee its resolution. The future looms over the heroes of tragedy, who are more aware of it than the heroes of other kinds of drama.

I propose to call this prediction of the future a forecast, which is a neutral concept. Meteorologists forecast sunshine or rain, west or north winds. A forecast is a conjecture; it can prove true or false. It foretells with a certain degree of probability, which may be calculated. It can have any value from "zero" to "one." A false forecast is still a forecast. Necessity is the forecast with a probability equal or close to "one." Improbability is a forecast with the value "zero" or close to "zero." Forecasts in tragedy come true or do not come true in a way that is different from what is expected.

Every tragedy can be considered in terms of sets: characters, actions, events. One can at any time select a definite element of such a set, and then all that remains in that set forms a "complementary set," to use mathematical terminology: "others" in relation to Orestes, Electra or Hamlet.

"Destiny," wrote Georg Lukács in his book on *The Sociology of Modern Drama*, "is what comes to man from outside." The complementary set is the destiny of a hero. His freedom is a freedom only in relation to the complementary set, in relation to "others." It is a decision, gesture or action, independent of the action of others, conducted on his own account. "Freedom" and "necessity" are the total relation between the hero and the complementary set. If there are gods in a tragedy, they are part of that complementary set. If there are no gods, if the tragedy takes place under empty skies, the complementary set means only people and their actions. A complementary set can be constructed for more than the protagonist of the tragedy. "Others" exist not only for Hamlet, Orestes or Oedipus; they also exist for Ophelia, Clytemnestra or Creon. "Others" are their dramatic destiny, too.

It follows that there can be at least two different forecasts: one for the set as a whole, the other for the hero, the protagonists or even the extras in a drama. The forecasts can be different or even contradictory to each other. In physics, there is a clear distinction between a prediction for the set and for one element only, for a series of events and for a single event. If a soldier throws a hand grenade, it is possible to calculate the diameter of the circle covered by its splinters, but it is not possible to predict the place where any one splinter will fall. We can predict the mortality rate for a region, but not the precise time of any individual's death. In a microcosm, the prediction for a series is determined, but the prediction for any particular electron—a prediction of its place and the time when it will find itself in a given place—has a probability of close to zero.

To give an even simpler example, in a game of roulette, the probability that the ball will stop on the red or the black equals one-half in every turn. In the history of roulette at Monte Carlo, however, the ball has never landed eighteen successive times in the red. Nevertheless, the probability of such a setup can be calculated, and it is precisely equal to the probability of every other alternating series of black and red being repeated.

Let us imagine a player who put his money on black seventeen times in succession, and every time the ball landed on the red. At the eighteenth turn, the player backed black again, and again the ball landed on the red. There is nothing unusual in this as far as probability is concerned; after a certain time, sooner or later, such a series has to come up. But what about the player? It happened to him, to him alone, to no one else but him, in a short series of eighteen games. He was the first to whom it happened at Monte Carlo. To all appearances, he is entirely justified in complaining of a peculiar malice of fate.

Unless he is a mathematician, it will be very difficult to convince him that three different predictions have been realized at the same time. The prediction that after seventeen reds, red will come up again; the prediction for the game that a calculable series of eighteen reds will come up; and the third and final prediction for himself, that while playing at Monte Carlo he will place his bet on the black eighteen times and lose eighteen times. The last prediction has, of course, a minimal probability. The "malice of fate" here is no more than a clash of two different series of probabilities—one for the mechanism and the player, the other for the world and the tragic hero.

Let us take another example. If there is a war and men die in it, someone has to be the last to die. The death of the last soldier is often felt by us as tragic. The prediction for war envisages the deaths of the first soldier and the last. But for an individual soldier the prediction that it is he who will die last has infinitesimal probability. Hence the feeling of tragedy in the case of the last victim, as if fate has been particularly malicious to him. Again, two different series of probabilities have clashed: that for the war and that for an individual who has a Christian name and a surname. It is both a tragic situation and a tragic opposition.

II.

The Greek tragedies about Orestes and the Elizabethan tragedies about Hamlet were preceded by earlier versions of the same basic plot.[2] The story of Agamemnon, Clytemnestra, Aegisthus and Orestes is mentioned by Homer in the *Odyssey;* the early-thirteenth-century Danish saga of Saxo Grammaticus is the first known version of the Hamlet story. The comparison of these two is significant; the names are different, but the development of action and the basic elements of drama are identical.

In the *Odyssey,* Agamemnon, setting out from Mycenae for the Trojan War, leaves behind him his wife, Clytemnestra. Aegisthus, his vassal and nephew, returns from exile, seizes the throne and the royal spouse. When at the end of the war Agamemnon returns, he is murdered by Aegisthus and his bodyguard. Seven years pass. When Agamemnon's son, Orestes, returns from exile, he kills Aegisthus. The fate of Clytemnestra is not clear, but the funeral feast is celebrated for both Aegisthus and Clytemnestra. "When Orestes had done the deed, he invited his friends to a funeral banquet for the mother he had loathed and the craven Aegisthus . . ." (*Odyssey,* III, 303 ff., Rieu's translation). When Menelaus returns with the fleet, bringing loot from Troy, wealth and order are restored to Mycenae. Orestes' deed is not questioned by anybody. Homer calls it "godlike," and Nestor in the *Odyssey* holds him up as an example for Telemachus. "You, my friend . . . must be as brave as Orestes. Then future generations will sing your praises" (*ibid.*, III, 193 ff.). Orestes inherits the throne.

In the Danish saga, the brave Viking Horwendil kills the king of Norway and later marries the daughter of the king of Denmark and with her begets a son, Amleth. Horwendil is then treacherously murdered by his brother, Fengo, who seizes the throne and marries the widow. The young Prince Amleth is exiled. Later Fengo issues orders to have him killed. Amleth escapes death, returns and kills Fengo. He becomes king, and order and wealth are restored, for a short time, to Denmark. The fate of Amleth's mother, Geruth, is not mentioned by the Danish chronicler. He ignores it, just as Homer ignores the fate of Clytemnestra.

Clytemnestra became a dramatic personage for the first time at the turn of the seventh and sixth centuries B.C. in the lyric poems connected with the Delphic oracle. In them, she takes part in the murder of Agamemnon, or murders him herself, and is in turn murdered by Orestes. Orestes is no longer alone; his sister Electra appears beside him. Orestes is now a matricide. He has to be punished. There are different versions of these *Oresteias*, but in every one of them the Erinyes appear. Orestes is defended by Apollo and persecuted by the Furies. He will be tormented to the end of his days, or ultimately purified. But he will never again be ruler of Mycenae.

In the Delphic versions of the *Oresteia*, the tragic opposition is sketched in for the first time. Before then there was an unbroken and unquestioned sequence of family vengeance. Orestes inherited the throne, and the story ends with that. From now on there are two stories: one of vengeance for a father's death, the other of responsibility. Orestes' situation becomes central and assumes key importance.

The epic and lyric records have only one tense: the past. They are a story told, a story that was. The beginning of tragedy is the division of the *Oresteia* into two tenses: what was and what is. Orestes arrives at Mycenae at daybreak and kills Clytemnestra and Aegisthus at dusk on the same day. The roulette wheel turns constantly; it has a past, a future and a present. Tragedy is in the present tense.

Every dramatic work exists in the present, but tragedy recalls the past and foretells the future. Tragedy is in a present suspended between a definite past and a definite future.

The *Oresteia* of Aeschylus is a trilogy *(Agamemnon, The Libation-bearers* and *Eumenides)* and thus has three present tenses: the situation of Clytemnestra before the murder of Agamemnon; the situation of Orestes before he has accomplished his revenge; and the situation of Orestes after the deed. Each part of the trilogy predicts the next. The Erinyes haunt Orestes for his mother's murder. In *The Libation-bearers* it is only Orestes who sees them. But they are not figments of the imagination. "Imaginings? They are real enough to me. Can you not see them? Hounds of a mother's curse!" (1053 f.).[3] In the *Eumenides* they are present onstage bodily and reeking of blood. In Sophocles there is only one present tense, the lifetime of Orestes and Electra, and they will remain forever in this present tense as two corpses. The Furies are not needed. There is no continuation. At the end of Euripides' *Electra*, the Erinyes are replaced by the divine twins, Castor and Pollux, who appear in a basket. They tell the terrified matricides that they have been victims of an error; Zeus did not want the crime to happen. From the outset it was all a mistake and misunderstanding. Gods make fools of men. The Trojan War was unnecessary, for Helen never set foot in Troy; the gods had carried her to Egypt, where she awaited the return of Menelaus. Iphigenia, Agamemnon's eldest daughter, was not sacrificed to Artemis; the gods saved her at the last moment and carried her away. The *Oresteia* is thus invested with irony and deprived of mystery.

The prediction, however, is fulfilled: Orestes has killed, and according to the forecast made by Castor and Pollux, he will be tormented by the Furies until he is cleared of guilt by the Council of the Areopagus, as in Aeschylus. Prediction means information. Thus we have, as always, the sender, the recipient, and the message communicated. Only in this tragedy the situation is exceptional: the recipient acts in good faith, the message communicated is true, but the sender turns out to be false. "A polluted demon spoke it in the shape of god," says Orestes in a sudden outburst of doubt (979).[4] In any case, Apollo had no right to push the children of Agamemnon to a new crime. In the epilogue, Castor in the basket authoritatively declares, on behalf of both twins: "On Phoebus I place all guilt for this death" (1296). This is divine irony translated into the language of communications theory.

In Shakespeare's treatment, all the predictions are also fulfilled, but for the first time Orestes-Hamlet dies. The cycle of vengeance has come to an end. Like Menelaus in the *Odyssey*, Fortinbras arrives at Elsinore and surveys the dead bodies. But will order and justice be restored to Danish Mycenae with his arrival? This we do not know.

Let us, however, refrain from any interpretations for the moment. First we have to extract the elements that do not change in various versions of the *Oresteia*, that is, its basic structure. There is the chain of three deaths: Agamemnon, Clytemnestra and Aegisthus, corresponding to the elder Hamlet, Gertrude and Claudius. In

Shakespeare, Gertrude's death is a chance one, perhaps a suicide, but the nature of her death does not change its structural character. Man's basic situation is the fact that he has to die. The kind of death does not alter the essential nature of human existence; in the final instance, it is of no importance. What matters is that we have to die, not how we are going to die.

The order in which the deaths occur, however, is important. In Aeschylus, Aegisthus is murdered first, then Clytemnestra; in Sophocles, first Clytemnestra, then Aegisthus; in Euripides, first Aegisthus, then Clytemnestra; in Shakespeare, Gertrude dies first, then Claudius. The assassination of a usurper ends the cycle of family vengeance; the murder of the mother, as the second victim, at the close of a tragedy, is particularly cruel. The killing of Aegisthus is the end of the tragedies dominated by the motive of revenge for the father; the murder of Clytemnestra brands Orestes additionally as a matricide. In this model of tragedy there are two conflicts and two themes.

Another element of the structure is the division into what *was* and what *is*. The dramatic action of the middle play of Aeschylus' Oresteian trilogy, of both *Electra*s, and of Shakespeare's *Hamlet* begins with the return of Orestes-Hamlet. What *was* is the history of the family and the chain of crimes passing from generation to generation, the story of kings who murder and are murdered. In Aeschylus the story begins with the gods and their human descendants. It is a theodicy which becomes history, beginning with the crime of Tantalus and ending with the calling of the Areopagus. The past is a prediction of the entire set and the dramatic destiny of Orestes. But Orestes' situation contains in it another prediction, that of responsibility and punishment. It is in the present, and so it is a situation of choice: to kill or not to kill. To kill is the prediction of the set. All the rest, all relationships between Orestes-Hamlet and the world, between Orestes-Hamlet and *others*, is changeable.

Unlike the Parthenon, Mycenae was not built of white marble. The royal palace of the accursed house of Atreus was built of huge blocks of gray and red stone and stood on top of a mountain which is bare today; there are no trees or bushes on it, only tufts of yellow grass burned by the sun. Even in the early hours of the morning the stones steam like hot ovens. The air is sultry. Agamemnon's tomb lies below, several hundred steps down the mountain. It is a chamber topped by a huge conelike cupola. A person's voice reverberates from its walls and comes back with a multiple echo. One enters it as one enters night.

In all these tragedies the father is present. Orestes sacrifices a lock of hair on the tomb of Agamemnon; Clytemnestra is afraid of the tomb. In Euripides, Aegisthus hates it and hurls stones at it. In Aeschylus, the tomb, in the shape of a mound, is present on the stage. If fate is "what comes from outside," the first place in the complementary set, in both Aeschylus and Shakespeare, is occupied by the father. In *Hamlet* he is even a dramatis persona who twice intervenes in the action. "Earth, send my father to look down on the battle!" (*The Libation-bearers,* 489). The oldest of the Hamlets, too, wants to transfer the burden of responsibility to his father.

Destiny in dramatic terms is a pressure exerted on the hero. In *The Libation-bearers,* the Chorus incites Orestes and Electra from the very first scene:

CHORUS:
Remember too those guilty of his murder.

ELECTRA:
What should I say of them? What do you mean?

CHORUS:
Ask them to grant that God or man may come.

ELECTRA:
May come to judge them, or to execute?

CHORUS:
Yes, say quite plainly, to take life for life.

(117 ff.)

The heroes always exist in the present, but the Chorus in Aeschylus incorporates all three tenses: past, present and future. The Chorus is the memory of the past present on the stage; a memory that constantly invokes all the links of the chain of crime and foretells the repetition of the cycle of vengeance. In Sophocles and Euripides, the Chorus is composed of Electra's friends and the women of Mycenae; in Aeschylus, the Chorus is composed of captive Trojan women. The hate of the Chorus for Clytemnestra and Aegisthus is dramatically motivated; these women remember the destruction of Troy, for that is their own past. The destruction of the house of Atreus will be their victory.

In Aeschylus, the Chorus is an actor in the tragedy; in both *Electras* the Chorus is only a witness and commentator. In Sophocles, the Chorus still fears the tyrant; they are almost real frightened village women. In Euripides, the Chorus is more lyrical. Its songs, like Brecht's, are on another level, outside the action.

The past has to be present in tragedy. The *praesens* of Orestes lasts from daybreak to dusk; he has only one meeting with Clytemnestra, in the scene in which he kills. The function of the Chorus is now taken up by a new character. Electra is not the one who will be its living presence on the stage. Orestes is the one who kills. Sophocles' Electra is the one who remembers and cannot kill.

ELECTRA:

Women, I am ashamed if I appear
to you too much the mourner with constant dirges.
What I do, I must do. Pardon me. I ask you
how else would any well-bred girl behave
that saw her father's wrongs, as I have seen these,
by day and night, always, on the increase
and never a check?
First there's my mother, yes, my mother, now become
all hatred. Then in the house I live with those
who murdered my father. I am their subject, and
whether I eat or go without depends
on them.
      What sort of days do you imagine
I spend, watching Aegisthus sitting
on my father's throne, watching him wear my father's self-
same robes, watching him
at the hearth where he killed him, pouring libations?
Watching the ultimate act of insult,
my father's murderer in my father's bed
with my wretched mother—if mother I should call her,
this woman that sleeps with him.

(254 ff.)[5]

Electra is a king's daughter, deprived of all the privileges of her birth and station. In Sophocles, she has been
made to remain a spinster. In Euripides, she has been
deprived of her rightful social position, forced to marry
a man beneath her, alienated in the literal, physical
sense. Electra has been placed in an enforced situation,
having to make the fundamental choice between total
acceptance and total refusal; acceptance of her fate, or
refusal to accept it; acceptance of a world in which her
mother has murdered her father, or rejection of that
world with all the consequences of such a decision. In
Electra's argument with her sister Chrysothemis, just as
in Antigone's argument with her sister Ismene, all the

great oppositions are presented: loyalty to the dead and loyalty to the living; revolt against authority and obedience to those in power; renunciation and compromise. Electra is asked to forget, but she is the one who remembers. Electra's memory is the presence of the past and the foretelling of vengeance.

Electra not only incites Orestes to vengeance, it is her situation that provides the psychological motivation for his deed. Orestes is to kill. The dramatic action of all tragedies requires a postponement of the moment of killing; the introduction of the character of Electra creates the necessary suspense. One can exactly define the point at which the real action of Orestes begins in Shakespeare's *Hamlet*. It is at the end of the first scene of Act V, when Hamlet jumps into Ophelia's grave. Electra is "seemingly alive," Orestes is "seemingly dead."[6] Hamlet, too, is seemingly dead; his leap into Ophelia's grave, as well as Laertes' descent into the same grave, are not merely a theatrical situation; they are a theatrical sign of an apparent death and the forecast of a real death. From that scene onward, Shakespeare maintains the unity of time and place. The forecast will come true. It will happen in the presence of the entire court, which, like a Greek chorus, performs the function of a witness. The forecast will come true in a solemn manner, accompanied by court ceremonial, with the ritual of a duel and the liturgy of a royal funeral, with trumpets sounding and drums beating. The body of Hamlet will be carried away, the bodies of Claudius and Gertrude will remain on the stage, as in Greek tragedy.

The dramatic construction of *Hamlet* is based, in a Greek manner, on the principle of retardation. According to the classic interpretations, dramatic suspense is created by Hamlet's hesitations; Hamlet is too weak to carry the burden of action. But this traditional interpretation seems to be insufficient. Hamlet's "hesitations" are the result not of his character but of his *situation*. From the end of the first scene of Act V, Hamlet is in the situation of Orestes, while through the first four acts he was in the situation of Electra—deprived of his rights, dependent on his father's murderer, threatened, like Electra, with exile or death. In Sophocles: ". . . if you don't give over your present mourning—they will send you where never a gleam of sun shall visit you" (379 ff.).

The similarities are not only on the external level of action. The psychological matter of both *Electras*— Sophocles' and Euripides'—is the conflict between daughter and mother, refusal to accept a mother who has been an accomplice in crime and betrayed her father. Hamlet's drama is developed on the same level of relationship with his mother. From Hamlet, as from Electra, forgetfulness is demanded by the mother, while Hamlet, like Electra, is all stubborn memory. Sophocles' Electra complains to the Chorus about her mother: "For this woman, all nobility in words, abuses me: 'You hateful thing, God-hated, are you the only one whose father is dead? Is there no one else of human kind in mourning? . . .'" (287 ff.). Similarly in Shakespeare:

QUEEN:
Good Hamlet, cast thy nighted colour off,
And let thine eye look like a friend on Denmark.
Do not for ever with thy vailed lids
Seek for thy noble father in the dust.
Thou know'st 'tis common—all that lives must die,
Passing through nature to eternity.

HAMLET:
Ay, madam, it is common.
. . .

KING:
. . .'tis a fault to heaven,

A fault against the dead, a fault to nature,
To reason most absurd; whose common theme
Is death of fathers . . .

(I, ii, 68–74, 101–4)

Hamlet, like Electra, refuses to accept the world in which a usurper and murderer is occupying the throne and bed of his father. "A bloody deed!—almost as bad, good mother, as kill a king, and marry with his brother" (III, iv, 28 f.). Both Electras, the tragic Electra of Sophocles, hermetically imprisoned in her hate, and the petty criminal of Euripides, neurotic, sexually frustrated, consider themselves daughters only of their father. Both Clytemnestras see this clearly. In Sophocles: "Your father, yes, always your father" (526). In Euripides: "My child, from birth you always have adored your father. This is part of life. Some children always love the male . . ." (1102).

Both Electras, like Hamlet, are continually tormented and humiliated, less by the murder of a father than by the image of a mother who shares her bed with another man. Sophocles' Electra shouts in Clytemnestra's face: ". . . tell me for what cause you now commit the ugliest of acts —in sleeping with him . . ." (585). Euripides' Electra shouts her complaint to the village women: "I in a peasant's hut waste my life wax in the sun . . . while my mother rolls in her bloody bed and plays at love with a stranger" (207 f., 211 f.). Hamlet in the closet scene finally asks only one thing of her: "Good night—but go not to my uncle's bed . . . Refrain to-night . . ." (III, iv, 159, 165). Sophocles' Electra identifies herself with Father so completely that mother is not Mother for her any more: "Mother! I do not count you mother of mine, but rather a mistress" (597). Hamlet repeats Electra's words almost literally: "You are the Queen, your husband's brother's wife; and—would it were not so!—you are my mother" (III, iv, 15 f.)[7]

From the situation of refusal, common to Electra and Hamlet, there follows the next choice, between suicide and revenge. That choice, too, is an enforced one, imposed, as it were, from outside. The moral order has been violated; one has to restore it or leave this world. It is a choice to which Electra and Hamlet in the first four acts are unequal. The choice looms over them, but both shrink from it. They feel too weak to carry it. "Evil is all around me, evil is what I am compelled to practice" (Sophocles' *Electra*, 308) recalls Hamlet's famous coda of the first act: "O cursed spite, that ever I was born to set it right!"

In no other of the great Shakespearean tragedies is the soliloquy so essential as it is in *Hamlet.* For the choice is in awareness, not in action. Hamlet can discuss it only with himself; Sophocles' Electra talks to the Chorus, but in fact she talks to herself. Her lament on receiving the news of Orestes' supposed death reminds one of Hamlet's greatest soliloquies in its tone, theme and even style.

> . . . I am alone,
> having lost both you and my father. Back again
> to be a slave among those I hate most
> of all the world, my father's murderers!
> Is this what is right for me?
>   No, this I will not—
> live with them any more. . . .
> Death is a favor to me, life an agony.
> I have no wish for life.
>
> (813 ff., 821 f.)

In the first four acts, Hamlet is in the situation of Electra, facing Electra's unmade choices. What happens in this model of tragedy to the empty space where Electra had been? Orestes-Hamlet acts on the level of the great prediction; Electra—let us repeat—provides the dramatic and psychological motivation for his deed. "Others" means to Orestes, first and foremost, Electra; "others" means to Hamlet, first and foremost, Ophelia. Ophelia, like Electra, is the daughter of a murdered father. Ophelia is an Electra who has passed through madness and chosen suicide.

The oppositions—Orestes-Electra, Hamlet-Ophelia—are subject to modifications, though they retain the same opposing signs. Hamlet is seemingly dead, Ophelia really dies; Hamlet is seemingly mad, Ophelia really goes mad. In Aeschylus and Euripides Orestes goes mad after his crime; in Sophocles, there is a sleepwalking Orestes, as Duvignaud calls him, who murders as if in a trance.[8] Shakespeare's Hamlet and his predecessors from the Nordic sagas pretend to be mad, or on occasion are really mad.

Of course, the word and concept of madness can mean different states and situations. To the Greeks, madness seems to have been above all a liturgical or ritual sign connected with the gods. There were two different kinds of madness: one sent by Apollo, the other by the Furies. The same distinction appears again in the Middle Ages and may even be found in the Renaissance tradition: divine madmen are opposed to those possessed by the devil. But madness has a third meaning. It is not only Electra who is and wants to be mad ("Terrors compelled me, to terrors I was driven . . . With terrors around me, I will not hold back these mad cries of misery, so long as I live" [Sophocles' Electra, 221 f., 223 f.]) Antigone, too, is considered mad; and Aeschylus' Prometheus replies to Hermes, who has called him a fool: "Yes, if it's madness to detest my foes" (978). Those who rebel against authority, against kings, who oppose their loyalty to the dead to their duties to the living, who refuse to accept the world, are mad. Madness signifies one of three things—anointment, punishment or revolt. The fool is mad too. Greek tragedy, apart from a few exceptions in Euripides, did not know the character of a tragic clown; it was Shakespeare who introduced him into tragedy. There is no court fool in *Hamlet,* though Hamlet plays the role of a tragic fool before others and sees himself in the clown's mirror.

The mad Electra is the sister of Orestes; the mad Ophelia is the sister of Laertes. In the Shakespearean system of mirrors, Laertes is Hamlet's reflection or double. He, too, avenges the death of his father, and it is by his hand that Hamlet dies, pierced by a poisoned rapier. The relationship between Ophelia and Hamlet is sexual, but in the Nordic sagas—as Gilbert Murray was first to point out—Amleth's mistress was also his foster sister. In myths and tragedies, a couple often appears in this double relationship of lovers and of brother and sister. Sophocles' Electra is to her brother more than a mother, more than a guardian, possibly more than a sister. "For never were you your mother's love as much as mine. None was your nurse but within that household. You called me always 'sister' . . ." (1146 ff.). Her attitude toward Orestes is almost erotic. "O brother, loved one, you have ended me. Therefore, receive me to your habitation, nothing to nothing, that with you below I may dwell from now on. When you were on earth, I shared all with you equally. Now I claim in death no less to share a grave with you . . ." (1163 ff.).

The suggestion of unfulfilled incest hanging over brother and sister appears even more strongly in Euripides, from the very first meeting, when Electra, who has not recognized Orestes, is unjustifiably afraid that the stranger wants to ravish her, until the final scene of farewell before parting forever: "Hold me now closely breast against breast, dear Brother. I love you. But the curses bred in a mother's blood dissolve our bonds . . ." (1321 ff.).

Orestes and Electra can be joined only in common death, or through the joint shedding of blood. The ambiguity in their relationship, however, seems intentional. In Aeschylus, at the decisive point when Orestes hesitates to murder his mother, Pylades speaks for the first and only time. He asks Orestes to kill in the name of obedience to the will of the gods. When, in Sophocles, Orestes goes through the same moment of hesitation, and the dying Clytemnestra's cries of fear are heard, Electra shouts in the climax of her frenzy: "If you have strength—again!" (1415). Electra is joined with Orestes by her mother's blood, instead of by her own.

III.

The murder at Mycenae was not only a family crime; the victim was a king and ruler. It meant not only a violation of family bonds, but the seizure of the throne by a usurper. Situations in tragedy exemplify both moral opposites and political conflicts, in the literal sense of the Greek *polis*—city and state. That is why Thebes is stricken with pestilence for the crimes of Oedipus, and Mycenae doomed for the crimes of the house of Atreus, and "something is rotten in the state of Denmark" after the murder of the elder Hamlet. The figure of the king and ruler is characterized by a double contradiction. He is a member of the community and is also outside it; he is a man like other men and a sacral figure. Rulers in Greek tragedies trace their descent from the gods; Christian kings are the Lord's anointed. But even when the sacral character of royal authority has been flouted, the transcendence of history remains. Crimes committed on the level of the throne mean not only a violation of the moral order but a disaster for the state. In both *Electra*s, Aegisthus is a tyrant; after the crime committed at Elsinore, "Denmark is a prison."

When in Aeschylus' *Agamemnon* Clytemnestra runs up the stairs of the palace after the murder of Aegisthus, she calls for an ax. She wants to defend herself. She wants the same ax she used to murder Agamemnon. In the Aeschylus trilogy that ax is a theatrical sign of the cycle of crime. I have seen such axes from the Trojan era at the Heraklion museum. They are heavy bronze double axes with long handles, rather like medieval halberds. With one edge of such a double ax one kills, with the other one is killed. Clytemnestra is the first personification of the tragic unity of executioner and victim.

In Euripides' *Electra,* for the first time the action takes place not in front of the palace of Atreus, but in a village on the edge of Mycenae, in front of a miserable hovel belonging to Electra's husband. The heroes are unheroic. Orestes is an ordinary tramp; Electra has been given in marriage to a peasant so that she cannot give birth to royal children. All the motivations here are direct, psychological, realistic. Electra hates her mother not so much for her father's death as for her own humiliations. That hate overshadows everything else. Clytemnestra is very human indeed. She complains of Agamemnon's past unfaithfulness and talks about unfaithfulness in Aegisthus. She is afraid of her lover but fears the return of Orestes even more. She simply wants to live.

Great origins and the Delphic oracle have been left far behind, before the opening of the action, outside the tragedy proper. Orestes' "destiny" is the role that has been imposed on him. He has to kill because he is called Orestes. He shudders at the murder demanded by Electra. He wants to have done with it as soon as possible. Later they become two frightened children on the stage. They have murdered their mother, but they do not really know why. The prediction has been fulfilled, but its sense, its validity, its necessity have been undermined even before the ironical divine twins, Castor and Pollux, descend in a basket from the roof of the palace.

In Shakespeare, as in Greek tragedy, all predictions are fulfilled. As in Aeschylus and Euripides, tragedy ends with a return to legality, but "necessity," "destiny" and even "legality" are questioned.

Hamlet's forecast is made by his father's ghost. The prediction for the set, for all events, is contained in Horatio's account in the first scene of Act I. Hamlet, the king of Denmark, killed old Fortinbras, the king of Norway, in a duel to settle a frontier dispute. Later Claudius poisoned old Hamlet, married his wife and ascended the throne of Denmark. What can we expect? Clearly the prognosis is a cycle of feudal revenge, which will include the murder of Claudius and Gertrude by Hamlet. Young Fortinbras, too, has grievances to be accounted for. The same prognosis foretells the murder of Hamlet by the son of the old king of Norway who has been killed in a duel. Young Fortinbras must become the king of Denmark. This is the superstructure of action in Shakespeare's *Hamlet.*

In this prognosis, only the order of the deaths is accurate. The reign of young Fortinbras has to be preceded by four deaths. Old Hamlet has been murdered before the action begins. When drumbeats announce the arrival of Fortinbras, there are three corpses on the stage. The deaths of Claudius and Gertrude are a repetition of the unchanging structure of Oresteian tragedy. But *Hamlet* is from the outset a history of the cycle of vengeance and its conclusion. In order that the cycle of vengeance may be ended, young Fortinbras has to ascend the throne of

Denmark without bloodshed. For this to happen, Hamlet must die without being killed by Fortinbras. Before Hamlet dies, he must avenge his father, but without being guilty of matricide or even consciously planned murder.

What is the choice facing Hamlet? There is a seemingly simple answer: he can either kill or not kill; avenge his father or leave Elsinore. Brecht wrote in his *Short Organum for the Theatre* that Hamlet is unable to make use "of the new approach to Reason which he has picked up at the university of Wittenberg. In the feudal business to which he returns it simply hampers him. Faced with irrational practices, his reason is utterly unpractical. He falls a tragic victim to the discrepancy between such reasoning and such action."[9]

Brecht's arguments are only partially right. The real choice facing Hamlet is quite different. He can and must choose between the Hamlet who will kill and the Hamlet who will not. He is in a compulsory situation involving two parts, both imposed from outside. Neither is acceptable to him. Both would alienate him from society, either as a man who has killed, or as a son who has not avenged his father. Euripides' Orestes formulates this contradiction of duties as precisely as if he had read Hegel. "What else *could* I have done? I had two duties, two clear choices, both of them conflicting" (551 ff.).[10]

Hamlet can neither accept this choice nor go away. He can never again be himself, that is, the Hamlet he was before, who did not have to make an impossible choice. Hence the thought of suicide arises as the only escape. Neither of the parts imposed on him is sufficiently justified, neither is authentic. Hamlet's freedom is an illusion, that is to say, he can decide not to kill; but that would mean to accept one of the parts imposed on him. Unlike Orestes, Hamlet will not accept the choice. He will be forced to make it—forced by "others." "Destiny is what comes from outside." The "destiny" that will make Hamlet avenge his father is an exchange of swords, one of which has been poisoned. The poisoned wine meant for Hamlet is also Gertrude's "destiny." "Necessity" is here a series of chances; there is no transcendence in it. Of all possible predictions, the ones saying that Hamlet will die and avenge his father in these ways would seem the least probable.

At Stratford in the autumn of 1965, David Warner played Hamlet in a production by Peter Hall. When all has been made clear—when the duel is over, Gertrude has died, and Claudius' deceit has been discovered by Laertes—Hamlet grabs the King, knocks him down, throws the poisoned wine in his face, and then slowly pours the remainder of the poison in his ear. In this interpretation, by killing Claudius in exactly the same way that Claudius killed his father, Hamlet fulfills the prediction in a ritual manner. In Aeschylus, after killing Clytemnestra, Orestes shows the Chorus the blood-stained net which she had thrown over Agamemnon at the moment of murder. In Sophocles, Orestes takes Aegisthus to the spot where Agamemnon died, and kills him there.

Hamlet dies. He had set a mousetrap and wanted to catch the royal murderer in it. But it is the world, the "others," who have turned out to be the real mousetrap. And he has been caught in it. He could not avoid making his choice; he has been trapped in spite of himself. In Hall's production, he speaks his last words and laughs. He laughs for a long time. Only terrible laughter has been left to him. The laughter signifies his refusal to identify with the part of Orestes; the part that has been forced on him; the Hamlet who has killed because the grand prediction foretold he would.

In Shakespeare's version, everyone loses. Claudius acts according to the principle of what will be most efficient: he wants first to win Hamlet over, then to get him out of the way, then to kill him. He dies. Polonius follows the same procedure: he wants to sound out Hamlet's intentions, render him harmless, perhaps even marry his daughter off to him. He, too, dies. Gertrude wants to avoid the cataclysm, to save her husband and her son. She is unable to save anybody, even herself. The complementary set, the "others," "destiny which comes from outside," the prediction for the entire set, turns out to be stronger than the most prudent counsels and the actions that would seem to be the most effective.

Fortinbras remains outside the action. He comes in literally to fill the gap. The return to legality is without any motivation, deprived of even a semblance of necessity. It does not mean anything. It follows from the logic of the structure, without any justification and without reference to any hierarchy of values. "I would not particularly like to live in a Denmark ruled by Fortinbras," declared Peter Hall, explaining his views on *Hamlet.*

IV.

The models of tragedy have two sets of references and two times: historic time and meta-historic time. In Aeschylus' *Oresteia,* as in a mountain slope uncovered by erosion, scholars have seen a dramatic opposition between the matrilineal and patrilineal concepts of family relationships, between the law of talion and the law of ransom, between religious purification of the murderer by priests in the temple and his exoneration by the Athenian court. The cycle of family vengeance in *Hamlet* represents, no doubt, the grand mechanism of feudal slaughter which Shakespeare dramatized so many times in his Histories. The arrival of Fortinbras is like the coming of the cold legalism of the Tudors. *Hamlet* was first performed in the year of Essex's execution. The Prince of Denmark, with a book of Montaigne in his hand, stood no chance of ascending the throne in the real world. He could not accept any of the historical choices. He could only die.

The oppositions contained in models of tragedy are also timeless. They are impoverished rather than enriched by historical interpretations. Antigone's conflict with Creon and her gesture of throwing a handful of dust on her brother's body contain all the antinomies between authority and morality, or, to put it more precisely, between the order of action whose measure is efficacy and the order of values in which all gestures count and a gesture dearly bought by death gives meaning to fleeting human existence. The dramatic model of Hamlet-Orestes contains all human situations in which choice is dictated by the past, but has to be made on one's own responsibility and on one's own account.

Tragedy, however, is more than a dramatic realization of an abstract model. Tragedy is visual form, and it is also theatre. I would say that it is, above all, theatre. In the theatre the present of the tragic heroes is also the present of the spectators. All times acquire concreteness. Past is what was, future is what can happen, what has been predicted. In all the great productions of *Hamlet* which have become part of theatre history—from Garrick and Kean to Jean-Louis Barrault, John Gielgud and Laurence Olivier—the Prince of Denmark has adopted the features and gestures of the actor's own generation. So must Orestes also have done in antiquity. The Greeks knew the characters, the plot and the resolution of the action; every new version of the old plot meant taking up anew the debate over Orestes and Electra. The same model of tragedy does not mean that performances are similar or the judgments identical, as may be clearly seen in the two *Electra*s, by Sophocles and Euripides.

Euripides' *Electra* is a violent polemic with Aeschylus and Sophocles. In spite of its psychological insight and propensity for realistic detail, it is really a parable or morality play about two unhappy children who are induced to commit a crime because of an old superstition. As in Brecht, the rationalistic morality play is accompanied by songs and music; as in Brecht's *The Good Woman of Setzuan,* the ironical gods who appear toward the end of the play could say: "Man is more inclined to good than to evil, but circumstances are against him."

In the earlier *Electra* by Sophocles, the living are fascinated by the dead. Here all is liturgy and ritual. Orestes offers a sacrifice on the tomb of his father; later Electra forbids Chrysothemis to offer a sacrilegious sacrifice and sends her to their father's tomb with a lock of her hair and her virgin girdle. The fascination with death continues. Electra survives the death of her brother and speaks her funeral laments holding the urn with his supposed ashes. Murder, too, is a liturgical sacrifice, offered ceremoniously. Of all the Oresteian tragedies, Sophocles' is the most monothematic. From the prologue to the *exodos*, it is a preparation and visualization of murder. Matricide is a tragic archetype of murder. There is no pity in Sophocles, only terror. Orestes and Electra infect each other with hate. The horrible dream really happens, accompanied by the cries of the murdered victim and Electra's frantic shouts.

The heroes do not wake from their murderous dream. The Furies do not appear, and after his last murder, Orestes does not speak a word. Even more curious is Electra's silence. Her first words in the play are uttered as a cry coming from the palace: "Ah! Ah!" Her last words are: "Kill him as quickly as you can. And killing throw him out to find such burial as suits him out of our sight. This is the only thing that can bring me redemption from all my past sufferings" (1486 ff.). She does not say another word. She remains alone on the empty proscenium, far from the Chorus. What else could she say? Only, like Hamlet, perhaps: "The rest is silence."

Consciousness means distance from one's own part. Hamlet is more than simply the Hamlet who has killed. The Greek Orestes experiences only two or three moments of doubt. He is the Orestes who has to kill. But as well as *Electra,* Euripides wrote his *Orestes.* Everything takes place after the murder. Orestes is mad, looked after by Electra. Menelaus comes and asks: "What is your sickness?" Orestes replies: "I call it conscience. The certain knowledge of wrong, the conviction of crime" (395 f.). These words could also be repeated by Hamlet. The Furies are the pangs of conscience.

Lucian in *Cymbeline*

Shakespeare's possible knowledge of the dialogues of Lucian has long been a subject of controversy. That Lucian was widely read in Elizabethan schools, primarily in Latin translation, has long been known.[1] We know also that Lucian was praised and quoted by Thomas Nashe[2]; Gabriel Harvey *(Foure Lectures)*; Thomas Dekker *(News from Hell* and *Devil Let Loose)*; Ben Jonson *(Volpone)*[3]; and John Webster *(The White Devil)*.[4] It has also been suggested that Lucian may have influenced the gravedigger scene in *Hamlet*[5] and even some of Berowne's jokes in *Love's Labour's Lost* (IV, iii, 166–70).[6] The strongest argument for Shakespeare's knowledge of Lucian has been the possibility that he provided a source for *Timon of Athens,* although this has never been established with certainty.

A debt (apparently hitherto unnoticed) to Lucian's *Charon* in *Cymbeline* may serve to reopen the entire question of Lucian's impact on Shakespeare. Guiderius says over what he takes to be the dead body of Imogen:

> Thersites' body is as good as Ajax',
> When neither are alive.
>
> (IV,ii,252–53)

These lines are based directly upon Lucian's *Charon, or the Inspectors,* 22:

> Θερσίτη δ ἶσος Θέτιδος παῖς ἠϋχόμοτο
> πάντες δ ἐισὶν ὁμῶς νεχύων ἀμενηνὰ χάρηνα
> γυμνοί τε ξηροί τε χατ'ἀσφοδελὸν λειμῶνα.

In modern English translation:

> Thersites and the son of fair-haired Thetis
> Are equals now, for all are dead . . .[8]

The lines in *Cymbeline* show their indebtedness to Lucian even more strikingly when we consider the speech of Guiderius in the light of the preceding lines from Belarius:

> . . . Though mean and mighty rotting
> Together have one dust, yet reverence—
> That angel of the world—doth make distinction
> Of place 'tween high and low. Our foe was princely;

And though you took his life, as being our foe,
Yet bury him as a prince.

GUIDERIUS:
                    Pray you fetch him hither.
Thersites' body is as good as Ajax',
When neither are alive.

(IV, ii, 247–54)

Shakespeare has substituted Ajax for Lucian's "Fair-haired Thetis' son" (Achilles) because the scene in *Cymbeline* deals with the problem of burying a foe as in Sophocles' *Ajax*. That Shakespeare knew the story of Ajax as it is told in Sophocles' play is made clear by a passage in *Titus Andronicus* where the plea of Ulysses for permission to bury the body of Ajax is mentioned:

The Greeks upon advice did bury Ajax,
That slew himself; and wise Laertes' son
Did graciously plead for his funerals.

(I, i, 379–81)

There also appears to be a striking reference to the prologue of Sophocles' *Ajax* in Shakespeare's *Rape of Lucrece:*

In Ajax' eyes blunt rage and rigour roll'd;
   But the mild glance that sly Ulysses lent
Show'd deep regard and smiling government.

(1400)

In no other account of Ajax known in Shakespeare's time, other than the tragedy of Sophocles, does the pleading of Ulysses for the burial of Ajax occur, although it is possible that it may have been in the now lost university play *Ajax Flageliter*,[9] of whose actual contents nothing, unfortunately, is known. We also know that in *Troilus and Cressida,* Shakespeare depicted Achilles as an effeminate coward, and thus the sinister strength of Ajax would make a more appropriate contrast to the weak foolishness of a Thersites. The allusion in *Cymbeline* may provide some further evidence for Shakespeare's knowledge of Sophocles, who, like Lucian, was read in Elizabethan grammar schools.[10] In the very next line of Lucian's text, moreover, Hermes mentions Ajax: "And now you've reminded me, let me show you the tomb of Achilles. There it is, beside the sea, on Cape Sigeum in the Troad. And Ajax is buried just across the way, at Rhoetium."

That Shakespeare could have read Lucian in Greek is extremely unlikely, but several Latin translations were available to him. The Latin translation by Erasmus of Rotterdam (1506), which included Lucian's dialogue of *Timon,* did not contain *Charon,* from which the passage in *Cymbeline* derives. *Charon* was printed in the collection of translations "by various hands," *Clarissimi Luciani Philosophia Cora,* published in Venice in 1494 and reprinted in Milan in 1497 by Uldericus Scinzeler. In this version the entire passage in question appears as follows:

> Nil inhumatus eo differt qui rite sepultus:
> Atqui eadem Atridae et Fortuna binominis Hyri:
> Non est deformi Thersite maior Achilles:
> Aeque imbecillum miseris caput omnibus: aeque
> Nudi omnes; arent herbosa ut prata calore.

> (1494 edition, sig. M$_3$^{r})

Another edition was prepared by Erasmus, Melanchton and Thomas More, and published in Frankfurt in 1538, in Paris in 1546, and in Basle in 1563. It was many times reprinted (London, 1664, 1694). Here the passage reads as follows:

Mortuus est aquae, tumuli qui nescit honorem,
Et qui sortitur spectandi funera saxi;
Atque honor unus adest et regi Agamemnoni, et Iro,
Thersitae, et similis Thetidos formosus Achilles.
Umbrae nam pariter siccae nudaeque; pererrent
Asphodeli campos, confracto vertice cunctae.

(Paris, 1546, folio 58ᵛ)

Close comparison of the language makes it likely that Shakespeare used the first of these versions for the passage in *Cymbeline*. But it was possible for him to have read the *Charon* in one of several Italian translations or in a French translation of Lucian's works by Filbert Bertin, published in 1582. The first English collection of Lucian by Francis Hickes (1566–1631) was published posthumously by his son, Thomas Hickes, in 1634 (reprinted Oxford, 1664). The translation by Hickes included *Menippus* and *Charon*.[11] Hickes translates the lines from *Charon* as follows:

No difference is, but all is one
Whether they have Tombes or none,
Poore Irus of as great a birth
As Agamemnon under Earth:
Thersites hath as good a feature
As Thetis sonne that comely creature.
All emptie skulls naked and drie
In Asphodelus medows lie.

(p. 105)

This new evidence of Shakespeare's debt to Lucian in *Cymbeline* poses some new and important questions. In all Latin editions of Lucian, from the first in 1494, the dialogue of *Timon* follows *Menippus* and *Charon*. These three dialogues were the three writings by Lucian most often referred to by writers in the sixteenth century.

These facts should establish Lucian's *Timon* as a source for Shakespeare's *Timon of Athens,* perhaps equal in weight to the account in Plutarch to which he certainly referred. It now seems likely that *Timon of Athens* and *Cymbeline* were written close to one another in time, although it is impossible to be certain of the exact date of either play.

NOTES

The Vertical Axis

1. The date of *Prometheus Bound* is still debated, but it is now
almost generally assumed that it was one of Aeschylus' last plays,
possibly performed after the *Oresteia* (458 B.C.). Three actors took
part in the performance, and the old hypothesis that in the prologue
and the epilogue the Titan was represented by a dummy has been
rejected. The rock on top of the Caucasus, writes Peter Arnott, was
"symbolized by an upright post to which the actor was bound" (*Greek
Scenic Conventions in the Fifth Century B.C.* [Oxford, Clarendon Press,
1962], Appendix i, "*Prometheus Bound:* The final scene," pp. 123 ff.).
The use of *machina* for the Chorus of the Oceanides, which descends
from above, seems doubtful. The most arguable point, however, is
the scenic treatment of the epilogue. The lightning and thunder were,
of course, only represented verbally and illustrated musically. The
earthquake was visualized in gestures of the chorus. The hurling
down of Prometheus must have been—in that theatre of stylized
gesture—symbolic. Arnott suggests that the Titan and the Chorus fell
flat on the ground. A spectacular fall would be possible only if Prome-

theus were placed on the *theologeion,* that is to say, on the roof of the *skene.* The actor could then jump six and a half feet down to the rear of the old *orchestra.* The *theologeion* was reserved for the gods, but Prometheus was a Titan and was struck by thunder direct from Olympus.

2. Mircea Eliade, *Cosmos and History: The Myth of the Eternal Return,* translated by Willard R. Task (New York, Harper, 1959), p. 13. See also his *The Sacred and the Profane: The Nature of Religion* (New York, Harcourt, 1959), pp. 34–37, 52–54.

3. Eliade, *Cosmos and History,* p. 14: "For Christians, Golgotha was situated at the center of the world, since it was the summit of the cosmic mountain and at the same time the place where Adam had been created and buried."

4. From *Hesiod. Theogony; Works and Days; Shield of Heracles,* in Richmond Lattimore's translation (Ann Arbor, University of Michigan Press, 1959). See *Theogony* (ll. 126–28).

5. The Greek and Biblical Genesis have the same character of a structural operation. The creation of the world meant arranging chaos according to the basic oppositions: bright—dark, stable—fluid, cold—hot, dry—wet. The most basic of all, however, is the spatial opposition of "above" and "below": "And God made the firmament and separated the waters which were under the firmament from the waters which were above the firmament. And it was so. And God called the firmament Heaven" (Gen. i. 7–8).

6. Richmond Lattimore's translation, *The Iliad of Homer* (Chicago, University of Chicago Press, 1951).

7. Northrop Frye, *Fables and Identity: Studies in Poetic Mythology* (New York, Harcourt, 1963), pp. 58–66.

8. Erwin Panofsky, *Studies in Iconology: Humanistic Themes in the Art of the Renaissance* (New York, Harper Torchbooks, 1962), p. 203: ". . . the Florentine Neoplatonists called the realm of matter *il mondo soterraneo* and compared the existence of the human soul, while it is 'imprisoned' in the body, to a life *apud inferos.*"

9. All quotations from *Prometheus Bound,* unless otherwise stated, are David Grene's translation in *The Complete Greek Tragedies, Aeschylus II* (Chicago, University of Chicago Press, 1956).

10. Northrop Frye, *Fools of Time: Studies in Shakespearean Tragedy* (Toronto, University of Toronto Press, 1967), p. 17.

11. *Ibid.,* pp. 44, 55.

12. Cf. William Chase Greene, *Moira: Fate, Good and Evil, in Greek Thought* (Cambridge, Mass., Harvard University Press, 1944), p. 123: "At first, Zeus had power, but not intelligence; Prometheus had intel-

ligence, but not power; man had neither; only a coalition of power and intelligence could result in goodness."

13. In Hesiod's *Theogony:* ". . . the Fates, to whom Zeus of the counsels gave the highest position: they are Clotho, Lachesis, and Atropos: they distribute to mortal people what people have, for good and for evil" (903 ff.). The Furies were born of blood or sperm of Uranus, when Cronos castrated his father and cast off his genitals. They inseminated Earth (182 ff.). It was the first artificial (and posthumous) insemination. The division of the "trio" of destiny into Fates and Furies was probably connected with the transition from matriarchate to patriarchate. The Erinyes in the *Oresteia* secure the revenge for the mother's murder. Fates, guardians of destiny and agents of inevitability, not merely of family revenge, are apparently of later origin. In Hesiod, the division of functions between Fates and Furies is not yet absolutely clear.

14. See Bernard M. W. Knox, *Oedipus at Thebes* (New Haven, Yale University Press, 1957), pp. 125, 145.

15. The attribution of the discovery of the alphabet to Prometheus was Aeschylus' own idea, which he perhaps felt was necessary for an intellectual anthropology of progress. Mythological sources attribute the discovery of the alphabet to the Three Parcae (or Fates), to Hermes and to Io. In this connection Io is the Moon; the first alphabet was connected with the moon calendar and was a religious mystery of the priestesses of Io-Moon. See Robert Graves, *Greek Myths*, Vol. I (Baltimore, Penguin Books, 1955), pp. 182–85.

16. Letters and numbers were media for Prometheus. He was almost a precursor of Marshall McLuhan, for whom the symbolic alphabet was a decisive medium in the uniformization of space and time, that is to say, in the visual concept of "topocosm."

17. Claude Lévi-Strauss, *Totemism*, translated by Rodney Needham (Boston, Beacon Press, 1963), p. 99. Rousseau quote is from Lévi-Strauss.

18. Knox, *op. cit.*, p. 144: *"Pronoia,* 'foreknowledge,' 'foresight,' is not only the basis of divine prophecy, it is also the ability which the physician, in the Hippocratic writings, is urged to cultivate above all others."

19. In the portion of a lost play by Aeschylus (A. Nauck, *Tragicorum Graecorum Fragmenta,* 2nd ed. [Hildesheim, G. Olms, 1964], fragment 205) which could have been the first part of the Promethean trilogy, we have something like a lesson in kindling a fire: "And do thou guard thee well lest a bubble strike thy face; for it is bitter, and deadly-scorching its vapors." Carl Kerényi, in his *Prometheus: Archety-*

pal Image of Human Existence (Bollingen Series; New York, Pantheon, 1963, pp. 70–71), supposes that these are instructions for operating a primitive iron-smelting furnace.

20. Claude Lévi-Strauss, *Mythologiques I: Le Cru et le Cuit* (Paris, Plon, 1964), p. 20; and for the succeeding passages, pp. 73, 200, and the entire chapter "Cantate de la sarigue." (Also available in translation by John and Doreen Weightman, *The Raw and the Cooked* [New York, Harper, 1969]).

21. Graves, *op. cit.*, p. 144.

22. With his astonishing intuition, Hegel was the first to discern in the Promethean myth the combination of the discovery of fire with the first animal sacrifice and the cooking of meat. See Hegel, *Vorlesungen über die Ästhetik*, edited by Fr. Bassenge (Aufbau-Verlag, 1955), pp. 435 and 447. See also Kerényi, *op. cit.*, pp. 53–54.

23. Eliade, *Cosmos and History*, p. 91: "In fact, the myths of many peoples allude to a very distant epoch when men knew neither death nor toil nor suffering and had a bountiful supply of food merely for the taking. . . . As a result of a ritual fault, communications between heaven and earth were interrupted, and the gods withdrew to the highest heavens. Since then, men must work for their food and are no longer immortal."

24. Hesiod, *Works and Days* (ll. 383–84): "At the time when the Pleiades, the daughters of Atlas, are rising,/begin your harvest, and plow again when they are setting." Cf. Lévi-Strauss, *Le Cru*, "L'Astronomie bien tempérée."

25. Claude Lévi-Strauss, *Race et histoire* (Paris, 1952), p. 19.

26. Knox, *op. cit.*, p. 148.

27. George D. Thomson, *Aeschylus, Prometheus Bound* (New York, Macmillan, 1932), and Anthony J. Podlecki, *The Political Background of Aeschylean Tragedy* (Ann Arbor, University of Michigan Press, 1966), Ch. 6, "Prometheus Bound."

28. Eric A. Havelock, *Prometheus* (Seattle, University of Washington Press, 1968), p. 96.

29. It is worth comparing the Aeschylean tower, in which gods dwell, with the image of bronze heaven and the divine citadel in Pindar (*Nemean VI*, 1–5):

> There is one
> race of men, one race of gods; both have breath
> of life from a single mother. But sundered power
> holds us divided, so that one side is nothing, while on
> > the other the brazen sky is established
> a sure citadel forever.

From *The Odes of Pindar,* edited and translated by Richmond Lattimore (Chicago, University of Chicago Press, 1947).

30. The first *stasimon* of the Chorus (353 ff.) from *Antigone* in Knox's prose translation, *op. cit.,* p. 108.

31. Martin Heidegger, "The Ode on Man in Sophocles' *Antigone,*" in *An Introduction to Metaphysics,* translated by Ralph Manheim (New Haven, Yale University Press, 1959), p. 147.

32. Io is also a mutation of the Egyptian Isis. Lucian was an experienced mythographer. In his *Dialogues of the Gods* (III) Zeus orders Hermes: "Fly down to Nemea . . . kill Argus, take Io across the sea to Egypt, and convert her into Isis. She shall be henceforth an Egyptian Goddess, flood the Nile, regulate the winds, and rescue mariners."

33. Havelock, *op. cit.,* pp. 60–61.

34. *Prometheus Bound,* in *Three Greek Plays,* translated by Edith Hamilton (New York, Norton, 1937), p. 141.

35. See Kerényi, *op. cit.,* pp. 120–22, and his *Asklepios: Archetypal Image of the Healer's Existence* (Bollingen Series; New York, Pantheon, 1959), pp. 95–100.

36. In the introduction to his doctoral dissertation; Marx-Engels, *Werke,* Ergänzungsband, Vol. I (Berlin, Dietz-Verlag, 1968), pp. 262 ff.

37. George D. Thomson, *Aeschylus and Athens: A Study in the Social Origins of Drama* (London, Lawrence & Wishart, 1941), p. 316.

38. Shelley's preface to his *Prometheus Unbound* is characteristic: "But, in truth, I was averse from a catastrophe so feeble as that of reconciling the Champion with the Oppressor of mankind. The moral interest of the fable, which is powerfully sustained by the sufferings and endurance of Prometheus, would be annihilated if we could conceive of him as unsaying his high language and quailing before his successful and perfidious adversary" (Shelley's *Prometheus Unbound,* edited by Lawrence J. Zillman [Seattle, University of Washington Press, 1969], p. 35).

39. Cf. Kerényi, *Prometheus,* p. 17: "Goethe's Prometheus is no God, no Titan, no man, but the immortal prototype of man as the original rebel and affirmer of his fate: the original inhabitant of the earth, seen as an antigod, as Lord of the Earth." Goethe wrote about himself: "I cut myself off, like Prometheus, from the gods." And this is how he ended his celebrated ode on Prometheus, published in 1785 (quoted in Kerényi, p. 6):

> Here I sit, shaping man
> After my image,

> A race that is like me,
> To suffer, to weep,
> To rejoice and be glad,
> And like myself
> To have no regard for You.

Marx, of course, knew Goethe's ode by heart.

40. In the same preface by Shelley: "The only imaginary being resembling in any degree Prometheus is, Satan; and Prometheus is, in my judgement, a more poetical character than Satan, because, in addition to courage, and majesty, and firm and patient opposition to omnipotent force, he is susceptible of being described as exempt from the taints of ambition, envy, revenge, and a desire for personal aggrandisement, which, in the hero of *Paradise Lost*, interefere with the interest" (Shelley, *op. cit.*, pp. 35, 37).

41. Cf. Eliade, *The Sacred and the Profane*, p. 203: "Modern nonreligious man assumes a new existential situation; he regards himself solely as the subject and agent of history, and he refuses all appeal to transcendence. . . . Man *makes himself*, and he only makes himself completely in proportion as he desacralizes himself and the world. The sacred is the prime obstacle to his freedom. He will become himself only if he is totally demysticized. He will not be truly free until he has killed the last god."

42. Eliade, *Cosmos and History*, p. 125.

43. Albert Camus, *The Myth of Sisyphus*, translated by Justin O'Brien (New York, Knopf, 1955), p. 65.

44. Amazingly and disturbingly close to Camus is the interpretation of the Prometheus myth by the Neo-Platonists, in Marsilio Ficino and in the famous panels of Piero de Cosimo. Panofsky, *op. cit.* (pp. 50–51): "The later mythographers, especially Boccaccio, have always insisted on the fact that, while Vulcan personifies the *ignis elementatus*, that is, the physical fire which enables mankind to solve its practical problems, the torch of Prometheus lighted at the wheels of the sun's chariot /'*rota solis, id est e gremio Dei*'/ carries the 'celestial fire' which stands for the 'clarity of knowledge infused into the heart of the ignorant,' and that this very clarity can only be attained at the expense of happiness and peace of mind. . . . In Piero's Strasburg panel this idea is beautifully expressed by the triumphal gesture of the statue which forms a striking contrast with the tortured position of Prometheus. The punishment of the latter symbolizes the price which mankind has to pay for its intellectual awakening, that is . . . to be tortured by our profound meditation, and to recover only to be tortured

again." This is already a pre-existentialist interpretation; Prometheus' torture is "unhappy awareness."

45. Cicero, *Tusculan Disputations* ii, 10.

46. See John H. Finley, Jr., *Pindar and Aeschylus,* Martin Classical Lectures, XIV (Cambridge, Mass., Harvard University Press, 1955), p. 231.

47. *Pythian* I, 6–7, in *The Odes of Pindar,* translated by C. M. Bowra (Penguin Classics; Baltimore, Penguin Books, 1969), p. 131.

48. Franz Kafka, *Wedding Preparations in the Country and Other Posthumous Prose Writings,* translated by Ernst Kaiser and Eithne Wilkins (London, Secker & Warburg, 1954), p. 95.

49. "Or take Beckett's *Happy Days:* has there been a comparable *stasis,* a comparable shape of action since the *Prometheus?*" George Steiner in reply to an *Arion* questionnaire, "The Classics and the Man of Letters," *Arion,* Vol. III (Winter 1964), p. 82.

Ajax Thrice Deceived

1. All quotations from *Ajax,* unless otherwise stated, are taken from John Moore's translation in *The Complete Greek Tragedies, Sophocles II* (Chicago, University of Chicago Press, 1957).

2. See Bernard M. W. Knox, *The Heroic Temper: Studies in Sophoclean Tragedy* (Berkeley, University of California Press, 1964), p. 42: "In all the seven plays of Aeschylus which have been preserved there is not one (though the Suppliants threaten suicide and Ajax, in a lost play, certainly committed it); in all the surviving plays of Euripides there are only four; but in the seven plays of Sophocles there are no fewer than six: Ajax, Antigone, Haemon, Eurydice, Deianira, and Jocasta— and in addition Philoctetes attempts suicide on stage, Oedipus *tyrannos* asks for a sword to kill himself, and Oedipus at Colonus prays for death in the opening scene of the play . . ." Heracles begs that his torments be cut short and demands of his son to burn him on the pyre while still alive.

3. Podaleirius, son of Asclepius, physician at the Greek camp, "first noticed Aias' [Ajax's] flashing eyes and clouded mind when he was enraged." Hesiod, *The Homeric Hymns and Homerica,* translated by Hugh G. Evelyn-White (Loeb Classical Library; Cambridge, Mass., Harvard University Press, 1967), p. 525.

4. Northrop Frye, *Fools of Time: Studies in Shakespearean Tragedy* (Toronto, University of Toronto Press, 1967), pp. 81–82: "The unburied body, 'a prey to dogs and birds,' in the Homeric phrase, is left

to dissolve in the flux of time; burial is, at least symbolically, real death, or deliverance from time. This dimension of the theme comes unobtrusively but palpably into *Antigone*. But of course there was still a shade that survived in the world below, and this shade still felt all the tragic emotions of enmity and revenge."

5. All quotations from the *Iliad* and the *Odyssey*, unless otherwise stated, are taken from E. V. Rieu's prose translations (Penguin Classics; Baltimore, Penguin Books, 1950 and 1946). I have added verse references.

6. William Sale, "Achilles and Heroic Values," *Arion*, Vol. II, No. 3 (Autumn 1963), p. 89: "The central concept is *geras*, the prize of honor, an object—material or human—granted by society to various of its members in token of their *areté*, which in the heroic world meant excellence in combat with the sword, spear and shield. Briseis, Achilles' mistress, is also his *geras*, given to him as a symbol of the prowess . . . Since the *geras* is granted as an indication of *areté* by society . . . it also functions as a status symbol, or . . . as a sign of *timé*, honor. When Agamemnon took away Achilles' *geras*, Briseis, he did the worst thing he could have done—he shattered the heroic value system." See also M. I. Finley, *The World of Odysseus* (New York, Viking, 1954), pp. 125–29.

7. Cedric H. Whitman, *Sophocles: A Study of Heroic Humanism* (Cambridge, Mass., Harvard University Press, 1951), p. 64: "Ajax is the first full-length portrait of a tragic hero in Western literature, and it is by no mere coincidence that both he and Achilles, the first epic hero, find themselves in identical situations. Both isolate themselves in the struggle with their own offended honor."

8. Walter Kaufmann, *Tragedy and Philosophy* (New York, Doubleday, 1968), p. 218: "In *The Women of Trachis* and in *Philoctetes* we are subjected both to poetic accounts of Heracles' and Philoctetes' sufferings and unbearable screams themselves. The result is far from what one would expect after reading Matthew Arnold, Nietzsche or Bradley."

9. Cf. J. C. Kamerbeek, *The Plays of Sophocles*, Part I, *Commentaries, The Ajax* (Leiden, 1963), p. 20: "The wording and the scene are reminiscent of the tracing satyr-chorus in the *Ichneutae.*" Of course, Kamerbeek is referring only to the wording and action, not the tone.

10. Antonin Artaud, *The Theatre and Its Double*, translated by M. C. Richards (New York, Grove, 1958), p. 108.

11. Some of the scant evidence of how *Ajax* had been performed in antiquity was left us by Lucian. In a performance, which may have been more of a mime-ballet than a spoken or sung performance—

though this is by no means certain—the actor fell into genuine frenzy (*Saltatio*, 83): "In presenting Ajax going mad immediately after his defeat, he so overleaped himself that it might well have been thought that instead of feeling madness he was himself insane; for he tore the clothes of one of the men that beat time with the iron shoe, and snatching a flute from one of the accompanists, with a vigorous blow he cracked the crown of Odysseus, who was standing near and exulting in his victory . . . The pit, however, all went mad with Ajax, leaping and shouting and flinging up their garments . . . They themselves applauded to cover the absurdity of the dancing, although they perceived clearly that what went on came from the madness of the actor, not that of Ajax" *Lucian*, Vol. V (Loeb Classical Library; Cambridge, Mass., Harvard University Press, 1936), pp. 285–86. Lucian was against exaggerated expression in dancing and mime, but he made the significant remark that in contemporary tragic performances the Chorus did "carry masculinity to the point of savagery and bestiality" (p. 285).

12. Frye, *op. cit.*, p. 8: ". . . being a man, his [Sarpedon's] life is death, and there is nowhere in life that is not a battlefield."

13. See E. R. Dodds, *The Greeks and the Irrational* (Berkeley, University of California Press, 1951), pp. 136–39. See also Eric A. Havelock, *Preface to Plato* (Cambridge, Mass., Harvard University Press, 1967), pp. 197–99, and Kaufmann, *op. cit.*, pp. 150–51.

14. Kaufmann, *op. cit.* p., 145: "In large parts of the Western World today one sees no vultures; and death, disease, and old age are concealed. In Calcutta, vultures still sit in trees in the city waiting for death in the streets; and sickness, suffering, and the disintegration of age assault the senses everywhere. But it is only in Homer that, while death is ever present to consciousness, the vultures in the tree are experienced as Athene and Apollo, delighting in the beautiful sight of a sea of shields, helmets, and spears. In this vision death has not lost its sting; neither has life lost its beauty; the very vultures are not the reproach to the world." In the *New York Times* of June 20, 1970, I read the following in an account of the military action in Cambodia: "The flies that swarm through the tilting barracks seem to be in control of the decaying army garrison in this town in Cambodia's northwest." The very flies are not the reproach to the world.

15. A tradition going back to Homer (*Odysseus*, XI, 547) attributed to Athene an active participation in the judgment assigning Achilles' armor to Odysseus. In Lucian's *Dialogues of the Dead* (XXIX) Ajax clearly refers to this: "Who inspired that verdict? I know, but about the gods we may not speak. Let that pass, but cease to hate Odysseus?

'Tis not in my power, Agamemnon, though Athene's self should require it of me" (*The Works of Lucian of Samosata*, Vol. I, translated by H. W. Fowler and F. G. Fowler [Oxford, Clarendon Press, 1905], p. 154.)

16. The Chorus from *Antigone* in Dodds's translation, *op. cit.*, p. 50.

17. The work of Exekias, a master of the black-figure style, potter and painter of vases. J. D. Beazley, *Attic Black-Figure* (New York, Oxford University Press, 1928), pp. 20–21: "It is not a mere coincidence that there should be at least five pictures of Ajax in the extant work of Exekias. There was something in Exekias of Ajax: so that he could admire and understand the hero slow, and strong, and at heart delicate." See also note 41.

18. John H. Finley, Jr., *Pindar and Aeschylus*, Martin Classical Lectures, XIV (Cambridge, Mass., Harvard University Press, 1955), p. 171.

19. In the chapter "From Shame-Culture to Guilt-Culture," p. 30., Dodds (*op. cit.*) quotes Theognis, who speaks like Athena in *Ajax*: "No man, Cyrnus, is responsible for his own ruin or his own success: of both these things the gods are the givers," and comments, "The doctrine of man's helpless dependence on an arbitrary Power is not new but there is a new accent of despair, a new and bitter emphasis on the futility of human purposes. We are nearer to the world of the *Oedipus Rex* than to the world of the *Iliad*. It is much the same with the idea of divine *phthonos* or jealousy . . . It is only in the Late Archaic and Early Classical time that the phthonos idea becomes an oppressive menace, a source—or expression—of religious anxiety."

20. Bernard M. W. Knox's translation in his influential *The Ajax of Sophocles*, Vol. LXV of *Harvard Studies in Classical Philology*, (Cambridge, Mass., Harvard University Press, 1961), pp. 1–37.

21. A key line for the understanding of *Ajax*. The Greek of line 126 is: *"eidola hosoiper zomen e kouphen skian"*—"like ghosts we live or like empty shadow." *Eidolon* (εἴδωλον)—a "dream-figure," an "image," a "phantom"; *skia* (ξκιᾱ)—a "shadow," an "image reflected by water," a "ghost." The ghost of King Hamlet would be *skia*. Often in Homer both *eidola* and *skiai* are used to refer to the shadowy shapes of the souls of the dead. Odysseus' mother flees from him like a *skia*. Athene demands of men to recognize themselves as *eidolon* and *skia*, while still alive. ("We are such stuff as dreams are made on; and our little life is rounded with a sleep," *The Tempest*, IV, i, 156–58.) In Pindar's *Pythian* VIII, quoted below, the word is the same: *skias onar* —"dream of a shadow." See Kamerbeek, *op. cit.*, pp. 44 and 238, and Dodds, *op. cit.*, pp. 104 and 122.

22. Cf. *Philoctetes* (133): "May Hermes, God of Craft, the Guide, for us be guide indeed, and Victory and Athene, the City Goddess, who preserves me ever."

23. Whitman, *op. cit.*, p. 70.

24. *Pythian* VIII, 95–99, *The Odes of Pindar*, translated by C. M. Bowra (Penguin Classics; Baltimore, Penguin Books, 1969), p. 237.

25. Schol. on Pindar, *Isthmian*, III, 53. *Hesiod, The Homeric Hymns and Homerica* (in Evelyn-White's translation), *op. cit.*, p. 509.

26. See G. M. Kirkwood, *Homer and Sophocles' Ajax* (Ithaca, Cornell University Press, 1958), p. 57: "As in Homer Hector reaches for his son (466), so Sophocles' Ajax calls for his son (530). Hector's son shrinks from his father waving plume (467–70), Ajax's son has been hidden away from the danger of his father's madness (531–3). Hector prays that his son may delight his mother's heart (461), Ajax bids Eurysaces bring joy to his mother (559). Finally, even as Hector at the end bids Andromache to go home to their work (490), so Ajax ends by bidding Tecmessa take the child and go into the hut (578–9). We are dealing, then, not with only rather close general likeness to the Homeric incident, but with a scene that borrows numerous precise details and locutions, and this fact puts it beyond doubt that the playwright wants to call attention to the borrowing, intends his audience to have the Homeric scene sharply in mind as a basis for the meaning of his own scene."

27. Richmond Lattimore's translation of *The Iliad of Homer* (Chicago, University of Chicago Press, 1951).

28. Erich Auerbach, *Mimesis: The Representation of Reality in Western Literature*, translated by Willard R. Trask (Anchor Books; Garden City, N.Y., Doubleday, 1957), "Odysseus' Scar," pp. 5–10. Cf. George Steiner, "Homer and the Scholars" in his *Language and Silence* (New York, Atheneum, 1970), p. 179: "The poet of the *Iliad* looks on life with those blank, unswerving eyes which stare out of the helmet slits on early Greek vases. His vision is terrifying in its sobriety, cold as the winter sun."

29. The beginning of Ajax's speech and the two fragments that follow in Humphrey D. F. Kitto's translation are from his *Ajax* in *Form and Meaning in Drama: A Study of Six Greek Plays and of Hamlet* (New York, Barnes & Noble, 1957), pp. 188–89.

30. This scene is among the most widely discussed in the work of Sophocles. Its dramatic function is the illusion of a happy end, but what did Ajax really say? One of the two traditional interpretations is that it is "Trugrede," that Ajax deliberately misled the Chorus and Tecmessa; the other, that Ajax gave up suicide. Both interpretations

are naïve, and remind one very much of the nineteenth-century ana-
lyses of what Hamlet had in mind in the "To be or not to be"
soliloquy. Instead of arguing whether Ajax said what he meant, it is
much more reasonable to accept that he meant what he said. Many
eminent philologists are like the Chorus of the sailors of Salamis, who
did not understand anything of what Ajax had said. The arguments
of C. M. Bowra, in his *Sophoclean Tragedy* (New York, Oxford University Press, 1944), are devastating as far as the followers of "Trugrede" are concerned, and ultimately Knox is right when maintaining
that it is Ajax's monologue. Ajax "speaks to himself," or rather, to the
audience. The audience has no illusions; they know that Ajax did not
surrender, but merely considered the conditions and consequences
of surrender. Ajax had learned how to be ironic.

31. Cf. *Oedipus at Colonus* (609 f.): "All other things almighty Time
disquiets. Earth wastes away; the body wastes away; faith dies; distrust
is born. And imperceptibly the spirit changes between a man and his
friend . . ."

32. See Georges Méautis, *Sophocle: Essai sur le héros tragique* (Paris,
Albin Michel, 1957), p. 41: *"Le choeur . . . se lance en une danse frénétique
de joie, un* Hyporchème, *dont l'effet de contraste avec les paroles sinistres
d'Ajax devait faire passer un frisson dans l'auditoire."* Similarly, the joyous
dance of the Chorus in *The Women of Trachis* precedes the return of
the son with the news that Heracles is dying, and in *Oedipus tyrannos*,
the tragic revelation of the secret of the king's birth.

33. *Ajax*, Sir Richard Claverhouse Jebb's translation, *The Complete
Plays of Sophocles*, newly edited by Moses Hadas (New York, Bantam
Books, 1967).

34. M. I. Finley, *The World of Odysseus*, p. 103: "In so permanently
hostile an environment the heroes were permitted to seek allies; their
code of honor did not demand that they stand alone against the
world. But there was nothing in their social system that created the
possibility for two communities, as such, to enter an alliance. Only
personal devices were available, through the channels of household
and kin." And on p. 107: "The stranger who had a *xenos* in a foreign
land . . . had an effective substitute for kinsmen, a protector, representative, and ally. He had a refuge if he were forced to flee his home,
a storehouse on which to draw when compelled to travel, and a source
of men and arms if drawn into battle."

35. William Arrowsmith, "A Greek Theater of Ideas," in *Ideas in
the Drama*, edited by J. Gassner (New York, Columbia University
Press, 1964).

36. Albert Camus, *The Myth of Sisyphus*, translated by Justin

O'Brien (New York, Knopf, 1955), p. 16, and further on: pp. 22 and 51.

37. Søren Kierkegaard, *The Sickness unto Death* (1849), translated by Walter Lowrie, in *A Kierkegaard Anthology*, edited by R. Bretall (Princeton, Princeton University Press, 1946), p. 369, and further on: p. 371.

38. In *Sickness unto Death* there rings a tone of a personal confession, as if wrested from his throat. Kierkegaard does not quote examples from literature, but says: "This sort of despair is seldom seen in the world, such figures generally are met with only in the works of poets, who always lend their characters this 'demoniac' ideality (taking this word in the purely Greek sense)" (p. 370).

39. Also in *Hippolytus,* of course (1. 178), but the Euripidean Phaedra is treated much more realistically.

40. One more tragic interpretation of the *Iliad.* When during a fight over Patroclus' body Zeus seemed to favor the Trojans and a dense fog reduced visibility, Ajax exclaimed: " 'Ah Father Zeus, save us from this fog and give us a clear sky, so that we can use our eyes. Kill us in daylight, if you must' " (*Iliad,* XVII, 645).

41. We do not know how the suicide scene was represented. Some commentators take the view that after the Chorus had departed, the painted panels representing Ajax's tent were changed to those depicting bushes in a "secluded place." This is not at all certain, at least as regards performances in Sophocles' lifetime. Realistically painted scenery was probably not introduced before the fourth century. In any event, the climax of the tragedy—Ajax falling on his sword—must have been seen. From the sixth century onward this scene had frequently been depicted in sculpture and on vases, and doubtless its visual image had shaped Sophocles' imagination.

Beazley, *op. cit.,* p. 20: "Another masterpiece by Exekias, unsigned this time, is an amphora in Boulogne. The theme of the picture is the Death of Ajax . . . The death of Ajax is often represented in archaic art: Ajax either riving himself on his sword, or fallen about it. Exekias, and he alone, shows not the dead hero, nor the moment of his death; but the preparation for the final act; Ajax, his resolution taken, methodically fixing the sword in the ground. Behind him a palm-tree, in front of him his armour—helmet, spears, the famous shield. The face is furrowed with grief."

Even more characteristic is a bronze statuette of early classic period, now at the Museo Archeologico in Florence (Gisela M. A. Richter, *The Sculpture and Sculptors of the Greeks:* [New Haven, Yale University Press, 1970], p. 43 and figs. 133 and 134). Ajax is represented in the moment of throwing himself on his sword. He is holding it with his left hand above the hilt, which is resting on the ground. The sword is short and aimed at the left side of his underbelly. His left leg is bent at the knee, his body arched. The sword is about to pierce the flesh. His right hand is lifted high with an open palm, as if in a gesture of farewell. Ajax looks into space; he is nude, only his head is covered by a heavy spiked helmet. In Sophocles' tragedy, Tecmessa will later cover Ajax's naked body (915). A scholiast commentary to line 864 is also significant: "We must surmise that he falls on his sword; and the actor must be someone powerful to lead the audience up to the revelation of Ajax as Timotheus of Zacynthus is said to have done. He led the audience on, and so inspired them with his acting that he was called 'Cut-throat.' "

Peter Arnott, in whose translation I am quoting the scholiast, in his excellent study *Greek Scenic Conventions in the Fifth Century B.C.* (Oxford, Clarendon Press, 1962), denies the use of *eccyclema* for the removal of Ajax's body backstage. He supposes the suicide scene to have taken place onstage, with him framed within the doorway (pp. 131–33). But this solution does not seem probable either. The actor would have to grasp his sword at the very last moment and hide behind the door, which would close behind him. The tension would have been destroyed and the effect could be ludicrous.

The main argument against the suicide taking place in view of the audience, one pointing to the difficulty of removing the body, is based on the three-actors principle. According to Gilbert Norwood, in his *Greek Tragedy* (London, 1920, 1928, p. 136), Ajax and Teucer were played by the same actor; the deuteragonist performed Odysseus and Tecmessa; the tritagonist, Athene, Messenger, Menelaus and Agamemnon. In the judgment scene, Ajax's corpse was a dummy, brought onstage. *Oedipus at Colonus*—it is generally assumed—was the only tragedy whose staging required four actors. It is possible that *Ajax* was another exception to the rule. After all, the entire suicide scene is exceptional for Greek tragedy. The scholiast observed: "Such things are rare in the old poets; they usually report what has happened through messengers." Personally I am inclined to think that the falling-on-the-sword scene was performed on the *orchestra*, in sunlight, and that Ajax's body remained on stage.

Also Tecmessa's presence in the epilogue is unclear, Teucer sends her to get her son (985). She brings Eurysaces (1168) and remains with him to the end. Her sudden departure would be unmotivated, since she would not leave her child behind. It would be the only other instance in all the extant plays—apart from *Alcestis*—that the same character would be performed by an actor and a walk-on.

42. *Ajax* is almost universally recognized to be the earliest of
Sophocles' extant tragedies and considered to have been written in
the early or late forties, between the death of Cimon (449 B.C.) and
Antigone (442 or 441 B.C). The following arguments are given: the
meter of choral odes, particularly the archaic structure of the *parados;*
the imagery and scenic arrangements recalling those of Aeschylus
(Jebb: "astonishing effects and Aeschylean flavour"); the active role
of the Chorus; the motive of the unburied corpse, close to that of
Antigone. Already in 1939 Kitto pointed out how deceptive it is to base
chronology on meter statistics. These methods were totally compromised when a papyrus published in 1951 caused the date of *The
Suppliants,* universally regarded as the earliest of the known tragedies
of Aeschylus, to be shifted at least a quarter of a century, to after 468
B.C. If only four plays of Shakespeare, one of Marlowe's, one of
Webster's, and a hundred pages of Samuel Johnson's critical writings
were extant, the chronology of plays and the line of development of
Elizabethan drama would be a big puzzle. *The Suppliants* had been
considered the earliest of the plays because of the importance of its
Chorus, as it used to be assumed that the role of the Chorus dimin-
ished as tragedy developed. If the date of *The Bacchae* were not known
it would, by the same token, be regarded as Euripides' earliest play,
because it too contains "Aeschylean flavour" and "astonishing
effects."
Aesthetic views and preconceived notions influence the dating of
works of art to a much higher degree than is revealed through arguments. *Ajax* had been considered an unsuccessful work, or at any rate
one seriously flawed in its structure, so it *had to* be the work of an
immature author. It seems, however, that there are equally serious
arguments for the shifting of the date of *Ajax* to the twenties, after
Oedipus, or perhaps even later, to the period preceding *Philoctetes.*
Similarities between *Ajax* and *The Women of Trachis* have often been
noted. The latter was considered to be both the earliest of Sophocles'
tragedies (in 1958 Kirkwood placed it before *Antigone,* in 1962 Mazon
and Dain placed it before *Ajax*) and as one of the latest (Kitto placed
it in the twenties, Perrotta toward the end of Sophocles' life).
The Chorus in *Ajax,* treated "realistically," is the closest to the
Chorus of sailors in *Philoctetes.* Even more important is the basic
similarity: the unheroic view of Homer's world in both tragedies, a
quite different tone than in *Antigone,* much more Euripidean. In the
prologue Athene has a "Euripidean touch," Kaufmann declared.
Spiteful allusions to Spartan autocracy were one of the arguments for
dating *Ajax* before 446, the date when thirty years' peace was con-

cluded with Sparta; but Reinhardt (1933) prudently added: "if the time of the Peloponnesian War is excluded." There is no reason, however, to exclude the possibility of *Ajax* having been written during the Peloponnesian War. And only if considered in the political climate of the late twenties does *Ajax* become fully intelligible. See John Jones, "The Matter of a Date," in his *On Aristotle and Greek Tragedy* (New York, Oxford University Press, 1962), pp. 65–72; Whitman, *Sophocles*, pp. 42–46; Kamerbeek, *The Ajax*, pp. 15–17.

43. See also Knox, *Heroic Temper*, pp. 121–23: "The contrasted figures of Odysseus and Achilles had become, for the fifth-century Athenians, mythical and literary prototypes of two entirely different worlds of thought and feeling . . . The aristocratic viewpoint in Greek literature (in Pindar especially, who has no use for Odysseus) is Achillean, an ideal of warlike generosity, of rigid standards of honor, of insistence on *timê*, the respect of the world—all this combined with the asceticism and physical beauty of the athlete and his all-too-frequent intellectual limitations. The democratic viewpoint . . . is Odyssean—an ideal of versatility, adaptability, diplomatic skill, and intellectual curiosity, insisting on success combined with glory rather than sacrificed for it."

44. Pindar's *Nemean* VII (24–27), quoted in the translation by C. M. Bowra, p. 159.

45. *Nemean* VIII (22–29), quoted in a prose translation by John H. Finley, from his *Pindar and Aeschylus*, p. 98.

46. Paraphrased by Shakespeare after Lucian, see Appendix "Lucian in *Cymbeline.*"

47. Cf. *Antigone* (1030): "What use to kill the dead a second time?"

48. Cf. Cedric H. Whitman, *Homer and the Heroic Tradition* (Cambridge, Mass., Harvard University Press, 1958), pp. 179–80. Whitman writes about Odysseus' meeting with Achilles in Hades: "He [Achilles] is emphasizing the cost of his greatness, the incurable sorrow of being Achilles. He is saying, I have suffered the worst, and identified myself with it; you have merely survived. And Odysseus, for his part, says: you are very honored indeed, but you are dead; I am doing the really difficult and great thing." The meeting with Ajax has incomparably greater impact.

49. Cf. note 21. Ajax is a corpse; Agamemnon uses the word *skia*, to refer to the dead man. Ajax is already a *skia* in Hades. Doubtless for Greek audiences who knew their Homer, this was preliminary to the next scene: the meeting of Odysseus with Ajax's *skia*, as in the *Odyssey*.

50. I quote Plato in B. Jowett's translation, from *Plato* (New York, Black, 1942), edited by Louise Rope Loomis, pp. 487–88. The choice of a lion's life by Ajax in Plato's story is certainly connected with Ajax's relationship to Heracles. The scholiast on Pindar, *Isthmian V*, 53 (*Hesiod*, in Evelyn-White's translation, p. 257): "The story has been taken from the *Great Eoiae:* for there we find Heracles entertained by Telamon, standing dressed in the lion-skin and praying, and there also we find the eagle sent by Zeus, from which Aias took his name (*Aietos*)." Finley, *Pindar*, p. 103, on *Isthmian IV:* "The injured Ajax of the beginning has become the triumphant Heracles of the end . . ."

51. Of all the heroes of the Trojan War, Ajax became the most ridiculed at the time of late Renaissance. Singularly cruel treatment was accorded to him in Elizabethan England. In *Troilus and Cressida*, Ajax is just a "valiant ass," "churlish as the bear, slow as the elephant" and "a chicken-brained heap of flesh," "all beef and no brains," "all eyes and no sight." A popular pun equated the stupid athlete with a privy, A-jax became a-jakes. Even Shakespeare did not spare himself this vulgar joke: "Your lion, that holds his pollaxe sitting on a close-stool, will be given to Ajax" (*Love's Labour's Lost*, V, ii, 570). Hence, probably, the most publicized detergent in the United States has been called Ajax. Until recently the plastic container of "Ajax" recalled a knight by their shape. Ajax became a "cleaner for all purposes." Character, indeed, is destiny. In a world where everything ends on a scrap heap, the only heroic role which still remains is to be the strongest detergent.

The Veiled Alcestis

1. All quotations from *Alcestis*, unless marked otherwise, are given in the translation by Richmond Lattimore, in *The Complete Greek Tragedies, Euripides I* (Chicago, University of Chicago Press, 1955).

2. *Euripides' Alcestis*, edited with introduction and commentaries by A. M. Dale (New York, Oxford University Press, 1954).

3. John Jones, *On Aristotle and Greek Tragedy* (New York, Oxford University Press, 1962), p. 25.

4. Bernard M. W. Knox, "Euripidean Comedy," in Alan Cheuse and Richard Koffler, *The Rarer Action: Essays in Honor of Francis Fergusson* (New Brunswick, N.J., Rutgers University Press, 1971), pp. 71 ff. In this impressive and sensible study Knox analyzes *Helen, Iphigenia in Tauris* and above all *Ion* as comedies leading directly to Menander

and Plautus. It is worth comparing the dirty floor in *Alcestis* with the Euripidean Electra's dirty hair: "Look at my hair; it's dirty. Look at these rags of clothes. Are they fit for Agamemnon's royal daughter?" (184 ff., p. 71.)

5. The time and circumstances of the bargain with death have no importance for Euripides. Heracles has known of Alcestis' decision for some time. In the versions of the myth known to us (Apollodorus and others), everything happened on the wedding night. Admetus did not offer a sacrifice to Artemis; the goddess foretold a speedy death for him; Apollo obtained a bond from the Fates; and Alcestis agreed to die for her husband when the appointed time came. See D. J. Conacher, *Euripidean Drama: Myth, Theme and Structure* (Toronto, University of Toronto Press, 1967), pp. 327 ff.

6. In Jones's translation, *op. cit.*, p. 255.

7. "... a self-centred, cowardly, and short-sighted man"—Wesley D. Smith, "The Ironic Structure in Alcestis," *The Phoenix*, Vol. XIV (1960), p. 129. "Admetus, to be sure, behaves like a cad"—Thomas G. Rosenmeyer, *The Masks of Tragedy: Essays on Six Greek Dramas* (Austin, University of Texas Press, 1963), p. 238. The only modern defense of Admetus is the essay by Anne Pippin Burnett, "The Virtues of Admetus," *Classical Philology*, Vol. LX (1965), pp. 240–55.

8. In the preface to *Iphigénie*, in *Théâtre Complet de Racine* edited by Maurice Rat (Paris, Classiques Garnier, 1960), p. 477. Racine intended to write his own *Alcestis*, perhaps even began to write it and destroyed the text. It is interesting, however, that in the preface he defended Admetus against Pierre Perrault, who saw in him not only a coward, but thought that he could not wait for his wife's death. To Racine, Admetus was a tragic hero.

9. Smith, *op. cit.*, p. 130. This also contains a very interesting analysis of the betrayal theme in *Alcestis*.

10. *Ibid.*, p. 131.

11. Humphrey D. F. Kitto, *Greek Tragedy*, 3rd ed. (New York, Barnes & Noble, 1961), p. 31.

12. Rosenmeyer, *op. cit.*, p. 239.

13. Cf. Smith, *op. cit.*, p. 156: "The spectators at first are led to expect that the restoration of Alcestis is to depend on a show of virtue by Admetus. And by a fine stroke Euripides arranges that the restoration itself is the test. At the crucial moment Admetus fails the test. He reaches out blindly for the unknown woman and in the act of betraying his wife receives her back."

14. A. W. Verrall, *Euripides, the Rationalist* (Cambridge, Cambridge University Press, 1895), pp. 120 ff.

15.   William Arrowsmith, "The Comedy of T. S. Eliot," in *English Stage Comedy* (New York, 1955), p. 148 ff.

16.   Hesiod, *Catalogues*, 90, in *Hesiod, The Homeric Hymns and Homerica*, translated by Hugh G. Evelyn-White (Loeb Classical Library; Cambridge, Mass., Harvard University Press, 1967), p. 213.

17.   From *Plato* (179b ff.), translated by B. Jowett, edited by Louise Rope Loomis (New York, Black, 1942), p. 168.

18.   Apollodorus, *Bibl.* 1.9.15.

19.   Kitto, *op. cit.*, p. 328.

20.   Robert Graves, *The Greek Myths*, Vol. II (Baltimore, Penguin Books, 1955), p. 93.

21.   Gisela M. A. Richter, *The Sculpture and Sculptors of the Greeks* (New Haven, Yale University Press, 1970), p. 139.

22.   *Cyclops* (336 ff.); see Knox, "Euripidean Comedy," p. 74.

23.   *Eumenides* (723 ff.), in Richmond Lattimore's translation, *The Complete Greek Tragedies, Aeschylus I* (Chicago, University of Chicago Press, 1953).

24.   Ivan M. Linforth, *The Arts of Orpheus* (Berkeley, University of California Press, 1941, pp. 16 ff.), suggests that a version of the myth existed in which Orpheus regained Euridice. Evidence is slight and rests on a rather debatable interpretation of the famous relief in Naples representing Hermes, Euridice and Orpheus. However, Admetus' ironically treated comparison of himself to Orpheus in *Alcestis* cannot in any way be regarded as confirming this optimistic version of the myth.

25.   "People who came back from there: Alcestis and Protesilaus of Thessaly, Theseus, son of Aegeus, Odysseus." Lucian, *On Funerals*, 5.

26.   Nauck, Euripides' *Tragediae* (1902), III.

27.   *Dialogues of the Dead, Protesilaus*, XXIII, in *The Works of Lucian of Samosata*, Vol. I, translated by H. W. Fowler and F. G. Fowler (Oxford, Clarendon Press, 1905), p. 145.

28.   Kitto, *op. cit.*, p. 322.

29.   Smith, *op. cit.*, p. 140.

30.   Cf. Conacher, *op. cit.*, p. 333: "In the folk tale no one ever wins the wrestling match with Death; nor would the somewhat sentimental 'moral' ending which Plato chose have suited the sinister figure of Death in Euripides' piece." See also Albin Lesky, *Alkestis, der Mythus und das Drama:* SB Wiener Ak., ph.-hist. Kl. CCIII, 2 (Vienna, 1925).

31.   The oldest iconographic sources date from the early eleventh century. See Erwin Panofsky, *Studies in Iconology: Humanistic Themes in the Art of the Renaissance* (New York, Harper Torchbooks, 1962), pp.

77 and 115. Even as late a writer as Lessing, in *How the Ancients Represented Death* (1769), contrasted the gentle, painless and dignified death in antiquity with the images of death in the Middle Ages and the Baroque. Schiller, following Lessing, wrote in his famous poem:

> Then no grisly skeleton to the dying
> Hideously appeared. The final breath
> Was taken by a kiss from lips scarce sighing,
> A torch extinguished by the god of death.

See Eliza Marian Butler, *The Tyranny of Greece over Germany*, 2nd ed. (Boston, Beacon, 1958), p. 70. Winckelmann's vision of monumental Greece, known only from plaster casts, concealed Euripides. Everyone forgot the grotesque, blood-drinking Death in *Alcestis*.

32. "Alcestis męża od śmierci zastąpiła" (ll. 73 ff.), in Jan Kochanowski, *Dzieła Polskie*, Vol. III (Warsaw, 1953), p. 200. Unfortunately Kochanowski translated only the prologue.

33. The author wishes to express his sincere thanks to Zbigniew Raszewski for information regarding Death in religious theatre.

34. Kitto, *op. cit.*, p. 315.

35. Alexander J. Tate, *The Alcestis of Euripides* (London, 1903), p. 54.

36. "Pan Painter," pl. 5, 1, in J. D. Beazley, *Attic Black-Figure* (New York, Oxford University Press, 1928). See also commentary by A. M. Dale to l. 1118 in her edition of *Alcestis (op. cit.)*, and Euripides' *Tro.*, 564 and *Rhesus* 606. The Freudian interpretation of the "Gorgon's head" can also help in the understanding of this scene; it seems to correspond amazingly to Admetus' situation. "The terror of Medusa is thus a terror of castration that is linked to the sight of something . . . The hair upon Medusa's head is frequently represented in works of art in the form of snakes, and these once again are derived from the castration complex. It is a remarkable fact that, however frightening they may be in themselves, they nevertheless serve actually as a mitigation of the horror, for they replace the penis, the absence of which is the cause of the horror . . . The sight of Medusa's head makes the spectator stiff with terror, turns him to stone. Observe that we have here once again the same origin from the castration complex and the same transformation of affect! For becoming stiff means an erection." (*The Standard Edition of the Complete Psychological Works of Sigmund Freud*, Vol. XVIII, translated from the German under the general editorship of James Strachey, [London, Hogarth Press, 1964], p. 273.)

37. Kurt von Fritz, "The Happy Ending of *Alcestis*" in *Euripides' Alcestis: Collection of Critical Essays* (reprinted from *Antike und moderne*

Tragödie, neun Abhandlungen [Berlin, 1962], edited by John R. Wilson
(Englewood Cliffs, N.J., Prentice-Hall, 1968), p. 81. See John R. Wilson's introduction, p. 11.

38. Dale, *op. cit.,* in commentary to l. 1146: "The mute Alcestis
was of course performed by a walker-on, the original actor being now
on stage as Heracles—but the perfect propriety of the reason here
invented and the advantage drawn from this limitation in terms of
drama, poetry and good taste, need not to be laboured."

39. Pippin Burnett, *op. cit.,* p. 250.

40. *Amphitryon,* translated by Paul Roche in *Three Plays by Plautus*
(New York, New American Library, 1968). It is interesting to note
that Hegel passes on to this quotation from *Amphitryon,* having discussed *Alcestis* in *Äesthetik.*

41. See below, p. 214 (and note 39 on p. 318) and p. 218.

42. T. S. Eliot, *The Cocktail Party* (New York, Harcourt, 1950),
p. 71.

43. Northrop Frye, *A Natural Perspective: The Development of Shakespearean Comedy and Romance* (New York, Harcourt, 1965), pp. 76 f.

44. Northrop Frye, "The Argument of Comedy," in *English Institute Essays,* edited by D. A. Robertson, Jr. (New York, Columbia University Press, 1944), p. 59.

45. The author wishes to express his most sincere thanks to Mr.
Bernard M. W. Knox for having directed his attention to the possibility of linking the unveiling scene with the *anakalypteria* ceremony. The
interpretation of this scene follows almost literally Mr. Knox's letter
to the author.

46. A Freudian interpretation is also possible. *Alcestis* may be a
"dream" of Alcestis herself, where she realizes her unconscious
desires. Alcestis, unhappy in her conjugal life with Admetus, wants
his death. But her desires are suppressed. Alcestis dreams that she
has sacrificed herself for Admetus and died for him. Later she returns
from her grave in "impenetrable disguise" and marries him as a
young girl. But this marriage-betrayal is the death of Admetus. This
would be similar, dramatically and psychoanalytically, to Doña Elvira's reappearance in *Don Juan,* also veiled, as a messenger of death.
In the oldest preserved Greek dream book, written by Artemidorus
in the second century B.C., we find: "A wedding and a death have the
same meaning, for the things that go with them are the same." (I
quote Rosenmeyer, *op. cit.,* p. 246.) It is strange that Nietzsche's
interpretation, in *The Birth of Tragedy,* of the returning Alcestis as the
mask of Dionysus, also envisages her as a figure of death:

Consider Admetus as he is brooding over the memory of his recently departed wife, Alcestis, consuming himself in her spiritual contemplation, when suddenly a similarly formed, similarly walking woman's figure is led toward him, heavily veiled; let us imagine his sudden trembling unrest, his tempestuous comparisons, his instinctive convictions—and we have an analogy with what the spectator felt in his Dionysian excitement when he saw the approach on the stage of the god with whose suffering he had already identified himself. Involuntarily, he transferred the whole magic image of the god that was trembling before his soul to that masked figure and, as it were, dissolved its reality into the unreality of spirits.

(Translated by Walter Kaufmann [New York, Doubleday, 1956], p. 66).

"But Where Now Is Famous Heracles?"

I. THE FACES OF HERACLES

1. All the quotations from the *Odyssey* and the *Iliad* are from the translations by E. V. Rieu, unless otherwise noted: *The Odyssey* (Penguin Classics; Baltimore, Penguin Books, 1946); *The Iliad* (Penguin Classics, 1950).

2. Richmond Lattimore's translation, *The Odyssey of Homer* (Chicago, University of Chicago Press, 1951).

3. See Bernard M. W. Knox, *The Heroic Temper: Studies in Sophoclean Tragedy* (Berkeley, University of California Press, 1964), p. 140.

4. Richmond Lattimore's translation, *The Iliad of Homer* (Chicago, University of Chicago Press, 1951).

5. "Canals, tunnels, or natural underground conduits were often described as the work of Heracles," wrote Robert Graves, *The Greek Myths*, Vol. II (Baltimore, Penguin Books, 1955), p. 124. And in Lucian's *Philosophies Going Cheap*, the following dialogue takes place between Customer and Diogenes during the sale of philosophy by Zeus and Hermes:

Customer: And who's your favorite character?
Diogenes: Heracles.
Customer: Then why aren't you wearing a lion skin? You've got his club all right!
Diogenes: This old blanket's my lion skin. Like Heracles I belong

to the Anti-Pleasure Brigade. And I'm not a conscript either—
I'm a volunteer, cleaning things up, that's my line.
(Lucian, *Satirical Sketches*, translated by Paul Turner [Penguin Classics; Baltimore, Penguin Books, 1961], p. 151.)

6. The quotations from *Hesiod* and from *The Homeric Hymns* are
from the translation by Hugh G. Evelyn-White, *Hesiod, The Homeric Hymns and Homerica* (Loeb Classical Library; Cambridge, Mass., Harvard University Press, 1967).

7. Erwin Panofsky, *Studies in Iconology: Humanistic Themes in the Art of the Renaissance* (New York, Harper Torchbooks, 1962): ". . . while the Roman relief represents Hercules carrying the Erymanthean boar to King Euristheus, the mediaeval master, by substituting billowy drapery for the lion's skin, a dragon for the frightened king, and a stag for the boar, transformed the mythological story into an allegory of salvation" (p. 19). ". . . the type of Hercules dragging Cerberus out of Hades was used to depict Christ pulling Adam out of Limbo" (*ibid.*). See also E. Panofsky, *Hercules am Scheidewege, und andere antike Bildstoffe in der neuren Kunst* (Leipzig, 1930), as well as Jean Seznec, *The Survival of the Pagan Gods: The Mythological Tradition and its Place in Renaissance Humanism and Art* (New York, Harper, 1961), pp. 30, 118, 155, 211.

8. Eugene M. Waith, *The Herculean Hero in Marlowe, Chapman, Shakespeare and Dryden* (New York, Columbia University Press, 1962), pp. 40 ff.

9. *Ode to Youth* in the translation of E. J. Czerwinski.

10. *Problemata* (author anonymous), attributed to Aristotle in Renaissance times; quoted from Roff Soellner, *The Madness of Hercules and the Elizabethans* (Comparative Literature X, 1958), p. 312.

11. In Robert Greene's *Orlando Furioso* (1594) the hero returns to the scene shaking the leg he has torn from his victim like a club. He imagines himself to be Hercules. To quote Soellner, p. 317:

> Villaine, prouide me straight a Lion's skin
> Thou seest I now am mightie Hercules
> Look wheres my massie club upon my necke.
>
> (II,i)

12. Bottom perhaps recalls from his grammar-school reading of Plautus how in the *Bacchides* young Pistoclerus threatens his tutor— saying that he'll kill him without any ceremony.

Lydus: Does a pupil dare to menace his own teacher?
Pistoclerus: I think I'll act like Hercules. You'll be my Linus.
(From the translation by Erich Segal, *Roman Laughter: The Comedy of Plautus* [Cambridge, Mass., Harvard University Press, 1968], p. 20.)
Plautus' heroes very often swear by Hercules, especially when someone suddenly loses his reason: "And since, by Hercules, you're certainly not sane . . . (*The Brothers Menaechmus* [313], in *Plautus: Three Comedies*, translated by Erich Segal [New York, Harper, 1969], p. 313). Bottom here is certainly recalling from his schooldays that the Latin curse "by Hercules" sounds like "Hercle," thus his "Ercles."

13. Thomas Heywood in *Apology for Actors*, written supposedly around 1607–8, published 1612, quoted from Waith, *op. cit.,* p. 53.

14. Seneca, *Tragedies*, 2 vols., translated by Frank Justus Miller (Loeb Classical Library; Cambridge, Mass., Harvard University Press, 1917, 1968).

15. Seneca, *Four Tragedies, and Octavia*, translated by E. F. Watling (Baltimore, Penguin Books, 1966).

16. A. J. Festugière, *De l'Essence de la Tragédie Grecque* (Paris, Aubier-Montaigne, 1969), p. 90.

17. *Nero*, 20 and 53; Suetonius, *The Twelve Caesars*, translated by Robert Graves (Penguin Classics; Baltimore, Penguin Books, 1957, 1965), pp. 219 and 240.

18. *Dialogues of the Dead*, XVI, in *The Works of Lucian of Samosata*, Vol. I, translated by H. W. Fowler and F. G. Fowler (Oxford, Clarendon Press, 1905), p. 134.

19. From .Hippolytus' *Refutation of All Heresies*: "Finally Elohim chose a prophet from the uncircumcision, Heracles, and sent him to contend with the twelve angels of Eden and to free the (spirit of the) Father from the twelve angels of the creation. These art twelve labours of Heracles in which Heracles contended in order, from the first to the last, the lion and the hydra and the boar and the rest; for these are the names of the nations which they were given from the power of the maternal angels. As he seemed to have been victorious, Omphale (Babel-Aphrodite) attacked him and seduced him and took of his power, the commandements of Baruch which Elohim commanded, and put on him her own robe, the power of Eden, which is the power from below. Thus the prophecy of Heracles and his works became ineffectual." ("Baruch by Justin," in *Gnosticism: A Source Book of Heretical Writings from the Early Christian Period*, edited by Robert M. Grant [New York, Harper, 1961], p. 98.)

20. Northrop Frye, *Anatomy of Criticism* (Princeton, N.J., Princeton University Press, 1957), p. 207.

21. "... to assure the birth of Hercules, she [Alcmena] had to be duped. No promise of immortality or deification can tempt Alcmena." From Laurent Le Sage, *Jean Giraudoux, His Life and Works* (University Park, Pa., Pennsylvania State University Press, 1959), p. 69.

22. In *The Brothers Menaechmus*, the twin from Epidamnus cites the example of Hercules when he steals his wife's dress in order to offer it to a courtesan: "What risks I ran in stealing this! Hercules in labor number nine was not as brave as I, when he stole the girdle from that Amazon Hippolyta" (199 ff.). *Plautus: Three Comedies*, translated by E. Segal, *op. cit.*

23. See Euripides: "O, young girl, given birth by Ether, whom mankind call Zeus" (Nauck, fragment 869).

24. Friedrich Nietzsche, *The Birth of Tragedy*, translated by Walter Kaufmann (New York, Random House, 1967), p. 75.

25. The metaphysical failure of the mythical Heracles occurs very clearly in Hegel's interpretation. See Hegel, *Vorlesungen über die Ästhetik*, edited by Fr. Bassenge (Aufbau-Verlag, 1955), III, 1, 744.

II. BLACK SOPHOCLES, OR THE CIRCULATION OF POISONS

1. *The Complete Plays of Sophocles*, translated by Sir Richard Claverhouse Jebb, edited by Moses Hadas (New York, Bantam Books, 1967).

2. All the quotations from *The Women of Trachis*, unless otherwise noted, are from the translation by Michael Jameson, in *The Complete Greek Tragedies, Sophocles II* (Chicago, University of Chicago Press, 1957).

3. Lucian apparently recalled Heracles' service and captivity. When Heracles wants to obtain a more honored place at the table of the gods, Asclepius answers him gruffly: "Anyhow, it would be enough to mention that I was never a slave like you, never combed wool in Lydia, masquerading in a purple shawl and being slippered by an Omphale, never killed my wife and children in a fit of spleen" (*The Works of Lucian: XIII, Dialogues of the Gods*).

4. Heracles' "I am nothing, nothing that can even crawl" is worth comparing with Macbeth's ". . . And nothing is but what is not" (I, iii, 141).

5. From Emily Townsend Vermeule's translation of *Electra* in *Euripides V, The Complete Greek Tragedies* (Chicago, University of Chicago Press, 1959).

6. Gilbert Murray, *Greek Studies* (Oxford, Clarendon Press, 1946), p. 126.

7. Racine wrote his comments in the Latin translation of Sophocles by the German philologist, Joachim Camerarius. Paul Estienne, in the commentary of his edition of Sophocles (1803), edited Racine's notations. The copy of Camerarius, which belonged to Racine, is now in the collection of the Toulouse Library. Cf. Racine, *Théâtre Complet*, edited by Maurice Rat (Paris, Classiques Garnier, 1960), p. 723.

8. Lucian in *Saltatio* (50) mentions among the dances in Aetolia, which certainly must have been a type of pantomime, "the wrestling match between Heracles and the river Achelous." (Loeb Classical Library; Cambridge, Mass., Harvard University Press, 1936.)

9. This was a stony brook, Evenus, flowing from the west wall of Zeus' Mount Oeta, which suddenly rose. The name of the centaur Nessus means "the roar of the angry torrent." (Jebb, *The Trachiniae* [Cambridge, 1892], commentary to line 557.)

10. Cf. Herbert Musurillo, *The Light and the Darkness: Studies in the Dramatic Poetry of Sophocles* (Leiden, Brill, 1967): "As the sun grows warm in the sky, the tuft disintegrates into a kind of powdery dust; but then, as it disappears, from the bare earth spurt up the foamy, blood-like clots which so terrify Deianeira (701 ff.). In Aeschylus (*Choëphori*, 66–70), blood on the ground that cannot be absorbed stands for a deed of blood that has not been avenged. Here the flecks of blood oozing from the earth stand for the unavenged death of the treacherous Nessus; they are a pledge of the oracle that Heracles once received from Zeus, that a power would emerge from Hades to destroy him. And so the bubbling blood becomes an oracular portent for Deianeira, even though she cannot understand its full significance" (p. 72).

11. Roman Jakobson (with Morris Halle), *Fundamentals of Language* (The Hague, Mouton, 1956). Especially the chapter "Two Aspects of Language."

12. From Musurillo's translation, *op. cit.* This line seems almost untranslatable. Jebb rendered it: "Thence may he come, full of desire, steeped in love by the specious device of the robe, on which Persuasion has spread her sovereign charm."

13. In the translation by Wesley Goddard, *Phaedra* (San Francisco, Chandler, 1961), p. 11.

> I saw again the enemy I had banished.
> My wound, still too fresh, bled again.
> It is no longer an ardor hidden in my veins;
> It is Venus clutching tight her prey.

14. Georges Méautis, in *Sophocle: Essai sur le héros tragique* (Paris, Albin Michel, 1957), was the first to recall these famous lines in his chapter on *The Trachinae* (p. 283). Racine's Venus *"toute entière a sa proie attachée"* is almost a literal transcription of Euripides' image: ". . . the Hydra, horrible and monstrous, has soaked in" (836).

In Racine's *Phèdre* one can come across scores of lines astonishingly close to *The Women of Trachis*. But the dependence is not only on the level of the text itself. It seems that in its "deep structure" *Phèdre* is closer to *The Women of Trachis* than to *Hippolytus* of Euripides. At the beginning of the first *stasimon* the Chorus speaks of the Sun-god. Heracles, theologically and structurally, is "torn" between the Hydra and Zeus, the sky and the Chthonic power, as Racine's Phèdre, *"la fille de Minos et de Pasiphaé,"* is divided between dark Venus and Sun-god. This correspondence seems not to have been noticed; the similarity in the structure of *The Women of Trachis* and *Phaedra* still awaits its own Barthes for further investigation.

15. Albert Camus, *The Myth of Sisyphus*, translated by Justin O'Brien (New York, Knopf, 1955), p. 95.

16. The predictions in *Macbeth*, that Macbeth will not die by the hand of a man born of woman, and that he shall rule "till Birnam wood do come to Dunsinane" (V, v, 44–45) comes true, but with a change of mood, from "supernatural" to "realistic." The world returned to its natural and legal order. An heir of the murdered ruler becomes anew the lord anointed: "Whom we invite to see us crown'd at Scone" (V, viii, 75).

17. Ezra Pound, *Women of Trachis* (New York, New Directions, 1957). In the commentary to this line Pound writes: "This is the key phrase, for which the play exists" (p. 50). Sophocles' *"tauta oun epeide lampra sumbanei,* Jameson translates literally: "since all this is coming true so clearly." Pound's version of *Women of Trachis* at times seems in its tone to come nearer to Wagner than Sophocles. But Pound has translated many passages with brilliant intuition, and Sophocles rings out in English like great poetry. For example, the following almost untranslatable line (1259 ff.): "And put some cement in your face, reinforced concrete . . ." (p. 54).

18. Gerhard Nebel in *Weltangst und Götterzorn*. Quoted from Jean-Marie Domenach, *Le Retour du tragique* (Paris, Seuil, 1967).

19. *The Portable Nietzsche*, selected and translated by Walter Kaufmann (New York, Viking, 1954), p. 299.

20. See Walter Kaufmann, *Tragedy and Philosophy* (New York, Doubleday, 1968), p. 226.

21. *The Odes of Pindar,* translated by C. M. Bowra (Penguin Classics; Baltimore, Penguin Books, 1969).

22. Heracles cries like a girl: "Pity me, for I seem pitiful to many others, crying and sobbing like a girl!" (1070 ff.). But Iole never cries. Deianira is also harder than Heracles. Cf. Leo Aylen, *Greek Tragedy and the Modern World* (London, Methuen, and New York, Barnes & Noble, 1964), p. 90: "Deianira and Heracles are the same actor. Feminine foolishness and masculine arrogance come to the same thing. Brutal man is loved, and loved for his brutality, by good hearted woman. That is the way things are. But Deianira faces adversity with silent courage, Heracles with womanly tears. This again is a paradox that speaks to us, though we cannot paraphrase what it says."

23. At least three times in the extant tragedies this special relation between two characters performed by the same actor seems worthy of consideration: Deianira-Heracles, Antigone-Teiresias, and Pentheus-Agave. On the same mask, which two different actors put on, see "The Veiled Alcestis" (p. 103 and note).

24. Cf. John Jones, *On Aristotle and Greek Tragedy* (New York, Oxford University Press, 1962), p. 175: "Sophocles' unforced catching up of the human here-and-now into the Bear's tune separates this from the familiar stellar image of transcendence . . . while we distinguish the turning Bear from the late classical Wheel of Fortune by the latter essential triviality (the wheel is a mere diagram of the prosperity-adversity rhythm observed in human affairs), and by the fact that the wheel's movement is on a perpendicular axis: prosperity at the top is antithetically opposed to adversity at the bottom—hence the wheel's long and close association with the Fall of Princes tradition in tragic theory and practice. The Bear, by contrast, is a deep-toned reality, up there for all to see, a living power as were all stars to the Greeks, active in bringing the seasons and not merely coming and going with them . . ."

25. The Hydra was a water dragon like the Biblical leviathan: "Can you draw out Leviathan with a fishhook, or press down his tongue with a cord? Can you put a rope in his nose, or pierce his jaw with a hook?" (Job, 41, 1-2). The Lernean Hydra was a fresh-water monster. She lived near Lerna, not far from Argos, where wide marshes spilled forth. She had hundreds of heads: "He seared each deadly hydra-head of Lerna's thousand-headed hound" (Euripides' *Heracles* (420 ff.); in William Arrowsmith's translation, *The Complete Greek Tragedies, Euripides I* (Chicago, University of Chicago Press, 1956).

26. *Thus Spoke Zarathustra* in *The Portable Nietzsche,* selected by Walter Kaufmann, *op. cit.,* p. 278.

27. Who speaks the last anapest (1275–78) has long been an object of debate among the editors of *The Women of Trachis.* See Jebb's commentary to these lines, and most recently, Musurillo's (p. 79). The logic of the drama and the endings in other Sophoclean tragedies demand that these lines be given to Coryphaeus. They sound amazingly like the last message of Horatio:

> So shall you hear
> Of carnal, bloody, and unnatural acts;
> Of accidental judgments, casual slaughters;
> Of deaths put on by cunning and forc'd cause . . .

(Hamlet, V, ii, 372–75)

What is also controversial is to whom the last words are directed. To the women of the Chorus? Or to Iole? The silent Iole is the most tragic figure in the play, and the coda of the drama is her presence in the funeral procession.

28. In Seneca's *Hercules Oetaeus,* Iole is not a mute part; she speaks, but the tension is immediately destroyed and everything becomes suddenly flat.

29. *Arthur Rimbaud, Complete Works with Selected Letters,* translated by Wallace Fowlie (Phoenix Books; Chicago, University of Chicago Press, 1966), p. 121.

III. "OH TO BE A STONE!"

1. All quotations from *Heracles,* unless otherwise noted, are from the translation by William Arrowsmith, *The Complete Greek Tragedies, Euripides II,* (Chicago, University of Chicago Press, 1956).

2. Murray, *Greek Studies,* p. 112: "I do not mean that I consider the *Heracles* of Euripides to be a very great work of art. I do not. It is broken-backed; it has too much conventional rhetoric; but for sheer loftiness of tragic tone the last act, after Heracles awakes . . . , will stand beside anything in ancient drama." H. D. F. Kitto, *Greek Tragedy* (New York, Barnes & Noble, 1961), p. 237: "There is no question that this is the most powerful thing of the kind that Euripides ever wrote, and that the last part of the play is, in a very different way, equally impressive; but what is the meaning of the play as a whole? Is it a whole? . . . [I]t is not a dramatic unity. Between the peril of Heracles' dependants . . . and the madness . . . there is no connection but juxtaposition, and the last scene . . . has no strict casual connection with the previous one." Only Arrowsmith in his marvelous introduc-

tion, which is a first attempt at interpreting *Heracles* as a unity of dramatic construction and design, shows the sense of breaking the play into two different stylistic parts: "Throughout the tragedy, gathering momentum by contrast, runs the rhythm of its minor terms: first despair, then hope, then again despair, and finally an endurance deeper than either; age and youth, weakness and strength, both pairs resolved in the condition that makes them one. Schematic, brilliant, savagely broken, the *Heracles* is a play of great power and . . . the most structural tour-de-force in Greek tragedy" (p. 45). About the first part, however, he writes: ". . . convention is everywhere visible. Character is essentially static, the action as a whole leached of any really tragic movement. All the emotional steps of a melodramatic situation have been pulled . . . If the action is not quite trite, it is at least customary and predictable, so predictable in fact that it might be regarded as a parody of a standard tragic movement" (p. 48).

3. Leon Parmentier dates *Heracles* from 424 B.C.; Arrowsmith sets it later, about 418.

4. *The Complete Writings of Thucydides: The Peloponnesian War,* in the unabridged Crawley translation (Modern Library; New York, Random House, 1951), pp. 188–89.

5. See Leo Aylen, *Greek Tragedy and the Modern World,* p. 128: "It is not one of Euripides' greatest lyrics, but I suspect that it did not need to be. It was presumably a great display of mime. This would have balanced the play where modern critics feel that is lacking, and made us realize that is a story of a great man. Reading the ode in the text, we tend to get the balance wrong."

6. About Prometheus and Oedipus as symbols of tragic "human things," see Maria Janion, "Edyp i Prometeusz" *Dialog,* Warsaw, No. 8 (1971), pp. 94–109.

7. Cf. Plato in *Timaeus* (29 E,1): "God is goodness. And thus in this which is goodness, never, for no reason, can jealousy arise."

8. Cf. Euripides' *Melanippus,* "Zeus. Who is Zeus? I know him only from rumors" (Nauck, fragment 483).

9. Nietzsche, *The Birth of Tragedy* (Kaufmann's translation), p. 69: ". . . that horrible triad of Oedipus' destinies: the same man who solves the riddle of nature—that Sphinx of two species—also must break the most sacred natural orders by murdering his father and marrying his mother."

10. This visionary line on Oedipus from Hölderlin's poem "In Lovely Blueness" was quoted and discussed by Heidegger in his *Introduction to Metaphysics.* André Green took the title for his psychoanalytical study of the Oedipus complex in Greek tragedy from

Hölderlin and called it *Un Oeil en trop* (Paris, Editions de Minuit, 1969).

11. In *Oedipus at Colonus* he says: "The bloody deaths, the incest, the calamities you speak so glibly of: I suffered them, by fate, against my will! It was God's pleasure . . ." (962 ff.). And once again: ". . . that was the sort of danger I was in, forced into it by the gods" (998). Robert Fitzgerald's translation in *Sophocles I, The Complete Greek Tragedies* (Chicago, University of Chicago Press, 1954).

12. Camus, *op. cit.*, p. 90.

13. Gilbert Murray's translation from his *Euripides and His Age* (New York, Oxford University Press, 1965), p. 49.

14. In Arrowsmith's introduction: ". . . the courage with which the hero meets his fate and asserts a moral order beyond his own experience is just as tragic and just as significant as that of Oedipus" (p. 57).

15. In *Hippolytus*, Artemis says to the dying Hippolytus: "Heavenly law forbids my tears" (1396).

16. See lines 2, 148 ff., 344 ff., 353 ff., 696, 798 ff.

17. Green, *op. cit.*, p. 228: *"Car le mythe d'Oedipe est le mythe exemplaire, puisqu'il est celui qui lie la question du 'qui suis-je?' avec celle du 'De qui le fils? De qui le père?'"*

IV. "PHILOCTETES," OR THE REFUSAL

1. All quotations from *Philoctetes*, unless otherwise noted, are from the translation by David Grene, in *Sophocles II, The Complete Greek Tragedies* (Chicago, University of Chicago Press, 1957).

2. Herman Melville, *Moby Dick*.

3. See R. C. Jebb, *The Philoctetes*, 3rd ed. (Amsterdam, 1966), commentaries to lines 2, 302, 800, 1000, 1455.

4. See Aeschylus, *Agamemnon*, 283.

5. Cicero (*Tusc.* 2.10.23): *"Quomodo fert apud eum Prometheus dolorem, quem excipit ob furtum Lemnium?"* See Carl Kerényi, *Prometheus*, (New York, Pantheon, 1963) p. 80.

6. See Knox, *Heroic Templer*, p. 145.

7. See Jebb, *op. cit.*, p. xxxviii ff. Just exactly what kind of cult existed on Chryse, and who Chryse was, for whom the island was named, is open to question. It is very tempting to speculate. Perhaps Chryse was a daughter of Pallas Athene who gave birth to Phlegyas and Ixion by the god of war, Ares. Phlegyas's daughter, Coronis, gave birth to Asclepius by Apollo. From the union of Ixion and the clouds changed into the shape of Hera, according to one of the mythological versions, Chiron the centaur was born. Philoctetes, whose incurable wound mythically relates to Chiron, is healed by Asclepius or by his

sons, a surgeon and physician serving in the Greek army at Troy. In this mythical infrastructure Neoptolemus too has his place: he is an anti-Apollonian figure like Phlegyas. After all, both set fire to Apollo's temple.

8.   See Claude Lévi-Strauss, *Structural Anthropology* (New York, Basic Books, 1963), pp. 210 ff.

9.   Graves, *The Greek Myths*, Vol. II, p. 293. The archetypal place of these wounds in the leg is interesting. In *The White Goddess*, rev. ed. (New York, Farrar, Straus, 1966), Graves writes: "In precisely what part of the heel or foot were Talus, Bran, Achilles, Mopsus, Cheiron, and the rest mortally wounded? The myths of Achilles and Llew Llaw give the clue. When Thetis picked up the child Achilles by the foot and plunged him into the cauldron of immortality, the part covered by finger and thumb remained dry and therefore vulnerable. This was presumably the spot between the Achilles tendon and the ankle-bone where, as I point out in my *King Jesus*, the nail was driven in to pin the foot of the crucified man to the side of the cross, in the Roman ritual borrowed from Canaanite Carthaginians; for the victim of crucifixion was originally the annual sacred king" (pp. 317 ff.).

10.   Kerényi, *Prometheus*, p. 122. It is astonishing that Kerényi, who gave so much attention to the wounded gods and the incurable wound of Chiron, did not point out his similarity to Philoctetes.

11.   Carl Kerényi, *Asklepios*, (New York, Pantheon, 1959) p. 98.

12.   André Gide was perhaps the first for whom the stinking wound of Philoctetes was the key to the understanding of the tragedy. His adaptation of *Philoctetes*, (Paris, 1947) published first in 1898 in *Revue Blanche*, was given the subtitle *"Traité de l'immonde blessure"* (Treatise on the Impure Wound). Philoctetes' wound, which cut him off from people, transformed him into an artist. On the deserted island the moans of Philoctetes became songs. *"Mais depuis que je ne m'en sers plus pour manifester ma souffrance, ma plainte est devenue très belle, a ce point que j'en suis consolé!"* (But since I stopped using it to manifest my suffering, my plaint has become very beautiful, to the point that I am consoled by it!)—p. 159. This modernistic Philoctetes from the end of the nineteenth century is a disinterested poet who found beauty, wisdom and finally his inner self in the desert: *"Je m'exprime mieux depuis que je ne parle aux hommes. Mon occupation, entre la chasse et le sommeil, est la pensée."* (I express myself better since I stopped talking to men. My occupation, between the hunt and sleep, is thought)—p. 160. Gide's Philoctetes voluntarily gives up the bow and remains alone on his glacial island. Gide's drama became the starting point for a brilliant essay on Philoctetes by Edmund Wilson in *The Wound*

and the Bow (New York, Oxford University Press, 1965). "With Gide we come close to a further implication, which even Gide does not fully develop but which must occur to the modern reader: the idea that genius and disease, like strength and mutilation, may be inextricably bound up together" (p. 237). Wilson's discussion of disease giving moral strength and of Sophocles' interest in psychological derangements ("a clinical Sophocles") is interesting, but what apparently escapes him is the fact that Philoctetes' wound is mythical.

13. Cf. Bernard M. W. Knox, "Euripidean Comedy," in *The Rarer Action* (New Brunswick, Rutgers University Press, 1971), p. 75.

14. Nadezhda Mandelstam writes in her memoir: "All of us were seized by the feeling that there was no turning back—a feeling dictated by our experience of the past, our forebodings about the future and our hypnotic trance in the present. I maintain that all of us—particularly if we lived in the cities—were in a state close to a hypnotic trance. We had really been persuaded that we had entered a new era, and that we had no choice but to submit to historical inevitability, which in any case was only another name for the dreams of all those who ever fought for human happiness. Propaganda for historical determinism had deprived us of our will and the power to make our own judgements . . ." (*Hope Against Hope*, translated by Max Hayward [New York, Atheneum, 1970], p. 44).

15. Thucydides (Crawley's translation), *op. cit.*, pp. 333–34.

16. Cf. Knox, *Heroic Temper*, pp. 138–39: "Philoctetes has won. The heroic will here wins a victory which outshines any that we have seen in the other plays. One man's stubbornness had defeated not only the whole Greek army but also the prophecy of Helenos and the will of Zeus, which is the pattern of history. It is an extraordinary moment in the theater of Dionysus, and we know, from the descriptions we have of the *Philoctetes* plays of Aeschylus and Euripides, that for the audience it must have been utterly unexpected. It is a theatrical *tour de force,* and we no sooner experience the shock of it than we realize that the play cannot end this way. For Philoctetes' victory is a terrible defeat. He will go home, a prey still to the monstrous pain of his sickness, to rot in idleness in Oeta as he did on Lemnos. And we know too that Troy did fall, and to Troy he must somehow go." In his commentary, Knox quotes from Kitto's *Form and Meaning in Drama* (New York, Barnes & Noble, 1957): "This is an occasion in which history is not so philosophic as poetry; Troy did fall." It is astonishing that almost all the critics consider that this moment when history is suspended precedes a happy ending brought about by Heracles' intervention. For example, Wilson *(op. cit.)* writes: "Instead

of winning over the outlaw, Neoptolemus has outlawed himself as well, at a time when both the boy and the cripple are desperately needed by the Greeks. Yet in taking the risk to his cause which is involved in the recognition of his common humanity with the sick man, in refusing to break his word, he dissolves Philoctetes' stubbornness, and thus cures him and sets him free, and saves the campaign as well" (p. 241). Even Knox, who characterizes Sophocles' tragic heroes as "recalcitrant" and "uncooperative" men who are forced to choose between "defiance and loss of identity" and who remain stubbornly unyielding to the end, writes: "It is a tragedy which, no matter how dramatic and painful its episodes, is bound to have a happy ending. . . . In true tragedy there can be no success, and we do not really want it; we are watching the fatal career of a hero whose obstinacy dooms him to defeat, but whom we do not wish to see surrender. As we watch Antigone, Ajax, or Oedipus, our deepest emotions make us hope that the compromise offered the hero *will* fail; in the *Philoctetes* we know that somehow they must and will succeed" (p. 118). Only William W. Flint, Jr. (*The Use of Myth to Create Suspense in Extant Greek Tragedy* [New York, Haskell, 1966], p. 16) calls Philoctetes' return to his homeland with Neoptolemus "the only human solution of the play," and Frye (*Anatomy of Criticism*, p. 207) feels that *Philoctetes* ends "in an ambiguous mood that is hard to define."

17. See Knox, *Heroic Temper*, pp. 121–22, and "Ajax Thrice Deceived," note 43.

18. Kitto, *Greek Tragedy*, p. 299. Also characteristic of his pious reading of Sophocles is this judgment on Philoctetes in *Form and Meaning in Drama*, p. 135: "The idea that Philoctetes is opposing the Will of the Gods creates in any case severe inconveniences. One is that Philoctetes is a character so entirely sympathetic that we do not easily see him in the guise of an obstructor of the gods who needs a lesson in modesty."

19. *The Little Iliad*, quoted by Tzetzes: *On Lycophron* 1268: "Then the bright son of bold Achilles led the wife of Hector to the hollow ships; but her son he snatched from the bosom of his rich-haired nurse and seized him by the foot and cast him from a tower" (in *Hesiod*, Evelyn-White's translation, p. 519).

20. William Arrowsmith's translation of *Hecuba*, in *Euripides III, The Complete Greek Tragedies* (Chicago, University of Chicago Press, 1958).

21. *The Aeneid of Virgil*, translated by C. Day Lewis (London, Hogarth Press, 1961), pp. 46 and 62.

22. Cf. Euripides' *Orestes:* "Neoptolemus hopes to make her

[Hermione] his wife, but never shall, for he is doomed to die when he comes to Delphi seeking justice for his father's death" (1655 ff., Arrowsmith's translation in *Euripides IV, The Complete Greek Tragedies* (Chicago, Chicago University Press, 1958).

23. Knox, *Heroic Temper*, p. 133.

24. *Ibid.*, p. 140; see also "The Faces of Heracles" (above), note 3.

25. Thucydides (Crawley's translation), *op. cit.*, p. 453.

26. See Jane Harrison, *Prologomena in the Study of Greek Religion* (Cambridge, 1922), p. 345, and William Scott Ferguson, "The Attic Orgeones" *Harvard Theological Review*, Vol. XXXVII, No. 2 (1944), p. 90: "Sophocles . . . whose interest in Asklepios was well known—he composed a paean in his honor . . . stepped into the breach and 'received' the snake in his own house . . . It is a precious detail to find the idol of the Athenians, then a genial, serene, dignified graybeard, conversant with, but untroubled by, the moral and religious contradictions of his great age, doling out eggs to a sacred snake and sacrificing cocks to Asklepios on a domestic altar." The sacred snake of Asclepius was, however, it seems, fed primarily mice. See also Kerényi, *Asklepios*, pp. 102 ff.: "Actually Vollgraff's finds show us how the mice were delivered to the snakes that were to devour them. One example makes it clear that the mouse could also be fastened by the tail."

27. Knox, *Heroic Temper*, p. 141.

28. *Ibid.*, p. 142.

29. Cf. Lucian: "The Celts call Heracles Ogmios in their native tongue, and they portray the god in a very peculiar way. To their notion, he is extremely old, bald-headed, except for a few lingering hairs which are quite gray, his skin is wrinkled, and he is burned as black as can be, like an old seadog" (*Heracles: An Introduction*, in *The Works of Lucian*, Vol. I, p. 63).

The Eating of the Gods, or *The Bacchae*

1. All quotations from *The Bacchae*, unless otherwise indicated, are given in the translation by William Arrowsmith from *The Complete Greek Tragedies, Euripides V* (Chicago, University of Chicago Press, 1959).

2. E. R. Dodds, in the introduction to the edition of *The Bacchae* (Oxford, Clarendon Press, 1944; 2nd ed., 1957), which became a milestone in the new understanding of Euripides, was the first to demonstrate decisively the importance of the Dionysian myth, par-

ticularly of the *sparagmos* and the *omophagia*, for the interpretation of *The Bacchae* and the bacchants' place in Greek culture. However, for all his sensitivity, intellectual insight, knowledge of Freudianism and new anthropology, Dodds remained a positivist to the end. *The Bacchae* was to him a historical and sociological representation of genuine ritual and mass psychosis. Because the Chorus in *The Bacchae* talks about the festival which takes place "each second year," and there is evidence that Dionysian festivals of an orgiastic nature took place every two years in midwinter, Dodds assumes that the rite in the tragedy is a winter one and therefore distinct from the fertility rites of the dying and reviving god which used to take place in the spring ("Maenadism" in his *The Greeks and the Irrational* [Berkeley, University of California Press, 1951], pp. 272–79). In spite of his impressive use of all available material, Dodds's thesis does not seem convincing. The Dionysian rite in *The Bacchae* is shown syncretically and is subject to the rigors of artistic construction. In Greek tragedy there are no seasons; time is syncretic too. *"The Bacchae,"* Arrowsmith writes in the introduction to his translation (p. 143), "is neither a study of Dionysiac *cultus* nor a cautionary essay on the effects of religious hysteria; nor, for that matter, however faithfully it may present the *hieros logos* or sacred myth of Dionysiac ritual, is it best read as an anthropological passion-play of the mystical scapegoat or the Year-Daimon."

3. As translated by Geoffrey S. Kirk, *The Bacchae* (Englewood Cliffs, N.J., Prentice-Hall, 1970).

4. This is one of the key lines for the interpretation of the tragedy. Kenneth Cavander translates it in a most brutal manner: "Come with me now . . . to the meal . . ." (unpublished manuscript). *The Bacchae* was produced in Cavander's translation at the Yale Repertory Theatre in 1969.

5. Kirk, *op. cit.*, in the introduction to his translation, points to the reversal of roles and situations: "Pentheus' temporal authority is progressively revealed as impotence in relation to the unfolding power of the god; and since king and god are in direct conflict it follows that the victim will become the aggressor, the hunted the hunter and vice versa." But although Kirk stresses the fact that both protagonists are contemporaries and cousins, and demonstrates with great precision the transformation of the hunter into the hunted, he is quick to withdraw from attributing any essential meaning to these. "Let us take note of these correspondences, but not exaggerate their significance. They do not of themselves imply that Pentheus was an aspect or perverted double of the god . . ." And a few lines further

on: "There is great subtlety and complexity, as well as great irony, in Euripides' description of the two opponents and their relationship: but although Pentheus may be thought of as dedicated to Dionysus as his victim by being dressed in the ritual apparel of Dionysus' worshippers, *there is little real evidence that he is a kind of aberrant incarnation of the power and personality* of the god himself" (my italics; pp. 14–15).

6. Pentheus, observes Arrowsmith *(op. cit.)*, is beardless at the time of his death, so he cannot be more than sixteen or seventeen (Introduction, p. 147).

7. Basic sources for the story of Lycurgus are Homer, *Iliad*, VI, 130 ff., [Apollodorus] 3, 5, 7; for the three daughters of Minyas in Orchomenus: Plutarch, *Quaestiones Graecae*, 38; for the frenzy of the women in Argos [Apollodorus] 2, 2, 2. See Dodds, *The Bacchae*, Introduction, p. xxiii, and Robert Graves, *Greek Myths*, Vol. I (Baltimore, Penguin Books, 1955), pp. 105 ff. Cf. J. G. Frazer, *The New Golden Bough*, edited by Theodore G. Gaster (New York, Mentor Books, 1964), p. 298: "The suspicion that this barbarous custom by no means fell into disuse even in later days is strengthened by a case of human sacrifice which occurred in Plutarch's time at Orchomenus, a very ancient city of Boeotia, distant only a few miles across the plain from the historian's birthplace. . . . Every year at the festival of the Agrigonia, the priest of Dionysus pursued these women with a drawn sword, and if he overtook one of them he had a right to slay her. In Plutarch's lifetime the right was actually exercised by a priest, Zoilus. Now, the family thus liable to furnish at least one human victim every year was of royal descent, for they traced their lineage to Minyas, the famous old king of Orchomenus . . . Tradition ran that the king's three daughters long despised the other women of the country for yielding to the Bacchic frenzy and sat at home in the king's house scornfully plying the distaff and the loom, while the rest, wreathed with flowers, their dishevelled locks streaming to the wind, roamed in ecstasy the barren mountains that rise above Orchomenus, making the solitude of the hills to echo to the wild music of cymbals and tambourines. But in time the divine fury infected even the royal damsels in their quiet chamber; they were seized with a fierce longing to partake of human flesh, and cast lots among themselves which should give up her child to furnish a cannibal feast."

8. Dodds seems to have been the first to question the so-called resistance theory which saw in those accounts a reflection of the historic invasion of Greece by the Dionysian cult. He writes: ". . . always it is the king's daughters who go mad; always there are

three of them . . . regularly they murder their children, or the child of one of them . . ." (Introduction, p. xxiv).

9. Kirk, *op. cit.*, p. 54, commentary to 1. 340.

10. Graves, *op. cit.*, Vol. I, p. 85, compares the Artemis of this myth to the Cretan "Lady of the Wild Things," whose cult was orgiastic. But he must be mistaken when he writes: "The Nymph properly took her bath after, not before, the murder." One should rather trust the myth. The ritual bath was a purification of the priestess *before* the sacrificial ceremony. Euripides' bacchants begin the sacred rites with "reverent purifications" (77). In the *Odyssey* (III, 439 ff.), ". . . Aretus came out from the store-room, carrying in his right hand a flowered bowl of lustral water, and in the other a basket with the barley corns . . . The old charioteer Nestor now started the ritual with the lustral water and the scattered grain, and offered up his earnest prayers to Athene as he began the sacrifice by throwing a lock from the victim's head on the fire." In Euripides' *Electra* the Messenger tells about the sacrifice offered by Aegisthus. He was a murderer and an adulterer, but he offered his sacrifices in a ritual manner: first he washed his hands in spring water, then he slaughtered a bull (800 ff.). In *Iphigenia in Aulis*, Achilles, who ultimately came to believe in the necessity of Iphigenia's murder, grasped the prepared bowl of spring water and rushed around the altar with it, sprinkling the warriors (1568 ff.).

11. Proclus, *Commentary on Plato's Politics*, quoted from Graves, *op. cit.*, Vol. I, p. 114.

12. The symbol of a saved head in the Orpheus and Dionysus myths merits a closer examination. The head of Orpheus, hurled by the Maenads into a river, did not sink but continued to sing until it drifted to the sea and waves took it to Lesbos, along with his lyre: ". . . his talking head voyaged on the lyre" (Lucian, *The Dance*, 51). According to another record, the head of Orpheus was deposited in the temple of Dionysus at Antyssa, where it talked day and night, forecasting the future, until Apollo silenced it, angered by the competition to other oracles. The lyre, through the intercession of the Muses, was later placed in the sky as a constellation by Apollo. The opposition of Dionysian head and Apolline lyre seems a very late interpretation.

For Graves, this myth tells of the sacral murder of a king. "A sacred king necessarily suffered dismemberment, and the Thracians may well have had the same custom as the Iban Dayaks of modern Sarawak. When the men come home from a successful head-hunting expedition the Iban women use the trophy as a means of fertilizing the rice crop by invocation. The head is made to sing, mourn, and answer questions, and nursed tenderly in every lap until it finally consents to enter an oracular shrine, where it gives advice on all important occasions . . ."(*ibid.*, p. 115).

The "severed head" belongs, it seems, to two different rites: to ensure harvest and fertility, and to forecast the future. C. G. Jung writes in "Transformation Symbolism in the Mass" (*Psyche and Symbol,* edited by Violet S. de Laszlo [Garden City, N.Y., Doubleday, 1958]): "Skull worship is widespread among primitives. In Melanesia and Polynesia it is chiefly the skulls of the ancestors that are worshipped, because they establish connections with the spirits or serve as tutelary deities, like the head of Osiris in Egypt. Skulls also play a considerable role as sacred relics. . . . Equally, the head or its parts (brain, etc.) can act as magical food or as a means for increasing the fertility of the land" (p. 193). Jung should have recalled the myth of Osiris, whom Greeks often identified with Dionysus and who also rose from the dead, having been torn to pieces. Like Dionysus, Osiris, the god of harvest and fertility, is connected with wine, trees and water (Nile floods).

Also interesting is the presence of the severed-head symbol in Jewish tradition. Jung quotes the twelfth-century legend, published by Bin Gorion in *Die Sagen der Juden:* "The teraphim were idols, and they were made in the following way. The head of a man, who had to be a first-born, was cut off and the hair plucked out. The head was then sprinkled with salt and anointed with oil. Afterwards a little plaque, of copper or gold, was inscribed with the name of an idol and placed under the tongue of the decapitated head. The head was set up in a room, candles were lit before it, and the people made obeisance. And if any man fell down before it, the head began to speak, and answered all questions that were addressed to it" (p. 190).

In this wide anthropological perspective, the severed head of St. John the Baptist suddenly resembles the head of Orpheus. They were both prophets and "doubles" of a god-man.

One other, modern interpretation of the severed head merits attention. "Onians [*The Origins of European Thought*, (New York, Cambridge University Press, 1951)], writes Jung, "rightly emphasises the fact that the psyche, whose seat was in the head, corresponds to the modern 'unconscious,' and that at that stage of development consciousness was identified with *thumos* (heart) and *phrenes* (lungs), and was localised in the chest or heart region. Hence Pindar's expression for the soul—*eiōnos eidōlon* (image of Aion)—is extraordinarily apt, for the collective unconscious not only imparts 'oracles' but forever represents the microcosm (i.e., the form of a physical man mirroring the Cosmos)" (p. 193). We are now back with the symbol of the cosmos, which perishes and dissolves in order to regenerate itself once more.

13. The basic sources for Dionysus-Zagreus *sparagmos* are Diodorus i, 96; Firmicus Maternus, *De err. prof. rel.* 6; Clemens Alexandrinus *Protrepticus*, ii, 18. A review and critical commentary of all accounts of the myth: Ivan M. Linforth, *The Arts of Orpheus* (Berkeley, University of California Press, 1941), particularly the chapter "Myth of the Dismemberment of Dionysus," pp. 307 ff.

14. *De E Delphico* 9, 388 E. I quote Linforth, pp. 317–8. E. Rohde, in *Psyche*, (Leipzig, 1898) takes the view that it was a myth about the unity and multigeneity of the cosmos (Vol. II, p. 119).

15. Frazer, *op. cit.*, p. 543: "It is now easy to understand why a savage should desire to partake of the flesh of an animal or man whom he regards as divine. By eating the body of the god he shares the god's attributes and powers. . . . Thus the drinking of wine in the rites of a vine-god like Dionysus is not an act of revelry, it is a solemn sacrament."

16. Mircea Eliade, *Myths, Dreams, and Mysteries*, translated by Philip Mairet (New York, Harper, 1960), pp. 46 and 183–84. In the same study Eliade describes the bloody rite of the Khonds in India, which is similar to the Dionysian *sparagmos:* "The *meriah* was a voluntary victim, bought by the community: he was allowed to live for years, he could marry and have children. A few days before the sacrifice, the *meriah* was consecrated, that is, he was identified with the divinity to be sacrificed; the people danced around and worshipped him. After this, they prayed to the Earth: 'O Goddess, we offer thee this sacrifice; give us good harvests, good seasons and good health.' And they added, turning to the victim: 'We have bought thee and have not seized thee by force: now we sacrifice thee, and may no sin be accounted to us.' The ceremony also included an orgy lasting several days. Finally the *meriah* was drugged with opium, and, after they had strangled him, they cut him into pieces. Each of the villages received a fragment of his body which they buried in the fields. The remainder of the body was burnt, and the ashes strewn over the land. This bloody rite evidently corresponds to the myth of the dismemberment of a primordial divinity" (pp. 187–88).

Jung *(op. cit.)* quotes the description by Bernardino de Sahagún, a Spanish missionary to the Aztecs six years after Mexico's conquest by Cortéz, of the "eating of the god"—*teoqualo*. In this rite, a statue of the god Huitzilopochtli is molded from the paste of the seed of prickly poppy.

And upon the next day the body of Huitzilopochtli died.

And he who slew him was the priest known as Quetzalcoatl.
And that with which he slew him was a dart, pointed with flint,
which he shot into his heart.

And he had died, thereupon they broke up his body of . . .
dough. His heart was apportioned to Moctesuma.

And as for the rest of his members, which were made, as it
were, to be his bones, they were distributed and divided up
among all. . . . Each year . . . they ate it. . . . And they divided
among themselves his body made of . . . dough, it was broken up
exceeding small, very fine, as small seeds. The youths ate it.

And of this which they ate, it was said: "The god is eaten." And
of those who ate it, it was said: "They guard the god." (p. 170)

Alfred Métraux describes in *Tupinamba: War and Cannibalism* (New
York, 1955) the ritual of cannibalism among American Indians:
"Tupinamba restricted their cannibalism to prisoners specially captured for this purpose. Once captured and brought back to the captor's community, the prisoner was allowed to roam around in relative
freedom during the weeks or months preceding his sacrifice. . . .
During his stay he was alternately teased, flattered, insulted, honored.
He in turn reciprocated by being as nasty toward his captors as he
could, throwing nuts, fruits, and stones at them when they danced,
foretelling their doom, boasting about his own bravery. The festivi-
ties surrounding his sacrifice would last from three to five days. He
was eventually put to death by his executioner, often the man who'd
touched him first at the time of his capture, which was a gruesome
affair, since this was done by clubbing him to death . . . When he
finally collapsed, dead from a cracked skull, his body was immediately
quartered and barbecued, and the tasty morsels were distributed to
the happy company. The prisoner's wife shed some tears over him,
and then joined in the banquet. . . . As for the executioner, he ran
away from the scene of the sacrifice . . . The flesh of the prisoner he
was absolutely forbidden to eat. For a period of time, he was forbidden from full participation in the community's affairs, had a restricted
diet, and had to keep to himself. His return to the tribe after the
designated period was celebrated by a big drinking bout, during
which he tattooed his body by slashing it. He came out of such an
experience with his prestige in the community substantially en-
hanced" (pp. 151–55). (The author is grateful to Dr. Sasha Weitman
for having drawn his attention to this text.)

17. Eliade, *Myths*, p. 80.

18. *Hesiod, The Homeric Hymns and Homerica*, translated by Hugh G.

Evelyn-White (Loeb Classical Library; Cambridge, Mass., Harvard University Press, 1967), p. 289.

19. Dodds, *op. cit.*, Introduction, p. xi: "Thus wine acquired religious value: he who drinks it becomes *ev θeos*—he has drunk deity."

20. Mircea Eliade, *Cosmos and History: The Myth of the Eternal Return*, translated by Willard R. Trask (New York, Harper, 1959), pp. 22 and 28.

21. *The Works of Lucian*, Vol. V, translated by A. M. Harmon and M. D. MacLeod (Loeb Classical Library; Cambridge, Mass., Harvard University Press, 1953), pp. 265, 269.

22. Eliade, *Myths*, p. 74.

23. Eliade, *ibid.*, pp. 47 and 196. On rites of initiation in Dionysian ceremonies, see H. Jeanmaire, *Dionysus* (Paris, 1951). See also Kirk's commentary *(op. cit.)* to 11. 857–60, p. 93.

24. Jung, *op. cit.*, p. 203. See also R. Eisler, *Orpheus—the Fisher* (London, 1923), pp. 280 ff.

25. Arnott writes in *Greek Scenic Conventions* about three scenes of earthquake, in *Prometheus*, in *Heracles* and in *The Bacchae:* "These three earthquake scenes use the same method and the same formula—promise, elaboration and anticipation, statement. The effect is threatened, its result forecast and dwelt on in detail, and then finally announced as happening. In *Heracles Furens* the emphasis is on Heracles' madness and on the earthquake as a natural phenomenon, but the technique is the same. Given a theatre without a realistic scenery, there is no other way in which the effect can be obtained. The *skene* cannot crumble, for it is a permanent part of the theatre, but when the chorus say that it does, then by all the rules of conventional drama, the audience must accept that it does. Accompanied by an evocative dance-movement, this would be enough. Jean-Louis Barrault once produced Pompey's galley scene in *Antony and Cleopatra* with a row of oarsmen at the back of the stage rocking rhythmically from side to side; this, with the characters' words, gave a perfect impression of movement on the water, although there was no other scenery. We must imagine a similar effect here; the chorus reel and swirl to illustrate their wild words, a balletic accompaniment to the action" (pp. 124 f.; Oxford, Clarendon Press, 1962).

26. On thunder as a mystic sign, see Eliade, *Myths*, pp. 81 ff.; on the symbolism of flight to the skies, *ibid.*, pp. 105 ff.

27. Kirk, *op. cit.*, writes in his commentary (p. 120): *"tendril:* the Greek word means anything shaped like a spiral—here, presumably, a curling shot of ivy. The 'lion's head' that Agave carries on her thyrsus-point (1141 f.), with its 'crest of soft hair' (1186), is described

as though it were ivy that was ordinarily fastened to the thyrsus-tip. Whether this is metaphor or delusion remains ambiguous."

28. *Brecht on Theatre: The Development of an Aesthetic,* edited and translated by John Willett (New York, Hill & Wang, 1964), p. 181.

29. Jung, *op. cit.,* p. 200.

30. O. B. Hardison, Jr., *Christian Rite and Christian Drama in the Middle Ages; Essays in the Origin and Early History of Modern Drama* (Baltimore, Johns Hopkins University Press, 1965), p. 55. (See also pp. 47, 63, 70.) For subsequent quotations, see pp. 130, 148.

31. "It has been suggested by Emil Forrer (in *Actes du XXème Congrès intern. des Orientalistes* [Louvain, 1940], pp. 124–28) that the ancient Hittite practice in certain rites of drinking out of a theriomorphic vessel (called *bibru*) is a survival or attenuation of an original drinking of the divine blood or essence, comparable to the Christian communion. Cf. also Chrysostom, *Homilectus in Joann:* 'He [Christ] hath given those who desire Him . . . to fix their teeth in His flesh.' " From Additional Notes in Frazer, *op. cit.,* pp. 586 f.

32. I quote from Jung, *op. cit.,* p. 162.

33. On theory of "mactation" and the symbolic "slaughter" of Christ, see *ibid.,* p. 161 f.; on symbolism of *Fractio, ibid.,* p. 165. Hardison, in accordance with medieval tradition, connects *Fractio* with the symbolism of resurrection (*op. cit.,* pp. 45, 75 f.).

34. Jung interprets the archetypal symbolism of bread and wine differently: "Grain and wine have something in the nature of a soul, a specific life principle which makes them appropriate symbols not only of man's cultural achievements, but also of the seasonally dying and resurgent god who is their life spirit. Symbols are never simple —only signs and allegories are simple. The symbol always covers a complicated situation which is so far beyond the grasp of language that it cannot be expressed at all in any unambiguous manner. Thus the grain and wine symbols have a fourfold layer of meaning: 1. as agricultural products; 2. as products requiring special processing (bread from grain, wine from grapes); 3. as expressions of psychological achievements (work, industry, patience, devotion, etc.) and of human vitality in general; 4. as manifestation of mana or the vegetation daemon" (*ibid.,* pp. 203–4).

35. Hardison, *op. cit.,* pp. 145–46, 217. Also: "The Church recognized the climactic nature of the Vigil Mass and placed it in the most splendid of all liturgical settings. Extraliturgical, representational, rememorative, and purely mimetic ceremonies are also used in greater profusion for this occasion than for any other of the year. Almost all of them involve death-rebirth symbolism, and several have

association linking them to the *Quem queritis* play—white robes, burial, and tomb symbolism; to name the most obvious" (p. 163).

36. Whom seek you in the tomb, O followers of Christ?

Jesus of Nazareth who was crucified, O Heaven-Dwellers.

He is not here, he has arisen as he said; go announce that he has arisen.

(The text of the earliest manuscript; in Hardison, pp. 178–79.)

37. *Ibid.*, p. 301.

38. *Ibid.*, p. 252. Not only did religious drama become more and more of a spectacle, Mass became theatre: "By the twelfth century Aelred, Abbot of Rievaulx, was complaining in his *Speculum charitatis* of singing suggestive of feminine voices, sighs, sudden dramatic silences, vocal imitations of the agonies of the dying and the suffering, and priests, who contort the whole body with histrionic gestures.' These practices, he observes, 'amaze the common people' but are proper 'to the theatre, not the oratory' " (*ibid.*, p. 78 f.).

39. Gilbert Murray, "Excursions on the Ritual Forms Preserved in Greek Tragedy," in Jane Harrison, *Themis* (Cambridge, 1912), p. 363: "Something like the old hierophant reappears at the beginning, something like the old rerisen god at the end; and, as we have seen, it is in plays of Euripides, and most of all in the very latest of his plays, that we find in most perfect and clear-cut outline the whole sequence of Contest, Tearing-asunder, Messenger, Lamentation, Discovery, and Resurrection which constituted the original Dionysus-mystery." See also Herbert Weisinger, "Ritual Origins of Drama" in *The Reader's Encyclopedia of World Drama*, edited by John Gassner (New York, Crowell, 1969).

40. Hardison, *op. cit.*, p. 291. Cf. Carl Kerényi, *Prometheus* (New York, Pantheon, 1963), p. 43: "Once Christ's action at the Last Supper took on the significance of a prototypical ritual act, it became a foundation sacrifice, the great sacrifice by which the world of salvation was established."

41. Honorius of Autun wrote about A.D. 1100 in *Gemma animae:* "When the sacrifice has been completed, peace and communion are given by the celebrant to the people. This is because after our accuser has been destroyed by our champion in the struggle, peace is announced by the judge to the people, and they are invited to a feast" (Hardison, *op. cit.*, p. 40).

42. *Ibid.*, p. 148.

43. Even if "the totemic banquet," the ritual eating of god the father by a primitive group, described in *Totem and Taboo*, is an anthropological fantasy, or—as Eliade calls it—"a gothic tale," Freud

had an amazing intuition when he discerned connections between the Dionysian rite and the religious drama of the Middle Ages. "In Greek tragedy the special subject-matter of the performance was the suffering of the divine goat, Dionysus, and the lamentation of the goats who were his followers and who identified themselves with him. That being so, it is easy to understand how drama, which had become extinct, was kindled into fresh life in the Middle Ages around the Passion of Christ" (*Totem and Taboo*, translated by James Strachey [New York, 1950], p. 156).

44. Hardison, *op. cit.*, p. 133.

45. The preserved text of *The Bacchae* numbers about 1,400 lines; the triumphant speech of Dionysus to the Chorus after emerging from the dungeon ends on line 642.

46. *Christus Patiens*, 1466 ff., from Kirk's commentary *(op. cit.)*, p. 131. See also Dodds *(op. cit.)*, Introduction, pp. li–lii.

47. There is yet another layer of myth in *The Bacchae*, which also merits closer examination. From the dragon's teeth scattered by Cadmus, men grew. One of them was Echion, father of Pentheus. When Pentheus has imprisoned Dionysus, the Chorus speaks: "He reveals his Khtonic race, and his descent from the dragon, does Pentheus, whom Echion the Khtonic one engendered as a wild-faced monster, not a human being . . ." (538 ff., Kirk's translation). In the epilogue Dionysus foretells that Cadmus and his wife, Harmonia, will be punished by being turned into snakes. Euripides was fond of brandishing his mythological erudition, but the "subterranean" origin of Pentheus is stressed in *The Bacchae* too often for it to be only a superfluous mythological embellishment. The archetypal adversary of god the creator is always a snake, or a dragon. "Now the serpent was more subtle than any other wild creature that the Lord God had made" (Gen. iii. 1).

48. The first stanza of the Easter hymn *Ad coenam agni*, attributed to St. Ambrose; Hardison, *op. cit.*, p. 95.

49. *The Second Shepherd's Play* from the Wakefield Cycle, the most amazing and perhaps the most brilliant of late medieval dramas (early fifteenth century), has a structure which is a total reversal of *The Bacchae*'s. The first part is mocking, the second is a traditional Nativity play about shepherds on their way to the manger. The death of a mythic "horned lad," actually a stolen sheep, precedes the birth of the Savior. The sheep, in a mock nativity, is placed in a manger. And prior to this mock nativity, in another version of the play there is a shepherds' feast with blood pudding and other pretended foods in what seems a mock *sparagmos*. The first part is almost blasphemous;

one could call it an anti–miracle play. Theophany, having been mocked, is then shown in the second part in a naïve manner, full of anachronisms. (The author wishes to extend his thanks to Mr. Martin Stevens for pointing to *The Second Shepherd's Play* as the structural reversal of *The Bacchae*.)

50. Hegel, *Vorlesungen über die Ästhetik* (Aufbau-Verlag, 1955), 1071.

51. Hartung, over a century ago. See Dodds, *op. cit.*, p. xl.

52. In Lucian's *Dialogues of the Dead* (XXVIII), Menippus says to Teiresias: "Ah, you love a lie still, Teiresias. But there, 'tis your trade. You prophets! There is no truth in you" (*The Works of Lucian of Samosata*, translated by H. W. Fowler and F. G. Fowler [Oxford, Clarendon Press, 1905], p. 153).

53. Northrop Frye, "Blake After Two Centuries," in *Fables of Identity: Studies in Poetic Mythology* (New York, Harcourt, 1963), p. 143.

54. After the second volume of *Mythologiques* by Claude Lévi-Strauss, *Du Miel au cendres*, the time has come to examine the place of honey in Greek myths, particularly in those of Dionysus. On the Nysa mountain, nymphs fed the saved Dionysus with honey, for which Zeus later turned them into the Hyades constellation. In the apocalypse of *The Bacchae*, honey trickles from the thyrsi. In the Middle Ages, proselytes and children were offered milk and honey after the Easter vigil. In *Exsultet* we find a passage of praise for the bees who have given the wax for the paschal candle: "Because it is fed by the melted wax which the mother bee made for the substance of the precious torch." Hardison, *op. cit.*, quotes (p. 149) the full Latin text, which is of immense interest in terms of the ancient and Christian mythology concerning honey. On the mythical relation between Orpheus, Euridice and Aristaeus, the raiser of bees, see M. Detienne, "Orphée au miel," *Quaderni Urbinati di Cultura Classica*, No. 12, (1971), pp. 7–23.

55. The letter of January 4, 1889, "To my maestro Pietro," in *The Portable Nietzsche*, selected and translated by Walter Kaufmann (New York, 1954), p. 685.

56. Compare the accounts in the *New York Times* (August, 1, 14, and December 2, 1970) of the trial of Charles Manson for the murder of Sharon Tate and six other persons:

FIVE GIRLS KEEP A THREE-MONTH VIGIL AT TATE TRIAL

Two of the girls are barefoot. Some have scars in the form of a cross between their eyes. They made the scars with heated screwdriver blades after Manson and his co-defendants scratched crosses on their foreheads early in the trial.

Occasionally the girls sing a song that was composed when the Manson Family lived on a ranch here. The lyrics go like this:

> Oh, love, I love the truth I've known.
> You are the king.
> My love, this word to you I bring.
> Now, you know you can be free.
> Look at your kind and come to me.

Key Witness Says That She Once Regarded Manson As a "Messiah"

Mrs. Kasabian said that Manson talked to her at length about his philosophy. "I felt he was the Messiah come again; you know, the second coming of Christ," she said. "I thought he was another Jesus Christ."

After questioning Mrs. Kasabian at length for the second day . . . Mr. Hughes, a large man with a blond beard and long hair, asked her: "Have you ever thought someone else was Jesus Christ besides Mr. Manson?"

"The Biblical Jesus Christ," she replied.

"Have you ever met Jesus Christ—besides Mr. Manson?" he asked.

"No," she said.

57. T. B. L. Webster, *Greek Art and Literature 700–530 B.C.* (New York, Ryerson Press, 1959), p. 66.

58. Jean Genet, *The Blacks: A Clown Show*, translated By Bernard Frechtman (New York, Grove, 1960), pp. 3, 84.

59. Arrowsmith writes in the introduction to his translation of *The Bacchae* (p. 148): ". . . the play employs Dionysus and Pentheus and the conflict between them as a bitter image of Athens and Hellas terribly divided between the forces that, for Euripides, more than anything else destroyed them: on the one side, the conservative tradition in its extreme corruption, disguising avarice for power with the fair professions of the traditional *aretai*, meeting all opposition with the terrible tyranny of popular piety, and disclosing in its actions the callousness and refined cruelty of civilized barbarism; on the other side, the exceptional individual, selfish and egotistical, impatient of tradition and public welfare alike, stubborn, demagogic, and equally brutal in action."

60. *Iphigenia in Aulis,* translated by Charles R. Walker, in *Euripides IV, The Complete Greek Tragedies* (Chicago, University of Chicago Press, 1958).

61. Plutarch, "Crassus," in *The Fall of the Roman Republic,* translated by Rex Warner (Baltimore, Penguin Books, 1958), p. 137.

ORESTES, ELECTRA, HAMLET

1. Humphrey D. F. Kitto, *Greek Tragedy,* 3rd ed. (New York, Barnes & Noble, 1961), p. 361.

2. The first Greek scholar to be interested in the similarity between Hamlet and Orestes was Tadeusz Zieliński, in his *Sofokles i jego twórczość tragiczna (Sophocles and His Tragic Works).* The Russian edition was published in 1914–15, the Polish edition in 1928. Zieliński was interested mainly in the development and transformations of the concept of vengeance and its Christian rendering in Shakespeare.

Prosser Hall Frye's work, "Shakespeare and Sophocles," in the volume *Romance and Tragedy* (Boston, 1922), recently republished (Lincoln, Nebr., University of Nebraska Press, 1961), is based on the parallel between Shakespeare and Sophocles. Frye is concerned with the differences between the *Weltanschauung* and artistic method of the two great tragic writers. H. D. F. Kitto made a detailed analysis of *Hamlet* as primarily religious drama and compared it with Greek tragedy in his *Form and Meaning in Drama: A Study of Six Greek Plays and of Hamlet* (New York, Barnes & Noble, 1957).

The most important and most detailed treatment of this theme, however, has been Gilbert Murray's excellent study "Hamlet and Orestes" in his book *The Classical Tradition in Poetry* (Cambridge, Mass., Harvard University Press, 1927). Murray deals not only with the *Oresteia* and the two *Electras* but also includes in his study Euripides' *Andromache, Iphigenia in Tauris* and *Orestes.* He was also the first to introduce to the study of the history of the Orestes myth the *Historia Danica: Gesta Danorum* by Saxo Grammaticus and the Icelandic *Ambales Saga.* He, too, as far as I know, was the first to compare the part of Ophelia with that of Electra, and Horatio with Pylades. His final conclusions are concerned with the universality and regeneration of myths.

3. All quotations from the *Oresteia (Agamemnon, The Libation-bearers, Eumenides)* are the translation by George D. Thomson, in *Aeschylus* (The Laurel Classical Drama; New York, 1965).

4. All quotations from Euripides' *Electra* are taken from the transla-

tion by Emily Townsend Vermeule in *The Complete Greek Tragedies, Euripides V* (Chicago, University of Chicago Press, 1959).

5. All quotations from Sophocles' *Electra* are taken from the translation by David Grene in *The Complete Greek Tragedies, Sophocles II* (Chicago, University of Chicago Press, 1957).

6. See Jacques Lacarrière, *Sophocle* (Paris, L'Arche, 1960), pp. 89 ff.

7. The Oedipus complex in Hamlet and Orestes has been analyzed copiously in modern criticism. Of particular interest are: Ernest Jones, *A Psycho-analytic Study of "Hamlet"; Essays in Applied Psycho-analysis* (London, Vienna, 1923); republished as *Hamlet and Oedipus* (New York, Norton, 1949), and Maud Bodkin, *Archetypal Patterns in Poetry* (New York, Oxford University Press, 1934), especially the chapter entitled "Examination of the Oedipus Complex As a Pattern Determining Our Imaginative Experience of Hamlet." Recently there has been a brilliant study by André Green, influenced by Lacan and the structuralists, entitled *Un Oeil en trop: Le Complexe d'Oedipe dans la tragédie* (Paris, Editions de Minuit, 1969). It is curious that all these studies leave out the striking resemblance between Electra's and Hamlet's relationship to the mother. Of course, Electra has a "negative Oedipus complex," but it does not seem to me that the psychoanalytic interpretation has taken us much farther in the understanding of the variable and constant elements in patterns of tragedy.

8. Jean Duvignaud, *Sociologie du Théâtre: Essai sur les ombres collectives* (Paris, 1965), pp. 242 ff.

9. *Brecht on Theatre: The Development of an Aesthetic*, edited and translated by John Willett (New York, Hill & Wang, 1964).

10. All quotations from *Orestes* are from the translation by William Arrowsmith in *The Complete Greek Tragedies, Euripides IV* (Chicago, University of Chicago Press, 1958).

LUCIAN IN "CYMBELINE"

1. T. W. Baldwin, *William Shakespeare's Small Latine and Lesse Greeke*, 2 vols. (Urbana, Ill., University of Illinois Press, 1944), Vol. I, pp. 103, 216, 374, 582, 734.

2. *The Works of Thomas Nashe*, edited by Ronald B. McKerrow, 2nd ed., revised by F. P. Wilson, 5 vols. (Oxford, Blackwell, 1958), Vol. I, pp. 283, 285; Vol. III, pp. 120, 126.

3. F. G. Allinson, *Lucian: Satirist and Artist* (New York, Cooper Square, 1963), pp. 156–58.

4. Baldwin, *op. cit.*, p. 732.

5. B. L. Gildersleeve, *Essays and Studies* (Baltimore, 1890) p. 343; W.

S. Fox, "Lucian in the Gravescene of Hamlet," *Transactions of the Royal Society of Canada*, 17 (1923), pp. 71–80.

6. Baldwin, *op. cit.*, p. 732.

7. *The Works of Lucian*, edited and translated by A. M. Harmon and M. D. MacLeod, 8 vols. (Loeb Classical Library; Harvard University Press, 1913–67), Vol. II, p. 440. The irreverent jokes of Charon are a part of a cento patched up out of the *Iliad*, IX, 319–20, and the *Odyssey*, X, 521, and XI, 539.

8. *Lucian's Satirical Sketches*, translated by P. Turner (Penguin Classics; Baltimore, Penguin Books, 1961), p. 95.

9. F. S. Boas, *University Drama in the Tudor Age* (Oxford, 1914), pp. 18 ff.

10. Baldwin, *op. cit.*, Vol. I, p. 457; Vol. II, p. 648.

11. These are strangely omitted in a description of the Hickeses' volume in Hardin Craig, "Dryden's Lucian," *Classical Philology*, Vol. 16 (1921), pp. 141–63. Necromantia was put into English translation for school use around 1530 (Baldwin, *op. cit.*, Vol. I, p. 734). In the third English translation of Lucian by Thomas Heywood in 1637, the Charon dialogue does not appear.

INDEX

Abraham (patriarch), 4, 61, 210
Achilles, 35, 44, 45–46, 50, 51, 53,
    57, 59, 61, 69, 73, 109, 110,
    112, 116, 162, 170, 171, 174,
    177–79, 270, 271
Actaeon, 195
Adam, 122
Admetus, 78–96, 98, 101–3, 106–8
Adonis, 230
Aeacus, 68
Aegeus, 236
Aegisthus, 44, 245, 247–52, 260,
    263
Aeneas, 49
Aeneid (Virgil), 5, 179
Aeschylus, 3–42, 49, 65, 93, 145,
    155, 157, 177, 192, 201, 204,
    222, 248–50, 251, 257, 259,
    260, 261, 263, 264, 266

Aethiopis, 57
Agamemnon, 31, 45, 46, 49, 57,
    70–71, 74, 75, 104, 129, 180,
    202, 229, 245, 248, 250, 260,
    263, 272
Agamemnon (Aeschylus), 247, 260
Agave, 186–87, 190–91, 193, 195,
    199, 205, 206, 220, 221, 230
Ajax, 43–77, 109, 137, 140, 154,
    166, 183, 269–70, 271
Ajax (Sophocles), 43–77, 126, 172,
    175, 270
Ajax Flageliter, 270
Alcestis, 78–108, 137
Alcestis (Euripides), 78–108
Alcides, 115, 116, 119
Alcmene, 113, 120, 122, 156
Alexander the Great, 116, 117,
    118–19

Almaviva, Count, 108
Amleth, Prince, 246, 258
Amphitryon, 122, 147–49, 150, 153, 155, 159, 161, 162
Amphitryon (Kleist), 122
Amphitryon (Plautus), 105
Andromache, 59, 178, 179
Antigone, 26–27, 137, 160, 166, 222–24, 240, 241, 252–53, 257, 265
Antigone (Sophocles), 26–28, 52–53
Antilochus, 183
Antony and Cleopatra (Shakespeare), 116
Aphrodite (Venus), 136, 188, 224
Apollo (Phoebus), 40, 51, 78, 79, 82, 83, 87, 90, 93, 96, 98, 99, 100–1, 103, 106, 153, 174, 179, 197, 246, 248, 257
Apollodorus, 91
Aquilea, 212
Argan, 87, 88
"Argument of Comedy, The" (Frye), 107
Argus, 29, 30
Aristophanes, 48, 85, 101, 123
Aristotle, 22–23
Armenius, 76, 157
Arnolf, 87
Arrowsmith, William, 66, 88
Artaud, Antonin, 49, 104, 203
Artemis, 54, 195, 224, 248
Asclepius, 90, 97, 167, 169, 184
Astyanax, 59, 178
Ate, 51, 153
Athamas, 193
Athene, 44, 46–48, 49, 51–55, 111, 153, 185, 196
Atlas, 13, 123
Atreus, 44, 46, 57, 58, 62, 63, 175, 250, 251, 259, 260
Attis, 230

Auerbach, Erich, 60, 61
Autonoë, 187, 193, 195

Bacchae, The (Euripides), 30, 105, 186–230
Bacchus, *see* Dionysus
Barrault, Jean-Louis, 265
Bassanio, 115
Beaumarchais, Pierre, 108
Beckett, Samuel, 42, 169
Belarius, 269
Bendis, 230
Bérénice, 236–37
Berowne, 269
Bertin, Filbert, 272
Beyond Good and Evil (Nietzsche), 140
Bible, 4, 5, 6, 20, 21, 60, 61, 113, 121, 226
Birth of Tragedy, The (Nietzsche), 124
Blacks, The (Genet), 228–29
Blake, William, 226
bororo (myth), 18, 19, 20
Bottom, 115
Brecht, Bertolt, 48, 85, 104, 149, 151, 207, 251, 262, 266
Briseis, 45, 46
Bromius, 190
Bundahisn (sacred book), 39
Byron, George Gordon, Lord, 38

Cabasilas, Archbishop of Thessalonica, 210–11
Cadmus, 186–87, 190, 191, 195, 204, 220, 221, 225
Caesar, Julius, 116, 117, 120
Calchas, 54
Caligula, Emperor, 236
Camus, Albert, 6, 33, 39, 40, 66, 67, 70, 139, 158, 169
Canace in Childbirth, 119
Castor and Pollux, 247, 248, 261

Catalogues (Hesiod), 112
Cerberus, 91, 111, 117, 123, 144
Charon, 94
Charon (Lucian), 269, 271, 272
Chiron (centaur), 34–35, 167, 168, 169, 174
Christian Rite and Christian Drama in the Middle Ages (Hardison), 209
Christus Patiens, 219
Chrysothemis, 252–53, 266
Cicero, 40, 41
Clarissimi Luciani Philosophia Cora, 271
Claudius, 10, 171, 248, 249, 253, 261, 263–64
Cleopatra, 116
Clytemnestra, 44, 129, 243, 245–51, 255, 259, 260, 263
Cocktail Party, The (Eliot), 106
Conquerors, The (Malraux), 66
Conrad, Joseph, 227–28
Cordelia, 70
Corneille, Pierre, 70
Cosmos and History (Eliade), 4
Crassus, 230
Creon, 148, 149, 223, 238, 243, 265
Cretans (Euripides), 196
Cromwell, Oliver, 6
Cronos, 7, 8–9, 11, 23, 24, 112, 113
Cru et le Cuit, Le (Lévi-Strauss), 18
Cybele, 201, 230
Cyclops, 90
Cyclops (Euripides), 93
Cymbeline (Shakespeare), 268–73

Dale, A. M., 80
David, King, 113
Days of Wrath (Malraux), 159–60

De E Delphico (Plutarch), 197–98
De Morbis Mulierum (Hippocrates), 114
Deianira, 112, 117, 124–38, 143, 144, 146, 151, 160
Dekker, Thomas, 268
Demeter, 225
Demosthenes, 184
Devil Let Loose (Dekker), 268
Dialogues of the Dead, The (Lucian), 95–96, 120
Dialogues of the Gods, The (Lucian), 19
Diogenes, 95–96, 120–21
Diomedes, 51, 91, 177
Dionysus (Bacchus), 133, 149, 186–88, 189, 191–98, 202, 204–6, 215–21, 224–30
Discours sur l'origine et les fondements de l'inégalité parmi les hommes (Rousseau), 16
Distraught Hercules, 119
Divine Comedy, The (Dante), 5
Dodds, E. R., 54, 194, 215
Domitian, Emperor, 119
Don Juan (Molière), 97, 102
Donne, John, 222
Dürrenmatt, Friedrich, 123
Duvignaud, Jean, 257

Echidna, 127
Eclogues (Virgil), 119
Edward II, King, 10
Electra, 43–44, 174, 222–23, 240–67
Electra (Euripides), 80, 129, 224, 247, 249, 251, 254, 260, 266, 267
Electra (Sophocles), 165, 249, 251, 254, 256, 260, 266
Eliade, Mircea, 4, 194, 198, 200, 203

Eliot, T. S., 106
Eluard, Paul, 159
Er (son of Armenius), 76
Erasmus, Desiderius, 271
Erinyes, *see* Furies
Eros, 33, 135, 144, 202, 224–25
Eumenides (Aeschylus), 14, 93, 247
Euridice, 96
Euripides, 23, 30, 78–108, 123, 124, 129, 136, 137, 147–62, 177, 178, 181, 186–230, 235, 249–51, 252, 254, 255, 257, 258, 261, 262, 266
Eurymedon, 149
Eurystheus, King, 91, 111, 113, 126, 148, 152, 154
Everyman, 100
"Excursus" (Murray), 214
Expérience du Théâtre (Ionesco), 108
Exsultet (hymn), 210, 215

Fall, The (Camus), 6
Fates, 87, 93
Fengo, 246
Ficino, Marsilio, 114
Finley, J. H., 54
Flaubert, Gustave, 47
Fortinbras, 10, 248, 261, 262, 264–65
Foure Lectures (Harvey), 268
Frazer, Sir James G., 134
Freud, Sigmund, 6, 155
Fritz, Kurt von, 101
Frogs, The (Aristophanes), 123
Frye, Northrop, 5, 8, 9, 22, 106, 107, 122, 123–24
Furies (Erinyes), 12–13, 43, 93, 144, 145, 246, 247, 248, 257, 266, 267

Gaea (Gaia), 5, 8, 121

Garrick, David, 265
Gaster, Theodore H., 5
gé (myth), 18, 19, 20
Genet, Jean, 228
Gertrude, 248–49, 253, 261, 263, 264
Geruth, 246
Geryon, 112
Gielgud, John, 265
Giraudoux, Jean, 71, 96, 122
Glauca, 236
Goethe, Johann Wolfgang von, 37, 38, 155
Gonzalo, 226
Good Woman of Setzuan, The (Brecht), 266
Gorgias (Plato), 28
Gorgon, 101, 107, 153
Graves, Robert, 196
Greek Studies (Murray), 130
Grene, David, 28, 29
Grotowski, Jerzy, 49
Guiderius, 269–70

Haemon, 137
Hall, Peter, 263, 264
Hamlet, Prince, 10, 27, 171, 235, 237, 240–67
Hamlet (Shakespeare), 10, 234, 237, 249, 250, 253, 256, 258, 261, 264, 265, 268
Happy Days (Beckett), 42
Hardison, O. B., 209, 210, 214
Harpagon, 87
Harrison, Jane, 105–6
Harvey, Gabriel, 268
Havelock, Eric A., 23, 32
Heart of Darkness, The (Conrad), 228
Hebe, 110, 113, 120
Hector, 46, 49, 50, 59, 61, 64, 65, 66–67, 69, 178
Hecuba (Euripides), 178

Hegel, Georg Wilhelm Friedrich, 13, 14, 38, 39, 153, 155, 159, 222–24, 262

Heidegger, Martin, 27

Helen of Troy, 248

Helena, 33

Henry III, King, 10

Henry IV, King, 10

Henry VII, King, 10

Hephaestus, 3–4, 9, 10, 23–25, 37, 44, 46, 155, 165, 185

Hera (Juno), 29–30, 110, 117, 122–23, 142, 144, 148, 153, 154, 156, 157, 193

Heracles (Hercules), 14, 32, 34, 35, 48, 79, 81, 85–89, 91–93, 96, 97–98, 101–2, 103, 106, 107, 109–85, 202, 224

Heracles (Euripides), 97, 123, 147–62, 181

Heracles and the Aegean Stable (Dürrenmatt), 123

Heraclitus, 73

Hercules, *see* Heracles

Hercules Furens (Seneca), 117

Hercules Oetaeus (Seneca), 117, 118, 119, 121

Hermes (Mercury), 23, 25, 29, 34, 36, 105, 106, 111, 257, 271

Hermione, 97

Herod, King, 99

Herodotus, 24, 166

Hesiod, 5, 7–8, 18, 20, 21, 26, 90, 112

Heywood, Thomas, 116

Hickes, Francis, 272

Hippocrates, 114

Hippolytus (Euripides), 224

Homer, 45, 49–53, 59–61, 65, 71, 75, 110, 111–12, 122, 126, 137, 153, 156, 164, 177, 181, 183, 221, 245, 246

Horatio, 261

Horwendil (Viking), 246

Hydra, 112, 114, 116, 127, 132, 134, 136, 138, 140, 143–44, 145, 151, 159, 167, 168, 174, 181

Hyginus, 96

Hyllus, 141–42

Hyrodes, 230

Iconology (Ripa), 114

Ida, 196

Iliad (Homer), 5, 46, 47, 49, 53, 57, 59, 60, 65, 69, 72, 111, 164, 183

Imogen, 269

Inachos, 29

Ino, 187, 193

Interpretation of Dreams (Freud), 6

Io, 13, 29–36

Iole, 124, 135–36, 138, 142–44, 146

Ionesco, Eugene, 108

Iphigenia, 54, 248

Iphigenia in Aulis (Euripides), 220, 229

Iris, 51, 153–54, 155

Isaac, 61, 210

Isaiah (prophet), 201

Ismene, 252–53

Isocrates, 118

Isthmians (Pindar), 142

Jacob, 4, 61

Jakobson, Roman, 134

Jason, 89, 166, 236–38, 239

Jason of Tralles, 230

Jebb, Sir Richard Claverhouse, 65, 68, 127, 129, 131, 143, 168, 169, 174

Jensen, Adolf E., 198

Jerusalem (Blake), 226

Jesus, 5, 113, 121, 122, 196, 204, 207–13, 215–19, 221, 238
Jocasta, 137, 160, 166
John (apostle), 213
John the Baptist, 195–96, 220
Jonson, Ben, 268
Jung, Carl G., 208
Juno, *see* Hera
Jupiter, *see* Zeus

Kafka, Franz, 41
Kean, Edmund, 265
Kerényi, Carl, 167
Kierkegaard, Søren, 67, 68
King John (Shakespeare), 10
King Lear (Shakespeare), 161
Kirk, G. S., 192, 195, 199, 205, 206, 218, 221
Kitto, H. D. F., 61, 62, 85, 91, 97, 100, 177, 178, 241
Kleist, Heinrich von, 122
Knox, Bernard M. W., 57, 62–63, 69, 73, 80, 170, 180, 184
Kochanowski, Jan, 98
Kurtz, 228

Labdacus, 167
Lachesis, 157
Laertes, 10, 47, 253, 258, 263, 270
Laius, 167
Laodamia, 95, 96, 108
Lattimore, Richmond, 90, 111, 112, 164
Lear, King, 127, 144
Lectures on the Philosophy of History (Hegel), 222
Leto, 90
Lévi-Strauss, Claude, 16, 18–20, 21
Libation-bearers, The (Aeschylus), 31, 202, 247, 250
Lichas, 116
Little Iliad, The, 178

"Little Organon" (Brecht), 207
Love's Labour's Lost (Shakespeare), 269
Lowell, Robert, 25
Lucian, 19, 95, 120–21, 151, 203, 268–73
Lucifer, 38
Lukács, Georg, 243
Lycurgus, King, 194
Lycus, 149, 152, 159, 162

Macbeth (Shakespeare,) 127, 133, 139, 141
Machiavelli, Niccolò, 24
Madness (goddess); 153, 154, 155
Maenads, 196, 206, 219, 227
Malraux, André, 38, 62, 66, 67, 69, 159–60
Man's Fate (Malraux), 62
Mao Tse-tung, 37
Marlowe, Christopher, 10
Marriage of Figaro, The (Beaumarchais), 108
Marx, Karl, 6, 35, 37, 155
Mary Magdalene, 213, 218
Medea, 83, 89, 90, 130, 224, 234–39
Medea (Euripides), 224, 233–39
Medusa, 101
Megara, 97, 147–49, 150, 153
Meges, 50
Melanchton, Philipp, 271
Melville, Herman, 165
Menander, 80
Menelaus, 45, 51, 53, 70–71, 74, 180, 229, 245–46, 248, 267
Menippus (Lucian), 272
Merchant of Venice, The (Shakespeare), 115
Mercury, *see* Hermes
Meriones, 50
Meyerhold, Vsevolod E., 104
Mickiewicz, Adam, 114

Midsummer Night's Dream, A (Shakespeare), 33, 115
Might (police official), 11, 24, 25, 155
Miller, Jonathan, 25
Mimesis (Auerbach), 60
Minos, 68
Moiras, 12–13
Molière, 84, 87, 102
Montaigne, Michel Eyquem de, 265
More, Thomas, 271
Moses, 4, 121
Murray, Gilbert, 106, 130, 214, 218, 258
Musurillo, Herbert, 137
Myth of Sisyphus, The (Camus), 66, 139, 158

Nashe, Thomas, 268
Natural History (Pliny), 19
Neleus, 112
Nemean (Pindar), 73
Nemesis, 10
Neoptolemus, 162–65, 167–75, 177–81, 183
Nero, Emperor, 117–19, 203, 236
Nessus, 116, 125, 132, 135, 167
Nestor, 246
News from Hell (Dekker), 268
Nichias, 184
Nietzsche, Friedrich, 124, 127, 140, 155, 227

Occhalia, 124
Oceanus, 13, 24, 25, 29, 36
Octavia, 117, 118
Ode to Youth (Mickiewicz), 114
Odysseus (Ulysses), 44–49, 52, 54, 55, 58, 61, 63, 72–77, 93, 109–11, 112, 126, 156, 162–64, 165, 170–74, 177, 179–81, 183, 184, 270

Odyssey (Homer), 20, 75, 109–11, 112, 119, 120, 126, 127, 245, 246, 248
Oeagrus, 94
Oedipus, 43, 44, 55, 130, 142, 155, 157–58, 160, 162, 166, 167, 222–23, 224, 240, 241, 243, 259
Oedipus (Sophocles), 6, 157–58
Oedipus at Colonus (Sophocles), 142, 160, 166
Oedipus Blinded, 119
Oedipus Rex (Sophocles), 23, 138–39, 142, 166, 202
Olivier, Sir Laurence, 265
Omphale, Queen, 126
Ophelia, 10, 243, 253, 257, 258
Oresteia (Aeschylus), 14, 104, 145, 246–48, 264, 267; see also *Agamemnon, The Libation-bearers, Eumenides*
Orestes, 43–44, 165, 179, 195–96, 202, 240–67
Orestes the Matricide, 119
Orpheus, 94, 96
Othello (Shakespeare), 152
Ouranos, *see* Uranus
Ovid, 192

Paris, 164, 174, 179
Pascal, Blaise, 34, 208
Pasiphaë, 33
Paradise Lost (Milton), 5
Patroclus, 46, 49, 50, 53, 57
Pausanius, 166
Pelias, 90
Pentheus, 186, 187–93, 195, 200, 203, 205–7, 215, 216–17, 219–23, 227, 230
Pericles, 184
Persephone, 91, 193
Perseus, 101
Peter (apostle), 213

Philoctetes, 48, 73, 124, 125, 162–85

Philoctetes (Sophocles), 73, 124, 125, 162–85

Phaedra (Euripides), 136

Phèdre (Racine), 68, 136

Pheres, 84–85, 93, 103

Philip of Macedon, 118

Phoebus, *see* Apollo

Pico della Mirandola, 114

Pindar, 40, 41, 55, 73, 142

Plato, 5, 28, 76, 90, 91, 94, 113, 157, 197

Plautus, 84, 105, 122, 123

Pliny, 19, 168

Plutarch, 118, 197–98, 230, 272

Pluto, 94, 95, 96

Podlecki, Anthony J., 23

Pollux, *see* Castor and Pollux

Polonius, 171, 264

Polyxena, 178

Pomaxathres, 230

Portia, 115

Priam, King of Troy, 178

Proclus, 196

Prometheus, 3–42, 112, 122, 155, 157, 162, 165, 167, 172, 174, 185, 222, 257

Prometheus Bound (Aeschylus), 3–42, 204

Prometheus Unbound (Shelley), 37, 38

Prospero, 226

Protesilaus, 95, 96, 108

Protesilaus (Euripides), 95, 97

Pylades, 259

Pythian (Pindar), 55

Quatrain (Rimbaud), 146

Quince, 115

Racine, Jean Baptiste, 56, 68, 83, 130, 236–37, 242

Radamanthos, 68

Rape of Lucrece, The (Shakespeare), 108, 270

Red Book (Mao), 37

Regnault, Maurice, 106

Republic (Plato), 5, 76, 157

Rhea, 196

Richard II (Shakespeare), 10

Richard III (Shakespeare), 10

Rieu, E. V., 126, 245

Rimbaud, Arthur, 146, 203

Ripa, Cesar, 114

Rousseau, Jean-Jacques, 16

Royal Way, The (Malraux), 67

Sabazius, 230

St. Christopher, 113

St. George, 113

St. John Chrysostom, 211

St. Luke, 216, 217

St. Matthew, 217

St. Michael, 113

Salome, 220

Saltatio (Lucian), 203

Samson, 113

Sartre, Jean-Paul, 33, 160

Satan, 38

Saturn, 98

Saxo Grammaticus, 245

Schiller, J. C. F. von, 114

Schopenhauer, Arthur, 33

Scinzeler, Uldericus, 271

Semele, 187, 188, 193, 195, 197, 201, 204

Seneca, 117, 118, 121, 192

Shakespeare, William, 9, 49, 70, 74, 97, 104, 108, 115–17, 119, 127, 179, 183, 237, 242, 248–249, 250, 253, 254, 257, 258, 261, 263, 264, 268–73

Shaw, George Bernard, 88

Shelley, Percy Bysshe, 37, 38

sherenté (myth), 18

Short Organum for the Theatre (Brecht), 262
Sickness unto Death (Kierkegaard), 67
Silenus, 93
Sillaces, 230
Smith, Wesley D., 83, 98
Sociology of Modern Drama, The (Lukács), 243
Sophocles, 6, 26–27, 43–77, 119, 123–25, 126, 130, 137, 142, 145, 154, 157, 160, 162–85, 223, 224, 235, 247, 249, 251, 252, 254, 255–59, 263, 266, 271
Sphinx, 130, 144, 157, 162
Stempowski, Jerzy, 229
Suetonius, 119
Symposium (Plato), 90, 94

Talthybius, 178
Tantalus, 249
Tate, Alexander J., 100
Tecmessa, 44, 48–49, 58, 59, 61, 64, 68
Teiresias, 225, 229
Telamon, 57, 75
Telemachus, 246
Tempest, The (Shakespeare), 162, 163, 183, 184, 185, 226
Tertullian, 208
Teucer, 44, 45, 65, 71, 74
Theogony (Hesiod), 5, 18, 112
Thersites, 184, 269–70, 271, 272
Theseus, 116, 155, 156, 158, 160, 161
Thespis (Gaster), 5
Thetis, 112, 269–70, 272
Thomson, George D., 23, 32, 35
Three Marys, 212, 213–14, 217
Thucydides, 149, 173, 182
Times of Contempt (Malraux), 38

Timon (Lucian), 271, 272–73
Timon of Athens (Shakespeare), 269, 272
Titus, Emperor, 236
Titus Andronicus (Shakespeare), 270
Tolstoy, Leo, 183
Troilus and Cressida (Shakespeare), 271
Trojan Women, The (Euripides), 178
Typhoeus, 13

Ulysses, *see* Odysseus
Uranus (Ouranos), 5, 7, 11, 121

Venus, *see* Aphrodite
Verrall, Arthur W., 88, 130, 150, 204
Virgil, 6, 119, 179
Visitatio Sepulchri, 212, 213, 214, 217
Volpone (Jonson), 268

War and Peace (Tolstoy), 183
Warner, David, 263
Webster, John, 268
Weird Sisters, 133
White Devil, The (Webster), 268
Whitman, C., 55
Wilson, John R., 101
Winter's Tale, The (Shakespeare), 97
Women of Trachis, The (Sophocles), 123, 133–35, 136, 139, 140, 142–44, 146, 159, 167, 168, 181
Works and Days (Hesiod), 20, 21
Worth, Irene, 30–31

Zarathustra, 145–46

Zeus (Jupiter), 5–13, 15, 19–21, 23–25, 28, 29–30, 34–36, 37, 40, 46, 53–55, 60, 65, 68, 72, 75, 90, 109–13, 118, 120, 122, 123, 125, 127, 130, 132, 134, 140, 142–48, 150, 151, 155, 162, 173, 181, 182, 185–87, 193, 196, 204, 216, 247

The Myth of Return in Early Greek Epic

The Myth of Return
in Early Greek Epic

Douglas Frame

New Haven and London
Yale University Press
1978

Designed by Thos Whitridge
and set in Times New Roman type.
Printed in the United States of America by
Vail-Ballou Press, Binghamton, New York.

Published in Great Britain, Europe, Africa, and Asia (except Japan) by Yale University Press, Ltd., London. Distributed in Latin America by Kaiman & Polon, Inc., New York City; in Australia and New Zealand by Book & Film Services, Artarmon, N.S.W., Australia; and in Japan by Harper & Row, Publishers, Tokyo Office.

Library of Congress Cataloging in Publication Data
Frame, Douglas, 1942-
The myth of return in early Greek epic
Includes bibliographical references and index.
1. Epic poetry, Greek—History and criticism.
2. Noos (The Greek word) I. Title.
PA3107.F7   883   77-76306
ISBN 0-300-01940-8

Contents

Acknowledgments   vii

Introduction   ix

1 Formal Evidence for the Etymology of Greek *nóos*   1

2 The Root **nes-* in Prehistoric Greek   6

  1 Evidence for the Primitive Meaning   6

  2 The Semantic Development of *ásmenos*   24

  3 The Relation Between the Greek Root **nes-*
    and *nóos*   28

3 The Return of Odysseus   34

  1 Introduction   34

  2 Circe, the Nekyia, and Helios   38

  3 The Ciconians, the Cyclops, and the
    Laestrygonians   53

  4 The Return to Ithaca   73

4 Nestor   81

  1 Introduction   81

  2 Nestor and the Greek Root **nes-*   82

  3 Nestor's Original Function   86

  4 A Closer Look at Nestor's Name   96

5 Achilles   116

6 Evidence for the Meaning of the Indo-European
  Root **nes-*   125

  1 Introduction   125

  2 Germanic   126

  3 Albanian   132

  4 Indic   134

7 Epilogue   153

Notes   163

Index   175

Acknowledgments

Two people have had a particularly large influence on this book. Gregory Nagy, with his insight into Greek epic tradition, inspired my efforts from the start, and Amy Sabatini, with her insight into comparative religions, gave focus to my efforts at an early and opportune moment; to both of these friends I am deeply grateful. I am likewise grateful to my former teachers, John Finley, Calvert Watkins, and Cedric Whitman, for their help along the way; because of them many an obstacle has proved to be not insurmountable. I owe a special debt to Deborah Boedeker, Linda Clader, Steven Lowenstam, Leonard Muellner, Richard Sacks, and Richard Shannon for the inspiration and support of their "Homeric companionship"; this book has benefited much from their thoughtful responses. Others as well have given welcome advice and encouragement; in particular, I would like to thank Ann Bergen, Charles Beye, Susan Edmunds, Barbara Folsom, Mary Lefkowitz, James Lesher, Patricia Marshall, Martha Nussbaum, Dan Petegorsky, Laura Slatkin, Edward Tripp, Emily Vermeule, and Thomas Walsh.

It remains to say that I alone am to blame that this is not a better book. Indeed time, while lending support to what I first set out to show, has also made me more keenly aware of shortcomings. Be these as they may, however, I still hold to the spirit in which the entire book was written, namely, that of a search. Whatever faithfully reflects that spirit, furthermore, I would like to dedicate to my father, who has followed my progress with interest, and to the memory of my mother, who encouraged me to see the work through to completion.

Introduction

Since much of the following study will have to do with the *Odyssey*, it is fitting to begin with an observation on the first line of this poem. When at the very outset Homer calls his hero *polútropos*, one cannot tell whether he intends this to mean "very wily" or "much-wandering," for both of these meanings are possible and both suit Odysseus equally well. One strongly suspects, however, that the ambiguity itself is what Homer intended—that he chose the word *polútropos* precisely because it captures two such basic features of his hero: what he is ("wily") and what he does ("wander").

The main argument of this book is that the connection suggested by Homer between the "wiles" and the "wanderings" of Odysseus in fact rested upon an earlier tradition both significant and deep. The origin of this tradition has to do with the etymology of the Greek word *nóos*, "mind," which I propose to connect with the Greek verb *néomai*, "return home." Such an effort requires that *nóos* be reconstructed as **nos-os*, a derivative from the verbal root **nes-*.

The significance of this proposal for the tradition underlying the *Odyssey* is clear. It implies that the connection still felt by Homer between the "wiliness" and the "wandering" of Odysseus goes back to a fundamental connection between "mind" and "returning home," and that the relation between what Odysseus "is" and what he "does" has a solid basis in the history of the Greek language.

It will not be denied that the words *nóos* and *néomai* come readily to mind in connection with Odysseus. By way of illustration, one may again consider the opening of the

Odyssey. The poem's first scene is a council of the gods. Athena intercedes here for Odysseus, accusing Zeus of having forgotten her protégé. But Zeus denies this charge, asking how he could forget godlike Odysseus, *hòs perì mèn nóon estì brotôn*, "who surpasses other mortals in his *nóos*" (*i* 66).[1] To judge by this passage, it is his *nóos* which chiefly characterizes what Odysseus "is."

The council of the gods also defines what Odysseus is to "do." Persuaded by Athena to end the long exile of Odysseus and to take thought for his future, Zeus bids the other gods as well to take thought for the hero's *nóston, hópōs élthēisi*, his "return, that he may come home" (*i* 77). What Odysseus is to "do," his destiny, is to "return home," and this is expressed by the word *nóstos*, a nominal derivative of *néomai*.

The crucial problem to be handled in this study concerns the original meaning of the verbal root *nes-*. This meaning must be carefully reconstructed in order to show how terms as semantically distinct in English as "mind" and "return home" were once closely related in the Greek language. Before tackling this problem, however, it will be useful to add a few remarks on methodology.

The major source of evidence in this investigation will be Homer, one reason for which is the very premise of the *Odyssey*: the "return" of the "intelligent" hero. But Homer's value also derives from the traditionality of his poetry; for traditional poetry, by its very nature, conserves much that is old. Given this, it is not rash to look to Homeric epic for traces of a derivation which Homer himself no longer perceived. His conservative tradition "remembered" more than he himself understood.

1. Lower case italicized Roman numerals refer to books of the *Odyssey*, small capitals to books of the *Iliad*.

However, problems of reconstruction require caution. It is true that Homer conserves much that is old, but this cannot always be easily isolated and evaluated. One must expect from the start that ancient patrimony in Homer will have survived in a fragmentary and disjointed form. Such a situation would, according to the thesis of this study, be graphically represented by the words *nóos* and *nóstos* in the first scene of the *Odyssey*. Although both words occur in the same significant passage, they of course remain separate and distinct lexical items. Homer could never fully re-integrate what had long since been split. He could only preserve such fragments as were embedded in a traditional context.

Only with the word *polútropos* does Homer seem to recapture something of a once coherent relation. In this word he does in fact combine notions of both *nóos* and *nóstos*. But it is important to notice how *polútropos* reinterprets both of these words. In contrast to the neutral terms "mind" and "return home," the meanings "very wily" and "much-wandering" (or "much-tossed about") are shaded toward "personality" and "suffering," respectively, and would seem to reflect Homer's own humanized view of his hero. An old combination of ideas has thus survived only in a reinterpreted form. Such survival through reinterpretation is an important phenomenon in Homer and will be met with again in this book.

These methodological points can all be reduced to the simple necessity of recognizing both synchronic and diachronic dimensions in Homer. On the one hand, the *Odyssey* is a highly unified work by a master poet, and one has to take account of this poet's understanding and use of his own material. On the other hand, one must also recognize that the poet's material was in large part traditional, and that it still bears the marks, however latent, of its previous history.[2]

It remains to indicate the order in which the various problems raised in this introduction will be considered. Chapter 1 presents the formal evidence for the derivation of *nóos* from the root *nes-*. Chapter 2 then investigates the root itself in order to determine its earliest meaning in Greek. Chapters 3–5 show how a latent connection between "mind" and "returning home" has been preserved by Homer. Chapter 6 then considers non-Greek evidence for the root *nes-* in order to determine its meaning in Indo-European. Chapter 7 returns to Greek to suggest further instances, in various traditions, where a connection between *nóos* and *néomai* has been preserved.

2. The terms synchronic ("with time," "at a given time") and diachronic ("through time") were coined by Ferdinand de Saussure to describe two distinct approaches to the study of language; the value of this distinction to the study of a traditional medium like Greek epic is well illustrated by Deborah Dickmann Boedeker, *Aphrodite's Entry into Greek Epic* (Leiden, 1974), and Leonard Muellner, *The Meaning of Homeric EYXOMAI through its Formulas* (Innsbruck, 1976).

1 *Formal Evidence for the Etymology of Greek* nóos

VARIOUS ATTEMPTS have been made to etymologize Greek *nóos*, but none of these has carried wide conviction. The word permits a large number of formal reconstructions, and this helps to explain both the number of attempted etymologies and the uncertainty of all of them.

The crucial problem is the hiatus, which may be accounted for by the loss of original -w-, -j-, or -s-, or may even be regarded as original itself. Complicating this situation is the ambiguity of the initial *n*, which may be either original or descended from an original *sn-* (as in *nípha*, "snow," from *snig^{w}h-m̥*). Multiplying the two uncertainties by each other produces a total of eight possible reconstructions.[1]

This field may be reduced sharply, however. The decipherment of the Linear-B tablets has produced a new and important piece of evidence regarding the hiatus. The evidence does not show which of the four possibilities is correct, but it does remove from consideration the one that has most often been assumed by etymologists.

---

1. For a discussion of the formal possibilities, see E. Schwyzer, *Festschrift für P. Kretschmer: Beiträge zur griechischen und lateinischen Sprachforschung* (Berlin, 1926), pp. 247 ff.

In the tablet KN V 962 is found the form *wi-pi-no-o*; this has been interpreted as the personal name *Wiphínoos*, classical Greek *Iphínoos*, a compound form with the word *nóos* as its second element. The spelling *no-o* of this element is decisive against the reconstruction **(s)now-os* for *-w-* is preserved in Mycenean (as in the first element *Wiphi-*), and the spelling would have been **wi-pi-no-wo*.[2] This factor immediately disposes of three attempted etymologies. Two of these, connecting *nóos* with *neúō*, "nod," and *néō*, "swim," were in any case unlikely.[3] But the third, proposing a connection with Gothic *snutrs*, "wise, intelligent," was defended by Eduard Schwyzer and is given preference by Hjalmar Frisk.[4] This too must now be abandoned.

Given the impossibility of connections with Gothic *snutrs* and Greek *néō*, there is no reason to postulate an original *sn-* initial. This was, in any case, unlikely on purely formal grounds, since there is no trace of a double consonant initial either in Homeric compounds or in the scansion of Homeric verse. As against the *-nn-* in for example, *agánniphos*, "very snowy," there is only *-n-* in *ankhínoos, anoémōn, anóētos, ánoos, Alkínoos, Antínoos, Arsínoos, Astúnoos, Autónoos, Hippónoos, Iphínoos, Pontónoos,* and *Prónoos.* Likewise, there is nothing corresponding to the scansion of *óreā niphóenta*, "snowy mountains," (*xix* 338) in sequences that involve *nóos.*[5] Admittedly, the treatment in these matters does not always correspond to etymological realities; but the onesidedness of the evidence cannot be ignored where there is no strong external reason for doubt.

2. The personal name *no-e-u, Noeús*, (PY Jn 431) is also generally connected with *nóos,* and again shows the lack of a *-w-*.

3. For the proposed connection with *neúō,* see W. Prellwitz *Etymologisches Wörterbuch der griechischen Sprache*[2] (Göttingen, 1905), s.v. *nóos*; and K. Brugmann, *Indogermanische Forschungen* 19 (1906): 213–14, 30 (1912): 371 ff. For the proposed connection with *néō,* see E. Kieckers, *Indogermanische Forschungen* 23 (1908–09): 362 ff.

4. E. Schwyzer, *Festschrift* (n. 1); H. Frisk, *Griechisches etymologisches Wörterbuch* (Heidelberg, 1960–71), s.v. *nóos.*

5. Cf. P. Chantraine, *Grammaire homérique* (Paris, 1958), 1 : 177.

These considerations reduce the possibilities to three: *no-os, *noj-os, and *nos-os. The first of these is in fact very unlikely, for nóos, as Frisk points out, is doubtless an old, inherited verbal noun ("zweifellos ein altererbtes Verbalnomen"), and as such should be connected with a verbal root—namely, with a root having the shape CeC- (where C = consonant).

The second form, *noj-os, satisfies this condition; it also conforms to the Mycenean evidence, since the loss of intervocalic yod is attributable to Common Greek. Furthermore, a root *nej- is attested with an appropriate meaning in Sanskrit. Related to the verb nayati, "lead," is the thematic noun naya-ḥ, which has the meanings "leading, performance, behavior, worldly wisdom, policy, fundamental principle, system, theory." According to McKenzie, who proposed this connection with Greek nóos, "it is not easy to see how far the resemblance of meaning between nóos and naya-ḥ is due to the survival of inherited senses in both cases, and how far to independent but parallel development of fresh meanings in each language. That the passage from 'lead' to 'think' was possible we know from Latin duco and Greek hēgéomai. It may have occurred independently in Greek and in Sanskrit."[6]

McKenzie's etymology is possible, but it has serious problems. Naya-h does not occur until the post-Vedic period, and may well be an independent formation in Sanskrit. The appropriate meanings, moreover, seem clearly derivative, and in any case are not very close to the meaning of Greek nóos. One might still suppose an independent semantic development in Greek, except for the most serious difficulty of all: one would be speculating about a verbal root which is otherwise unattested in Greek. As far as we know, there was no Greek root nej-.

6. R. McKenzie, Classical Quarterly 17 (1923): 195–96. It should be noted that the Greek and Latin parallels cited by McKenzie represent different semantic developments, one from the other; cf. É. Benveniste, Le vocabulaire des institutions indo-européennes (Paris, 1969), 1 : 151 ff.

The form that remains is *nos-os. This, too, conforms to the Mycenean evidence, since the loss of intervocalic s is also attributable to Common Greek. In Mycenean this s probably survived as h in pronunciation, but the feature is usually not represented in the writing system (cf. the s-stem dative we-te-i, later Greek (w) étei, from *wetesi). Furthermore, there is a well-attested verbal root nes- in Greek: namely the root of néomai, "return home," in which etymological s is guaranteed by the nominal form nóstos.

The formal evidence thus indicates that nóos and néomai have the same relation to each other as lógos and légō, phóros and phérō, phóbos and phébomai. This situation has already been recognized, as is indicated by Hugo Mühlestein's remark that, in the opinion of Ernst Risch and Alfred Heubeck, "noûs could, in spite of the semantic difficulty, belong to the same root as néomai" ("noûs könnte, trotz der semantischen Schwierigkeit, zur gleichen Wurzel gehören wie néomai").[7]

Mühlestein himself connects the element -noos in names like Iphínoos with the verb néomai in a transitive sense, "bring home," and he would like to distinguish these from other compound names which clearly have to do with nóos, "mind,"[8] His translation "he who brings safely home by means of his strength" ("der mit Kräften heim rettet") for Mycenean Wiphínoos in fact puts the present argument in danger of circularity, since it was merely assumed that this proper name has to do with nóos, "mind." The circularity can be overcome only by showing that in reality there is only one class of compounds in -noos, insofar as the root is concerned. This, in turn, can be shown only when the "semantic difficulty" of connecting nóos and néomai is removed. Such, in any case, is the

7. H. Mühlestein, "Namen von Neleiden auf Pylostäfelchen," Museum Helveticum 22 (1965): 158, n. 18. C. J. Ruijgh and P. Frei have also discussed the possible derivation of nóos from nes-; for their solutions to the semantic problem see, respectively, nn. 27 and 32 below, chap. 2.

8. Mühlestein, p. 158.

main problem to be solved in establishing the proposed
etymology of *nóos*. The danger of circularity in the formal
argument gives appropriate emphasis to the need for convincing
semantic arguments. On the success of the latter the whole case
must rest.

2 *The Root* *nes- *in Prehistoric Greek*

1 EVIDENCE FOR THE PRIMITIVE MEANING

IN ORDER TO CONNECT *nóos* with *néomai* one must first reconstruct the primitive meaning of Greek *nes-*. Other Indo-European families (notably Germanic) contain valuable comparative evidence, and some of this evidence will enter the present discussion. The bulk of the Indo-European evidence, however, will be treated separately in chapter 6. The first step is one of internal reconstruction.

For the primitive Greek meaning there is one piece of evidence with singular importance. This is the old participial form *ásmenos*, which occurs first in Homer and then, with considerable frequency, in later Greek. This form deserves close attention, and, in fact, most of this chapter will be devoted to it. The points to be considered are, first, the etymology of the form; second, its place in the formulaic diction of Greek epic; and third, its meaning in primitive Greek. As will be seen, these three points are to a large extent overlapping.

The basic question concerns the etymology of *ásmenos*. On this question there has been a persistent debate, which can be described briefly.[1]

---

1. The two derivations to be discussed are both given, with no decision made, by H. Frisk, *Griechisches etymologisches Wörterbuch* (chap. 1, n. 4), s.v., E. Boisacq, *Dictionnaire étymologique de la langue grecque*[2] (Paris, 1916), s.v., and P. Chantraine, *Dictionnaire étymologique de la langue grecque*, vol. 1 (Paris, 1968), s.v. Yet another derivation (connection with Greek *ãsai*, "satisfy") has been proposed by L. R. Palmer, *Sprache* 5 (1959): 136 n. 21; while possible, this derivation still calls for a satisfactory explanation of the form *ãsai* itself (see Chantraine, s.vv. *ãsai*, *ásmenos*, who reviews Palmer's proposals).

6

The first etymology proposed for *ásmenos* connected this participle with the root **swād-* of, for example, Greek *hḗdomai*, "enjoy," and *handánō*, "please."[2] The form was reconstructed as **swad-s-menos*, representing an archaic sigmatic aorist. The chief merit of this derivation from *swād-* is that it provides a basis for the meaning "pleased" or "happy," which is regular for *ásmenos* in classical Greek.

But this etymology has a serious problem in that *ásmenos* has a smooth-breathing in Attic as well as Ionic, which conflicts with a derivation from an original *sw-* (cf. Attic *handánō*).[3] It has further been shown that in all manuscript traditions of all Greek authors only the form *ásmenos* is correct.[4]

This problem was pointed out by Wackernagel, who then proposed a new derivation from the root *nes-*.[5] He too reconstructed a sigmatic aorist participle, of the form **ns-s-menos*, and he defended his etymology by citing passages in Homer and later authors where *ásmenos* apparently means "saved" and not "happy." For the meaning "saved" of the root *nes-* he compared the important Gothic cognates *nasjan*, "save," and *ganisan*, "be saved," and proposed that *ásmenos* originally had the same sense. To account for the later meaning "happy," he supposed either a semantic development from the basic meaning "saved," or a cross-etymology with an original **swad-s-menos*, with generalization of the smooth-breathing.

Two derivations for *ásmenos* have been given, only one of which can be correct. I will argue that the derivation from the root *nes-* is correct but that Wackernagel's arguments as to

2. The derivation goes back to P. Buttmann, *Ausführliche griechische Sprachlehre*[2] (Berlin, 1839), 2: 10; cf. also J. Schmidt, *Zeitschrift für vergleichende Sprachforschung* 27 (1882–85): 320; it has been accepted by E. Schwyzer, *Griechische Grammatik* (Munich, 1939), 1: 749, n. 3.

3. Only the unlikely assumption that Attic *ásmenos* was an Ionic or epic borrowing evades this problem.

4. See R. McKenzie, "ΆΣΜΕΝΟΣ or ΆΣΜΕΝΟΣ?" *Classical Quarterly* 20 (1926): 193–94.

5. J. Wackernagel, *Vermischte Beiträge zur griechischen Sprachkunde* (Basel, 1897), p. 6 [= *Kleine Schriften* (Göttingen, 1953), 1: 767].

form, meaning, and semantic development are in need of modification.

The reconstruction *ns-s-menos has a formal problem. It posits a zero-grade of the root, which, because of its samprasārana ablaut, would have to be very old. But the sigmatic aorist middle, to judge from the evidence of Vedic Sanskrit, originally had a full-grade of the root.[6] The Sanskrit forms in which a zero-grade appears are late and seem to have been based on original root-aorist middles.

A solution for Greek ásmenos is suggested by this mention of the root-aorist. One may in fact regard this form as simply a root-aorist, in which an archaic zero-grade would be entirely natural (cf. Homeric phthímenos and ktámenos). To account for the preservation of the consonant group -sm-, one may assume the same paradigmatic pressure as restored the form esmén on the basis of esté, or created pepusménos on the basis of pépustai.[7] In just this way, ásmenos could have been restored on the basis of a third-singular *asto. If phonology thus offers no real problem, the morphology of ásmenos would seem to demand the reconstruction *ns-menos.

The next problem is that of meaning. I suggest that "saved" may be close to the original meaning of ásmenos but that it is not exact. Wackernagel took this meaning directly from Germanic, but it will later be argued that even Gothic nasjan and ganisan contain (or at least go back to) more "primitive" meanings than "save" and "be saved." Reserving this matter for chapter 6, we must first consider the most important evidence, which is to be found in Greek itself.

This evidence has to do with the use of ásmenos in Homer. The word is in fact relatively rare (it occurs only five times),

6. See J. Narten, Die sigmatischen Aoriste im Veda (Wiesbaden, 1964), pp. 23–36.

7. Cf. M. Lejeune, Phonétique historique du mycénien et du grec ancien (Paris, 1972), pp. 122–24.

but it is possible, by means of formulaic analysis, to establish a chronological hierarchy of what occurrences there are. This has important consequences in that the oldest use can be shown to be very old indeed and to contain the original meaning of the root *nes-*.

The following formulaic line accounts for three of the five occurences of *ásmenos* in Homer:[8]

> *ásmenoi ek thanátoio, phílous olésantes hetaírous*
> *ásmenoi* from death, having lost dear companions.

Wackernagel thought that the collocation *ásmenoi ek thanátoio* meant "having been *saved* from death." I propose, however, that the original meaning was simply "having *returned* from death," which keeps *ásmenoi* in line with Homeric *néomai*. This may be disappointing from the point of view of *ásmenoi* alone, but from the point of view of the whole collocation the result is startling. The words *ásmenoi ek thanátoio*, interpreted as "having returned from death," reveal the primitive context in which the verb *néomai* appeared, and this context is of the greatest importance. To "return from death" is clearly not the same as to "return home."

The argument sketched above must now be filled out and defended. Three immediate points require demonstration, all concerning the line:

> *ásmenoi ek thanátoio, phílous olésantes hetaírous.*

First, does the word *ásmenoi* in this line in fact derive from the root *nes-*? Second, does the first half of this line in fact mean "having returned from death"? Third, is the whole line an inheritance from an earlier period in the epic tradition?

---

8. The line is part of a two-line refrain at the end of the Ciconian episode (*ix* 62–63), the Cyclops episode (*ix* 565–66), and the Laestrygonian episode (*x* 133–34).

The demonstration for each of these points emerges from another formulaic line in Homer, which has never been considered in this connection before. The line, which occurs twice in the *Odyssey* (*xi* 114 and *xii* 141), is the following:

opsè kakôs neîai, olésas ápo pántas hetaírous.

You will return late and in evil condition, having lost all your companions.

The crucial point to be noticed is the resemblance between this line and that which includes *ásmenoi*. In the latter half of the two lines the resemblance is unmistakable. Is it, then, a coincidence that the second line contains a form of *néomai*, namely *neîai*, "you will return"? On the contrary, this fact indicates that *ásmenoi* also belongs to the paradigm of *néomai*, and that the two lines in question are ancient formulaic variations of one pattern.

The justification for this view involves a number of different considerations. The most important point concerns the meaning of the forms *ásmenoi* and *neîai*. It is obvious that if the two lines in question originated as variants of each other, then the two forms of *néomai* must have had the same meaning. It was proposed above that *ásmenoi* should be rendered as simply "having returned." The connection with the form *neîai*, "you will return," would now seem to support this. More important, however, is the question of context. In the case of *ásmenoi* the context is made explicit by the words *ek thanátoio*: the "return" is "from death." It is of great significance that for *neîai* the context is likewise a "return from death," with the difference, however, that the context in this case remains implicit.

What must be taken into account is the larger context in which the line with *neîai* appears. As stated earlier, the line occurs twice. Both occurrences are significant, but for the sake of clarity only the first need be considered here.[9] The context in which

9. *xi* 114 is in question here; *xii* 141 forms part of the Circe episode.

this is found is the prophecy Teiresias gives to Odysseus in the underworld. The implication here is clear. When Teiresias says "you will return," he means, implicitly, "you will return from death."[10]

Comparison with the line containing *neîai* has already indicated the answer to two important questions about the collocation *ásmenoi ek thanátoio*. There is now a compelling reason to believe that *ásmenoi* contains the root *nes-* and that the whole collocation once meant "having returned from death." The relevance of this meaning to the Homeric contexts where the collocation appears is a separate and important problem, which will be considered thoroughly in chapter 3. At present, however, more discussion is required to elucidate the formulaic relationship of the two lines in question.

There is, first of all, a difference between the two lines that must be explained. One line contains the root *nes-* in a participial form and fails to make a complete statement; the other line contains the root in a finite form and is thus self-contained. The explanation for this would seem to be formulaic expansion. The line with *ásmenoi* in fact forms the second part of a two-line unit; this unit, which does not vary, functions as a "refrain" at the end of three episodes in the *Odyssey*. The complete traditional unit is therefore the following:

ἔνθεν δὲ προτέρω πλέομεν ἀκαχήμενοι ἦτορ,
ἄσμενοι ἐκ θανάτοιο, φίλους ὀλέσαντες ἑταίρους.

From there we sailed onward grieving at heart, *ásmenoi* from death, having lost our dear companions.

10. This is the time to counter an immediate objection—namely, that the prophecy of Teiresias does not refer to Odysseus's return from the underworld but to the dangers he will encounter afterward, on the "way home"; this merely shows us that Homer understood *neîai* to mean "you will return home," not that this was the intended meaning when the line was first composed (see below in text on this point).

Further objections might be raised by analyst critics, who view the Nekyia (*Odyssey* 11) as a late addition to the poem; for a discussion of how this view affects my argument, see end note 1.

The first line in this refrain contains a further link with the line beginning *opsè kakôs neîai*; the word *kakôs*, "in evil condition," and the phrase *akakhḗmenoi ḗtor*, "grieving at heart," both suggest a negative aspect to "returning."

There are other obvious differences between the two lines. Person, number, and tense are all different for the two forms *ásmenoi* and *neîai*. Formulaic flexibility can again be invoked to explain this, though the precise mechanism need not be specified.[11] It is enough to realize that basic differences in situation are involved.

One hesitates to be overly specific because the two lines in question must have been composed at a very early time and should not therefore be explained in terms of Homer's own improvisational techniques. The question that now remains, however, has to do precisely with the antiquity of these lines. How old do they seem to be?

The fact that they are variations of each other means they originated more or less together. When they were composed, moreover, the form *ásmenos* was necessarily still a part of the paradigm of *néomai*.[12] At this time, therefore, the whole root-aorist paradigm of *néomai* must still have been intact. This establishes as a terminus ante quem for the composition the point at which the root-aorist died out. This development, in turn, has a terminus post quem on the basis of an earlier argument. According to this argument, the consonant group -*sm*- was preserved through pressure from other parts of the root-aorist paradigm. Hence this paradigm must still have been

11. Formulaic flexibility can be analyzed in detail only for the period of the final composition of the *Iliad* and the *Odyssey*; cf. J. B. Hainsworth, *The Flexibility of the Homeric Formula* (Oxford, 1968), for such an analysis.

12. Hainsworth, pp. 36–38, in defining a "formula," counts variations within the same paradigm (inflection) but excludes variations between forms from the same root which belong to different paradigms; with *ásmenos*, however, it is a case of having belonged to the same paradigm as *neîai*, or of having ceased to belong to any paradigm at all.

intact when the alteration of original -sm- took place in Greek. This development belongs to the second millennium B.C.[13]

Two things are uncertain in this, and the possible period of composition is thus somewhat broad. One cannot tell how long before the death of the root-aorist paradigm the line with *ásmenoi* was composed; and, at the other end, one cannot tell how long after the alteration of original -sm- this paradigm died. It is enough to say that the period of composition could easily have been in the second millennium B.C.

By the Homeric period, at any rate, the form *ásmenoi* no longer belonged to the same paradigm as *neîai*. This point has not yet been discussed, and it should now be emphasized. Since the two forms in question no longer belonged to the same grammatical system, the lines in which they occur inevitably ceased to belong to the same formulaic system. Instead the two lines went their separate ways, creating new "subsystems" of their own. This development is worth demonstrating in detail.

The development is especially apparent in the case of the line beginning *opsè kakôs neîai*. As argued above, this line properly and traditionally formed an essential part of a *Nekuomanteía*.[14] In one crucial instance (*xi* 114) Homer preserves this context. In the line's only other occurrence (*xii* 141) the context is still "prophecy," but the implication of "returning from death" is less apparent.[15]

The first formulaic variation of the line appears in *ii* 174 ff., where again the context of prophecy is preserved without further implications. The seer Halitherses, warning the suitors that Odysseus will soon be home, says that everything he once

13. Cf. E. Risch, "Die Gliederung der griechischen Dialekte in neuer Sicht," *Museum Helveticum* 12 (1955): 67–68 [= *Language and Background of Homer*, ed. G. S. Kirk (New York, 1964), pp. 96–97].

14. See n. 10 and accompanying text above, and end note 1 as well.

15. For a discussion of the Circe episode, see chap. 3, sect. 2.

prophesied has come to pass; he repeats his prophecy in indirect discourse:

> φῆν κακὰ πολλὰ παθόντ', ὀλέσαντ' ἄπο πάντας ἑταίρους,
> ἄγνωστον πάντεσσιν ἐεικοστῷ ἐνιαυτῷ
> οἴκαδ' ἐλεύσεσθαι.

I said that he, having suffered many evils and having lost all his companions, would come home unrecognized by all in the twentieth year.

In modifying his basic pattern, Homer has changed *neîai*, "you will return," into *oíkad' eleúsesthai*, "he would come home"; *kakôs*, "in evil condition," into *kakà pollà pathónt'*, "having suffered many evils"; and *opsé*, "late," into *eeikostôi eniautôi*, "in the twentieth year." The secondary nature of the above passage is evident, just as it is evident that in it there is no conscious suggestion of "returning from death." Only the prophetic context is traditional.

In a second passage, *ix* 532ff., there is less modification of the basic pattern but the context has been changed from prophecy to curse. In this passage the Cyclops prays that the fleeing Odysseus, even if he is not prevented by Poseidon from returning home, may at least suffer great misfortune on his way:

> ἀλλ' εἴ οἱ μοῖρ' ἐστὶ φίλους ἰδέειν καὶ ἱκέσθαι
> οἶκον ἐϋκτίμενον καὶ ἑὴν ἐς πατρίδα γαῖαν,
> ὀψὲ κακῶς ἔλθοι, ὀλέσας ἄπο πάντας ἑταίρους.

But if it is his destiny to see those dear to him and to reach his well-founded home and fatherland, may he come late and in evil condition, having lost all his companions.

Here Homer has substituted *élthoi*, "may he come," for the traditional *neîai*. The fact that *élthoi* depends for its sense on the previous mention of "home" and "fatherland" shows the secondary nature of this passage.

A final variation occurs in *xiii* 339–40, where Athena has met Odysseus upon his return to Ithaca and apologizes for her apparent neglect during his voyages:

αὐτὰρ ἐγὼ τὸ μὲν οὔ ποτ᾽ ἀπίστεον, ἀλλ᾽ ἐνὶ θυμῷ
ᾔδε᾽, ὃ νοστήσεις ὀλέσας ἄπο πάντας ἑταίρους.

I never doubted it, but knew in my heart that you would return home, having lost all your companions.

Here Homer omits any suggestion of the traditional words *opsè kakôs*, "late, in evil condition" (which would be tactless in this context), and he substitutes the derivative form *nostêseis* for the older *neîai*. It is also worth noticing that the word *êide'*, "I knew," goes syntactically with what precedes, and that Homer has thus used less than a full hexameter in modifying his inherited model. What was expanded in the first two passages has here been contracted, and the latter process, as much as the former, indicates a secondary status. As for context, this is traditional only insofar as Athena's statement has a future reference (cf. *nostêseis*). The element of prophecy has again been weakened, if not eliminated.

The dependence of the above passages on the line beginning *opsè kakôs neîai* argues strongly for the traditionality of this line. Each modification, moreover, makes it clear that Homer understood the word *neîai* as meaning, simply, "you will return home" (cf., for example, *oikad' eleúsesthai* in *ii* 176). If the word originally meant "you will return from death," then Homer, while preserving a traditional line, has understood something new by it. The three dependent passages bear witness to this reinterpretation.

When we turn to the line beginning *ásmenoi ek thanátoio* the factor of reinterpretation becomes more important still. Whereas *neîai* meant something new to Homer, it at least still belonged to the paradigm of *néomai*. As argued above, however, the same was not true of *ásmenos*. This old participle had in fact already lost its verbal force, acquiring instead the adjectival meanings "pleased" and "happy." An isolated occurrence in Homer shows this; in xiv 107–08, Agamemnon appeals to his counselors to suggest some better plan than his own:

νῦν δ᾽ εἴη ὃς τῆσδέ γ᾽ ἀμείνονα μῆτιν ἐνίσποι,
ἢ νέος ἠὲ παλαιός· ἐμοὶ δέ κεν ἀσμένῳ εἴη.

Would that there were someone, either young or old, who might utter a better plan than this; it would make me *ásmenos*.

Even if a weakened notion such as "relieved" might still be present, the form *asménoi* functions as an adjective, just as in classical Greek. The meaning is probably no more than "happy."

If *ásmenos* functioned only as an adjective by Homer's time, then Homer can no longer have understood the syntax, let alone the meaning, of the traditional refrain. This is in fact borne out by the one formulaic adaptation of the phrase *ásmenoi ek thanátoio* which occurs in Homer. Homer must have felt the lack of a verb in the refrain; this he supplies in the following passage (xx 349–50), part of the speech Achilles utters when he realizes that Aeneas, snatched by Poseidon, has escaped to safety:

ἐρρέτω· οὔ οἱ θυμὸς ἐμεῦ ἔτι πειρηθῆναι
ἔσσεται, ὃς καὶ νῦν *φύγεν* ἄσμενος ἐκ θανάτοιο.

Let him go; he will no longer have the heart to make trial of me who has just now *escaped ásmenos* from death.

The fact that Homer has added the verb *phúgen*, "escaped," indicates strongly that he felt no verbal force in *ásmenos*. Equally important, the verb *phúgen* reveals how Homer has reinterpreted the very context of the collocation *ásmenoi ek thanátoio*. What was originally a "return from death" has become simply an "escape from death."

Homer's use of the verb *pheúgein* is to be stressed here, for it is a constant feature in a whole series of reinterpreted contexts that will be considered in the course of this study. One such context may be considered immediately because it has to do with another, as yet unanswered, question. The collocation *phúgen ásmenos ek thanátoio* shows that *ásmenos* no longer had its verbal force. How, then, did Homer understand this adjective? The phrase *emoì dé ken asménōi eíē* in XIV 108 has already indicated the meaning "happy." The same meaning is therefore more than likely in the derivative collocation *phúgen ásmenos ek thanátoio*. But can Homer have understood the same meaning in the traditional refrain, where there is no form of *pheúgein* to rescue the syntax?

That he in fact did so is indicated by the lines in the *Odyssey* which conclude the Laestrygonian episode. These lines, which are followed immediately by the traditional refrain, serve to adapt this refrain to the particular occasion. Homer thus offers his own reinterpretation of the refrain, a practice which he follows consistently,[16] and which in this case is very revealing. The Laestrygonian episode ends as follows (*x* 131 ff.):

> ἀσπασίως δ' ἐς πόντον ἐπηρεφέας φύγε πέτρας
> νηῦς ἐμή· αὐτὰρ αἱ ἄλλαι ἀολλέες αὐτόθ' ὄλοντο.
> ἔνθεν δὲ προτέρω πλέομεν ἀκαχήμενοι ἦτορ,
> ἄσμενοι ἐκ θανάτοιο, φίλους ὀλέσαντες ἑταίρους.

Happily my ship *escaped* from the overhanging rocks into the sea; but all the other ships *perished* there together. From there we sailed onward grieving at heart, *ásmenoi* from death, *having lost* our dear companions.

The correspondence between the last line and the first two lines is apparent. But while the forms *olésantes*, "having lost," and *ólonto*, "perished," balance one another completely, the form

---

16. The specific instances are discussed in chap. 3, sect. 3.

ásmenoi has been reinterpreted by the words *aspasíōs . . . phúge*, both of which are significant. *Phúge* shows that the context is now simply one of "escape"; *aspasíōs* indicates that Homer did in fact understand *ásmenoi* to mean "happy."[17]

A phrase meaning "happy from death" must have seemed odd to Homer but not impossible. This would have been justification enough for preserving a line that was hallowed by tradition. The crucial factor in this preservation was the very possibility of reinterpretation. Had the form *ásmenos* not acquired a new meaning and a new grammatical function, and thus survived, the line containing it would doubtless have disappeared long before Homer. But since *ásmenos* did survive in the ordinary language apart from its original paradigm, the line containing it was able to survive in the epic language apart from its original formulaic system. It is thus an accident of linguistic history that the lines with *ásmenoi ek thanátoio* and *opsè kakôs neîai* both appear in the same Homeric poem, for the lines no longer have anything to do with one another.

This completes my analysis of the formulaic factors involved in the interpretation of the form *ásmenos*. Before proceeding to other matters, however, I shall consider briefly an alternative explanation of these factors.

Friedrich Bechtel sought to disprove Wackernagel's contention that *ásmenos* must sometimes mean "saved."[18] Realizing that the correct reconstruction for *ásmenos* depends ultimately on a correct interpretation of the formulaic refrain, he argued that the second line of this refrain is a late interpolation. The supposed interpolator did two things. He first modified the phrase *phúgen ásmenos ek thanátoio* found in xx 350 by pluralizing *ásmenos* and

---

17. The word *aspásios* also occurs in the reinterpretation of the refrain in the Cyclops episode; see p. 64 below.

18. F. Bechtel, *Lexilogus zu Homer* (Halle, 1914), s.v. *ásmenos*.

omitting the finite verb *phúgen*. He then took the formulaic phrase *olésas ápo pántas hetaírous*, "having lost all your (his) companions," and adapted it to a plural context: *phílous olésantes hetaírous*, "having lost our dear companions."

There are serious problems with both parts of this argument. As far as *ásmenos* is concerned, the supposed interpolator did all in his power to create nonsense if this word meant "happy" to him. Not only is the syntagma "happy from death" abnormal in the extreme, but also its juxtaposition to *akakhḗmenoi êtor*, "grieving at heart," would have required an ineptitude that is difficult to imagine. As far as *olésas ápo pántas hetaírous* is concerned, Bechtel failed to realize that the basic line containing this formula contains the word *neîai* as well, which all but proves what he sought to disprove concerning the root of *ásmenos*. The only plausible explanation of the relation between the lines with *ásmenoi* and *neîai* is that they both go back to the same primitive source.

With this point established, one may look more closely at the original meaning of the Greek root *nes-*. The earliest context in which this root appears is a "return from death." What must now be asked, therefore, is precisely what it means to "return from death." How is this meaning, which seems implicit in the primitive root, to be interpreted?

The enquiry into this matter can best begin with a further observation on the two lines:

ásmenoi ek thanátoio, phílous olésantes hetaírous

and

opsè kakôs neîai, olésas ápo pántas hetaírous.

What must now be taken into account are the contents of these two lines in their entirety. Both lines contain two distinct ideas: on the one hand a "return" and on the other hand a "loss of companions." The opposition between these two ideas, further-more, is one that has a profound relevance to the basic plot of the first half of the *Odyssey*. The essential result of the adventures of Odysseus is the gradual "loss of companions," until all have perished and the hero alone is left to "return."

The importance of this opposition may be judged by the opening passage of the *Odyssey*, which presents a synopsis of the action, and which deals almost exclusively with the different fates of Odysseus and his companions. Odysseus is said to have suffered much "while winning his life (*arnúmenos hến te psukhến*) and the return of his companions (*kaì nóston hetaírōn*)."[19] However, the companions are then said not to have returned but to have perished through their own foolishness.

The lines describing the companions' fate contain an important clue for our present enquiry. The lines (*i* 6ff.) are as follows:

ἀλλ' οὐδ' ὣς ἑτάρους ἐρρύσατο, ἱέμενός περ·
αὐτῶν γὰρ σφετέρῃσιν ἀτασθαλίῃσιν ὄλοντο,
νήπιοι, οἳ κατὰ βοῦς Ὑπερίονος Ἠελίοιο
ἤσθιον· αὐτὰρ ὁ τοῖσιν ἀφείλετο νόστιμον ἦμαρ.

Even so he did not save his companions, hard though he tried; for they perished through their own recklessness, the fools, when they ate the cattle of Hyperion Helios and he took away their day of return.

The poet has here singled out the god Helios as the agent who prevented the companions from returning. The importance of this for the tradition behind the *Odyssey* and for the original meaning of the root *nes-* can be suggested here by anticipating one conclusion of chapter 6—namely, that the Indo-European root *nes-* meant not only "return from death" but also, implicitly,

19. *i* 5; notice the parallelism between *psukhến* and *nóston* in this line, both used as objects of *arnúmenos*. Does the expression "winning his life" imply "winning his life back again" or merely "remaining alive"? Such ambiguity could well be the reflection of a traditional "return from death" motif.

"return from darkness." The same composite meaning was also present in the Greek root,[20] on the evidence of the *nóstos* of Odysseus. One purpose of chapter 3 will be to show that this *nóstos* is a "return from darkness" as well as a "return from death"; for now, however, attention can at least be drawn to the name *Kalupsó*. The name of Odysseus's captor for seven years, related as it is to the verb *kalúptō*, suggests both "darkness" and "death."[21]

If the root *nes-* originally had to do with "returning from darkness," it is not difficult to believe that the role of Helios, the Sun, is somehow relevant to the present discussion. I wish to suggest, however, that this role, more than being relevant, is absolutely central to a correct understanding of the root *nes-*. We know that the earliest context for this root was a "return from death" accompanied by a "loss of companions." This context, I suggest, originated as a direct reflex of primitive sun worship. What leads to this conclusion is not only the role of Helios in the *Odyssey* and the meaning "return from darkness" of the root *nes-*; the assumed hierophany of the sun also explains what it means to "return from death," and why this return is accompanied by a "loss of companions." An explanation which takes account of both of these patently old features is very compelling.

The easiest way to explain what is involved in primitive sun worship is to quote from the work of a scholar who has made a comparative study of the phenomenon. The following paragraphs are taken from Mircea Eliade's *Patterns in Comparative Religion*.[22] The first paragraph describes primitive conceptions of the sun in a general way, while the final two paragraphs are particularly relevant to our problem.

20. The notions of "death" and "darkness" are of course closely connected in Greek generally (cf. the noun *erebos*).
21. Cf. chap. 3, n. 68 below.
22. M. Eliade, *Patterns in Comparative Religion*, trans. R. Sheed (New York, 1963), pp. 136–37.

Sunset is not recognized as a "death" of the sun (unlike the moon's three days in hiding) but as a descent into the lower regions, into the kingdom of the dead. Unlike the moon, the sun has the privilege of passing through hell without undergoing the condition of death. Nonetheless, its pre-destined journey through the lower regions still confers on it the prerogatives relating to death and burial. Thus even when it no longer holds a front place in the pantheon or in the religious experience of a given civilization, as the Supreme Being who has become a sun god or a fecundator, the sun still manifests a certain ambivalence which makes it capable of undergoing yet further developments.

This ambivalence might be expressed rather like this: though immortal, the sun descends nightly to the kingdom of the dead; it can, therefore, take men with it and, by setting, put them to death; but it can also, on the other hand, guide souls through the lower regions and bring them back next day with its light. That is its twofold function—as psychopomp to "murder" and as hierophant to initiate. It explains the belief, so widely held in New Zealand and the New Hebrides, that merely to glance at the setting sun may induce death. The sun draws things, it "sucks in" the souls of the living with as much ease as it guides the souls of the dead to whom it acts as psychopomp through the western "gate of the sun." . . .

. . . Clearly, the fate of all the souls who plunge into the setting sun is not the same; not all gain what we may call "salvation." That is the point at which the redemptive power of initiation enters, and the part played by the various secret societies in choosing the elect and separating them from the amorphous mass of common men (the separation expressed in the mystique of sovereignty and the "children of the sun").

This description makes clear why the role of Helios is central to an understanding of the root *nes-*. Helios takes away from the companions their day of return (*autàr ho toîsin apheíleto nóstimon êmar*) because they are the "amorphous mass of common men" from whom the hero must be separated. The hero, on the other hand, is one of the "elect," and may thus gain "salvation."[23]

Eliade's description also reveals what it means to "return from death" in the context of a solar hierophany: "the sun has the privilege of passing through hell without undergoing the condition of death. Nevertheless, its predestined journey through the lower regions still confers on it the prerogatives relating to death and burial." Thus the hero, too, can pass through the regions of death without actually dying; he can, without violating nature, "return from death," because he has had only the prerogatives, and not the actual condition, of death.

It is appropriate to mention here the Gothic verb *ganisan* in its meaning "get well, recover." The verb contains the IE root *nes-*, and the context of illness is the easiest in which to grasp the root's underlying meaning, "return from death, return to life."

This section has shown that the earliest reconstructable context of the Greek root *nes-* is a "return from death and darkness," and that this context was hieratic. It is possible, however, that the root also appeared in secular contexts from an early time. If so, it would be overly restrictive to render the meaning of the root as "return from death and darkness." It is worth noting that, in the phrase *ásmenoi ek thanátoio*, the hieratic context has been specified through the words *ek thanátoio*. Similarly, in the frequent Homeric verse cadence *oíkónde néesthai*, "to return homeward," the word *oíkónde*, "homeward," may once have served to specify a secular context.

Émile Benveniste has reconstructed the original meaning of Greek *néomai* and its Sanskrit cognate *nasate* as "return to a familiar state" ("revenir à un état familier"),[24] which is perhaps

23. According to Pausanias 8.31.7, Helios was called *Sōtḗr*, "Savior," in Arcadia.

24. É. Benveniste, "Actif et moyen dans le verbe," *Journal de Psychologie* (Jan.-Feb. 1950) [= *Problems de linguistique générale* (Paris, 1966), p. 172].

broad enough to accommodate a variety of specific contexts. It does not, however, do justice to the hieratic context in early Greek. Since this context is of first importance to this study, I will refer only to the hieratic acceptation of the root *nes-*, which may indeed be rendered as "return from death and darkness."

2 THE SEMANTIC DEVELOPMENT OF *ásmenos*

The previous section showed that the word *ásmenos* had undergone a semantic development even before the Homeric period. To Homer the word already meant "happy." As soon as the rest of the root-aorist paradigm of *néomai* died out, the old participle from this paradigm could survive only because of its acquired adjectival meaning.

It was also shown that the original hieratic meaning of *ásmenos* was "having returned from death and darkness." This meaning could as accurately be rendered as "having returned to life and light." What is the connection between this meaning and the meaning "happy"? I suggest that for this connection one need only take into account the Greek word *pháos*. *Pháos* of course means "light," but throughout ancient Greek it also has the metaphorical meanings "deliverance" and "happiness" (see *LSJ* s.v.). The triple notion of "light," "deliverance," and "happiness" exactly covers what has been reconstructed and what is attested for the meaning of *ásmenos*.

There is evidence in post-Homeric Greek of a connection between the words *pháos* and *ásmenos*. The following passage in Plato (*Cratylus* 418c) is very revealing. In this passage Socrates mentions an old pronunciation of iota for eta, which allows him to derive *hēméra*, "day," from *himeírō*, "desire." What interests us is the way in which he glosses his explanation:

ὅτι γὰρ ἀσμένοις τοῖς ἀνθρώποις καὶ ἱμείρουσιν ἐκ τοῦ
σκότους τὸ φῶς ἐγίγνετο, ταύτῃ ὠνόμασαν "ἱμέραν"

Men named it day (himéran) because when the light (phôs)
emerged from the darkness they were happy (asménois) and
longing for it (himeírousin).

The fact that Socrates uses *ásmenos* as his gloss indicates that
this word was the *vox propria* in the context of "light." A
passage in Herodotus (8.14.1) exemplifies the implied association in the phrase: *hós sphi asménoisi hēméra epélampse*, "as
day broke to their happiness (relief)."

Equally striking are the following passages from Euripides. In
the first, *pháos* is used metaphorically. The passage is *Bacchae*
608–09, in which the Chorus, terrified by the destruction of the
royal palace, hails Dionysus as he emerges unharmed:

ὦ φάος μέγιστον ἡμῖν εὔιου βακχεύματος,
ὡς ἐσεῖδον ἀσμένη σε.

O greatest *light* to us of the Bacchic revelry, how *happily* have
I set my eyes on you.

The next two passages are more striking still, in that they involve
not only "light" but also a "return from death." The first is *Ion*
1437ff., in which Creusa and Ion, discovering that they are
mother and son, have the following dialogue:

I. ὦ φιλτάτη μοι μῆτερ, ἄσμενός σ' ἰδὼν
    πρὸς ἀσμένας πέπτωκα σὰς παρηίδας.
C. ὦ τέκνον, ὦ φῶς μητρὶ κρεῖσσον ἡλίου–
    συγγνώσεται γὰρ ὁ θεός–ἐν χεροῖν σ' ἔχω,
    ἄελπτον εὕρημ', ὃν κατὰ γᾶς ἐνέρων
    χθόνιον μετὰ Περσεφόνας τ' ἐδόκουν ναίειν.

(Ion) "My dearest mother, *happily* seeing you I have fallen on your *happy* cheeks." (Creusa) "O child, O *light* which to your mother is better than the sun—for this the Sun God will forgive me—I have you in my hands, an unexpected godsend, you who I thought were dwelling dead and buried beneath the earth in the kingdom of Persephone."

The second passage is *Hercules* 523–24, in which the hero, emerging from the underworld, addresses his palace as follows:

ὦ χαῖρε, μέλαθρον πρόπυλά θ᾽ ἑστίας ἐμῆς,
ὡς ἄσμενός σ᾽ ἐσεῖδον ἐς φάος μολών.

Hail to you, my gateway and palace, how *happily* have I set my eyes on you as I come into the *light*.

The expression *es pháos molón*, literally "having come into the light," could serve as an etymological definition of *ásmenos*.

One may speculate about another element which the three Euripidean passages have in common—namely, the collocation of *ásmenos* with the verb *horân*, "to see." This collocation is frequent in post-Homeric Greek. Along with *ásmenos pheúgein*, "to escape happily," it is in fact the only recurring collocation involving *ásmenos*. The instances with *horân*, moreover, considerably outnumber those with *pheúgein*.[25] One wonders, therefore, whether the collocation is old. Since the faculty of vision is inseparable from "light," one suspects that it is. I suggest that the collocation may actually go back to a fuller, more explicit form, **ásmenos horân pháos*, in which *ásmenos* still contained the notion of "returning to life." It should be noticed that the latter part of the suggested collocation is closely connected with "life" in the following Homeric formula: *zóei kaì horâi pháos ēelíoio*, "he *lives* and *sees the light* of the sun." It is easy to see

25. Examples of *ásmenos horân* are found in Sophocles *Trachiniae* 755, *Philoctetes* 271; Euripides *Iphigenia Aulidensis* 640, 644, *Troades* 21, *Hypsipyle* 1.4.20; Plato *Protagoras* 346a; Lysias 1.12, 3.29, 21.18; Demosthenes 37.15; Isocrates *Philippus* 50, 104. See below in text for *ásmenos pheúgein*.

how, in a collocation *ásmenos horân pháos* (which *Bacchae* 608–09 would still reflect), *ásmenos* could develop the meaning "happy," and how *ásmenos horân* could then be applied to objects other than *pháos*.

But one need not insist upon a precise channel for the semantic development of *ásmenos*. It is enough to recognize that the meaning "having returned to light" could develop the adjectival meaning "happy" as easily as the word *pháos* could stand metaphorically for "happiness."

It remains to give a brief discussion of the phrase *ásmenos pheúgein*. This collocation adds nothing to our understanding of the semantic development of *ásmenos*, but in some instances at least the context is worthy of note.

The complicating factor in the collocation *ásmenos pheúgein* is the possibility that it has been based on the Homeric phrase *phúgen ásmenos ek thanátoio* (xx 350), which is itself already secondary (cf. section 1 above). Thus, for example, Euripides *Helen* 398 probably owes something to the Homeric model:

τοὺς δ' ἐκ θαλάσσης ἀσμένους πεφευγότας
those who have *escaped happily* from the sea.

It is interesting, however, that the collocation twice appears in erotic contexts, where death imagery is otherwise common in Greek literature. The first instance is Theognis 1337–38:

οὐκέτ' ἐρῶ παιδός, χαλεπὰς δ' ἀπελάκτισ' ἀνίας
μόχθους τ' ἀργαλέους ἄσμενος ἐξέφυγον.

I no longer love the youth, but have shaken off the bitter sorrows, and have *escaped happily* from the painful troubles.

The second passage is Plato *Republic* 1.329c4, an anecdote according to which Sophocles, when asked if he missed love-making in his old age, replied in the negative: ἀσμενέστατα μέντοι αὐτὸ ἀπέφυγον, "most *happily* have I *escaped* from it."

In the next passage, Euripides *Hercules* 619ff., the context is explicitly a "return from death." In this passage the hero has just brought Theseus from the underworld, and in telling his father where Theseus is now, he says that he is in Athens, *nérthen ásmenos phugṓn*, "having fled *ásmenos* from the world below."

One final passage may be mentioned, in which the verb *anabaínein*, "to ascend," is used instead of *pheúgein*, but where the context is once again a "return from death." The passage is Plato *Republic* 10.616a7, in that part of the myth of Er where the torments of the wicked souls in Tartarus are described; it is reported that the worst torment of all was a "mouth" leading out of Tartarus which would roar whenever those below tried to ascend through it, and that therefore "each of them ascended *asmenéstata* whenever the mouth was silent."

In the last two passages cited, the words *ásmenos* and *asmenéstata* would seem to mean "happy" and "most happily," but it is also likely that the words were felt to be particularly appropriate to their contexts. Counting two of the Euripidean passages quoted earlier (*Ion* 1437ff. and *Hercules* 523–24), we have thus seen four instances where the classical Greek *ásmenos*, through whatever channel, has preserved a connection with its etymological meaning, "having returned from death."

3. The Relation Between the Greek Root *nes-* and *nóos*

I have reconstructed the original meaning of the Greek root *nes-* as "return to life and light." If the word *nóos* is to be explained as an old verbal noun from this root, then it too should have had to do with a "return to life and light". The plausibility of this reconstruction of *nóos* can be supported in this place by a number of general observations.[26]

26. From a formal standpoint, it is the whole series *néomai nóos noéō* which must be explained semantically. The nearest formal parallel is the series *phébomai phóbos phobéō*, in which the forms are related as follows: *phóbos*, "panic flight,"

In the last section attention was drawn to the inseparable relation between "vision" and "light." This establishes an immediate point of contact with *nóos*, for it is well known that *nóos* and denominative *noéō* are intimately connected with the

---

"panic fear," is an action noun, and corresponds closely in meaning to the primary verb *phébomai*, "flee in terror;" *phobéō*, "put to flight," "terrify," is a causative verb formed directly from the root, though it was later regarded as a denominative from *phóbos* (cf. H. Frisk [chap. 1, n. 4], s.v. *phébomai*).

Here the parallel with *nóos* breaks down, since *noéō* is generally taken as an originally denominative verb (see P. Chantraine [n. 1], s.v. *nóos*, who comments on the similar semantics of *noéō* and *nóos*). If this is correct, the basic meaning of *noéō*, "perceive closely," must derive from the meaning of *nóos*. Now *nóos* itself seems to be an action noun (cf. Chantraine); but it may be that the verbal notion in *nóos* was not "return to life" (intransitive) but "bring back to life" (transitive); a reconstructed Greek verb *néō*, with just such a transitive meaning, will be discussed in chap. 4, sect. 4 below. If the verbal notion was indeed transitive, a better comparison for *nóos* is the noun *gónos*. Although there is no Greek verb *génō*, *gónos*, in the meaning "procreation," is an action noun from the root *gen-*, to "procreate"; just so, on the strength of the conjectural verb *néō*, "bring back to life," the noun *nóos* may be taken to mean a "bringing back to life," and a "bringing back to the light." Now "bringing back to the light," as the description of a mental process, is easily related to "perceive closely," the meaning of denominative *noéō* (see below in text for both *nóos* and *noéō* in connection with verbs of perception, especially "seeing").

In the meaning "mind" it is possible that *nóos*, in addition to expressing an action, also expresses the result of an action (is not only a *nomen actionis*, but also a *nomen rei actae*: see E. Schwyzer, *Griechische Grammatik*[2] [Munich, 1953], 1: 457, 458–59). This is the case for *gónos*, which means not only the act of "begetting," but also "that which is begotten," namely, "offspring." Just so *nóos*, in the meaning "mind," may have been "that which is brought back to life." This meaning suggests certain contexts of *noûs* in classical Greek. Aristotle, for example, in *The Generation of Animals* 736[b]28, reasons that at birth "*noûs* alone enters in, as an additional factor, from outside, and it alone is divine" (τὸν νοῦν μόνον θύραθεν ἐπεισιέναι καὶ θεῖον εἶναι μόνον).

Euripides, on the other hand, in *Helen* 1014ff., represents *noûs* as departing at death (the speaker, significantly, is the priestess *Theo-nóē*):

> ὁ νοῦς
> τῶν κατθανόντων ζῇ μὲν οὔ, γνώμην δ' ἔχει
> ἀθάνατον εἰς ἀθάνατον αἰθέρ' ἐμπεσών.

The *noûs* of those who have died does not remain alive, but rather preserves an immortal intelligence, having fallen into the immortal ether.

faculty of vision. In Bruno Snell's terms, the verb *noéō* designates a "seeing," but a "mental" or "spiritual" seeing which is independent of the eye.[27]

But it is difficult to say more precisely what the noun *nóos*, involving a "return to life and light," in the first instance designated. The meaning "return to life" suggests more than mere vision. Perhaps "consciousness" would be the closest equivalent, inasmuch as one "returns" to consciousness, or consciousness "returns" to one. Consciousness is also closely related to vision, but is at the same time broader and more internal than vision alone. The term includes the other senses as well, and it suggests the mental quality inherent in *nóos*.

Whether contexts like these have to do with the original semantics of *nóos* is of course a matter for conjecture. For possible interpretations of the Euripidean passage, see A. M. Dale, *Euripides: Helen* (Oxford, 1967), p. 132. The passage may allude vaguely to Anaxagoras and a cosmic *Noûs*; Dale, on the other hand, sees no close parallels, and regards the passage as a "piece of high-toned but vague mysticism appropriate to Theonoe." Since *noûs* is at least a minor theme in the play (cf. *Theonóē*), one wonders if Euripides may have drawn on a piece of old solar tradition in the lines quoted.

27. B. Snell, *Gnomon* 7 (1931): 77: "Das νοεῖν steht . . . in naher Beziehung zum Organ des Auges. Nur dass die Funktion des Auges (das Sehen) in dem Wort erscheint als abgelöst von dem Organ. Das νοεῖν ist ein 'Sehen,' aber ein 'geistiges' Sehen." See also K. von Fritz, "ΝΟΥΣ and NOEIN in the Homeric Poems," *Classical Philology* 38 (1943): 88, and "ΝΟΥΣ, NOEIN, and their Derivatives in Pre-Socratic Philosophy," *Classical Philology* 40 (1945): 223. C. J. Ruijgh. *Études sur la grammaire et le vocabulaire du grec mycénien* (Amsterdam, 1967), pp. 371–72, has proposed a direct connection between Greek *noéō*, "to observe," and the Gothic causative verb *nasjan*, "to save"; he argues that the original meaning of *noéō* was likewise "to save," and he cites such parallels as Latin *servo*, "to save" and "to observe," to explain the subsequent semantic development of *noéō*. The verbal noun *nóos* would have undergone the same semantic development, and both noun and verb would ultimately have lost their original meanings completely. This argument is attractive for its simplicity, but it does not, in my opinion, do justice to the Indo-European meaning of the root *nes-*, which had to do with more than simply "saving" and "protecting." I also doubt that *noéō* is a real equivalent of the Gothic causative *nasjan*; *noéō* is more likely to be a denominative formation from *nóos*, as is usually assumed (see n. 26 above).

It is worth noting that in Homer the Sun seems to be endowed with an all-embracing consciousness in the line:

Ἥλιος θ’, ὃς πάντ’ ἐφορᾷς καὶ πάντ’ ἐπακούεις

and Helios, you who see everything and hear everything.[28]

To be sure, there is no mention of *nóos* here, but the idea may not be far away. One thinks of Xenophanes' description of God (frag. 20 [Diehl]), which greatly resembles the Homeric line but which contains a new element:

οὖλος ὁρᾷ, οὖλος δὲ νοεῖ, οὖλος δέ τ’ ἀκούει

He entirely sees, entirely *perceives*, entirely hears.

This line shows how closely allied *noéō* is with verbs of perception.[29] Xenophanes, moreover, has placed this verb iconically; it occurs "internally," between verbs of sense perception, because it designates what Snell calls "ein 'geistiges' Sehen," or what we might simply call "consciousness."

To mention the sun in this discussion is not amiss. There is already good reason to believe that sun symbolism is important

28. III 277; the same line, with slight variations, occurs in the prophecies of Teiresias (*xi* 109) and Circe (*xii* 323). R. Schmitt, *Dichtung und Dichtersprache in indogermanischer Zeit* (Wiesbaden, 1967), p. 164, argues, on the basis of the vocative *Ēélios*, that this line is archaic.

29. Consider also the following texts:
Hesiod, *Works and Days* 267:

πάντα ἰδὼν Διὸς ὀφθαλμὸς καὶ πάντα νοήσας

The *eye* of Zeus which *sees* all and *clearly perceives* all;

Epicharmus, frag. 249 (Kaibel):

νοῦς ὁρῇ καὶ νοῦς ἀκούει· τἄλλα κωφὰ καὶ τυφλά

The *mind sees* and the *mind hears*; all else is deaf and blind;

Sophocles, *Oedipus Tyrannos* 371:

τυφλὸς τά τ’ ὦτα τόν τε νοῦν τά τ’ ὄμματ’ εἶ

In your *ears, mind*, and *eyes*, you are *blind*;

Euripides, *Helen* 122:

αὐτὸς γὰρ ὅσσοις εἰδόμην, καὶ νοῦς ὁρᾷ

I myself *saw* with my *eyes*, and the *mind sees* too.

in understanding the root *nes-*. If *nóos* contains this root, then sun symbolism must also be taken into account in explaining the origin and development of this word.

Eliade's comparative study again proves useful. It emphasizes that hierophanies of the sun have achieved real importance in few cultures, being all but limited to Egypt, Asia, and primitive Europe.[30] Where they have become important, however, they have consistently gone hand in hand with a development toward rationality; hence the phenomenon that sun worship habitually ends by rationalizing itself out of existence, at least from the standpoint of its originally "ambivalent" nature. What remains of it tends to become the secret possession of a small "elite."

The "rationalizing" tendency of sun worship has an obvious bearing on the word *nóos*, which in attested Greek designates the "rational" faculty. When we consider the importance that this word attained in the Greek philosophical tradition, the notion of a rational "elite" also becomes important. Eliade himself makes some useful comments on this matter:[31]

> It is worth underlining the close connection between solar theology and the elite—whether of kings, initiates, heroes or philosophers. Unlike other nature hierophanies, sun hierophanies tend to become the privilege of a closed circle, of a minority of the elect. The result is the hastening of the process of rationalization. In the Graeco-Roman world the sun, having become the "fire of intelligence," ended by becoming a "cosmic principle"; from a *hierophany* it turned into an *idea*. . . . The philosophers, last among the "elect," . . . at last completed the secularization of what was one of the mightiest of all the cosmic hierophanies.

I suggest that the history of Greek *nóos* also followed a course from "hierophany" to something more strictly rational. It is the

30. Eliade, *Patterns in Comparative Religion* (n. 22), p. 124.
31. Ibid., pp. 150–51.

former stage in which I am interested, and for which I shall seek traces in Homer.

But it must be remembered that the Homeric poems are themselves well along in the development of Greek rationalism. This indicates in itself that Homer's understanding of *nóos* will no longer correspond to the word's original significance. The traces left in Homer are only those which have been preserved by his conservative tradition.[32] One such has been encountered already, although attention was not drawn to it. In the first section of this chapter I spoke at length of the companions of Odysseus who are "murdered" by the Sun. When Homer refers to this event at the beginning of the *Odyssey*, he calls the companions "foolish" (*i* 8–9):

*νήπιοι, οἳ κατὰ βοῦς Ὑπερίονος Ἠελίοιο
ἤσθιον.*

The significance of this in terms of tradition is that the companions lost their *nóstos* for their lack of *nóos*.

Unlike his companions, Odysseus himself is one of the arch-embodiments of intelligence in ancient legend. In the next chapter I shall examine the relation between Odysseus's *nóos* and his "return from death."

32. Some of the Homeric evidence that will concern us has already been noticed by P. Frei, "Zur Etymologie von griech. νοῦς," *Lemmata W. Ehlers* (Munich, 1968), pp. 48–57. Frei argues that *nóos* is derived from the root *nes-*, and he proposes "safe homebringing, safe return from danger" as the noun's original meanings; he then points out a few Homeric passages where such meanings are still suggested by the context, e.g. the speech of Zeus to Athena in *v* 23–24:

οὐ γὰρ δὴ τοῦτον μὲν ἐβούλευσας νόον αὐτή,
ὡς ἦ τοι κείνους Ὀδυσεὺς ἀποτίσεται ἐλθών;

Did not you yourself devise this plan (return?), that Odysseus might come and take revenge on them?

The semantic development which Frei proposes for *nóos* is: (1) "an escape from danger"; (2) "a plan to escape from danger"; (3) "plan" or "purpose" in a general sense. The difficulty, however, is to explain the development from "escape" to "plan to escape," and Frei does not attempt to do this.

3 *The Return of Odysseus*

In the last chapter two Homeric verses, each with a form from the root *nes-*, were seen to have a common origin in the early history of Greek epic. It was argued that these forms from *nes-* originally had to do with "returning to life and light" and that this meaning can best be understood in the context of solar symbolism. The first purpose of this chapter will be to amplify and support the two parts of this argument, in regard both to the proposed meaning and to its interpretation, by considering various episodes in the first half of the *Odyssey*. The second purpose will be to show how *nóos*, "mind", is involved in the same episodes.

When attempting to carry out these two purposes it is best to recognize certain limitations from the outset. The first has to do with the nature of the material to be considered. It is well known that the adventures of Odysseus reflect diverse folktale motifs;[1] hence it would be a mistake to try to reduce these adventures to a single formula. My object is, therefore, not to show that the "return to life and light" is the *only* strand in the tradition behind the *Odyssey*, but rather that this is one important strand, which may be only latently present in diverse contexts. The second limitation, which has already been discussed, is that Homer no longer understood the connection between *nóos* and

---

1. For a short bibliography of literature on this subject, see E. R. Dodds, "Homeric," in M. Platnauer, ed., *Fifty Years of Classical Scholarship* (Oxford, 1954), pp. 7, 32 n. 19 [= *Language and Background of Homer* (Chap. 2, n. 13), pp. 7, 18 n. 19].

néomai. It is therefore to be expected that traditional material which preserved the etymological connection has been altered and obscured in Homer's own creation.

Before entering the main body of this chapter it will be useful to comment upon an episode that illustrates the latent form in which our traditional material may appear. In Book 9 Odysseus encounters the Lotus-eaters, whose food causes anyone who eats it to lose his desire to return home. This loss of desire is a kind of "forgetfulness," as is revealed by two closely related collocations, both in verse-final position: *nóstou te lathésthai*, "to forget their homecoming," in line 97 and *nóstoio láthētai*, "that he might forget his homecoming," in line 102. What is suggested by the forms of *lanthánomai*, "to forget," in these collocations is that the loss of a "return" is at the same time a loss of "mind."

The objection to this theory is that the lotus blossom, an integral feature of the episode, is a drug, and this fact sufficiently explains the use of the verb *lanthánomai*. One could compare the phrase *lathoíato patrídos aíēs*, "that they might forget their fatherland," in *x* 236, which describes the effect Circe intends her drugs to have on the companions of Odysseus. But the situation is more complex than this. Another factor to be considered is the existence of another set of collocations complementing those already given. Balancing *lathoíato patrídos aíēs* in *x* 236 is the phrase *mimnéskeo patrídos aíēs*, "remember your fatherland," in *x* 472, and balancing *nóstou te lathésthai* and *nóstoio láthētai* is the phrase *nóstou te médēai*, "(if) you are mindful of your homecoming," in *xi* 110 and *xii* 137. The verbs *mimnéskomai*, "remember," and *médomai*, "be mindful of," have as much significance for the connection of *nóos* with *néomai* as does the verb *lanthánomai*. It should be stressed that the former verbs are associated with the noun *nóstos* more than once in Homer; the remaining examples are the phrases *nóstoio medoíato* in ix 622, *nóstou dè mnêsai* in x 509, *nóstou hupomnésousa* in *xv* 3, and *nóstou mimnéskesthai* in *iii* 142.

The above evidence suggests that Greek epic diction contained a regular opposition between "remembering" and "forgetting" one's "return," and that the phrases *nóstou te láthesthai* and *nóstoio láthētai* are to be seen in terms of this opposition. Their significance, in other words, transcends the context in which they occur.

The argument may now be carried a step farther. Just as the connection between *nóos* and *néomai* is only latent in the encounter with the Lotus-eaters, so is the idea that a *nóstos* was originally a "return from death." But this idea, however latent, is still suggested by the verb *lanthánomai*. The noun associated with this verb is *léthē*, "forgetfulness," and this noun, in post-Homeric Greek, designates a place of oblivion in the lower world. The land of the Lotus-eaters, since it is also a place of oblivion, likewise suggests a kind of death.

A passage in Theognis offers a striking illustration of what is only remotely implied in Homer. This passage (Theognis 702ff.) describes how Sisyphus alone among mortals achieved a "return from death" by means of his "intelligence." Particular attention is drawn to line 705, in which *léthē* is associated with a loss of *nóos* in the context of "death"; attention is also drawn to the several words designating the "intelligence" which enabled Sisyphus to "return from death":

> . . . Σισύφου Αἰολίδεω,
> ὅς τε καὶ ἐξ Ἀΐδεω *πολυϊδρείῃσιν* ἀνῆλθεν
> πείσας Περσεφόνην αἱμυλίοισι λόγοις,
> ἥ τε βροτοῖς παρέχει *λήθην* βλάπτουσα *νόοιο* –
> ἄλλος δ᾽ οὔπω τις τοῦτό γ᾽ *ἐπεφράσατο*,
> ὅντινα δὴ θανάτοιο μέλαν νέφος ἀμφικαλύψῃ
> ἔλθῃ δ᾽ ἐς σκιερὸν χῶρον ἀποφθιμένων
> κυανέας τε πύλας παραμείψεται, αἵ τε θανόντων
> ψυχὰς εἴργουσιν καίπερ ἀναινομένας·
> ἀλλ᾽ ἄρα καὶ κεῖθεν πάλιν ἤλυθε Σίσυφος ἥρως
> ἐς φάος ἠελίου σφῇσι *πολυφροσύναις.*

. . . Sisyphus the son of Aeolus, who came up from the house of Hades by means of his *great intelligence*, persuading

Persephone with wily words, _she who gives forgetfulness to mortals, unhinging their minds_—no other man had ever _devised_ this thing once the black cloud of death covered him over and he had come into the shadowy region of the deceased, passing by the dark gates which restrain the unwilling spirits of the dead. But even from that place Sisyphus came back into the light of the sun by means of his _great shrewdness._

The connection between _nóos_ and "returning from death" could not be more strongly suggested than it is by this passage. This in itself is important, and helps to bring out what is latent in Homer. But the passage also suggests another preliminary point. It is very significant that _nóos_ is associated with a "return from death" in a myth concerning a figure other than Odysseus.[2] This reveals that the association transcends the characterization of a particular figure, Odysseus, just as the significance of the collocations _nóstou te lathésthai_ and _nóstoio láthētai_ transcends the contexts in which they occur. What makes Odysseus our principal object of study is the fact that an entire epic is extant of which he happens to be the hero.

The possibility that this epic may contain material borrowed from other epic traditions also becomes irrelevant in light of the above remarks. It has been suggested that two of our key episodes, those involving Helios and Circe, have been based on a lost _Argonautica_; in these episodes Helios becomes the divine adversary, whereas in the more "genuine" parts of the _Odyssey_ Poseidon plays this role.[3] Considerations such as this, however,

2. According to one tradition, Sisyphus was the father of Odysseus (cf. Sophocles _Ajax_ 189–90). A fragment of Alcaeus (B 6A in Lobel-Page) seems to represent Sisyphus as having succumbed to death in spite of his wisdom; cf. lines 5–8:

$$\kappa\alpha\grave{\iota}\ \gamma\grave{\alpha}\rho\ \Sigma\acute{\iota}\sigma\upsilon\phi o\varsigma\ A\grave{\iota}o\lambda\acute{\iota}\delta\alpha\iota\varsigma\ \beta\alpha\sigma\acute{\iota}\lambda\epsilon\upsilon\varsigma\ [$$
$$\check{\alpha}\nu\delta\rho\omega\nu\ \pi\lambda\epsilon\hat{\iota}\sigma\tau\alpha\ \nu o\eta\sigma\acute{\alpha}\mu\epsilon\nu o\varsigma\ [$$
$$\grave{\alpha}\lambda\lambda\grave{\alpha}\ \kappa\alpha\grave{\iota}\ \pi o\lambda\acute{\upsilon}\iota\delta\rho\iota\varsigma\ \check{\epsilon}\omega\nu\ \grave{\upsilon}\pi\grave{\alpha}\ \kappa\alpha\rho\iota\ [$$
$$\delta\iota\nu\nu\acute{\alpha}\epsilon\nu\tau'\ A\chi\acute{\epsilon}\rho o\nu\tau'\ \grave{\epsilon}\pi\acute{\epsilon}\rho\alpha\iota\sigma\epsilon,\ \mu[$$

3. Cf. D. Page, _The Homeric Odyssey_ (Oxford, 1955), p. 2.

pertain to a late stage in the formulation of the great Greek epics. It is a particular tradition that could have been the common patrimony of many such epics in which I am interested.

The remainder of this chapter will be divided into three parts. Section 2 will deal with those episodes in the *Odyssey* which involve the line beginning *opsè kakôs neîai*, namely Circe, the Nekyia, and the cattle of Helios. Section 3 will deal with the episodes which involve the line beginning *ásmenoi ek thanátoio*, namely the Ciconians, the Cyclops, and the Laestrygonians. Section 4 will deal with the final home-coming of Odysseus, his journey from Ogygia to Ithaca via Phaeacia.

2 CIRCE, THE NEKYIA, AND HELIOS

The episodes to be considered here are closely connected in the narrative. It is Circe who both sends Odysseus to the underworld and receives him back again, and it is in the underworld that Odysseus is warned about the cattle of Helios.[4] In this group of episodes events occur in a literal way and, on some points, do not require much comment. There could be no more emphatic evidence for a "return from death" than the Nekyia. The meaning of this event is clear from Circe's words to the returning hero and his companions in *xii* 21–22:

> σχέτλιοι, οἳ ζώοντες ὑπήλθετε δῶμ᾽ Ἀΐδαο,
> δισθανέες, ὅτε τ᾽ ἄλλοι ἅπαξ θνήσκουσ᾽ ἄνθρωποι.

> Rash men, you who while still alive have gone down into the house of Hades, thus *having two deaths* while other men die once.

In the Helios episode the hero again seems to pass through death unharmed, although in a less literal fashion: so I would interpret the "sleep" which the gods cast over Odysseus while

---

4. For the connection among these episodes, cf. end note 1.

his companions slaughter the Sun's cattle.[5] It is unconsciousness such as this, from which *nóos* is the "return."

The actual role of *nóos* in the episodes as they stand is less obvious, but there are traces. The first of these are negative. As was suggested earlier, only the privileged can pass through death unharmed; thus is the hero increasingly separated from his companions. In the Circe episode and the Nekyia only one companion is lost, and this is the foolish Elpenor, described in *x* 553 as *oúte phresìn hêisin arērós*, "not sound in his wits." Elpenor, who met his fate by falling from the roof of Circe's palace in a drunken stupor, has seemed to some to be a curious element in the *Odyssey*.[6] From the point of view of tradition, however, his presence can easily be explained as a survival of the idea that a lack of *nóos* meant a loss of *nóstos*: only the foolish Elpenor cannot "return from death."

As mentioned earlier, the rest of the companions are also characterized by their lack of *nóos* when they slaughter the cattle of Helios. The opening of the *Odyssey* calls them "foolish" (*nḗpioi*) in connection with this deed.

The case with Odysseus is just the reverse. The purpose of his trip to the underworld is to hear the prophecy of Teiresias. There is every reason to believe that this "oracle from the dead" was a deeply traditional part of the Nekyia; the future reference of the verse:

opsè kakôs neîai, olésas ápo pántas hetaírous

You will return late and in evil condition, having lost all your companions,

5. *xii* 338–39. For a sleep which is like death, cf. the final return of Odysseus to Ithaca, discussed in sect. 4 below. *Húpnos* "Sleep," is called the brother of *Thánatos* "Death," in Hesiod *Theogony* 756; both are the children of *Núx*, "Night," (*Theogony* 758–59). *Húpnos* and *Thánatos* are also mentioned together in xvi 672, where both are charged with the duty of bearing Sarpedon back to Lycia.

6. According to Page, *Homeric Odyssey*, pp. 44–46, Elpenor was a traditional part of the Nekyia who was used by Homer to connect the Nekyia with the rest of the *Odyssey*. Page, however, does not offer any explanation of Elpenor's original role.

is consistent with little but a prophetic context, and it has been shown that this verse is very old. Whether the prophecy always contained a description of the way home cannot be known for sure, but this seems doubtful. The emphasis in the first instance would have been on the "way back to life."[7] The acquiring of prophetic knowledge such as this would at the same time have been the acquiring of *nóos*.[8] This explains, at least in terms of tradition, the motivation for the Nekyia. Originally, the return from death was tightly bound up with *nóos*, and *nóos* was tightly bound up with a prophecy from the dead. In the *Odyssey* as it stands, the connecting link (*nóos*) has dropped out, and only a vague sense remains that the "return home" is dependent upon a prophecy from the dead. In fact, the main prophetic duties are taken over by Circe, who belongs to the upper world. There is, however, an indication of the importance of *nóos*, the connecting link, in the role Teiresias plays. In *x* 494–95, Homer reveals that what distinguishes Teiresias from the rest of the dead is precisely his retention of *nóos*:

> τῷ καὶ τεθνηῶτι νόον πόρε Περσεφόνεια
> οἴῳ πεπνῦσθαι· τοὶ δὲ σκιαὶ ἀΐσσουσιν.

> To him even when dead Persephone granted mind, to him alone, so that he might have sound wits; but the others flit about as shadows.

The next question concerns the role of the sun. Like the return from death, this is for the most part quite plain. Helios causes the ultimate destruction of the "amorphous mass" of companions.

---

7. Even in the poem as we have it, Teiresias has less to say about the "way home" than Circe does (cf. end note 1); another detail showing that Teiresias's prophecy has more to do with "life and death" than with the "way home" is his mention of the *thánatos . . . ex halós*, "death from the sea" (*xi* 134) which will overcome Odysseus in his old age.

8. Homer emphasizes that the journey to Hades is undertaken to "gain knowledge from Teiresias" (*x* 537, *Teiresíao puthésthai*; the formula is repeated at *xi* 50 and 89). For the importance of secret knowledge with respect to sun symbolism, see chap. 2, sect. 3 above.

What is most apparent is thus the negative side of the sun's ambivalent powers. The companions are to be equated with sunset, the passing of the sun into the infernal regions. A reminiscence of this equation may well be contained in *xii* 382–83, where Helios threatens to descend into Hades if the offending companions do not die for him:

εἰ δέ μοι οὐ τίσουσι βοῶν ἐπιεικέ᾽ ἀμοιβήν,
δύσομαι εἰς Ἀΐδαο καὶ ἐν νεκύεσσι φαείνω.

If they do not pay me a fitting recompense for the cattle, I will sink into the house of Hades and shine among the dead.

What is presented in these lines as a threat was perhaps once, when the sun's negative aspect was still a powerful force on the imagination, more the means by which Helios put the companions to death.[9]

The positive side of the sun's twofold nature is not emphasized in the Helios episode. Odysseus escapes death because he has had no part in the offense of his companions. In this limited sense, Helios may be said to "save" the hero. But there is, I think, another indication of the sun's saving aspect, an indication which is only latent and which is unfortunately ambiguous. In *xii* 131 ff. the divine guardians of the Sun's cattle are mentioned; they are daughters of Helios himself and are named *Phaéthousa* and *Lampetíē*. In the same passage their mother is mentioned, whose name is *Néaira*:

θεαὶ δ᾽ ἐπιποιμένες εἰσί,
νύμφαι ἐϋπλόκαμοι, Φαέθουσά τε Λαμπετίη τε,
ἃς τέκεν Ἠελίῳ Ὑπερίονι δῖα Νέαιρα.

Their herdsmen are goddesses, the fair-tressed nymphs Phaethousa and Lampetia, whom shining Neaira bore to Helios.

9. For this idea, cf. the paragraphs quoted from Eliade on p. 22 above.

Phaéthousa and *Lampetíē* are plainly "significant names" having to do with the *brightness* of Helios, their father. Hence it is natural to assume that the name *Néaira* also has to do with some characteristic of the sun. This assumption has been made by others, who explain the name as a derivative of *néos*, "new," and as referring to the "new" light of day.[10] I suggest, however, that the name may be related to the verb *néomai*, just as the hieratic epithet *iokhéaira*, "pouring arrows," is related to the verb *khéō*, "to pour."[11] Thus explained, the name *Néaira* would still refer to the returning light of day, but more pointedly so. It would refer to this light in the context of "salvation." This would suit Neaira's role as the provider of guardians for the cattle of Helios.[12]

The cattle of Helios are themselves worth considering more closely, as they are an apparently old feature of Greek sun mythology, and will be encountered again in this study. In the *Odyssey* Helios has not only cattle but sheep as well; when Circe first describes Thrinacia to Odysseus, she says that there is an equal number of the two species (*xii* 127 ff.):

Θρινακίην δ᾽ ἐς νῆσον ἀφίξεαι ἔνθα δὲ πολλαὶ
βόσκοντ᾽ Ἠελίοιο βόες καὶ ἴφια μῆλα,
ἑπτὰ βοῶν ἀγέλαι, τόσα δ᾽ οἰῶν πώεα καλά,
πεντήκοντα δ᾽ ἕκαστα.

You will come to the island of Thrinacia; many cattle and sturdy sheep of Helios graze there, seven herds of cattle and as many beautiful flocks of sheep, with fifty head in each.

10. See W. B. Stanford, *The Odyssey of Homer*[2] (London, 1959) 1:410, where a proposed connection with *neíaira* in the unattested sense, "depths of the sea" (from which the sun seems to rise), is also mentioned.

11. So P. Chantraine, *Formation des noms en grec ancien* (Paris, 1933), p. 104; for a different interpretation of the epithet, cf. R. Schmitt, *Dichtung und Dichtersprache in indogermanischer Zeit* (chap. 2, n. 28), pp. 177–78. One may also compare the name *Dáeira*, related to *daênai* (Chantraine, ibid.).

12. In later Greek mythology, there were ten or so figures with the name Neaira; see, W. Roscher, *Ausführliches Lexikon der griechischen und römischen Mythologie* (Leipzig, 1897–1909), vol. 3, cols. 43–44.

Outside the *Odyssey* as well, Helios has both sacred cattle and sacred sheep, and these appear in contexts that serve to broaden our perspective on the Homeric episode. Perhaps the most important source for our purposes is Herodotus 9.92.2–95. This passage tells the story of Euenius, a prophet from the Corinthian colony of Apollonia who lived in the generation before the Persian wars. According to this story, Euenius acquired the gift of prophecy as a direct consequence of his role as the guardian of sheep that were sacred to Helios. Euenius's story has the qualities of a legend about it, and would seem to contain traditional elements of sun mythology as preserved in an actual cult to Helios. The account in Herodotus is as follows (de Sélincourt translation):

> Euenius' story was an odd one and I will here relate it. In Apollonia there is a flock of sheep sacred to the sun; during the daytime these sheep graze along the banks of the river which rises on Mt Lacmon, and, after running through Apollonian territory, joins the sea by the harbor of Oricus; at night, however, they are looked after by men specially chosen from the wealthiest and most distinguished families— each man having one year's spell of duty. The people of Apollonia value these sheep very highly because of an oracle they once received concerning them. The place where they are penned for the night is a cave, a long way from the town, and here it was that Euenius, who had been chosen for the task, was keeping watch. One night he fell asleep on duty, and some wolves got in and killed about sixty of the sheep. When, on waking, he saw what had happened, Euenius kept silent and told nobody about it, intending to buy some more sheep to make good the losses; but the people of the town got to know of the disaster, and at once brought the culprit to trial and condemned him to have his eyes put out for sleeping at his post. The sentence was carried out, and immediately afterwards the sacred ewes had no more lambs, and the land ceased to produce the normal harvests. The oracles both at Dodona and Delphi were consulted upon the reason for this calamity, and the answer in each case was

that it was due to the fact that Euenius, the guardian of the sacred sheep, had been unjustly deprived of his sight; it was the gods themselves who had set the wolves on the sheep, and they would continue to punish the people of Apollonia for the wrong they had done Euenius, until they made him such amends as he himself might choose; and when this was done, they, too, would give him something, for the possession of which many men would call him blessed.

The gift Euenius received from the gods was that of prophecy, and this gift, as the oracles had foretold, made him famous.[13]

Like Odysseus, Euenius was asleep when the beasts of Helios were destroyed, and—again like Odysseus—Euenius was not blamed by the gods for what happened. The parallels between the two stories are strong enough to suggest that Euenius's gift of prophecy, which has to do with "intelligence," is also important for the traditions which lie behind *Odyssey 12*.[14]

That "intelligence" was a highly traditional element in myths of the Sun's cattle is supported by a comparison with Vedic Sanskrit. In Vedic mythology cattle are closely associated with the phenomenon of sunrise;[15] in particular, the "winning of cattle" and the "winning of light" are closely related mythical

13. Herodotus tells the story of Euenius after mentioning that a prophet named Deiphonus, who claimed to be the son of Euenius, was with the Greek fleet at Samos between the battles of Salamis and Mycale. Herodotus ends his account in 9.95 by stating that he had heard that Deiphonus was not in fact the son of Euenius, but claimed to be in order to trade on the name of a famous man. Given Euenius's fame, it is easy to understand how he became the subject for legend.

14. The blinding of Euenius, which has no parallel in *Odyssey* 12, has a more distant parallel in the Indic myth of Ṛjrāśva, which is referred to twice in the *Rig-Veda*. According to *RV* 1.116.16 and 1.117.17–18, Ṛjrāśva was blinded by his father for having slaughtered one hundred and one rams to a she wolf, and the Aśvins—divine twins—restored his eyes when the wolf intervened on his behalf; for the connection of the Vedic twins with sheep and cattle, sunrise, intelligence and the root *nes-*, see chap. 6, sect. 4 below. For the theme of blinding as a solar motif, consider also the Cyclops in *Odyssey* 9, whose solar origins are discussed in section 3 below.

15. The "ruddy cows" of the Dawn goddess Uṣas are frequently referred to in the *Rig-Veda*; see A. A. Macdonell, *Vedic Mythology* (Strassburg, 1897), pp. 46–47.

deeds.[16] Both of these deeds, furthermore, depend on "intelligence" rather than "strength"; this is clear from the myth of the Panis, which I shall consider briefly.[17]

The Panis are a band of demons who live at the ends of the earth, beyond the world-encircling river Rasā, where they keep rich herds of cattle hidden in a cave. The guardian for these cattle is a demon named Vala (the "encloser") who was originally, perhaps, the cave itself.[18] Although it is Indra who wins back the cattle of the Panis, the deed really belongs to various mythical priests who accompany him—the Angirases and the seven Ṛsis, representing the original divine and human priesthoods, and Bṛhaspati, who is also a divine priest.[19] These figures use their priestly knowledge as if for a sacrifice in order to free the imprisoned cattle. *RV* 2.24.3 says that Bṛhaspati "drove the cows out, rent Vala asunder with his magic word, removed the darkness, and allowed the sun to shine." *RV* 6.65.5 attributes similar means to the Angirases: "at this hour, O Dawn, who dwell on the mountain heights, the Angirases praise your herds of cattle. They rent (the cave) with their song and with the power of their prayer." *RV* 6.13.3, which says that "the prince slays his enemy with might, the priest carries off the wealth of the Paṇi," shows clearly that the Paṇi myth had to do with priestly "intelligence" rather than warrior "strength."

Although the Paṇi myth bears a peculiarly Indic stamp,[20] the association between "intelligence," the "winning of light," and the "winning of cattle" is probably old.[21] Another feature of the

16. See H. Oldenberg, *Die Religion des Veda* (Berlin, 1894), p. 147.
17. For Vedic references, see Macdonell, *Vedic Mythology*, pp. 63–64, 157.
18. For Vala, see ibid., pp. 159–60.
19. See ibid., p. 142 for the Angirases, p. 144 for the seven Ṛsis, and pp. 101–04 for Bṛhaspati.
20. The very name Paṇi means "niggard," and reflects the preoccupation of the Vedic poet/priests with large rewards of cattle; see Oldenberg (n. 16), pp. 143–50.
21. See Oldenberg, p. 144 for evidence that the myth of the winning of the cattle belonged to a priestly class at least as early as Common Indo-Iranian.

myth that is probably old is the cave in which the Paṇis hide their cattle. This cave, which is located at the ends of the earth, suggests the "darkness" and "death" characteristic of primitive sun mythology. Greek tradition also associates a cave with the sheep of Helios in the story of Euenius. The location of this cave, far from the town of Apollonia, may well be significant;[22] in any case, the cave is explicitly a place of death for the sacred sheep under Euenius's care.

The cattle of Geryon, which Heracles drives off from the island of Erytheia in the far west, resemble the cattle of the Paṇis. Further, they seem to be connected with the cattle of Helios,[23] and to have to do with darkness and death. Hesiod refers to Geryon's "gloomy stable,"[24] and Geryon himself has been interpreted as a transposed god of the underworld.[25] Thus, when Heracles drives off Geryon's cattle, it is a virtual "return from darkness and death."

Our final source is the Homeric Hymn to Apollo, which locates sacred sheep of Helios on Cape Taenarum in the southern Peloponnesus (411 ff.):

> ἷξον καὶ χῶρον τερψιμβρότου Ἡελίοιο
> Ταίναρον, ἔνθα τε μῆλα βαθύτριχα βόσκεται αἰεὶ
> Ἡελίοιο ἄνακτος.

> They came also to the land of man-delighting Helios, Taenarum, where the deep-fleeced sheep of lord Helios graze forever.

---

22. The expression in Herodotus 9.93.1 is ἐν δὲ ἄντρῳ αὐλίζονται ἀπὸ τῆς πόλιος ἑκάς, "they are stabled in a cave far away from the city."

23. Apollodorus 1.6.1 mentions cattle of Helios on the island of Erytheia that were driven off by the giant Alcyoneus; these seem to be equivalents of the cattle of Geryon, and vice versa. Heracles himself, in order to reach Erytheia, uses the golden cup of Helios (see Apollodorus 2.5.10).

24. σταθμῷ ἐν ἠερόεντι, *Theogony* 294.

25. See U. von Wilamowitz-Moellendorff, *Glaube der Hellenen* (Berlin, 1931), 1:276, and H. J. Rose, *Handbook of Greek Mythology*[5] (London, 1953), pp. 214–15.

Taenarum was not only the location of these sacred sheep but was also supposed to contain a cave that led to the underworld.[26] Whether this cave was associated with the sheep of Helios is unknown, but it is an attractive hypothesis.

The evidence we have surveyed suggests that two traditional elements in myths of Helios's cattle and sheep were the role of the hero's "intelligence" and a cave representing darkness and death. Neither of these elements is overtly present in *Odyssey 12*,[27] and this fact calls for an explanation. The explanation probably has to do with the Cyclops episode, which fully exploits both mythic elements in question. The Cyclops episode also has to do with solar mythology, as will be discussed in the next section, and it should be viewed as a complement to Odysseus's adventure with the cattle of Helios in *Odyssey 12*.

It remains to say something more about Circe. Homer says in *x* 138 that she was the daughter of Helios. Thus her episode in the *Odyssey* also has to do with symbolism of the sun. As has been seen, this symbolism has an eastern and a western aspect. One wonders whether this is not the reason that her home, the land of Aeaea, is variously located in both east and west. It is remarkable that when Odysseus lands in Circe's domain he can no longer tell where the sun sets and where it rises (*x* 190 ff.):

ὦ φίλοι, οὐ γὰρ ἴδμεν ὅπη ζόφος οὐδ᾽ ὅπη ἠώς,
οὐδ᾽ ὅπη ἠέλιος φαεσίμβροτος εἶσ᾽ ὑπὸ γαῖαν
οὐδ᾽ ὅπη ἀννεῖται.

O friends, we do not know where the darkness is and where the dawn, we do not know where the sun that shines on men goes beneath the earth and where it returns.

26. It was through this entrance that Heracles is said to have descended to Hades to fetch Cerberus (see Apollodorus 2.5.12).

27. As Odysseus's ship approaches Thrinacia, he hears the lowing of "stabled cattle" (βοῶν αὐλιζομενάων, *xii* 265), but we hear no more about their stable.

According to Hesiod (*Theogony* 1011 ff.), Circe lived in the west among the Etruscans, a tradition which Latin authors followed. But when Odysseus returns from the underworld, her land is placed at the "rising of the sun" (*xii* 1 ff.):

αὐτὰρ ἐπεὶ ποταμοῖο λίπεν ῥόον Ὠκεανοῖο
νηῦς, ἀπὸ δ' ἵκετο κῦμα θαλάσσης εὐρυπόροιο
νῆσόν τ' Αἰαίην, ὅθι τ' Ἠοῦς ἠριγενείης
οἰκία καὶ χοροί εἰσι καὶ ἀντολαὶ Ἠελίοιο . . .

But when our ship left the stream of the river Oceanus, and returned to the waves of the wide-pathed sea and to the island of Aeaea, where the Dawn has her house and dancing places and where Helios has his risings . . . .

This discrepancy is easily explained. Circe's role in the *Odyssey* is both to usher the hero into the underworld and to receive him back again from it. When Odysseus and his men "return to life and light," she is naturally equated with the dawn. The complement to this would be that she is equated with sunset when Odysseus and his companions venture into "death and darkness."

For Homer, however, to whom realism was a concern, this ambivalence would have been difficult to manage. The Homeric version, in fact, seems to represent a compromise. Odysseus and his men do venture into darkness, but the text suggests a northerly direction. Their ship takes them to the land of the Cimmerians, upon whom the sun never shines (*xi* 13 ff.):

ἡ δ' ἐς πείραθ' ἵκανε βαθυρρόου Ὠκεανοῖο.
ἔνθα δὲ Κιμμερίων ἀνδρῶν δῆμός τε πόλις τε,
ἠέρι καὶ νεφέλῃ κεκαλυμμένοι· οὐδέ ποτ' αὐτοὺς
Ἠέλιος φαέθων καταδέρκεται ἀκτίνεσσιν,
οὔθ' ὁπότ' ἂν στείχῃσι πρὸς οὐρανὸν ἀστερόεντα,
οὔθ' ὅτ' ἂν ἂψ ἐπὶ γαῖαν ἀπ' οὐρανόθεν προτράπηται,
ἀλλ' ἐπὶ νὺξ ὀλοὴ τέταται δειλοῖσι βροτοῖσι.

Our ship came to the boundary of deep-flowing Oceanus. There lie the land and city of the Cimmerian men, who are covered in mist and clouds; neither does shining Helios ever look down on them with his rays, either when he climbs into the starry sky, or when he turns back from the sky toward earth, but baneful night lies stretched over these wretched mortals.

The Cimmerians were a historical people who moved from the north into Asia Minor in the eighth and seventh centuries and who therefore must be a late feature in Greek epic. It is also worth noting that the reading *Kimmeriōn* in line 14 was much disputed in antiquity.[28] On the basis of these observations, it is plausible to think that the Cimmerians in Homer have replaced something older and more clearly symbolic of sunset.

The same conclusion is strongly suggested by a very revealing passage in Hesiod's *Theogony,* which should be compared carefully with the passage in Homer. Hesiod first mentions the "house of Night" (744), in front of which Atlas stands supporting the heavens (746 ff.); this is the point at which Night and Day pass each other, one entering the "house," the other leaving it (748 ff.).[29] Hesiod continues his description of this twilight region as follows (758 ff.):

ἔνθα δὲ Νυκτὸς παῖδες ἐρεμνῆς οἰκί' ἔχουσιν,
Ὕπνος καὶ Θάνατος, δεινοὶ θεοί· οὐδέ ποτ' αὐτοὺς
Ἠέλιος φαέθων ἐπιδέρκεται ἀκτίνεσσιν
οὐρανὸν εἰσανιὼν οὐδ' οὐρανόθεν καταβαίνων.

There the children of dark Night have their house, the dread gods Sleep and Death; *neither does shining Helios ever look upon them with his rays,* either ascending into the sky or descending from the sky.

28. See W. B. Stanford, *The Odyssey of Homer* (n. 10), p. 382, for the five variant readings in antiquity. On an etymological connection of Κιμμέριοι with Hesych. κέμμερος· ἀχλύς, ὀμίχλη. "mist," and Hittite *kammara-*, "fog, darkness," see G. Neumann, *Untersuchungen zum Weiterleben hethitischen und luvischen Sprachgutes in hellenistischer und römischer Zeit* (1961), pp. 31–32; A. Heubeck, *Hermes* 91 (1963): 490–92; C. Nylander, *Hermes* 93 (1965): 131–32; M. L. Mayer, *Acme* 20 (1967): 289–90.
29. For further discussion of this passage in Hesiod, see sect. 3 below.

The similarity of the emphasized phrase to *xi* 15–16 is un-mistakable; at the same time, the variation *epidérketai*, "looks upon," for *katadérketai*, "looks down upon," and the difference in the line that follows do not make it seem that Hesiod has imitated Homer. On the contrary, Hesiod has preserved the original context of the underlined phrase (sleep, death, the region beyond sunset), whereas Homer has sacrificed part of this context (the extreme west) for the sake of realism.

If it is true that the fluctuation from east to west is an essential part of Circe's nature, it is tempting to see this action reflected in her name. The Greek word for "ring" is *krikos*, which is also attested as *kirkos*. The name *Kirke* could be simply the feminized form of the latter, and refer to the circular path of the sun from east to west.

Circe's twofold nature is apparent in matters other than geography. Initially she is a very hostile figure to Odysseus and his companions. This is her chthonic aspect, which is explained by her close relationship to Helios—so Eliade explains it. In describing the place of the sun in Greek mythology and religion, he comments that "Helios is not only *pythios, chthonios, titan,* and so on; over and above all this, he is in communication with the chosen world of darkness: sorcery and hell. He is the father of the sorceress Circe, and the grandfather of Medea, both illustrious specialists in nightplant philtres."[30] It is by means of such philtres that Circe turns the companions into swine, and when in *x* 283 the "swine" are said to be pent up in hidden places:

ἔρχαται, ὥς τε σύες, πυκινοὺς κευθμῶνας ἔχοντες

there would seem to be a connection with the imprisoned beasts of the Sun. If this is so, the symbolism of the imprisoned beasts

30. M. Eliade, *Patterns in Comparative Religion* (chap. 2, n. 22), p. 143.

has become very literal in the land of magic potions and incantations.[31]

Circe's positive aspect is equally plain. After "imprisoning" the companions, she also sets them free by returning them to human form. She becomes the lover of Odysseus, moreover, and helps him with his journey home by describing the dangers he will encounter. Like Teiresias, she gives Odysseus a necessary fore-knowledge, which can be interpreted as a kind of *nóos*.

The role of *nóos* is perceptible throughout the Circe episode. In the case of the companions this role is predictably negative. When in *x* 231 they first follow Circe into her palace, they do so out of "witlessness":

οἱ δ᾽ ἅμα πάντες ἀϊδρείῃσιν ἕποντο.

More telling is the fact that Circe uses her drugs to make the companions "forget" their fatherland (*x* 236):

ἵνα πάγχυ λαθοίατο πατρίδος αἴης.

The collocation *lathoíato patrídos aíēs*, "that they might forget their fatherland," is balanced by the collocation *mimnḗskeo patrídos aíēs*, "remember your fatherland," in *x* 472, where the companions bid their leader to leave Circe's island; the significance of these collocations was discussed at the beginning of this chapter.

Odysseus, on the other hand, is saved from Circe by receiving the necessary occult knowledge before he enters her palace from Hermes, who serves as his guide in this dangerous encounter.[32]

31. Notice also that when Odysseus himself "returns" (*x* 419) unharmed from Circe's palace, his remaining companions, who are said to be as happy as if they had "returned home" (*x* 416ff.), are compared to heifers that have been freed from their pens (*x* 410ff.).

32. The presence of Hermes at this moment is significant, for he both leads to death (as psychopomp) and brings back to life; see sect. 4 below for his role in bringing Odysseus back from Ogygia, and chap. 7 for his role in guiding Priam in *Iliad* 24. Notice what Hermes says to Odysseus in the present episode (l. 286):

ἀλλ᾽ ἄγε δή σε κακῶν ἐκλύσομαι ἠδὲ σαώσω.

But come, I will *free* you *from evils* and *save* you.

At first Odysseus too is ignorant. Hermes asks him in *x* 282 where he is going *khórou áïdris eón*, "being ignorant of the land," and warns him that in such ignorance not even he will "return" (*x* 284–85):

οὐδέ σέ φημι
αὐτὸν νοστήσειν, μενέεις δὲ σύ γ᾽ ἔνθα περ ἄλλοι.

I say that not even you will return (*nostésein*), but you will remain where the others are.[33]

Hermes enables Odysseus to "return" by explaining beforehand Circe's wiles and the antidote to them. In both cases he "tells" the hero what he must know (*x* 289, 291–92):

πάντα δέ τοι ἐρέω ὀλοφώϊα δήνεα Κίρκης. . . .
ἀλλ᾽ οὐδ᾽ ὣς θέλξαι σε δυνήσεται· οὐ γὰρ ἐάσει
φάρμακον ἐσθλόν, ὅ τοι δώσω, ἐρέω δέ ἕκαστα.

I will *tell* you about all the cunning wiles of Circe. . . . She will not be able to charm you, for the good drug, which I will give to you and *tell* you all about, will not allow it.

In lines 302–03, the hero says that Hermes gave him a *phármakon* and "explained its nature" (*kaí moi phúsin autoû édeixe*). Its nature is very interesting. The *phármakon* is a plant with a black root and a white blossom, a color-contrast entirely appropriate to the underlying meaning of the Circe episode[34]; one also notes

33. The verb *nostésein* is significant; Homer seems to realize that merely by emerging alive from Circe's palace Odysseus accomplishes a *nóstos*, originally a "return to life." In order to reconcile this with his own understanding of *nóstos*, Homer has the remaining companions say to Odysseus when he "returns" unharmed from the palace (*x* 419–20):

σοὶ μὲν νοστήσαντι, διοτρεφές, ὣς ἐχάρημεν,
ὡς εἴ τ᾽ εἰς Ἰθάκην ἀφικοίμεθα πατρίδα γαῖαν.

We rejoiced at your return (*nostésanti*), O Zeus-nourished king, as if we had arrived in Ithaca our fatherland.

34. For the significance of the color white in Indo-European tradition, see L. Gerschel, "Couleur et teinture chez divers peuples indo-européens," *Annales Économies Sociétés Civilisations* 21 (1966): 608–31.

that the use of the magic plant seems to be restricted to the chosen few (304 ff.):

ῥίζῃ μὲν μέλαν ἔσκε, γάλακτι δὲ εἴκελον ἄνθος·
μῶλυ δέ μιν καλέουσι θεοί· χαλεπὸν δέ τ᾽ ὀρύσσειν
ἀνδράσι γε θνητοῖσι· θεοὶ δέ τε πάντα δύνανται.

On the root it was black, but its flower was like milk: moly is the name the gods give to it, and it is difficult for mortal men to dig up; the gods, on the other hand, are able to do everything.

It seems clear that Hermes gives Odysseus exclusive knowledge with which to pass through darkness to light, or through death to life. In an underlying sense, therefore, *nóos* is the *nóstos* in the Circe episode.[35]

3 THE CICONIANS, THE CYCLOPS, AND THE LAESTRYGONIANS

The episodes just considered provide explicit evidence for the "return from death" and for the role of sun symbolism in the *nóstos* of Odysseus; in the next group of episodes these features are less explicit. What binds these episodes together for us is the fact that they all end with the refrain containing the line:

ásmenoi ek thanátoio, phílous olésantes hetaírous.

On the basis of this refrain, one might expect the "return from death" to be a particularly marked feature in each episode. That

35. In *x* 240 the companions, who have been turned into swine, are described as in all respects swinelike, except that their "mind was intact as before" (*noûs ên émpedos hōs tò páros per*). It is hard to tell whether *noûs* has any traditional significance here. The form (only here in Homer is *nóos* contracted) is late, but the companions do in fact "return" to human form. Probably the poet only meant to say that the companions had not irrevocably been turned into swine; it remains unclear how he related *noûs* to their eventual "return."

it is not is explained by the fact that Homer no longer understood the original meaning of the word *ásmenos*. Much of the content in these episodes, especially the two minor ones, must have been fashioned after the refrain had lost its original meaning. Such material would be too late, not only to be concerned with a return from death, but also to grant much scope to the role of the sun. Nevertheless, the episodes in question, particularly that of the Cyclops, do contain significant traces of what we are looking for.

The Ciconians come first; they provide Odysseus with his first adventure after his departure from Troy. It is this fact, moreover, which chiefly determines the character of the episode. Since the Ciconians stand closest to Troy and the world of the *Iliad*, Homer has made them reflect the character of that world.[36] They are described as conventional warriors (*ix* 49–50):

> ἐπιστάμενοι μὲν ἀφ᾽ ἵππων
> ἀνδράσι μάρνασθαι καὶ ὅθι χρὴ πεζὸν ἐόντα

Knowing how to fight against men both from chariots and, where need be, on foot,

and Odysseus sacks their city in the conventional way (*ix* 40 ff.):

> ἔνθα δ᾽ ἐγὼ πόλιν ἔπραθον, ὤλεσα δ᾽ αὐτούς·
> ἐκ πόλιος δ᾽ ἀλόχους καὶ κτήματα πολλὰ λαβόντες
> δασσάμεθ᾽, ὡς μή τίς μοι ἀτεμβόμενος κίοι ἴσης.

Then I sacked the city and killed the men; we carried off their wives and all their possessions from the city and we divided them up so that no one would be deprived of an equal share.

The scene of this sack could be any of the towns near Troy.

The departure from this scene could hardly be called a "return from death" in any full sense. The refrain expressing this idea

36. Cf. C. H. Whitman, *Homer and the Heroic Tradition* (Cambridge, 1958), p. 298.

in latent form is merely tacked on at the end, after its substance, significantly, has been reinterpreted in the lines immediately preceding. In *ix* 60–61 it is said that six companions were "lost" from each ship, while the rest "escaped death":

ἓξ δ᾽ ἀφ᾽ ἑκάστης νηὸς ἐϋκνήμιδες ἑταῖροι
ὤλονθ᾽· οἱ δ᾽ ἄλλοι φύγομεν θάνατόν τε μόρον τε.

Six well-greaved companions from each ship were lost, but the rest of us escaped death and doom.

The form *ólonth'*, "were lost," corresponds to the form *olésantes*, "having lost," in the refrain, while the phrase *phúgomen thánaton*, "we escaped death," corresponds to and reinterprets the meaning of the phrase *ásmenoi ek thanátoio*, "having returned from death." The significance of the verb *pheúgein*, "to escape," in this context was commented upon earlier: to "escape death" is clearly not the same as to "return from death."[37]

In spite of these remarks, however, the refrain is not wholly inappropriate to its present context. For the Ciconians do not belong completely to the world of the *Iliad*, but are, rather, a bridge from this world to the fabulous world of the *Odyssey*. In fact, an element from the latter world—the slaughter of the Sun's cattle—seems to have been adapted to the Ciconian episode. All would have escaped unharmed following the sack had the companions not stopped to slaughter and eat their booty; Odysseus bids them to flee, but they, in their witlessness, do not obey (*ix* 44 ff.):

τοὶ δὲ μέγα νήπιοι οὐκ ἐπίθοντο.
ἔνθα δὲ πολλὸν μὲν μέθυ πίνετο, πολλὰ δὲ μῆλα
ἔσφαζον παρὰ θῖνα καὶ εἰλίποδας ἕλικας βοῦς.

But they, the great fools, did not obey. Much wine was then drunk, and along the shore they slaughtered many sheep and shambling cattle with curved horns.

37. See pp. 17–18 above.

The cause of destruction here, just as in the slaughter of the Sun's cattle, is the mindlessness of the companions. The word *nḗpioi*, "fools," in line 44 echoes *i* 8–9:

> νήπιοι, οἳ κατὰ βοῦς Ὑπερίονος Ἠελίοιο
> ἤσθιον
> The fools (*nḗpioi*), who ate the cattle of Helios.

The suggestion of drunkenness in line 45 provides another indication of "mindlessness."

It is also possible that the poet who constructed this episode still had some sense of the role of the sun. One should note that the stages of the Ciconian battle follow the course of the sun, with disaster coming at nightfall (*ix* 56 ff.):

> ὄφρα μὲν ἠὼς ἦν καὶ ἀέξετο ἱερὸν ἦμαρ,
> τόφρα δ᾽ ἀλεξόμενοι μένομεν πλέονάς περ ἐόντας·
> ἦμος δ᾽ ἠέλιος μετενίσσετο βουλυτόνδε,
> καὶ τότε δὴ Κίκονες κλῖναν δαμάσαντες Ἀχαιούς.

> While it was dawn and the sacred daylight was increasing, we held our ground and kept them off, even though there were more of them; but when the sun began to set, the Ciconians put us Achaeans to flight and overcame us.

It is peculiar that the poet says "dawn" in line 56, since much has happened on this day before the battle begins; it appears that a formulaic passage has been used somewhat inappropriately. Perhaps this can be explained as a license which a deeper appropriateness, based on tradition, would have justified.[38]

---

38. The passage is similar to XVI 777 ff., describing the course of the battle in which Patroclus dies:

> ὄφρα μὲν Ἠέλιος μέσον οὐρανὸν ἀμφιβεβήκει,
> τόφρα μάλ᾽ ἀμφοτέρων βέλε᾽ ἥπτετο, πῖπτε δὲ λαός·
> ἦμος δ᾽ Ἠέλιος μετενίσετο βουλυτόνδε,
> καὶ τότε δή ῥ᾽ ὑπὲρ αἶσαν Ἀχαιοὶ φέρτεροι ἦσαν.

Before discussing the Cyclops episode, which is the most important in this group, we will first consider that of the Laestrygonians; it occurs last and, like the Ciconian episode, is relatively minor. It does, however, parallel the adventure with the Cyclops in several details, both latent and explicit, and thus serves as a good introduction to that adventure.

Certain general similarities between the Laestrygonians and the Cyclopes are obvious. Both of these fabulous peoples are of giant stature, herd sheep rather than farm, hurl rocks as weapons, and eat human flesh.[39] Even the cave of the Cyclops is to a degree paralleled by the Laestrygonian harbor, which is given a very cavelike description in x 87 ff.:

> ἔνθ' ἐπεὶ ἐς λιμένα κλυτὸν ἤλθομεν, ὃν πέρι πέτρη
> ἠλίβατος τετύχηκε διαμπερὲς ἀμφοτέρωθεν,
> ἀκταὶ δὲ προβλῆτες ἐναντίαι ἀλλήλῃσιν
> ἐν στόματι προὔχουσιν, ἀραιὴ δ' εἴσοδός ἐστιν

When we had entered the famed harbor, around which a towering cliff is placed on either side without a break, and two jutting promontories, face to face, extend to form the mouth, and the entrance is a slender opening. . . .

It is in this harbor that Odysseus loses all the ships except his own.

I shall presently argue that the Cyclops' cave was originally a place of death—an "underworld"—from which the hero

---

While Helios was covering mid-heaven the weapons of both sides took hold and men fell; but when Helios began to set the Achaeans were stronger, beyond their destiny.

The line describing the movement of the sun as it begins to set, which is virtually the same in the two passages (ix 58 = xvi 779), contains the peculiar word *boulutónde*, "to the time for the unyoking of oxen;" see end note 2 for a discussion of the possibility that this word has been reinterpreted by the Homeric poets, and that the "oxen" in question were originally the cattle of Helios himself.

39. Compare x 112–13 and 120; 121–22; 82ff. and 98; 116 and 124 with ix 190ff.; 481ff. and 537ff.; 108, 167, and 187–88; 291.

"returned." One is thus tempted to see the Laestrygonian harbor in the same terms. At the same time, one of course realizes that this would no longer have been Homer's own conception. The reinterpretation of the formulaic refrain with which the Laestrygonian episode ends was considered fully in chapter 2 and need not be reconsidered here. What emerged was simply that what was once a "return from death" had become a matter of "escape" in Homer's understanding.

In light of this it is not surprising that Odysseus himself never enters the Laestrygonian harbor, the place of death; he alone keeps his ship outside (x 95):

αὐτὰρ ἐγὼν οἶος σχέθον ἔξω νῆα μέλαιναν.

This detail makes his ultimate "escape" still less a "return from death."

Concerning the role of *nóos* in the Laestrygonian episode there is little to say. The most that can be said is that Odysseus, in mooring his ship outside the harbor, displays his usual prudence.

Thus far the Laestrygonian episode seems to have little to offer. But by looking more closely at certain details in the narrative, one can discover traces of this episode's original nature. A minor detail which suggests an "underworld" context appears in the companions' encounter with the Laestrygonian queen (x 112–13):

οἱ δ' ἐπεὶ εἰσῆλθον κλυτὰ δώματα, τὴν δὲ γυναῖκα
εὗρον ὅσην τ' ὄρεος κορυφήν, κατὰ δ' ἔστυγον αὐτήν.

When they entered the famed halls they found the (king's) wife, large as a mountain peak, and they *shrank* from her *in fear.*

The verb *stugéō*, "shrink in fear," has unmistakable connotations;[40] the reaction of the companions strongly suggests that they have come face to face with the queen of the underworld.

40. Cf. the name *Stúx*, "Styx," and the adjective *stugerós*, "dreaded," in the expressions *stugeròs d' ára min skótos heîle*, "dreaded darkness seized him" (in, e.g., v 47) and *stugeroû Aḯdao*, "dreaded Hades" (vIII 368).

Much more important, however, are the obscure lines at the beginning of the episode that describe the Laestrygonian kingdom (*x* 81 ff.):

ἑβδομάτῃ δ᾽ ἱκόμεσθα Λάμου αἰπὺ πτολίεθρον,
Τηλέπυλον Λαιστρυγονίην, ὅθι ποιμένα ποιμὴν
ἠπύει εἰσελάων, ὁ δέ τ᾽ ἐξελάων ὑπακούει.
ἔνθα κ᾽ ἄϋπνος ἀνὴρ δοιοὺς ἐξήρατο μισθούς,
τὸν μὲν βουκολέων, τὸν δ᾽ ἄργυφα μῆλα νομεύων·
ἐγγὺς γὰρ νυκτός τε καὶ ἤματός εἰσι κέλευθοι.

On the seventh day we came to the steep citadel of Lamus, Laestrygonian Telepylos, where shepherd calls out to shepherd as he drives his flocks in, and the other, driving his flocks out, hears him. There a sleepless man would earn two wages, one by herding cattle, and the other by pasturing silvery sheep, for the paths of night and day are close together.

Particularly obscure is the poet's precise meaning in line 86, when he says that "the paths of day and night are close together." W. B. Stanford takes this to be a "muddled reference" to the short nights of northern latitudes.[41] This interpretation would seem to be right in view of the preceding lines, which state that "in this place a sleepless man might earn a double wage." By working all the daylight hours of summer in the extreme north, one would in fact earn a "double wage."

But if Homer is suggesting a northern location, this conflicts with what is otherwise known about the Laestrygonians. Thucydides 6.2.1 attests the apparently orthodox tradition, according to which the Laestrygonians (together with the Cyclopes!) dwelt in Sicily—that is, in the West:

παλαίτατοι μὲν λέγονται ἐν μέρει τινὶ τῆς χώρας Κύκλωπες καὶ Λαιστρυγόνες οἰκῆσαι, ὧν ἐγὼ οὔτε γένος ἔχω εἰπεῖν οὔτε ὁπόθεν ἐσῆλθον ἢ ὅποι ἀπεχώρησαν· ἀρκείτω δὲ ὡς ποιηταῖς τε εἴρηται καὶ ὡς ἕκαστός πῃ γιγνώσκει περὶ αὐτῶν.

41. W. B. Stanford, *The Odyssey of Homer* (n. 10), p. 368.

It is said that the earliest inhabitants of any part of the country were the Cyclopes and Laestrygonians. I cannot say what kind of people these were or where they came from or where they went in the end. On these points we must be content with what the poets have said and what anyone else may happen to know.

The discrepancy between Homer's apparent view and other traditions concerning the Laestrygonians invites us to return to the "muddled" opening passage in search of something latent. Line 82 reveals that the name of the Laestrygonian city was *Tēlépulos*, "far gate."[42] One may reasonably ask to what "gate" or "gates" this name refers. The "gates," I suggest, are those "of the paths of day and night." In chapter 7 I shall examine the very significant "proem" of Parmenides, which describes the philosopher's own mythical "return to light." This journey begins at a set of gates, which are described as follows, in line 11:

ἔνθα πύλαι Νυκτός τε καὶ Ἤματός εἰσι κελεύθων.
There are the gates of the paths of Night and Day.

This line is the same as *x* 86, with only a case variation in the final word and with *éntha púlai* for *engùs gàr* at the beginning. Parmenides, I suggest, has preserved the older form of a traditional line; more than this, he has preserved this line's original context, a "return to light," which has become "muddled" in Homer.

This argument can be carried a step farther. The gates described by Parmenides stand at the entrance to the "house of Night" (*dṓmata Nuktós*, in l. 9). Hesiod, in the *Theogony*, also speaks of the "house of Night," which he designates with the words *Nuktòs d' erebennês oikía deiná*, in line 744; following this the

---

42. I believe that, *tēlépulos* was originally an epithet ("far-gated") describing *Laistrugoníē*, and not a proper noun; nevertheless, I have followed the usual interpretation in the text.

poet gives a very explicit description of how day and night pass as they enter and leave this house. This description implies the "gates of the paths of day and night," although Hesiod himself refers to the meeting-point as a "threshold."[43] I shall quote the entire passage here, since it conveys so eloquently the mythic background that is latent in Homer; one detail, however, is particularly important, and will be emphasized:

Νυκτὸς δ' ἐρεβεννῆς οἰκία δεινὰ
ἔστηκεν νεφέλης κεκαλυμμένα κυανέῃσιν.
τῶν πρόσθ' Ἰαπετοῖο πάις ἔχει οὐρανὸν εὐρὺν
ἑστηὼς κεφαλῇ τε καὶ ἀκαμάτῃσι χέρεσσιν
ἀστεμφέως, ὅθι Νύξ τε καὶ Ἡμέρη ἆσσον ἰοῦσαι
ἀλλήλας προσέειπον, ἀμειβόμεναι μέγαν οὐδὸν
χάλκεον· ἣ μὲν ἔσω καταβήσεται, ἣ δὲ θύραζε
ἔρχεται, οὐδέ ποτ' ἀμφοτέρας δόμος ἐντὸς ἐέργει,
ἀλλ' αἰεὶ ἑτέρη γε δόμων ἔκτοσθεν ἐοῦσα
γαῖαν ἐπιστρέφεται, ἣ δ' αὖ δόμου ἐντὸς ἐοῦσα
μίμνει τὴν αὐτῆς ὥρην ὁδοῦ, ἔς τ' ἂν ἵκηται,
ἣ μὲν ἐπιχθονίοισι φάος πολυδερκὲς ἔχουσα,
ἣ δ' Ὕπνον μετὰ χερσί, κασίγνητον Θανάτοιο
Νὺξ ὀλοή, νεφέλῃ κεκαλυμμένη ἠεροειδεῖ.

Here stands the dread house of dark Night covered with black clouds. Before the house stands the son of Iapetus, holding fast the wide heaven on his head and untiring arms, *at the place where Night and Day address each other as they pass, crossing over the great bronze threshold*: one of them goes down within while the other comes out, so that the house never contains both of them, but one is always outside the house traveling over the earth, while the other is inside the house waiting for the time of her journey to come; one of them brings the far-seeing light to those on earth, while the other, baneful Night covered with murky clouds, carries Sleep, the brother of Death, in her hands.

43. Hesiod mentions "gates" (*puléōn*) in l. 741, but it is not clear whether these gates are related to the "threshold" in l. 749.

When "Night and Day address each other as they pass, crossing over the great bronze threshold," we cannot help but be reminded of *Telépulos*, "where shepherd, driving in his flocks, cries out to shepherd, and the other, driving his flocks out, hears the call." The Homeric and Hesiodic passages cannot be separated.

At this point let us consider where Parmenides and Hesiod imagine the "gates" (or the "threshold") of day and night to be. Since Parmenides is "returning to light," his gates are presumably on the *eastern* shore of the world. Hesiod, on the other hand, mentions Atlas (*Iapetoîo páis* in l. 746), whom he has previously (l. 518) placed "at the ends of the earth, in front of the Hesperides," in other words, on the *western* shore of the world. This discrepancy arises from the very concept of a single point at which day and night pass, for, in reality, there are two such borders between darkness and light—one in the east, the other in the west. Thus the very concept of "gates of day and night" is anything but realistic.[44]

The unrealistic quality of the Hesiodic passage provides the key to understanding what Homer has done. It was seen earlier in this study that Circe belongs to both east and west at the same time, and that Homer, seeking a rational solution to this incongruity, has Odysseus enter the underworld from her domain by sailing northward past the Cimmerians. There is now every reason to believe that the same thing has happened in Homer's handling of the Laestrygonian episode. The tradition behind this episode represented *Telépulos Laistrugoníe* as that nonexistent

44. Cf. the discussion of the Hesiodic passage by Hermann Fränkel, *Dichtung und Philosophie des frühen Griechentums,* Philological Monograph no. 13, American Philological Association (1951), p. 147: "Es ist immer Tag oder Nacht, und die Schwelle repräsentiert das Oder, in einem mehr metaphysischen als räumlichen Sinn. Sie müsste sonst im Westen und Osten zugleich liegen. Hesiods Schilderung der Unterwelt ist nicht als Topographie gemeint." ["It is always day or night, and the threshold represents the 'or' (the alternative between the two) in a more metaphysical than spatial sense. Otherwise it would have to lie in both west and east at the same time. Hesiod's description of the underworld is not meant as topography."]

point where the sun both rises and sets. Homer's only rational recourse was to picture the Laestrygonians as dwelling in the extreme north.

Before we move on to the Cyclops episode, one final point deserves notice. In the Hesiodic passage, Day and Night call out to each other, whereas in Homer "shepherds" do this. If "shepherds" are traditional in this context, do they not recall the cattle and sheep of Helios investigated earlier? Of course Homer, in the lines concerning the possibility of a "double wage," takes a rational and realistic view toward these shepherds. But what if the same shepherds were once represented as passing each other on their way into and out of the "house of night"? This house can have been nothing other than the cave at the ends of the earth which enclosed the herds and flocks of the sun.[45] On this note we may move on to the Cyclops episode, where there is no doubt about the importance of "shepherds" and a "cave" to the underlying myth.

From the time Odysseus leaves Troy until he reaches the land of Circe, he has five encounters. The first and the last are with the Ciconians and the Laestrygonians, and in both cases Odysseus loses some of his companions. The second and the fourth are with the Lotus-eaters and the winds of Aeolus, but in these no companions are lost. Occupying a monumental place in the center is his encounter with the Cyclops, in which the hero again loses companions.[46] More than its central position, the length and elaboration of this episode show that Homer intended it to be monumental. It is on this adventure that our main attention should focus.

---

45. In *Theogony* 740, Hesiod refers to a *khásma méga*, "great chasm," which seems to be the same as the "house of night" (but cf. n. 43 above).

46. Notice that whereas the full traditional refrain is given at the end of the first, third, and fifth episodes, only the first line of it is given after the second and fourth episodes (*ix* 105 and *x* 77). For a discussion of the "geometric" arrangement of all the episodes in the first half of the *Odyssey*, see C. H. Whitman, *Homer and the Heroic Tradition* (n. 36), p. 288.

Part of the elaboration of the Cyclops episode is that it has a separate point of entry and exit. Serving as a threshold to the encounter is an offshore island where Odysseus and his men spend a day both before and after they meet the Cyclops (*ix* 116ff. and *ix* 543ff.). Significantly, the traditional refrain occurs at the final departure of Odysseus from this island (*ix* 565–66). Homer has again simply tacked the refrain on at the end of his own (in this case elaborate) creation.

But Homer also repeats his practice of reinterpreting and incorporating the refrain into his story. Unlike in the minor episodes, however, the reinterpretation and the refrain no longer occur side by side. In this case the familiar substitute appears immediately after the "escape" from the Cyclops' cave. Odysseus says that he loosened himself and his companions from beneath the sheep, which they then drove off to his ship where other companions were waiting; and then, in *ix* 466–67, come the words:

> ἀσπάσιοι δὲ φίλοις ἑτάροισι φάνημεν,
> οἳ φύγομεν θάνατον· τοὺς δὲ στενάχοντο γοῶντες.

> We were a welcome sight to our dear companions, those of us who had escaped death; for the others they mourned and wept.

Again there is the contrast between those who survived and those who perished, and again the words *ásmenoi ek thanátoio*, "having returned from death," have been recast as (*aspásioi*) . . . *phúgomen thánaton* "(a welcome sight) . . . we escaped death."[47]

The preceding observations imply two things: first, that the "return from death," however traditional in the Cyclops episode,

---

47. This recasting, since it stands farther from the traditional refrain than in the other two cases (see pp. 17–18 and 55 above), is somewhat looser; there is no form of *óllumi*, "to lose," and the word *aspásios*, "welcome," in contrast to the Laestrygonian episode, is dissociated from the verb *pheúgo*, "to escape," and is used in a different sense ("welcome" rather than "happy").

has become as latent here as in the minor episodes; and second, that this latent feature is to be connected closely with the Cyclops' cave.

A number of traces still remain which suggest that this cave was once a realm of the dead. One of these is the name *Oûtis*, "no one," by which Odysseus calls himself in the cave. Besides providing the means for a clever stratagem, this name suggests that its bearer really is "no one."[48] The name is really no name at all, and Odysseus, in the cave, is "anonymous." He loses his anonymity only when he emerges and shouts to the Cyclops that he is (*ix* 504–05):

'Οδυσσῆα πτολιπόρθιον . . .,
υἱὸν Λαέρτεω, Ἰθάκῃ ἔνι οἰκί' ἔχοντα

Odysseus, sacker of cities . . . the son of Laertes, having a home in Ithaca.

This regaining of his name is a kind of rebirth for Odysseus; one might recall the words of King Alcinoos on another occasion (*viii* 552–53):

οὐ μὲν γάρ τις πάμπαν ἀνώνυμός ἐστ' ἀνθρώπων,
οὐ κακὸς οὐδὲ μὲν ἐσθλός, ἐπὴν τὰ πρῶτα γένηται.

No man, either base or noble, is entirely *nameless* once he has been *born*.

Another indicative trace appears in line 421, where Odysseus says that he took counsel with himself in the cave in order to find a *thanátou lúsin*, a "loosening of death," for himself and his companions; and he goes on to say that he wove all manner of tricks and devices *hôs te perì psukhês*, "as if for my *psukhê*."

48. Cf. C. H. Whitman, *Homer and the Heroic Tradition* (n. 36), pp. 299–300.

These expressions could scarcely come much closer to equating the Cyclops' cave with death without explicitly doing so.[49] Homer has created a kind of suggestive ambiguity in which there is still a glimmer of the tradition that preceded him.

These indications will suffice for the "return from death."[50] The next question concerns the role of the sun. That this is important in understanding the Cyclops there is every reason to believe, but *how* it is important is a disputed point. The question centers on the etymology of the name *Kúklōps*. Three derivations of this name have been proposed, and each of these, in one way or another, involves the sun.

According to the oldest view, going back to the Greeks themselves, the name means "circle-eyed."[51] Adalbert Kuhn proposed to take the first element of the name, *kúklos*, in connection with the "wheel of the sun," an Indo-European designation for the sun itself, to judge by the cognate phrases *cakrám súryasya* in Vedic Sanskrit, *sunnan hwéol* in Old English, and *kúklos hēlíou* in Greek tragedy.[52] The connection with the sun would explain why the Cyclops has only one eye—namely,

---

49. With *psukhês* in this passage, compare the expression *arnúmenos hên te psukhên*, "winning his life," in *i* 5 and the discussion of this in chap. 2, n. 19. With *thanátou lúsin*, "release from death," compare the same expression and its context in Theognis 1009–10:

οὐ γὰρ ἀνηβᾶν
δὶς πέλεται πρὸς θεῶν οὐδὲ λύσις θανάτου.

There is from the gods no growing young again for a second time, nor a release from death (*lúsis thanátou*).

The verb *anēbân*, "grow young again," strongly suggests "rebirth."

50. It should be emphasized that of the episodes which end with the traditional refrain only the present one contains a graphic "return"; the cave of the Cyclops, more than anything else, illustrates what the refrain originally meant.

51. This interpretation begins at least with Hesiod *Theogony* 144.

52. A. Kuhn, *Die Herabkunft des Feuers und des Göttertrankes* (Berlin, 1859), p. 54 [=A. Kuhn, *Mythologische Studien* (Gütersloh, 1886), p. 51]; cf. also R. Schmitt, *Dichtung and Dichtersprache in indogermanischer Zeit* (chap. 2, n. 28), pp. 167–69.

because he stands for the sun itself; this feature is otherwise left unexplained, since all eyes are "circular," and the description "circle-eyed" does not imply one eye as opposed to two.[53]

Kuhn's argument has been attacked because it seems to have little to do with the Cyclops as depicted by Homer.[54] But such attacks are unjustified. The fact that the Cyclops is a murderous monster accords well with the sunset aspect of solar mythology. Presumably, it is this fact that has eluded scholars,[55] for otherwise the Cyclops, entering his cave by night and leaving it by day, is an apt symbol for the sun. Kuhn's explanation is probably the correct one.

Another derivation has recently been suggested by Rüdiger Schmitt, who proposes that *Kúklōps* was reduced by haplology from **kukló-klōps*, "robber of the (sun's) wheel."[56] Schmitt adduces Vedic parallels in which the wheel of the sun is stolen, and he draws attention to the character of the Cyclopes as storm-demons. The oldest evidence for this is in the names *Bróntēs, Sterópēs,* and *Árgēs,* which Hesiod, *Theogony* 140, gives

---

53. Notice that in Hesiod *Theogony* 144–45:

Κύκλωπες δ᾽ ὄνομ᾽ ἦσαν ἐπώνυμον, οὕνεκ᾽ ἄρα σφέων
κυκλοτερὴς ὀφθαλμὸς ἔεις ἐνέκειτο μετώπῳ

They were called by the name Cyclopes because one circular eye had been placed in their forehead,

the fact of having one eye is expressed by the word *héeis*, "one," and not by the word *kukloterés*, "circular."

54. Cf. the discussion of R. Schmitt, *Dichtung und Dichtersprache in indo-germanischer Zeit* (chap. 2, n. 28), p. 167; so I also interpret the remark "sachlich unbefriedigend" of H. Frisk, *Griechisches etymologisches Wörterbuch* (chap. 1 n.4), s.v.

55. For the difficulties which the negative aspect of sun symbolism might create for the rational mind, cf. the following remark of M. Eliade, *Patterns in Comparative Religion* (chap. 2, n. 22), p. 144: "The hierophanies of the sun display, indeed, dimensions that the sun merely as such would lose in any purely rational or profane perspective. But those dimensions hold a definite place in any primitive system of myth and metaphysic."

56. R. Schmitt, *Dichtung und Dichtersprache in indogermanischer Zeit* (chap. 2, n. 28), p. 168.

to three of the Cyclopes.[57] It is clear why storm-demons might be called "robbers of the (sun's) wheel." It is less clear, however, how Schmitt's derivation fits the story in the *Odyssey*. Do storm-demons also murder men? This is the dominant feature of the Cyclops in the oldest Greek evidence, and it is better explained by Kuhn's derivation than by Schmitt's.

Paul Thieme has proposed a third derivation.[58] He posits an original form *Pku-klōps*, meaning "cattle-thief." In this case, the first element of the compound would descend from Indo-European *pku-*, a zero-grade of *peku*, "cattle."[59] Thieme argues the existence of the Indo-European zero-grade on the basis of Vedic and Avestan compounds, in which the meaning "cattle" had been forgotten, but for which Thieme's reconstruction is convincing.[60]

On the basis of his derivation Thieme argues that the Cyclops is the Greek equivalent of the Vedic Paṇis, discussed earlier in this study. This argument fits exceedingly well with the nature of the Homeric episode. As in the Paṇi myth, there is a demon dwelling in a cave; this demon, moreover, has flocks which he encloses in his cave by night and releases by day.[61]

57. The three names have to do, respectively, with "thunder," "lightening," and "brightness."

58. P. Thieme, "Etymologische Vexierbilder," *Zeitschrift für vergleichende Sprachforschung* 69 (1951): 177–78 [= *Kleine Schriften* (Wiesbaden, 1971), 1: 62–63].

59. The meaning in Indo-European seems in fact to have been "moveable property" rather than "cattle"; cf. n. 64 below.

60. In addition to the article cited above (n. 58), see also P. Thieme, "Beiträge zur Vedaexegese, 2. *śurúdh*," *Zeitschrift der deutschen morgenländischen Gesellschaft* 95 (1941): 338 ff. [= *Kleine Schriften* 1 : 42 ff.].

61. Notice the initial description of the cave (*ix* 182 ff.):

ἔνθα δ' ἐπ' ἐσχατιῇ σπέος εἴδομεν, ἄγχι θαλάσσης,
ὑψηλόν, δάφνῃσι κατηρεφές· ἔνθα δὲ πολλὰ
μῆλ', ὄϊές τε καὶ αἶγες ἰαύεσκον.

There at the edge of the land we saw the cave, close to the sea, high, covered with laurels; there many small animals, sheep and goats, passed the night.

The fact that the rams are left outside the cave on the first night (*ix* 238) and are brought inside on the second night (*ix* 337) has to do mainly with a plot device.

A further correspondence is that these flocks are ultimately driven off by a hero who relies on his intelligence rather than his might.[62]

From the point of view of content and meaning Thieme's derivation has much to recommend it. But the important question remains whether the derivation is at all likely from a formal standpoint. There are two serious difficulties. The first is that no other form from Indo-European *peku is attested in Greek; the second is that the type of zero-grade represented by *pku- is rare in Greek.[63] While neither of these difficulties is insurmountable,[64] they do render Thieme's derivation very uncertain.

For this reason Kuhn's explanation of the name *Kúklōps* remains the simplest and the best. The Cyclops, as "circle-eyed," would originally have symbolized the sun itself; this connection accounts for the similarity between the Cyclops and the Panis sufficiently well, for the Panis, like the Cyclops, apparently have to do with an archaic myth of the sun and the sun's cattle.

Two points have now been considered in connection with the Cyclops: a latent "return from death" and the latent role of the sun. The remaining point is the role of *nóos*. That this is very important in the Cyclops episode requires no lengthy proof, for the famous intelligence of Odysseus is nowhere more prominent

62. See sect. 2 above for the role of knowledge in the Pani myth, and below in text for the role of "mind" in the escape of Odysseus from the cave.

63. The type does exist, however; cf. the pair *méli, blíttō*.

64. A recent study by É. Benveniste makes it probable that a Greek form *peku once existed. In *Le vocabulaire des institutions indo-européennes*, vol. 1 (chap. 1, n. 6), chap. 4, "Le bétail et l'argent: *pecu* et *pecūnia*," Benveniste shows that Indo-European *peku did not mean "cattle," but "moveable property" in general; in chap. 3, "*Próbaton* et l'économie homérique," he shows that the Greek words *próbasis* and (*tà*) *próbata* likewise originally meant "moveable property." On the basis of this, he draws the following conclusion (p. 59): "Il est intéressant de noter—les comparatistes n'y ont pas prêté assez d'attention—que *peku manque en grec. Ce n'est pas un hasard. Une notion aussi importante ne pouvait simplement disparaître. Le terme indo-européen a été, en fait, remplacé en grec par une désignation nouvelle, qui porte le même sense; c'est hom. *próbasis*, avec son équivalent beaucoup plus commun, *próbata*."

than in the escape from the Cyclops's cave. One first notices how tightly the latent "return from death" is connected with words denoting intelligence in the following lines (*ix* 420ff.):

αὐτὰρ ἐγὼ βούλευον, ὅπως ὄχ' ἄριστα γένοιτο,
εἴ τιν' ἑταίροισιν θανάτου λύσιν ἠδ' ἐμοὶ αὐτῷ
εὑροίμην· πάντας δὲ δόλους καὶ μῆτιν ὕφαινον,
ὥς τε περὶ ψυχῆς· μέγα γὰρ κακὸν ἐγγύθεν ἦεν.

But I *took counsel* so that what was best might come about, to see if I could find some *release from death* for my companions and myself; I wove all sorts of *plots* and *schemes, as if for my life*, for a great evil was near at hand.

Other examples of "intelligence" may also be cited. Odysseus says that the Cyclops tried to trick him into revealing where his ship was, but did not succeed because he (Odysseus) was too wise (*ix* 281):

ὣς φάτο πειράζων, ἐμὲ δ' οὐ λάθεν εἰδότα πολλά.

So he spoke, testing me, but he did not escape my notice since I *knew many things*.

When Odysseus forms his plan to blind the Cyclops, and again when he devises an escape by clinging beneath the Cyclops's sheep, there is an emphasis on his mental deliberation in the following repeated line (*ix* 318, 424):

ἥδε δέ μοι κατὰ θυμὸν ἀρίστη φαίνετο βουλή.

This *counsel* seemed best to me in my heart.

Between these two instances of "best counsel," the *Oûtis* stratagem works, and the Cyclops is abandoned by his neighbors. Odysseus comments on this as follows (*ix* 414):

ὣς ὄνομ' ἐξαπάτησεν ἐμὸν καὶ μῆτις ἀμύμων.

Thus my name and faultless plan deceived him.

In this line one should note what seems to be an intentional pun between *mêtis*, "plan," and the name *Oûtis*. The pun is set up four lines earlier when the other Cyclopes say:

εἰ μὲν δὴ μή τίς σε βιάζεται οἶον ἐόντα

If *no one* (*mḗ tis*) is doing violence to you and you are alone,

and proceed to bid their neighbor farewell. Paralleling the equation between *oú tis*, "no one" and *mḗ tis*, "no one," an equation is established between *Oûtis*, "No one," and *mêtis*, "shrewd plan." The suggestion of "death" in *Oûtis* thus quickly changes to the notion of "mind." It would seem from this that Homer, in his own way, has preserved the relation between death and *nóos*, the "return from death."

The importance of "mind" in the Cyclops episode can also be judged from references occurring elsewhere in the *Odyssey*. On the night before Odysseus kills the suitors, he steels himself by recalling how he took courage even in the Cyclops's cave (*xx* 20–21):

σὺ δ᾽ ἐτόλμας, ὄφρα σε μῆτις
ἐξάγαγ᾽ ἐξ ἄντροιο ὀϊόμενον θανέεσθαι.

But you took courage until intelligence led you out of the cave, although you thought you would die.

The word *mêtis* is again used, and Homer could not have done more to connect "mind" with "return" than he does by using the words *se mêtis exágag'*, "intelligence led you out." Again, when Odysseus approaches Scylla and Charybdis, he encourages his companions with the thought that nothing could be worse than the Cyclops; he then adds (*xii* 211–12):

ἀλλὰ καὶ ἔνθεν ἐμῇ ἀρετῇ βουλῇ τε νόῳ τε
ἐκφύγομεν.

But we escaped from that place by means of my valor, my *plan*, and my *intelligence*.

These passages reveal that Homer was still dimly aware of the relation between "mind" and the "return from death." Significantly, however, the word *nóōi* in the last passage represents the only time that *nóos* is used in relation to the escape from the cave. The word *nóos* has largely been replaced by a new vocabulary, by words such as *boulé* and, in particular, *mêtis*.[65]

The reason for the change in vocabulary is easy to see. In the first instance, *nóos was* the "return from death," but Homer was at most only dimly aware of this. One detail alone in his story suggests the original relation between "mind" and "return." This, significantly, appears at the very moment when Odysseus emerges from the cave. At this point (*ix* 444–45) the text reads:

> ὕστατος ἀρνειὸς μήλων ἔστειχε θύραζε,
> λάχνῳ στεινόμενος καὶ ἐμοὶ πυκινὰ φρονέοντι.

Last among the sheep the ram went out of the doorway, loaded with his own fleece, and with me, and my close counsels.

With the words *pukinà phronéonti, "having close counsels,"* which refer to no definite "thought" or "plan," Homer comes closest to realizing the originally neutral sense of *nóos*.

Otherwise, however, Homer had lost this sense. From the substitution of the phrase *phúgomen thánaton*, "we escaped death," for the traditional phrase *ásmenoi ek thanátoio,* "having returned from death," it is clear that Homer no longer thought in terms of an actual "return from death." Once the notion of "death" had become latent, the relation between "returning" and *nóos* was bound to change. We see the result of this change in Homer, where "mind" no longer *is* the "escape" but is, rather, the *means* of "escape." This was a natural development, and, given this development, it was also natural that the word *nóos* should have been replaced by a more descriptive vocabulary.

65. For another instance in which *mêtis* is the significant word, see chap. 4, sect. 2, on Nestor in *Iliad* 23.

Words like "counsel," "plot," and "device" were far more suited to describing the means of escape than was the neutral word *nóos*.[66] The change from *nóos* to *mêtis* should be seen in connection with the change from *ásmenoi ek thanátoio* to *phúgomen thánaton*; the root *nes-* in both of the traditional expressions had lost its original meaning, and this necessitated the substitution of a new vocabulary.

4 THE RETURN TO ITHACA

Until now I have been concerned only with the adventures Odysseus relates to the Phaeacian court in Books 9–12 of the *Odyssey*.[67] These adventures have provided the basic evidence for the "return from death," the role of the sun, and the role of *nóos* as related features in the *nóstos* of Odysseus. I shall now consider the final stage of this *nóstos*, which begins in Ogygia, includes Phaeacia, and ends in Ithaca. Here too there is evidence of the features mentioned above. It is fitting that such remaining evidence be surveyed in the final section of this chapter.

That the return from Ogygia has been poetically conceived as a return from death is very clear. The goddess who dwells on this island is a solitary figure who lives far from men and the other gods; she inhabits a cave, and her name, *Kalupsố*, suggests the darkness of death.[68] As long as Calypso keeps

66. Cf. the discussion of *polútropos* in the introduction to the book above.

67. The adventures in Books 9–12 which have not been discussed in the preceding are the Sirens, Scylla and Charybdis, and the winds of Aeolus. The Aeolus adventure, it may be noted, provides another instance of the "mindlessness" of the companions (cf. *x* 27 and 46).

68. The name is connected with the verb *kalúptein*, "to cover;" for the connotations of the latter, cf. the Homeric formulas *tòn dè skótos ósse kálupse(n)*, "darkness covered his eyes," and *télos thanátoio kálupse(n)*, "the end of death covered (him)." For the relevance of the verb for *nóos*, cf. Aristotle, *de Anima* 429ª7: *dià tó epikalúptesthai tòn noûn eníote páthei ề nósois ề húpnōi*, "on account of the *mind's* being *covered over* at times by passion, diseases, or sleep."

Odysseus with her, he is like the shades of the underworld in his listlessness and sorrow. Hence it is significant that when Hermes is sent to free him, the god takes with him his "ambivalent" staff (*v* 47–48):

> εἵλετο δὲ ῥάβδον, τῇ τ᾽ ἀνδρῶν ὄμματα θέλγει
> ὧν ἐθέλει, τοὺς δ᾽ αὖτε καὶ ὑπνώοντας ἐγείρει.

He took the staff with which he charms the eyes of those whom he wishes, and awakens others from their sleep.

In this case, of course, Hermes does not use his staff to "awaken" Odysseus in a literal fashion. But by mentioning the staff, Homer still suggests that the return of Odysseus is a return to consciousness and to life.[69]

During the final voyage from Phaeacia to Ithaca, on the other hand, sleep and the return to consciousness become literal motifs. When this voyage begins Odysseus falls into a deep sleep, and remains there until he reaches home. Homer prepares for this feature of the story well in advance. At an early point King Alcinoos takes measures to ensure that the gifts given to Odysseus will not be harmed when he "sleeps" on his return (*viii* 444–45):

> ὁππότ᾽ ἂν αὖτε
> εὕδῃσθα γλυκὺν ὕπνον ἰὼν ἐν νηῒ μελαίνῃ

. . . whenever you fall into a sweet sleep going on the black ship.

The Phaeacians, moreover, carefully prepare a bed for Odysseus before the voyage begins. These details show that "sleep" was to be a basic part of the "return."

Calypso's connection with death is further indicated by a series of striking parallels between her and the underworld river goddess Styx—these are listed and interpreted in end note 3.

69. For Hermes' role, cf. chap. 3, sect. 2 on the Circe episode, and chap. 7 below on Priam's ransom of Hector in *Iliad* 24, where the same lines describing the staff of Hermes occur.

More significant is the fact that the sleep which falls upon Odysseus is all but equated with death in the following lines (*xiii* 79–80):

καὶ τῷ νήδυμος ὕπνος ἐπὶ βλεφάροισιν ἔπιπτε,
νήγρετος ἥδιστος, θανάτῳ ἄγχιστα ἐοικώς.

And upon his eyes there fell a gentle sleep, the sweetest sort of sleep with no awakening, *which was most like death.*

The sleep of Odysseus also contains a suggestion of *lēthē*, the "forgetfulness of death," in the following description of the sleeping hero (*xiii* 90ff.):

ὃς πρὶν μὲν μάλα πολλὰ πάθ᾽ ἄλγεα ὃν κατὰ θυμὸν
ἀνδρῶν τε πτολέμους ἀλεγεινά τε κύματα πείρων,
δὴ τότε γ᾽ ἀτρέμας εὗδε, λελασμένος ὅσσ᾽ ἐπεπόνθει.

He who before this had suffered many woes in his heart, the battles of men and crossing the hard seas, now slept still, *forgetting* all that he had suffered.

The virtual equation between sleep and death is very revealing. It was suggested earlier in this chapter that when Odysseus falls asleep in Thrinacia he is experiencing a kind of passage through death. The description of the hero's final voyage supports this suggestion.

The equation is also highly relevant to the original meaning of the word *nóos*. In chapter 2 it was suggested that the word originally designated something close to "consciousness." The role of sleep during the final voyage supports this suggestion as well.

One may now observe more closely how the final voyage preserves the connection between *nóos* and the "return to consciousness." The last passage quoted above suggests that when the hero falls asleep, his *nóos* is removed by *lēthē*. He forgets his past sufferings, whether in Troy or on the way home.

But Odysseus is now on his final "return to life," and his *nóos* should therefore be ready to reemerge. This is in fact suggested in the lines immediately preceding the last passage quoted above; the lines refer to the speeding Phaeacian ship which carries Odysseus (*xiii* 88–89):

ὡς ἡ ῥίμφα θέουσα θαλάσσης κύματ' ἔταμνεν,
ἄνδρα φέρουσα θεοῖς ἐναλίγκια μήδε' ἔχοντα.

Thus the quick-running ship cut across the waves of the sea, carrying a man *whose counsels were like the gods'.*

One is strongly reminded of the return from the Cyclops's cave (*ix* 444-45):

ὕστατος ἀρνειὸς μήλων ἔστειχε θύραζε,
λάχνῳ στεινόμενος *καὶ ἐμοὶ πυκινὰ φρονέοντι.*

Last among the sheep the ram went out of the doorway, loaded with his own fleece, *and with me, and my close counsels.*

But this is only an intermediate stage. The *nóos* of Odysseus should properly reappear only when he reawakens in his homeland. And so it seems to happen in the Homeric poem. Waiting to give Odysseus advice when he returns is the goddess Athena. The striking feature of the encounter that follows is the attention given to "intelligence," particularly through the words *nóos* and *nóēma*. Before Odysseus recognizes Athena, he tries to deceive her with one of his Cretan tales. Homer comments on this as follows (*xiii* 254–55):

οὐδ' ὅ γ' ἀληθέα εἶπε, πάλιν δ' ὅ γε λάζετο μῦθον,
αἰεὶ ἐνὶ στήθεσσι *νόον* πολυκερδέα νωμῶν.

He did not tell the truth, but held back his speech, always plying his clever *mind* within his breast.

When Athena reveals herself and puts the lie to this tale, she continues (*xiii* 296 ff.):

ἀλλ' ἄγε, μηκέτι ταῦτα λεγώμεθα, εἰδότες ἄμφω
κέρδε', ἐπεὶ σὺ μέν ἐσσι βροτῶν ὄχ' ἄριστος ἁπάντων
βουλῇ καὶ μύθοισιν, ἐγὼ δ' ἐν πᾶσι θεοῖσι
μήτι τε κλέομαι καὶ κέρδεσιν.

But come, let us no longer say these things when *both of us know cunning ways*, since you among all mortals are by far the best in *counsel* and speech, and I among all gods am famed for my *intelligence* and *craft*.

And when Odysseus demands assurance that he himself has not been deceived about his finally being home in Ithaca, Athena gently rebukes him as follows (*xiii* 330 ff.):

αἰεί τοι τοιοῦτον ἐνὶ στήθεσσι *νόημα*·
τῷ σε καὶ οὐ δύναμαι προλιπεῖν δύστηνον ἐόντα,
οὕνεκ' ἐπητής ἐσσι καὶ *ἀγχίνοος* καὶ ἐχέφρων.

The *intention* in your breast is always such, and thus I cannot abandon you in your plight, for you are reserved, *close-witted*, and shrewd.

It should be noted that Athena and Odysseus are closely identified with each other in this scene. The second passage quoted above shows this clearly. The main advice Athena has come to give to Odysseus is to conceal his identity until the suitors have been killed. Remarkably, Odysseus has just tried to conceal his identity from Athena.[70] Thus, as frequently in Homer, the divinity in this scene seems to represent a specific aspect of the hero. Athena, who has come to advise Odysseus, represents intelligence—the intelligence of Odysseus. Thus explained, her presence is a sign that the *nóos* of Odysseus was indeed a basic feature of his return to Ithaca. Homer uses this feature as an

70. I am grateful to John Finley for this observation.

opportunity to have Odysseus devise his "plot" against the suitors. But the feature itself was undoubtedly older than this adaptation of it. The emphasis placed on *nóos* in the initial sparring between Odysseus and Athena indicates this.

There is less to say about the role of the sun in the final voyage of Odysseus. This voyage takes place by night, and the Phaeacian ship approaches Ithaca just as the daystar appears in the east (*xiii* 93ff.):

εὖτ᾽ ἀστὴρ ὑπερέσχε φαάντατος, ὅς τε μάλιστα
ἔρχεται ἀγγέλλων φάος Ἠοῦς ἠριγενείης,
τῆμος δὴ νήσῳ προσεπίλνατο ποντοπόρος νηῦς.

When the brightest star arose, the foremost messenger of the light of early-born Dawn, then did the sea-faring ship approach the island.

The arrival of Odysseus thus coincides with the rising of the sun.[71]

It now remains only to say something more about the Phaeacians. The first point of interest is their ships, which are described in such a way as to reveal once again the close connection between *nóos* and *néomai*. They are described in *viii* 556ff., where Alcinoos says that his ships do not require helmsmen or rudders but will send Odysseus on his way by "taking aim in their minds," *tituskómenai phresí*; for these ships "themselves know the thoughts and minds of men," *autaì ísasi noḗmata kaì phrénas andrȭn*. The word *nóēma* occurs again in relation to the Phaeacian ships in *vii* 36, in a brief simile describing their speed:

τῶν νέες ὠκεῖαι ὡς εἰ πτερὸν ἠὲ νόημα.

Their ships are as swift as a wing or a thought.

71. Notice also that upon his arrival Odysseus is first surrounded by a mist (*xiii* 189), which Athena ultimately removes (*xiii* 352).

The simile "as quick as thought" is unique in Homer.[72] That it should be used to describe the ships in which Odysseus "returns" is significant. It seems equally significant that the same ships are said to "know the thoughts and minds of men." Possessing minds of their own and knowing the minds of others, the Phaeacian ships could not be a more apt symbol of the relation between *nóos* and *néomai*.

Homer indicates that it was the special pride of the Phaeacians to send people safely on their way. On two occasions Alcinoos refers to this function (*viii* 566 = *xiii* 174):

πομποὶ ἀπήμονές εἰμεν ἁπάντων.

We are harmless escorts for all.

The Phaeacians are thus a sea-faring people, and most of their names (*Nausíthoos, Pontónoos,* etc.) reflect this fact. The one major exception to the rule seemed to be King *Alkínoos* himself, until his name was correctly explained by Hugo Mühlestein.[73] The second part of his name is to be connected with the verb *néomai* in a transitive sense, which gives to the first element its proper instrumental force. Like the name *Iphínoos,* the name *Alkínoos* must have meant "he who brings back by his might."[74]

So explained, the name of the Phaeacian king harmonizes excellently with the special function of his people, which was to "bring back" strangers like Odysseus. This correspondence lends great conviction to Mühlestein's argument that the name *Alkínoos* should be dissociated from the noun *nóos*; the only

72. Cf., however, the phrase ὡς δ' ὅτ' ἂν ἀΐξῃ νόος, "as when the mind (*nóos*) darts," in a simile describing Hera's speed as she returns to Olympus (xv 80).

73. H. Mühlestein, "Namen von Neleiden auf Pylostäfelchen" (chap. 1, n. 7), p. 158; *Arétē,* the name of the Phaeacian queen, does not refer to sea-faring but is nonetheless significant—*Arétē* is "prayed to" by Odysseus (cf. the verb *aráomai,* "to pray").

74. Underlying the form *Alkínoos,* which has the usual accentuation of personal names, there may also have been an epithet *alkinoós.* For more on the transitive sense of the root *nes-* in Greek, see chap. 4, sect. 4 below.

necessary qualification is that, while the name and the noun are not immediately related, they both still contain the same root, *nes-*.

In conclusion, attention may be drawn to another aspect of the Phaeacians; namely, their peculiar status, which seems to be halfway between gods and men.[75] For the most part they are as unhardened and frivolous as the Homeric gods, but they also experience suffering through their contact with Odysseus. For giving him safe conduct they are punished by Poseidon.

The ambiguous status of the Phaeacians prepares the way for my next chapter, the subject of which will be Nestor, a figure who, like the Phaeacians, often seems somewhat remote from the hard concerns of mortal life. It should emerge from the following pages that the similarity between Nestor and the Phaeacians is not accidental, but has to do with their originally common function.

75. In *v* 35 they are called *ankhítheoi*, "close to the gods."

4 *Nestor*

1 INTRODUCTION

THE FOCUS OF ATTENTION in the last chapter was Odysseus, whose adventures preserve a latent relation between "mind" and "return." In this chapter I shall consider another Homeric figure, who by his very name—*Néstōr*—tightens the connection between the words *nóos* and *néomai*.

Much of the scholarly work necessary to understanding Nestor's name has already been done, and this work is fundamental to the present study. Nevertheless certain misconceptions have arisen, first of all with regard to the precise interpretation of Nestor's name and, as a result of this, the interpretation of Nestor's original nature. Oddly, what has helped to obscure these matters is an achievement which has shed light on so many other things—namely, the archeological discovery of the Bronze Age city of Pylos.

The discovery that Pylos once really existed has not unnaturally led to the assumption that Nestor was once really its king. The possibility that there was such a historical figure must in fact be granted; but this possibility, even if it became fact, would not explain the name *Néstōr* or the original function of the figure so called in Homer. One purpose of this chapter will be to show that at least the "original" Nestor must have been a purely mythological figure.

2 NESTOR AND THE GREEK ROOT *nes-

The view has long been held that the name *Néstōr* contains the verbal root *nes-* (followed by the agent suffix *-tōr*). This derivation was first proposed by Curtius and has since been accepted by such scholars as Kretschmer, Hofmann, Palmer, Heubeck, Mühlestein, Durante, Ruijgh, and Frisk.[1] The derivation is thus solidly established.

Nevertheless, there has been disagreement on the interpretation of the name. The predominant modern view is that the root *nes-* in *Néstōr* has a transitive sense and that the name therefore means "he who brings [his people] home." Kretschmer, in his time, offered a different interpretation. He retained the intransitive sense of *néomai* by proposing that *Néstōr* simply meant "he who returns" and that the figure so called was originally a vegetation deity. This view has been supported most recently by Hofmann (see n. 1).

Significantly, the predominant view has established itself as such only since the decipherment of Linear-B. One of the Pylos tablets has in fact furnished a new piece of evidence. Ventris and Chadwick were the first to draw attention to the form *ne-e-ra-wo* in Fn 79. 5.[2] They compared this form, which the context shows to be a personal name in the dative case, with the name *Neíleōs* in later Greek. The Mycenean name would be *Neélāwos* on the basis of this comparison.

1. G. Curtius, *Grundzüge der griechischen Etymologie*[5] (Leipzig, 1869), p. 294; P. Kretschmer, "Mythische Namen," *Glotta* 4 (1913): 308–09; J. B. Hofmann, *Etymologisches Wörterbuch des Griechischen* (Munich, 1949), s.v. *néomai*; L. R. Palmer, *Eranos* 54 (1956): 7ff., also his *The Interpretation of Mycenean Greek Texts* (Oxford, 1963), pp. 79–80; A. Heubeck, *Beiträge zur Namenforschung* 8 (1957): 28; H. Mühlestein, "Namen von Neleiden auf Pylostäfelchen" (chap. 1, n. 7), p. 158; M. Durante, "Νείλεως e Νηλεύς," *Studi Micenei ed Egeo-Anatolici* 21, no. 3 (1967): 36; C. J. Ruijgh, *Études sur la grammaire et le vocabulaire du grec mycénien* (chap. 2, n. 27), pp. 369–70; H. Frisk (chap. 1, n. 4), s.v. *néomai*.

2. M. Ventris and J. Chadwick, *Documents in Mycenean Greek*[2] (Cambridge, 1973), p. 421.

The implications of this comparison were first seen by Palmer,[3] who pointed out that the name *Neíleōs* belonged to the supposed *oikist* of Miletus, and that this figure, according to Greek tradition, was a direct descendant of Neleus, the founder of the Pylian dynasty. The second member in this dynasty, moreover, was Nestor, whose name contains the root *nes-*. This suggests that the name *Neíleōs* also contains the root *nes-*, and that its Mycenean equivalent should be transcribed as *Nehé-lāwos*, both forms meaning "he who leads the war-folk home."

The importance of the Mycenean form and its Ionic equivalent is that they attest a transitive use of the root *nes-*. This springs directly from the form of the first element in the name, which is composed of the verbal root followed by *e*. One may compare the name *Agé-lā(w)os*, "he who leads the war-folk."[4]

This makes it probable that the name *Néstōr* also had a transitive meaning. For the present, however, I shall go no further than this. Other aspects of Palmer's argument require more caution and will be considered later in detail. Among these is the view—probable in itself—that the name of Nestor's father, *Nēleús*, stands for the Mycenean form *Nehélāwos*. Improbable, however, is the view that this is a crucial factor in determining what the name *Néstōr* originally meant. Arguments will later be given for rejecting Palmer's view that *Néstōr* is only a "short form" of *Nehélāwos*, and that it therefore has the same meaning, "he who leads the war-folk home."

But two points have been firmly established: the first, that *Néstōr* is related to the verb *néomai*, and the second, that the name could have been understood in a transitive sense at an early period. One half of our problem has thus already been eliminated through previous scholarship. The other half, however,

---

3. L. R. Palmer, *Eranos* (n. 1), pp. 9ff.

4. On the archaic form of these compounds, see C. Watkins, *Indogermanische Grammatik*, vol. 3, pt. 1 (Heidelberg, 1969), pp. 94–95.

has never been recognized; it has to do with *nóos*. But this part of the problem, once it is recognized, all but solves itself.

It requires little argument to become convinced that Nestor has as strong a connection with *nóos* as he does with *néomai*. The figure who is known to us from Homer is the very embodiment of wisdom. In the *Iliad* he is the wise old counselor of the Greeks, and his subsequent fame derived from this role above all. Nor does it matter that his advice to the Greek princes often seems old-fashioned and long-winded, for his role is rather to symbolize *nóos* than to make *nóos* effective.

A few passages from the *Iliad* may be quoted to show Nestor's clear connection with *nóos*. His most important advice (although it ultimately fails) is to send the embassy to Achilles. He introduces this proposal as follows (IX 103 ff.):

> αὐτὰρ ἐγὼν ἐρέω ὥς μοι δοκεῖ εἶναι ἄριστα.
> οὐ γάρ τις *νόον* ἄλλος ἀμείνονα τοῦδε *νοήσει*,
> οἷον ἐγὼ *νοέω*, ἠμὲν πάλαι ἠδ᾽ ἔτι καὶ νῦν,
> ἐξ ἔτι τοῦ ὅτε, διογενές, Βρισηΐδα κούρην
> χωομένου Ἀχιλῆος ἔβης κλισίηθεν ἀπούρας
> οὔ τι καθ᾽ ἡμέτερόν γε *νόον*.

> I will speak as seems best to me. For no one else *will conceive* a better *plan* than this one, such as I *have in mind*, either now or long before now, ever since the time when you, O Zeus-born king, went and took the maiden Briseis from the tent of angry Achilles, which was not at all according to my *advice*.

When the embassy fails, Nestor slips into the background for a while, at least as the wise counselor. When the Greeks reach the point of full retreat, however, he is at hand again to suggest that Agamemnon call a council, phrasing his advice as follows (XIV 61–62):

> ἡμεῖς δὲ φραζώμεθ᾽ ὅπως ἔσται τάδε ἔργα,
> εἴ τι *νόος* ῥέξει.

> Let us take counsel as to how these matters will be, if *intelligence* may accomplish anything.

In this case it is very plain that Nestor is only the symbol of *nóos*. In actuality it is Diomedes rather than Nestor who proposes the measure which is adopted—that the wounded champions should encourage their men from behind the lines.

A third passage dwells on the word *mêtis* rather than *nóos*. When, during the funeral games for Patroclus, Nestor instructs his son Antilochus how best to compete in the chariot race, he introduces his advice as follows (XXIII 313 ff.):

ἀλλ᾽ ἄγε δὴ σύ, φίλος, μῆτιν ἐμβάλλεο θυμῷ
παντοίην, ἵνα μή σε παρεκπροφύγῃσιν ἄεθλα.
μήτι τοι δρυτόμος μέγ᾽ ἀμείνων ἠὲ βίηφι·
μήτι δ᾽ αὖτε κυβερνήτης ἐνὶ οἴνοπι πόντῳ
νῆα θοὴν ἰθύνει ἐρεχθομένην ἀνέμοισι·
μήτι δ᾽ ἡνίοχος περιγίγνεται ἡνιόχοιο.

But come, dear son, and put into your mind all sorts of *intelligent schemes* so that the prizes do not escape you. It is by *intelligence* rather than strength that a woodcutter becomes much the better, and it is again by *intelligence* that a helmsman on the wine-dark sea holds his ship on course when it is battered by the winds. It is also by *intelligence* that charioteer surpasses charioteer.

Once again Nestor seems to be present mainly as the symbol of "intelligence." In the lines immediately preceding what is quoted above, he in fact recognizes that Antilochus already has *mêtis* enough of his own, at least in relation to his competitors:

οὐδὲ μὲν αὐτοὶ
πλείονα ἴσασιν σέθεν αὐτοῦ μητίσασθαι.

They do not know how to *devise* more *schemes* than you yourself.

It is unnecessary to give further examples of this sort. What Nestor symbolizes is already perfectly clear; Nestor is in fact among the strongest single arguments for the derivation of *nóos* from the root *nes-*.

3 Nestor's Original Function

A significant problem was ignored in the previous section. I stated that the name *Néstōr* contains the root *nes-* but did not explain how the verbal notion of this root is relevant to understanding the Homeric figure so called.

Hugo Mühlestein has drawn attention to the place in Homer where Nestor truly exemplifies his name, namely, Book 11 of the *Iliad*.[5] In this book Nestor tells a long story concerning a battle between Pylos and Elis, which occurred when he was young and in which he played the leading role. It is widely assumed that this story was adapted by Homer from a lost "Pylian epic," which undoubtedly had its own long tradition and of which Nestor was the hero.[6] These assumptions make the story in *Iliad* 11 the most likely repository of ancient lore concerning Nestor.

Mühlestein has followed Palmer in equating the names *Néstōr* and *Nehélāwos*, and has therefore tried to find an instance in which Nestor "brings the war-folk safely home." He argues that such an instance appears in xi 759 ff., when Nestor has slain his last victim and the "Achaeans" return to Pylos:

αὐτὰρ Ἀχαιοὶ
ἂψ ἀπὸ Βουπρασίοιο Πύλονδ᾽ ἔχον ὠκέας ἵππους,
πάντες δ᾽ εὐχετόωντο θεῶν Διὶ Νέστορί τ᾽ ἀνδρῶν.

But the Achaeans headed their swift horses back from Bouprasion to Pylos, and they offered prayers to Zeus among gods and to Nestor among men.

It is in fact plausible to see Nestor as a kind of *Nehélāwos* in this passage.

But this final moment does not exhaust the relevance of Nestor's story to his name. The mere fact that Nestor is involved with the

---

5. H. Mühlestein, "Namen von Neleiden auf Pylostäfelchen" (chap. 1, n. 7), p. 158.

6. For a detailed investigation, see R. Cantieni, *Die Nestorerzählung im XI. Gesang der Ilias* (Zurich, 1942).

word *nóos* indicates that he is a deeply traditional figure, whose roots go back to a time when the relation between *nóos* and *néomai* was still perceived. At this time, moreover, the root *nes-* still signified a "return to life" and was used in the context of sun symbolism, the dominant feature of which, in Homer, involves the sun's "cattle." These observations determine what we should be looking for in Nestor's story.

His story does not disappoint us. The first episode he describes is in fact a *boēlasíē*, a "cattle-raid" (cf. XI 671–72). Under the leadership of Nestor, a band of Pylians stages this raid against one of the Epeians and drives the captured spoil home to Pylos (XI 671 ff.). The rest of the narrative springs from this beginning. In the next section (683–707) the spoil is divided at Pylos. We learn that the Pylians, first weakened by their conflict with Heracles, had been abused by the Epeians; the Epeians had probably been engaged in raiding the cattle of the Pylians, since the latter (the Pylians) regard the newly won spoil as their rightful due. In the next section (707–61) the Epeians attack and the Pylians hasten from their city by night to meet them. The battle takes place on the next day and the Pylians are victorious.

This is the structure of Nestor's story. There are two major episodes, a cattle-raid and a battle, and in trying to understand Nestor's function, the first deserves at least as much attention as the second. For while Nestor may bring the war-folk home from battle, he also "rescues" from the Epeians the herds and flocks which rightfully belong to Pylos. He is the foremost figure in the cattle-raid, insofar as he kills Itymoneus, who is present to protect his "cattle" (*ho d' amúnōn hêisi bóessin*, in l. 674). In the following lines we see Nestor, as the first among his companions, bringing huge flocks and herds home to Pylos; the elaborateness of the description is itself a sign that this function is important (XI 677 ff.):

λη̈ΐδα δ' ἐκ πεδίου συνελάσσαμεν ἤλιθα πολλήν,
πεντήκοντα βοῶν ἀγέλας, τόσα πώεα οἰῶν,
τόσσα συῶν συβόσια, τόσ' αἰπόλια πλατέ' αἰγῶν,

ἵππους δὲ ξανθὰς ἑκατὸν καὶ πεντήκοντα,
πάσας θηλείας, πολλῇσι δὲ πῶλοι ὑπῆσαν.
καὶ τὰ μὲν ἠλασάμεσθα Πύλον Νηλήϊον εἴσω.

We drove together from the plain an immense amount of spoil: there were fifty herds of cattle, as many flocks of sheep, as many droves of pigs, and as many wide-ranging flocks of goats; there were also a hundred and fifty brown horses, all of them mares, and many of them with foals following underneath. All of these we then drove into Pylos, the city of Neleus.

When *Nés-tōr* kills the guardian of the "cattle" and drives the rescued herds home, we are immediately disposed to see this, at least in part, as the reflex of a solar myth.[7] This idea, moreover, is soon seen to be more than a prejudice. For lurking in the background of Nestor's story is the Epeian king, whose name is *Augeías*. In xi 701 he is mentioned as having once robbed the four race-horses of Neleus, an example, apparently, of the grievances Pylos held against Elis.[8] In xi 739 he is mentioned as the father-in-law of the first hero slain in battle, whose horses and chariot are taken and used by Nestor.

The name *Augeías* is related to the noun *augé*, which in turn suggests the "radiance" of the sun.[9] It is clear that this figure was originally connected, or even identical, with the sun itself. Homer indicates as much in the description of his daughter Agamede, the spouse of the first hero slain (xi 739 ff.):

γαμβρὸς δ᾽ ἦν Αὐγείαο,
πρεσβυτάτην δὲ θύγατρ᾽ εἶχε ξανθὴν Ἀγαμήδην,
ἣ τόσα φάρμακα ᾔδη ὅσα τρέφει εὐρεῖα χθών.

7. The actual description of the spoil, including cattle, sheep, pigs, and goats, seems to be stock in nature; cf. the parallel description of Odysseus's possessions in *xiv* 100ff.
8. According to R. Cantieni (n. 6), p. 64, mention of this incident represents a later interpolation into Nestor's original story; see sect. 3 below for further suspected interpolations.
9. Cf. the frequent Homeric formula *hup' augàs ēelíoio*, "under the rays of the sun."

He was the son-in-law of Augeias, and had as wife his oldest
daughter, the fair-haired Agamede, who knew all the drugs
which the wide earth nourishes.

Agamḗdē, who is well-versed in all manner of drugs, is just
another form of *Mḗdeia*. In later Greek tradition Medea was
thought to be the granddaughter of Helios. If this was also
Homer's view, then he perhaps considered Augeias to be the son
of Helios. Probably, however, the name *Augeías* originated as an
epithet belonging to Helios himself.

In later Greek myth, at any rate, Augeias was said to be the
son of Helios. More importantly, the significance of "cattle" in
relation to Augeias becomes clearer at this stage. It was the cattle
of Augeias whose stables Heracles had to clean. Theocritus 25 is a
long epyllion which uses this particular labor as its background.
The second part of the poem is devoted to an elaborate
description of the prodigious herds as they return at night; they
are like endless clouds driven on by the wind.[10] That these herds
have to do with the cattle of the Sun is apparent throughout, but
especially in the description of the twelve white bulls (129 ff.):

ἄλλοι δ᾽ αὖ μετὰ τοῖσι δυώδεκα βουκολέοντο
ἱεροὶ Ἡελίου· χροιὴν δ᾽ ἔσαν ἠύτε κύκνοι
ἀργησταί

Pasturing among the other bulls were twelve sacred to Helios;
in color they were like shining white swans,

and in the following lines as well (118 ff.):

10. Theocritus 25. 88 ff.:

αὐτὰρ ἔπειτα βόες μάλα μυρίαι ἄλλαι ἐπ᾽ ἄλλαις
ἐρχόμεναι φαίνονθ᾽ ὡσεὶ νέφη ὑδατόεντα,
ἄσσα τ᾽ ἐν οὐρανῷ εἰσιν ἐλαυνόμενα προτέρωσε
ἠὲ Νότοιο βίῃ ἠὲ Θρηκὸς Βορέαο.

Then the cattle came thousand upon thousand like watery clouds driven
forward through the sky by the force of the south wind or the north wind
from Thrace.

Ἥλιος δ' ᾧ παιδὶ τόγ' ἔξοχον ὤπασε δῶρον,
ἀφνειὸν μήλοις περὶ πάντων ἔμμεναι ἀνδρῶν,
καί ῥά οἱ αὐτὸς ὄφελλε διαμπερέως βοτὰ πάντα
ἐς τέλος.

Helios gave this special gift to his son, to be rich in flocks beyond all men, and he himself made all the animals prosper for him continually without end.

In light of the above it becomes highly plausible that Nestor, by capturing the Epeian herds, in effect rescues the cattle of the Sun. It is true that the herds seem to belong, not to Augeias, but to the figure named Itymoneus. But Helios also remains in the background in Book 12 of the *Odyssey*, where he has other guardians to tend his cattle on Thrinacia. Perhaps Itymoneus stands for what was once the sort of monstrous guardian that would fittingly be slain.[11] But details such as this need not be pressed.

This interpretation of Nestor's story is supported by a passage in Pausanias, from which we learn that there was a cave outside the Messenian city of Pylos in which the cattle of Nestor, and earlier those of Neleus, were said to have been stabled.[12] Nothing could bring Nestor into closer relation with the cattle of the Sun than this piece of information. The importance of the cave in Greek and Sanskrit myths has already been discussed.

Pausanias goes on to conjecture that the cattle in question were those which had earlier belonged to the Thessalian Iphiclus, and

11. As Geryon, for example, is slain by Heracles; cf. chap 3, sect. 2 above.
12. Pausanias 4.36.2–3:

κἀὶ σπήλαιόν ἐστιν ἐντὸς τῆς πόλεως· βοῦς δὲ ἐνταῦθα τὰς
Νέστορος καὶ ἔτι πρότερον Νηλέως φασὶν αὐλίζεσθαι· εἴη δ᾽ἂν
Θεσσαλικὸν τὸ γένος τῶν βοῶν τούτων, Ἰφίκλου ποτὲ τοῦ
Πρωτεσιλάου πατρός· ταύτας γὰρ δὴ τὰς βοῦς Νηλεὺς ἕδνα ἐπὶ
τῇ θυγατρὶ ᾔτει τοὺς μνωμένους.

And there is a cave inside the city; they say that here the cattle of Nestor, and earlier those of Neleus, were stabled; these cattle would have been Thessalian in origin, as they once belonged to Iphiclus, the father of Protesilaus; for Neleus demanded these cattle as the bride-price for his daughter from her suitors.

which Neleus had demanded as the price for his daughter's hand. It is worth considering this legend more closely. Homer refers to it twice in the *Odyssey*, in Books 11 and 15. According to these accounts, Bias wanted to marry the daughter of Neleus. His brother Melampus, a prophet, therefore undertook to bring back the cattle of Iphiclus. Melampus, however, was captured in the attempt and imprisoned for a year before being released with the cattle.

The language used to describe the imprisonment is striking. One instance occurs in *xi* 292–93:

> χαλεπὴ δὲ θεοῦ κατὰ μοῖρα πέδησε,
> δεσμοί τ' ἀργαλέοι καὶ βουκόλοι ἀγροιῶται.

The hard destiny of the god, painful bonds, and rustic cow-herds shackled him.

There is another description in *xv* 231 ff.; here Phylacus, the father of Iphiclus, is mentioned:

> ὁ δὲ τῆος ἐνὶ μεγάροις Φυλάκοιο
> δεσμῷ ἐν ἀργαλέῳ δέδετο, κρατέρ' ἄλγεα πάσχων
> εἵνεκα Νηλῆος κούρης ἄτης τε βαρείης.

He meanwhile was tied in painful bonds in the house of Phylacus, suffering harsh woes because of the daughter of Neleus and the heavy ruin.

Words like *moîra*, "destiny," and *átē*, "ruin," suggest that the imprisonment was somewhat extraordinary. More suggestive still is the description of the release of Melampus in *xv* 235–36:

> ἀλλ' ὁ μὲν ἔκφυγε κῆρα καὶ ἤλασε βοῦς ἐριμύκους
> ἐς Πύλον ἐκ Φυλάκης.

But he escaped death and drove the loud-bellowing cattle from Phylaca to Pylos.

Melampus is said to have driven the cattle *ek Phulákēs*, "from the town of imprisonment" (cf. also *Phúlakos*); first, however, he "escaped death," *ékphuge kêra*. The latter phrase is similar to the second-level expression *phúgomen thánaton*, "we escaped death," which has replaced the notion of "returning from death" elsewhere in the *Odyssey*.[13] One is inclined to think that this was also the original notion in the Melampus legend. Even the role of *nóos* seems to have been preserved. In *xi* 296–97, Iphiclus is said to have released Melampus when the latter had "told all the oracles," *thésphata pánt' eipónta*. The significance of prophecy in the context of "returning from death" has already been seen in connection with Teiresias.[14]

It is interesting that Pausanias connects the myth of Melampus with the cave of Nestor. But the "myth" in which Nestor himself is involved seems primary to the myth of Melampus[15] and therefore has a still greater right to be connected with this cave. Nestor's original function was presumably to release the sun's cattle from this place, although such a detail is no longer suggested by his story and had perhaps long since vanished from the tradition behind it.[16]

It was pointed out earlier that flocks of the Sun were associated with Taenarum, and that in Taenarum there was a cave which was thought to connect with the underworld (see pp. 46–47). It is therefore plausible that Nestor's cave was also once thought to be an entrance to the underworld. No such tradition has survived, but there are still many indications that Pylos in general was associated with this domain. The very name suggests the "gates"

13. See pp. 55 and 64 above; cf. also pp. 17–18.

14. See chap. 3, sect. 2 above, where the Apollonian prophet Euenius is also discussed.

15. The myth in which Melampus is involved seems to reflect historical ties between Thessaly and the western Peloponnesus in the Mycenean age; cf. M. P. Nilsson, *The Mycenean Origin of Greek Mythology* (Berkeley, Calif., 1932), pp. 141–47.

16. In *Iliad* 11, Nestor brings the cattle back from Elis, whereas his cave is in Pylos. Perhaps relevant to discovering the underlying myth is the fact that there were three cities in the western Peloponnesus named Pylos, in Messenia, Triphylia, and Elis; the name Pylos appears to have a mythological connection with the "gates" to the underworld (see below in text), and the fact that there was more than one city of this name perhaps suggests a belief in different points of entrance and exit from the underworld.

(*púlai*) of Hades. Homer must have had this in mind when he related (v 397) how Heracles wounded the death-god Hades *en Púlōi en nekúessin*, "in Pylos among the dead." Mühlestein, furthermore, draws attention to "the remarkable fact that several names found around Pylos and Neleus express connections with Hades: Klymenos, Klymene, Periklymenos, Khloris, Anax, Pylartes, Ekhelos, among others, . . . and also *po-ro-u-te-u*/Pluteus, and *e-ru-si-jo*/Elysios."[17] From this list of names it is apparent that Homer, even if he had overextended the relation between Pylos and Hades, was nevertheless following a tradition.

It is not unnatural that Nestor, whose function had to do with "returning to life," was associated with Pylos. Sun symbolism is characterized by its two opposed aspects. If Nestor stands for the positive aspect, one might see in his brother Periclymenus the negative aspect; the latter's name was also an epithet for the god of the underworld.[18] Of all the sons of Neleus, in fact, only Nestor was associated with life. According to tradition, he alone survived the attack of Heracles on Pylos (xi 692–93):[19]

δώδεκα γὰρ Νηλῆος ἀμύμονος υἱέες ἦμεν·
τῶν οἶος λιπόμην, οἱ δ' ἄλλοι πάντες ὄλοντο.

There had been twelve sons of blameless Neleus, but of these only I was left; the others had all perished.

This raises the final point to be considered in this section. In addition to evidence for his freeing of the cattle of the sun, can one also find signs in Book 11 that Nestor's original function was to restore mortals to life and to light? I suggest that there are traces of this.

17. "Die merkwürdige Tatsache, dass mehrere Namen um Pylos und Neleus Hadesbeziehungen ausdrücken. . . .": H. Mühlestein, "Namen von Neleiden auf Pylostäfelchen" (chap. 1, n. 7), p. 169 n. 49.

18. Cf. Hesychius, *periklúmenos: ho Ploútōn* (god of the underworld).

19. Hesiod says that Nestor was in Gerenia at the time of Heracles' attack, cf. frags. 34 and 35 in *Fragmenta Hesiodea,* ed. R. Merkelbach and M. L. West (Oxford, 1967).

One finds a latent sense that Nestor restores the Pylians to light in the following curious details. Because the Epeians attack suddenly, the Pylians, forewarned by Athena,[20] must set forth by night (xi 714 ff.):

ἀλλ' ὅτε πᾶν πεδίον μετεκίαθον, ἄμμι δ' 'Αθήνη
ἄγγελος ἦλθε θέουσ' ἀπ' 'Ολύμπου θωρήσσεσθαι
ἔννυχος, οὐδ' ἀέκοντα Πύλον κάτα λαὸν ἄγειρεν.

But when they had crossed the entire plain, Athena rushed from Olympus by night to give us the message to arm, and throughout Pylos she gathered the willing host.

At this point, moreover, Neleus tries to prevent his son from going to battle by "hiding" his horses: *apékrupsen dé moi híppous* (718). But Nestor goes on foot, and when the sun rises and the battle begins, he immediately acquires horses by slaying the son-in-law of Augeias (735 ff.). Then the rout begins. In all of this there is a latent sense that Nestor is leading his people from the dark night of danger to the daylight of victory.[21]

There is also a sense in which Nestor brings the Pylians back to life. If one considers the narrative in Book 11 as a whole, it becomes clear that Nestor, far more than "bringing his people home from battle," effectively restores his people to life. The following lines (xi 689 ff.) show how close to extinction Pylos was before Nestor accomplished his cattle-raid and subsequent battle-rout:

ὡς ἡμεῖς παῦροι κεκακωμένοι ἐν Πύλῳ ἦμεν·
ἐλθὼν γάρ ῥ' ἐκάκωσε βίη Ἡρακληείη
τῶν προτέρων ἐτέων, κατὰ δ' ἔκταθεν ὅσσοι ἄριστοι·

---

20. The fact that it is Athena who comes with the "forewarning" seems significant, since the patron deity of Pylos was Poseidon; perhaps Athena's role has to do with *nóos* in this episode, as it does in the final homecoming of Odysseus (see chap. 3, sect. 4 above).

21. That *hippóta Néstōr*, "the horseman Nestor," is deprived of his own horses and forced to get new ones is an interesting, and perhaps a significant, detail. See chap. 6, n. 72 below for remarks on the possible significance of Nestor's epithet "the horseman."

δώδεκα γὰρ Νηλῆος ἀμύμονος υἱέες ἦμεν·
τῶν οἶος λιπόμην, οἱ δ' ἄλλοι πάντες ὄλοντο.

There were few of us left in Pylos and we were badly off,
for Heracles had come in earlier years and hurt us badly—
all the bravest men were killed. There had been twelve sons of
blameless Neleus, but of these only I was left; the others had
all perished.

The narrative in Book 11 suggests that the hostilities between
Pylos and Elis, the cattle-raids in particular, were of a recurrent
nature; this fits well with the original meaning of the myth. But
the myth has become historicized. A highly convincing study by
Räto Cantieni[22] has shown how this process, even at a relatively
late date, was still at work. One of his arguments is particularly
worth mentioning. According to Cantieni, the passages in Nestor's
story which contain detailed geographical references are late
additions to the basic narrative. These passages (711–13, 722–34,
and 757–58) represent the battle as taking place on the border
between Pylian and Elian territory. This is inconsistent with the
fact, which Cantieni demonstrates, that Bouprasion was on the
far side of Elis from Pylos.[23] When the later passages are removed,
it becomes clear that the battle originally covered the whole
territory between Pylos and the far side of Elis. This in turn
highlights the significance of the name *Bou-prásion*, from which
Nestor returns with his victorious people.[24]

I would suggest that at an earlier stage as well a historical
dimension began to replace the original myth. The myth was
recast as the hostility between two peoples, with the conflict
between Heracles and Pylos occupying the background. When
this happened the role of the "return from death" became obscure;
the idea could survive only as suggested above—namely, as a
return from virtual extinction by Nestor's people.

22. See n. 6 above.
23. For the location of Bouprasion, see Cantieni, pp. 43ff.; for his discussion
of the interpolated passages, pp. 36–57.
24. Whatever the second element of this name has to do with (*práson,* "leek"?),
the first element has to do with "cattle."

4 A CLOSER LOOK AT NESTOR'S NAME

In the previous section I have argued that the essential part of Nestor's story in *Iliad* 11 descends from an original myth of the sun. This would imply that Nestor himself came to be viewed as "historical" only when his myth had first been historicized. The trend of modern scholarship since the discovery of Pylos has been to historicize Nestor even more, and a pivotal argument in this trend has to do with the interpretation of Nestor's name. In this section, therefore, I shall reexamine this matter in some detail.

I shall begin by putting the case for a historical King Nestor as strongly as possible. As far as the name is concerned, the case may be summarized as follows. The crucial factor is the tradition, already well established in Homer, that Nestor was the son of Neleus. The next step must be to show that the name Neleus actually stands for an original *Nehélāwos*. If this can be done, there is then some basis for believing that a King Nehelawos once existed, given the fact that this name is already attested on the Pylos tablets, although apparently not for a king.[25] If we are thus led to believe Homer concerning Neleus, we may also be led to believe that Neleus had a son named Nestor. The presence of the root *nes-* in both names becomes an argument for the accuracy of Homer's picture of the Pylian dynasty. Leonard Palmer phrases this view as follows: "in the names of *Néstōr* and his father *Nēleús* we find further exemplification of the common practice of giving to the son a part of his father's name."[26] This, with certain reservations, is a plausible argument.

Marcello Durante has made the best case for the above interpretation of the name *Nēleús*.[27] He first points out that *Neíleōs*, the name of the Milesian *oikist*, sometimes appears as *Nēleús*,

25. Cf. M. Durante (n.1), p. 34: "Si tratta di una persona di condizione modesta, che viene citata a proposito di una assegnazione di frumento e di olive." ["It is a matter of a person of modest state, who is cited in connection with an allotment of grain or olives."]

26. L. R. Palmer, *Eranos* (n.1), p. 7.

27. M. Durante (n.1); Palmer, *Eranos* (n.1), p. 7, simply calls *Nēleús* a "short form" of *Nehélāwos*.

and more rarely as *Neileús* (a composite of the first two forms). This suggests from the start that the forms *Nēleús* and *Neíleōs* may represent the same thing.[28] A major problem, however, is the explanation for the *-ē-* in *Nēleús*. Wackernagel first suggested that this represents an Aeolic contraction of original *-ee-* (as in Aeolic *kênos* vs. Ionic *keînos*, "that one"), and Durante has substantially agreed.[29]

Durante's main contribution has been to explain the suffix *-leus* in a plausible way. His argument may be summarized as follows.[30] The form *Nēleús* is actually based on the patronymic *Nēlḗïos*. *Nēleús* occurs in only a limited number of Homeric contexts, which Durante views as late, and when it occurs the first syllable is usually in arsis.[31] This is difficult to reconcile with an underlying vowel contraction. In contrast, the patronymics *Nēlḗïos* and *Nēlēïádēs* have a broad distribution and necessarily accommodate an underlying vowel contraction in every occurrence. One may therefore suppose that Homer had inherited only the patronymics, and that when he went to recreate Nestor's father for a few brief moments he invented the form *Nēleús*. His model can be seen in the pairs *Odussḗïos*: *Odusseús*, *Pēlḗïos*: *Pēleús*, etc. No longer, however, did a model exist for recreating the original *o*-stem name. But significantly, such a model is found in Mycenean, in a form like *adaratijo, Adrástios*, from *Ádrastos*. The argument therefore is that in Mycenean the name *Nehélāwos* led to the patronymic *Nehelā́wios*, and that only the latter survived in the epic tradition. It should be noted that such an adjectival patronymic represents a great archaism in Homer.

This explanation of *Nēleús* seems convincing. But the crucial problem is how to understand the relationship between the names *Nehélāwos* and *Néstōr*. Palmer, Durante, and Mühlestein all rely

28. Durante, p. 33.
29. J. Wackernagel, *Berliner philologische Wochenschrift* (1891), cols. 6–7; Durante, p. 40 n.29 allows other possibilities as well.
30. Summarized from Durante, pp. 35–41.
31. Durante says eight of ten instances (p. 37); the figures should be seven of eleven.

heavily on the view that the latter is a "short form" of the former.[32] Parallels can supposedly be seen in such name-pairs as *Menélā(w)os* : *Méntōr*, *Ekhélā(w)os* : *Héktōr*, and *Agélā(w)os* : *Áktōr*. On the basis of this view, it is then thought likely that a real King *Nehélāwos* gave the name *Néstōr* to his son. Palmer's judgment to this effect was quoted above; Durante is even more emphatic, calling the two names "a beautiful example of the custom, both Greek and Indo-European, of giving to the son a name which repeated in part that of the father."[33]

That there was such a Greek and Indo-European custom is not to be doubted. The question is simply whether Greek names ending in *-tōr* reflect such a custom. The specific argument for this goes back to an article by Grace Macurdy;[34] but this article was reviewed soon after by Paul Kretschmer, who immediately saw an important weakness in it. His judicious remarks suggest the solution to both parts of our problem: how Nestor can be the very old mythological figure he seems to be, without simultaneously eliminating the possibility that he was also a historical personage. In response to Macurdy's argument, Kretschmer pointed out that a suffix like *-tōr*, which has its own well-preserved function, would be highly unusual in genuine "short forms"; one could at most assume that, for the sake of brevity, compounds were replaced by agent nouns with the same meaning.[35]

32. Palmer, *Eranos,* p. 7; Durante, p. 36; Mühlestein (chap. 1, n.7), p. 158.
33. "Un bell'esempio della consuetudine, greca e indoeuropea, di dare al figlio un nome che ripetesse in parte quello paterno": Durante, p. 36.
34. G. Macurdy, "Homeric Names in -tor," *Classical Quarterly* 23 (1929): 23–27.
35. P. Kretschmer, *Glotta* 20 (1932): 230: "Ich meine, es handelt sich hier nicht um gewöhnliche Kurzformen, für die ein Suffix mit einer stets bewahrten Funktion wie—τωρ sonst nicht üblich ist, sondern man könnte höchstens annehmen, der Kürze halber sei das Kompositum durch ein gleichbedeutendes Nomen agentis ersetzt worden"; cf. also A. Heubeck (n. 1), p. 29, who agrees with Kretschmer, and who also draws attention to Illyrian names ending in *-tor* (*Aetor, Buctor, Daetor, Veitor,* among others) as showing the antiquity of these names.

The crucial point is the independence of the *-tōr* agent suffix. This liberates *Néstōr* from *Nehélāwos*, and allows Nestor to be as old and as mythological as necessary. At the same time, however, a name like *Néstōr* could have "replaced" a name like *Nehélāwos*, if the former had the *same meaning* as the latter. We already have reason to believe that originally the name *Néstōr* referred to more than "bringing the war-folk safely home," and more reasons will emerge from the discussion to follow. But it is also possible that by the late Mycenean era the name *Néstōr* had lost its full original meaning, and was perceived as an equivalent of *Nehélāwos*. This would leave open the possibility of there having been a real King Nestor. The case for such a loss of original meaning will be developed further in the discussion to follow.

In the meantime, the name *Néstōr* stands alone and must be interpreted alone. In arguing that Nestor's original function was to "bring back to life and light," I have already committed myself to a transitive force of the root *nes-* in his name. This may be related to the conjecture of other scholars that the name *Nehélāwos* presupposes a transitive form **néō*, which has been lost. It is my contention, however, that the form has not been completely lost but has actually survived, disguised as something else, in one Homeric passage. To validate this claim I shall have to leave Nestor for a while and return to Odysseus. But the results of this shift will ultimately be important for Nestor.

In a passage of *Odyssey* 18, Penelope repeats to one of her suitors what Odysseus had said to her when he left for Troy, namely (*xviii* 259 ff.), that he did not think all the Achaeans would "return home":

ὦ γύναι, οὐ γὰρ ὀΐω ἐϋκνήμιδας Ἀχαιοὺς
ἐκ Τροίης εὖ πάντας ἀπήμονας ἀπονέεσθαι.

O woman, I do not think that all the well-greaved Achaeans
will return home safe and unharmed from Troy.

For (he said) the Trojans are skilled in the arts of war—spear-throwing, archery, and horsemanship—and they can therefore quickly decide the issue of a battle. In conclusion to this, Odysseus then added (*xviii* 265–66):

> τῷ οὐκ οἶδ᾽ ἤ κέν μ᾽ ἀνέσει θεός, ἤ κεν ἁλώω
> αὐτοῦ ἐνὶ Τροίῃ.

> Therefore I do not know if a god will *anései* me, or if I will die in Troy.

This conclusion is plainly a reversion to the initial point. Odysseus began by saying that he did not think all the Achaeans would "return home." He must therefore now be saying that he does not know whether he himself will "return home" or die in Troy. This much is clear; but it is not immediately clear how this meaning can be extracted from the Greek. What stands in the way is the peculiar verbal form *anései* in line 265.

I propose that the two words *m' anései* actually stand for an original **me nései*, which gives us a future form of the hitherto hypothetical verb *néō*. The meaning of lines 265–66 would then be: "therefore I do not know whether the god will *bring me home* or whether I will die in Troy," and the root *nes-* would be present at the end as well as the beginning of Odysseus's statement. But to defend this proposal we must first see how the form *anései* has been explained in the past.

It has traditionally been explained as an irregular future of *aniēmi*. But everywhere else the future of this verb is *anésō* with a long vowel, and the irregularity raises serious doubts. The advantage of this explanation, on the other hand, is that *aniēmi* supplies at least a vaguely appropriate sense. Homer uses the verb with the meaning "release" (cf. *emè d' oud' hôs thumòn aníei . . . odúnē*, "but even so the pain would not let go of my spirit," in xv 24–25), and Odysseus could conceivably be wondering whether the god will "release" him from Troy.

The short vowel of *anései*, however, destroys the traditional explanation. Realizing this, Monro proposed to derive the form from the root **sed-* of Greek *hízō*, "to seat," and *hézomai*, "to sit."[36] Homeric Greek possesses an old simplex aorist from this root in the forms *heîsa* and *hés(s)ai*. Monro therefore proposed the existence of a compound form with the preverb *an(á)*, and in fact demonstrated the existence of such a form in two Homeric lines which had previously been thought to contain aorists of *aniēmi*. The first example occurs in XIII 657: *es díphron d' anésantes ágon protì Ílion hirḗn*. This line concerns the rescue of a wounded hero, and the meaning can only be, "*having set* (him) *upon* the chariot, they took (him) to Troy." The same verb, with the same meaning, can be seen in XIV 209: *eis eunḕn anésaimi homōthḗnai philótēti*. In this line Hera is the speaker, and she refers to the possibility of *placing* Tethys and Oceanus *on* their bed of love again by reconciling them. The forms *anésantes* and *anésaimi* thus have nothing to do with *aniēmi*, the aorist of which is seen in *xxi* 537 in the phrase *ánesán te púlas*, "and they *opened* the gates." The forms are clearly compounds from the root *sed-*; the compound verb in fact occurs elsewhere, in tmesis, without the least ambiguity as to the root involved (I 310–11): <u>anà</u> *dè Khruseḯda kallipárēion/<u>heîsen</u> ágōn*. These lines refer to the *placing* of Chryseis *upon* a ship.

This much of Monro's argument seems perfectly correct. But he also wished to explain *anései* in *xviii* 265 in the same way, and that is a different matter. For the aorist forms, both the forms and the meaning are transparently accurate, and they are also otherwise attested. But not so for the future in *xviii* 265. The only evidence for a future *hésō* from the root *sed-* is the form *kathésō* in the comic playwright Eupolus. This could be overlooked were it not for the question of meaning. Monro's

<hr/>

36. Cf. D. B. Monro, *Homer, Iliad Books XIII-XXIV*[2] (Oxford, 1890), commentary on XIII 657 and XIV 209; I have been unable to find where Monro first proposed this derivation.

own examples show that his compound verb means to *place* or *set upon*. To make sense in *xviii* 265, this meaning must be extended to "set up" and then interpreted as "restore." But even the meaning "restore" does not really convey what Odysseus intends to say in *xviii* 265.

Thus, Monro's explanation seems as impossible semantically as does the traditional explanation formally, and the way is clear for the new proposal offered above. Phonologically, the form *nései* is an acceptable future for *néō*. Homer fluctuates between a single and a double sigma in forms from an original configuration (-)VssV-; for example, he uses both *ésomai* and *éssomai*, "I will be." The difference is one of dialect. In ancient Greek the dialects with single sigma are Attic, Ionic, and Arcadian,[37] which would suggest that the form *nései* in Homer is Ionic; but it is also possible that the form goes back to a common ancestor of the three dialects in question, and this possibility should be left open.[38] To explain the reading *m' anései* in *xviii* 265, one simply assumes what is already evident from the lack of other examples, namely, that the verb *néō* no longer existed in Homer's time. A traditional line containing this verb was therefore reinterpreted and thus allowed to survive. What Homer may have had in mind, if it was he who effected the change, was the future of *aniēmi* in the meaning "release."

According to the argument above, *xviii* 265 was a traditional epic line which contained a forgotten form from the root *nes-*. This should remind us of another traditional line, that which begins *ásmenoi ek thanátoio*, "having returned from death." We have already seen that on more than one occasion Homer reinterprets the latter phrase with the words *thánaton phúgomen*,

---

37. Cf. M. Lejeune, *Phonétique historique du mycénien et du grec ancien* (Paris, 1972), p. 102.

38. See below in text for further discussion.

39. This would, in fact, have been close to the original sense of *nései* which I propose (see below in text).

"we escaped death."[40] Hence it is very significant that in *xv* 300 Telemachus, sailing for home by night, is described as:

> *hormaínōn ế ken thánaton phúgoi ế ken halóēi*
> Pondering whether he would escape death or die.

The similarity of this to the reconstructed line:

> *tôi ouk oîd' ế kén me nései theòs ế ken halóō*

is unmistakable. In the first part, *hormaínōn*, "pondering," balances *tôi ouk oîd'*, "therefore I do not know," in expressing uncertainty. The last part, *ế ken halóēi*, "or die," is the same as *ế ken halóō* except for a change of person. The only significant variation occurs in the middle, where *ế ken thánaton phúgoi*, "whether he would escape death," contrasts with *ế kén me nései theós*, "if a god will *nései* me." At this point such a variation is almost predictable and confirms beyond reasonable doubt the interpretation proposed for *xviii* 265.

The inevitable question now is whether *thánaton phúgoi* has replaced a phrase containing the root *nes-* for the same reason that *thánaton phúgomen* has replaced *ásmenoi ek thanátoio*. In other words, does the transitive verb *néō* in *xviii* 265 mean "to bring back from death" just as *ásmenoi* means "having returned from death"? I suggest that it does, and that this can be seen by considering the line *xviii* 265 as a whole.

What must be considered more closely is the verb *halóō* at the end of the line. This is an aorist form of *halískomai*, which means "to be seized" or "to be captured." But in *xviii* 265 and in a few other Homeric occurrences, the verb clearly means "to be killed" or simply "to die." How is this meaning to be explained?

---

40. See n. 13 above for page references.

With only one exception,[41] the meaning "to die" is not attested after Homer. In classical Greek the basic meaning "to be seized" or "captured" is always obvious. Homer, too, attests this meaning in a few phrases: for example, in the formula used of a city which has been "captured" and "sacked"—namely, *haloûsá te perthoménē te*.[42] Since the meaning "to die" is all but limited to Homer, one suspects from the outset that it is an artificial product of the epic *Kunstsprache*. This suspicion is increased by the fact that the meaning "to die" is limited to two basic formulaic patterns.

The first pattern in fact reveals immediately how the meaning "to die" developed. The original notion was "to be seized by death," as in the following lines (*v* 312 = xxi 281 and *xxiv* 34):

νῦν δέ με λευγαλέῳ θανάτῳ εἵμαρτο ἁλῶναι
But now it is my fate to be seized by a grievous death,

νῦν δ' ἄρα σ' οἰκτίστῳ θανάτῳ εἵμαρτο ἁλῶναι
But now it is your fate to be seized by a most pitiable death.

The phrase *thanátōi . . . halônai*, "to be seized by death," is perfectly understandable as an equivalent for *thaneîn*, "to die." But it is obvious that the word *thanátōi*, "by death," is necessary to the sense. How, then, can the second formulaic type, in which *thanátōi* is no longer present, be explained? This type is exemplified by *xviii* 265 and *xv* 300, and by a few other passages to be discussed below. The essential feature of this pattern is the occurrence of a form of *halônai* as the second member in a set of alternatives, the alternatives being marked by the particles *ḗ* (or *ēé*) and *ê*.

I suggest that the semantic ellipsis began in *xviii* 265 or in a line like *xviii* 265. If the form *nései* meant "will bring back from death," then it would have been unnecessary to make "by death"

41. See below in text.
42. Formulaic in ii 374, iv 291, and xiii 816.

explicit in the alternative; the alternative would naturally have been understood as "or be caught by death." It should be noted that the meaning "be caught" is a very fitting alternative to the proposed meaning of *nései*. Earlier parts of this study have shown that the root *nes-* originally pertained to a kind of "safe passage" through death; such a safe passage would seem to imply not being "caught" by death.[43]

Once the ellipsis of *thanátōi* had begun in a line like *xviii* 265, it could then spread. A line in which the ellipsis was necessarily continued was *xv* 300, which was patterned directly on a line like *xviii* 265. In this line the expression *thánaton phúgoi*, "would escape death," makes the notion of death explicit; but in spite of this, the meaning of *halóēi* is no longer quite accurate. The line now means literally "pondering whether he would escape death or be caught," and it is not clear who or what threatens to catch him (viz. Telemachus). The line plainly depends on *xviii* 265: "therefore I do not know whether the god will bring me back from death or whether I will be caught," where no such ambiguity exists.

Homer, too, may have felt that the opposition between "escaping death" and "being caught" was somewhat imprecise. A solution would have been to vary the second member in the opposition, as in the following lines where Penelope "ponders" the *nóstos* of Telemachus (*iv* 789–90):

ὁρμαίνουσ' ἤ οἱ θάνατον φύγοι υἱὸς ἀμύμων,
ἤ ὅ γ' ὑπὸ μνηστῆρσιν ὑπερφιάλοισι δαμείη.

Pondering whether her blameless son would escape death or be overcome by the arrogant suitors.

---

43. For the notion of death as "seizing" its victims, cf. Hesiod *Theogony* 765–66, regarding *Thánatos*, "Death":

ἔχει δ' ὃν πρῶτα λάβῃσιν
ἀνθρώπων.

He holds fast any man that he first *seizes*.

These lines clearly have to do with *xv* 300, but the ambiguity of the latter has been removed. *Dameíē*, "be overcome," is clearer than *halóēi* in the meaning "be killed," and specific agents, who come to mind already in *xv* 300, have replaced the latent *thanátōi* of the latter line; it is specifically the suitors who threaten Telemachus.

Again in the following example it is not at once clear whether *halônai* means "to be killed" or "to be captured." In this passage Eumaeus is speaking to Odysseus about the *nóstos* of Telemachus (*xiv* 183–84):[44]

ἀλλ' ἦ τοι κεῖνον μὲν ἐάσομεν, ἤ κεν ἁλώῃ
ἦ κε φύγῃ καί κέν οἱ ὑπέρσχῃ χεῖρα Κρονίων.

But let us not concern ourselves with him, whether he should be killed (captured) or whether he should escape and the son of Cronus protect him.

Only the evidence of other related lines tells us that the meaning here is "be killed" and not "be captured." In this passage one should also note the mention of Zeus, which may well be a survival of the tradition represented by the word *theós*, "a god," in *xviii* 265.

The last passage quoted above shows that the opposition between *pheúgein* and *halônai*, even without the mention of death, had become firmly established as an opposition between "escaping" and "dying." The following line (XIV 81), in which *pheúgein*, "to flee from, escape," is doubly emphasized and *thánaton*, "death," has been replaced by *kakón*, "evil," shows the same thing:

---

44. This passage is in fact a conflation of formulaic patterns; cf. IX 701–02:

ἀλλ' ἤτοι κεῖνον μὲν ἐάσομεν, ἤ κεν ἴῃσιν,
ἤ κε μένῃ.

But let us not concern ourselves with him, whether he comes or stays.

῀βέλτερον ὃς φεύγων προφύγῃ κακὸν ἠὲ ἁλώῃ.

It is better that one escape evil by fleeing than that one be killed.[45]

The meaning of *halônai*, "to be killed," was so firmly established in this opposition that the opposition could itself be renewed with a first member meaning "to kill" (XII 172):

πρίν γ᾽ ἠὲ κατακτάμεν ἠὲ ἁλῶναι.[46]

Before either killing or being killed.

It is clear that the opposition between *kataktámen*, "to kill," and *halônai*, "to be killed," in the last line is the final result of an artificial development which can be explained only in terms of a *Kunstsprache*. This suggests one final observation. The verb to which *halískomai* is genuinely opposed is *hairéō*, "to seize" or "capture."[47] This genuine opposition seems to have asserted itself in the following isolated expression, spoken by Hector to Achilles in XXII 253: *héloimí ken, é ken haloíēn*. This phrase means "I will slay or be slain." I suggest that it was through the natural opposition of the verbs *halískomai* and *hairéō* that *haireō* acquired the meaning "slay," a meaning which is common in the aorist form *héle(n)*, as in the phrase *hélen ándras*

---

45. There is a similar opposition in XXI 493ff., in which a divinity is indirectly involved:

θεὰ φύγεν ὥς τε πέλεια
ἥ ῥά θ᾽ ὑπ᾽ ἴρηκος κοίλην εἰσέπτατο πέτρην,
χηραμόν· οὐδ᾽ ἄρα τῇ γε ἁλώμεναι αἴσιμον ἦεν.

The goddess *fled* like a dove that flies into a hollow rock, a cave, away from a hawk; it is not destined for the dove to be *caught* (*killed*).

Since the opposition does not apply directly to the "immortal" in question, *halómenai* here, too, can mean "to be killed."

46. For a second instance of the opposition between *katakteinai* and *halônai*, cf. XVII 506.

47. Cf. Attic legal usage, in which *hairéō* means "convict", *halískomai* "be convicted."

aristous, "he slew the best men," in v 541. The suggestion that this usage originated as a euphemism[48] will convince no one who recalls the explicit battle descriptions of the *Iliad*. Like *halískomai*, *hairéō* has its special meaning only in Homer; the two words should be explained together. It is natural that one member of a genuinely opposed pair should have affected the other.

The above discussion has shown the meaning "to die" of Homeric *halônai*, when used alone, can best be explained by starting from a line like *xviii* 265. The development of this meaning begins with an ellipsis of *thanátōi*, "by death," which is understandable only if the verb *nései* has to do with "bringing back from death." In support of this argument may now be mentioned the only example known to me where *halískomai* means "to die" in later Greek. The example occurs in Pindar *Pythian* 3. 54 ff., in which the perfect participle *halōkóta* is used to mean "dead." The context concerns Asclepius, whose fame as a physician has just been celebrated, but who is now censured for an unholy deed:

> ἀλλὰ κέρδει καὶ σοφία δέδεται.
> ἔτραπεν καὶ κεῖνον ἀγάνορι μισθῷ
>   χρυσὸς ἐν χερσὶν φανεὶς
> ἄνδρ' ἐκ θανάτου κομίσαι
> ἤδη ἁλωκότα.

But even wisdom is subject to greed. When he saw gold in his hands, he was perverted by this lavish pay to *bring back from death* a man who had already been *caught*.

Greedy for profit, Asclepius used his wisdom "to bring back from death" a man who had already been "caught," and for this impiety (as the following lines inform us) both he and the

48. Thus *LSJ*, s.v. αἱρέω.

rescued man were struck down by Zeus. The phrase *ek thanátou komísai*, "to bring back from death," gives the precise meaning that has been proposed for transitive *néō*. What is equally striking, however, is the clear opposition between this phrase and the word *halōkóta*. One could not "bring back from death" a man who had already been "caught (by death)."[49] It is also well worth noting the role of *sophía*, "wisdom," in this passage. With different words Pindar seems to have preserved something very old—namely, the connection between *nóos* and *néomai*. Wisdom is connected with "bringing back from death," although not even the wisdom of Asclepius could bring back one who was caught by death.[50]

The meaning "he will bring back from death," of the form *nései* in *xviii* 265, brings transitive *néō* in line with intransitive *néomai*. It is significant that *xviii* 265 pertains to Odysseus, whose "return from death" was studied in the last chapter. Of course Homer, who uses this line in connection with a "return from war," has lost the line's original context along with its original wording. From the point of view of context, the secondary line *xv* 300—*hormaínōn ḗ ken thánaton phúgoi ḗ ken halṓēi*, "pondering whether he would escape death or die," has remained closer to the original meaning of the root *nes-*. In the passage preceding *xv* 300, Telemachus takes on board his ship the seer Theoclymenus, and following Athena's command (*nuktì d' homôs pleíein*, in *xv* 34) he sails for home by night (*xv* 296). His voyage home is thus a passage through darkness to light, and is made in the company of one whose presence reflects the original role of *nóos*.

In light of these remarks the line *tôi ouk oîd' ḗ kén me nései theòs ḗ ken halṓō* may justly be separated from its context. Like

49. In *LSJ* (s.v. ἁλίσκομαι), *nósōi*, "by disease," rather than *thanátōi*, "by death," is suggested as the word lost by ellipsis, but this would imply that any recovery from illness would offend Zeus.

50. Another point to be noticed in this passage is the context of illness and healing, for this is the semantic sphere of German *genesen*, "get well," one of the cognates of *néomai* to be discussed in chap. 6.

the refrain containing the phrase *ásmenoi ek thanátoio*, *xviii* 265 no longer fits its context if the root *nes-* is given its full force. It was argued earlier that the line containing *ásmenoi* goes back far beyond the Homeric period; it is now suggested that *xviii* 265, with some variation in the first foot-and-a-half, is likewise very old. Some points in the language cause uncertainty, but nothing more; the formulaic pattern of the line is a stronger argument for its antiquity.[51] If this view is correct, then one point in my previous argument should be modified. The syntax of *xviii* 265 would be more archaic if *nései* were a subjunctive rather than a modal indicative.[52] As it happens, the form may easily represent an original subjunctive of the sigmatic aorist.[53] The ultimate status of *nései* (or *anései*) as a future form would have to do with subsequent changes in both the morphological and syntactic systems of Greek.

The next problem is to determine the relative age of transitive *néō* and, if its antiquity be granted, of the line represented by

51. The alternative question markers ἤ κεν and ἦ κεν require some comment. It is assumed that Homeric ἦ and ἤ represent contractions of ἠέ and ἦε (cf. H. Frisk, *Griechisches etymologisches Wörterbuch* [chap. 1, n. 4], s.v. ἦ); the latter particles are from *ἠ-Ϝε and *ἦ-Ϝε, both containing the alternative marker *-*we*, as in Latin *sive*. It should be noted, however, that in Homer the particle κεν also serves as an alternative marker (cf. P. Chantraine, *Grammaire homérique* [Paris, 1963], 2: 211 and 295). In the sequence ἤ κεν . . . ἤ κεν, the particle -Ϝε would therefore be redundant, and it is best simply to posit the particle ἤ by itself; for this interjectional and interrogative particle, see E. Schwyzer and A. Debrunner, *Griechische Grammatik* (Munich, 1950), 2: 546–47.

The Homeric formulaic evidence, furthermore, favors ἤ κεν and ἦ κεν as older forms than (ἠέ κεν) and ἦέ κεν. Further examples of ἤ κεν and ἦ κεν, to add to those quoted in the text above, are found in XIII 742–43, xx 311, and XXI 226; cf. also XXII 244 ff. By contrast, ἠέ κεν seems to occur only once (*xxiv* 218).

It is also necessary to draw attention to the etymological digamma in the verb ἀλώω in *xviii* 265, and to suggest that the sequence ἤ κεν ἀλώω, if it is old, must originally have contained a preconsonantal form of the particle *kn (∅-grade of κεν); see L. R. Palmer, "The Language of Homer," in *A Companion to Homer*, ed. A. J. B. Wace and F. H. Stubbings (London, 1963), pp. 90ff.

52. Cf. P. Chantraine, *Grammaire homérique*, 2: 225.

53. The sigmatic aorist, as an athematic formation, originally had a short-vowel subjunctive; for dialect forms of a third-singular subjunctive in -σει, see C. D. Buck, *The Greek Dialects*[2] (Chicago, 1955), pp. 119–20.

xviii 265. From the Indo-European standpoint, Greek *néomai* belongs to a class of verbs that are *media tantum*. When such verbs develop active forms, this process occurs only within the individual languages. Hence the verb *néō* must have been created within Greek itself. Whether it was created during or after the period of common Greek cannot be told.

The form *nései* in *xviii* 265, at any rate, must be later than the supposed dialectal split into northern and southern Greek,[54] for the form would otherwise have preserved its original double sigma. The important question now is how early the double sigma was simplified in the southern group. Although this cannot be dated precisely, a recent study makes it appear that the simplification took place before the attested stage of Mycenean Greek.[55] This means that in theory the line represented by *xviii* 265 could be older than the Linear-B tablets.

On the basis of these observations, one may attempt a relative chronology for the development of transitive *néō*. At this point we return to Nestor, who in fact occupies a crucial place in the chronology to be proposed. I suggest that one should begin with the name *Néstōr*, composed of nothing more than the verbal root and the agent suffix *-tōr*; this name could go back to Common Greek if not beyond.[56] The figure to whom this name belonged was doubtless mythological, and his function was conceived to be that of "bringing back to life and light." The suffix *-tōr*, moreover, gave to his name a strong verbal rection.[57] Thus the transitive force of his name could easily have led to the creation of a new transitive verb *néō*, which was almost certainly restricted to hieratic contexts. Such a context is still

54. I.e., the split proposed by E. Risch, "Die Gliederung der griechischen Dialekte in neuer Sicht," (chap. 2, n. 13).

55. G. Nagy, *Greek Dialects and the Transformation of an Indo-European Process* (Cambridge, 1970), pp. 135, 142.

56. Cf. n. 35 above for Illyrian names in *-tor*.

57. See É. Benveniste, *Noms d'agent et noms d'action en indo-européen* (Paris, 1948), pp. 28 ff., 62.

apparent in *xviii* 265, where the subject of *nései* is *theós*, "the god."[58]

The implication of this argument is that *Néstōr* was once a hieratic name, reflecting the hieratic connotations of the root *nes-*. But the same is not true of the name *Nehélāwos*, attested for Mycenean Greek. This name, which from its form also appears to be old,[59] attests a secular acceptation of the root *nes-* (see p. 23). Thus the two names in question are on very different levels, and it is difficult to see how they could have belonged to an actual father and son, by the method so often assumed, in the late Mycenean era. For this to be the case would one not have to assume a previous effacement of the hieratic acceptation of the root *nes-*? Such an eventuality is possible if *xviii* 265 goes back to a very early time; whether or not this eventuality is likely is a question for others to decide.[60]

58. Gregory Nagy has pointed out to me a strong parallel for the active formation. Aristotle, *de Caelo* 305ª11, distinguishes between the two verbs *sbénnusthai* and *marainesthai*—whereas *sbénnusthai* is used in relation to a fire which is put out *by someone, marainesthai* is used of a fire which goes out *by itself*; nevertheless, *marainesthai* is put in an active form in *Hymn to Hermes* 140, with Hermes (i.e., a god) as the subject: *anthrakiēn d' emárane*, "he extinguished the burning embers." There is another interesting example in the verbs *khráomai*, "to consult an oracle," and *khráō*, "to give an oracle"; the active verb *khráō* was created from the middle verb *khráomai*, and the subjects of the active verb are limited to the gods and their prophets.

59. See n. 4 above.

60. For another attempt to explain the development of a transitive *néō*, cf. A. Heubeck (n.1), p. 30. Heubeck starts from the Mycenean form *netijano*, interpreted as *Nestiánōr*, the first part of which was originally an abstract noun (*néstis), representing either an action noun or a personification within the compound itself; the name would thus have originally meant "happy home-coming of men." Subsequently, however, the first member would have been felt to have a transitive verbal force. While this argument is plausible in itself, it does not explain the transitive force of the root *nes-* in the old name Nestor, which should be reckoned with first.

This is an appropriate place to mention another Mycenean name that may contain the root *nes-*. Mühlestein (chap. 1, n.7), p. 157, cites a form *pironeta*, which he interprets, hesitantly, as *Philo-nes-tas, "he who saves his dear ones" ("der seine Lieben rettet.") If this is correct, one should note (as Mühlestein does) the similarity in formation to *Polu-dék-tēs*, an epithet of the god Hades (cf. sect. 3 above for remarks on Nestor and his brother Periclymenus).

Since Nestor's origins are to be found in myth, a final question arises concerning his original mythological status. Are we entitled to consider him a god? Since we know so little about the period of his origin, the question is perhaps presumptuous, but attention can at least be drawn to certain indications. The first of these is the word *theós* in *xviii* 265; as subject of a verb which is closely related to Nestor's name there appears the word "god." A second indication is the impression gained from Homer that Nestor alone defied the famous dictum of Glaucus (VI 146ff.) that the generation of men is like the generation of leaves. For Nestor, when he is met in Homer, has survived the passing of not only one, but two generations. In the following lines from the *Iliad* (I 250ff.) Nestor is represented as the *sole* survivor from a former era:

τῷ δ᾽ ἤδη δύο μὲν γενεαὶ μερόπων ἀνθρώπων
ἐφθίαθ᾽, οἵ οἱ πρόσθεν ἅμα τράφεν ἠδ᾽ ἐγένοντο
ἐν Πύλῳ ἠγαθέῃ, μετὰ δὲ τριτάτοισιν ἄνασσεν.

For him two generations of mortal men had already passed away, those born and raised with him in holy Pylos, and now he was king among the third.

Taking this passage literally, one cannot think that Homer simply means that Nestor is over sixty years old, for two entire generations do not vanish in so short a time.

There is a second reference to Nestor's survival from generation to generation in the *Odyssey*. Of the following lines (*iii* 245–46) which Telemachus addresses to Athena, the second is especially revealing:

τρὶς γὰρ δή μίν φασιν ἀνάξασθαι γένε᾽ ἀνδρῶν,
ὥς τέ μοι ἀθάνατος ἰνδάλλεται εἰσοράασθαι.

They say that he has ruled during three generations of men; thus he seems to me to be an immortal to look upon.

When Telemachus gazes at Nestor, the latter seems to him to be "immortal." We already share this impression ourselves, but what makes us do so the more is the fact that no tradition has survived concerning Nestor's death. The only minor blemish on this *argumentum ex silentio* is the mention in Pausanias 4. 62. 3 of a *mnêma*, "monument, tomb," within the Messenian city of Pylos which was said to belong to Nestor.

Thus Nestor "seems" to have been immortal. But there may be other reasons for hesitating to call him a god. Benveniste has argued that the suffix *-tōr* serves to signify "un mérite actuel, non une virtualité," which makes it an appropriate component of a man's name.[61] One wonders whether the same factor does not render the suffix inappropriate in a god's name. A name that comes to mind is *Kástōr*, but this example is ambiguous in that Castor was considered the mortal son, and Polydeuces the immortal son, of their fathers Tyndareus and Zeus.

Another name that comes to mind is *Méntōr*. Mentor is not a god in the *Odyssey*; but, significantly, it is his likeness that Athena assumes when she accompanies Telemachus. The name is a very close parallel to *Néstōr*; it, too, contains the root of an intransitive verb in a transitive sense—the sense "to put in mind"—and its meaning is likewise connected with mental activity. Perhaps we should view Nestor, like Mentor, as neither wholly human nor wholly divine, but as something in between.

This, at any rate, accords with the picture Homer gives of Nestor when the latter, at the end of his story in *Iliad 11*, says that his restored people gave glory to *Zeus among gods* and to *Nestor among men* (761):

πάντες δ᾽ εὐχετόωντο θεῶν Διὶ Νέστορί τ᾽ ἀνδρῶν.

Nestor includes himself among men, but the mere fact that he is glorified like Zeus raises him toward Zeus's level.

61. É. Benveniste (n. 57), p. 55.

Even if a good possibility remains that Nestor was originally a god, we may rest content with what clearly emerges from *Iliad 11*—namely, that he was at least mythological. Like the Phaeacians, who were seen in the last chapter to perform the same function of "bringing back to life," the Homeric Nestor does not belong entirely either to the world of gods or to the world of men.

5 Achilles

THE TWO PRECEDING CHAPTERS have dealt with a pair of Homeric figures who show in a very positive way the connection between *nóos* and *néomai*. As far as the verb is concerned, it is Nestor in whose name the very root of *néomai* is contained, and it is Odysseus who was celebrated beyond all others for his "return home." Both of these figures, moreover, were renowned for their *nóos*. Nestor, as seen in the last chapter, is the very symbol of *nóos* whenever he appears in the role of the wise counselor; Odysseus, too, was famous for his counsel, although his role was less to symbolize *nóos* than to make it effective. Nestor himself, in harkening back to the Trojan War, makes the following appraisal of Odysseus (*iii* 120ff.):

> ἔνθ' οὔ τίς ποτε μῆτιν ὁμοιωθήμεναι ἄντην
> ἤθελ', ἐπεὶ μάλα πολλὸν ἐνίκα δῖος Ὀδυσσεὺς
> παντοίοισι δόλοισι.

No one there wished to compete against him in shrewdness, since shining Odysseus was by far the best with his tricks of all kinds.

Odysseus, in recounting the virtues of Neoptolemus, ranks himself and Nestor as the foremost Greek counselors (*xi* 510ff.):

> ἦ τοι ὅτ' ἀμφὶ πόλιν Τροίην φραζοίμεθα βουλάς,
> αἰεὶ πρῶτος ἔβαζε καὶ οὐχ ἡμάρτανε μύθων·
> Νέστωρ ἀντίθεος καὶ ἐγὼ νικάσκομεν οἴω.

Whenever we took counsel around the city of Troy he always spoke first and he never failed in his words; only godlike Nestor and I surpassed him.

Achilles, the subject of this chapter, is a very different figure from Nestor and Odysseus. For one thing, his reputation has nothing whatever to do with wise counsel. Achilles himself admits this at one point, after first drawing attention to his own particular virtue (XVIII 105–06):

τοῖος ἐὼν οἷος οὔ τις Ἀχαιῶν χαλκοχιτώνων
ἐν πολέμῳ· ἀγορῇ δέ τ' ἀμείνονές εἰσι καὶ ἄλλοι.

Being such in battle as no one else among the bronze-clad Achaeans; in the assembly, however, there are others who are better.

One may justly infer from this that the virtues of Achilles do not include *nóos*.

At the same time Achilles is more emphatically barred from a "return home" than any other hero. Thus, he is as much dissociated from the verb *néomai* as from the noun *nóos*.

In the *Odyssey* it becomes clear that Achilles cannot "return home" because he cannot "return from death." This is the dramatic point of the confrontation between Achilles and Odysseus in the Nekyia. Odysseus remarks that even in the underworld Achilles is a king (*xi* 485–86); but Achilles responds bitterly that he would rather be a serf among the living than the king of the dead (*xi* 488 ff.). Unlike Odysseus, he cannot "return to life."

The antithetical fates of Achilles and Odysseus could not be more strongly contrasted than in this meeting. Their difference with respect to *nóos* is also immediately apparent from the words with which Achilles greets Odysseus (*xi* 473 ff.):

Διογενὲς Λαερτιάδη, πολυμήχαν' Ὀδυσσεῦ,
σχέτλιε, τίπτ' ἔτι μεῖζον ἐνὶ φρεσὶ *μήσεαι* ἔργον;
πῶς ἔτλης Ἄϊδόσδε κατελθέμεν, ἔνθα τε νεκροὶ
ἀφραδέες ναίουσι, βροτῶν εἴδωλα καμόντων;

Zeus-born son of Làertes, resourceful Odysseus, how will you, incorrigible man, *devise* in your mind a still greater deed than this? How have you dared to come down to the house of Hades where the *mindless* dead dwell, the ghosts of men who have perished?

Odysseus is immediately characterized by his "wits," while Achilles numbers himself among the "mindless dead." [1]

The essential point of this chapter is contained in the foregoing analysis. Hitherto we have encountered three figures (Nestor, Odysseus, and Sisyphus) whose *nóos* is intimately connected with a "return from death." We now meet another figure who, by his lack of *nóos* and his failure to "return from death," demonstrates what might be termed the negative corollary to this relation.

But Achilles also offers a more specific kind of evidence for the connection between *nóos* and *néomai*. In the *Iliad*, Achilles refers three times to the fact that he will not "return home"; it is very significant that in each case he also alludes to a loss of "mind" in one form or another. In the second and third speeches, the words *nóos* and *nóēma* actually appear, and these speeches therefore have the greatest probative value. In the first speech, only the idea of a loss of "mind" is present; the interest of this speech will therefore lie in seeing how Homer has reinterpreted a traditional motif to suit his own ends.

1. In XIX 216ff., where Odysseus addresses Achilles before the final battle of the *Iliad*, there is a pointed contrast between Odysseus's *nóēma*, "wisdom," and Achilles' strength:

ὦ Ἀχιλεῦ, Πηλῆος υἱέ, μέγα φέρτατ' Ἀχαιῶν,
κρείσσων εἰς ἐμέθεν καὶ φέρτερος οὐκ ὀλίγον περ
ἔγχει, ἐγὼ δέ κε σεῖο *νοήματί* γε προβαλοίμην
πολλόν, ἐπεὶ πρότερος γενόμην καὶ πλείονα οἶδα.

Achilles, son of Peleus, far greatest of the Achaeans, you are stronger than I am and greater by not a little with the spear; but I in turn might surpass you by far in *wisdom*, since I was born before you and have learned more things.

In XI 786ff. there is a similar contrast between the *bíē*, "strength," of Achilles and the greater age and superior counsel of Patroclus.

All three speeches occur in the context of the death of Patroclus and the vengeance Achilles takes against Hector. By the time of the final two speeches, Achilles realizes that by killing Hector he will lose his own "return"—hence he may refer to this loss as a certainty. The third speech is in fact delivered following the death of Hector, when Achilles' fate has been forever sealed. The setting for the speech is the funeral of Patroclus; Achilles has cut from his own head a lock of hair that was formerly dedicated to the river Spercheius in his homeland, and, in rededicating the lock to Patroclus, he begins by addressing the distant river (XXIII 144 ff.):

Σπερχεί᾽, ἄλλως σοί γε πατὴρ ἠρήσατο Πηλεύς,
κεῖσέ με νοστήσαντα φίλην ἐς πατρίδα γαῖαν
σοί τε κόμην κερέειν ῥέξειν θ᾽ ἱερὴν ἑκατόμβην,
πεντήκοντα δ᾽ ἔνορχα παρ᾽ αὐτόθι μῆλ᾽ ἱερεύσειν
ἐς πηγάς, ὅθι τοι τέμενος βωμός τε θυήεις.
ὣς ἠρᾶθ᾽ ὁ γέρων, σὺ δέ οἱ νόον οὐκ ἐτέλεσσας.
νῦν δ᾽ ἐπεὶ οὐ νέομαί γε φίλην ἐς πατρίδα γαῖαν,
Πατρόκλῳ ἥρωϊ κόμην ὀπάσαιμι φέρεσθαι.

Spercheius, in vain did my father Peleus pray to you, vowing that *if I returned* to my dear fatherland he would cut off this lock of hair for you and offer up a holy hecatomb, and that he would sacrifice fifty uncastrated sheep to your springs, there where your holy ground and smoking altar are. So the old man prayed, but *you have not brought about his intention.* Now, since *I will not return* to my dear fatherland, I would give this lock to the hero Patroclus to bear.

This passage should be directly compared with Achilles' second speech, which is delivered shortly after the body of Patroclus has been retrieved from battle; at this point Achilles is already intent on slaying Hector, and thus on forsaking his own "return" (XVIII 324 ff.):

ὢ πόποι, ἦ ῥ᾽ ἅλιον ἔπος ἔκβαλον ἤματι κείνῳ
θαρσύνων ἥρωα Μενοίτιον ἐν μεγάροισι·

φῆν δέ οἱ εἰς Ὀπόεντα περικλυτὸν υἱὸν ἀπάξειν
Ἴλιον ἐκπέρσαντα, λαχόντα τε ληΐδος αἶσαν.
ἀλλ᾽ οὐ Ζεὺς ἄνδρεσσι νοήματα πάντα τελευτᾷ·
ἄμφω γὰρ πέπρωται ὁμοίην γαῖαν ἐρεῦσαι
αὐτοῦ ἐνὶ Τροίῃ, ἐπεὶ οὐδ᾽ ἐμὲ νοστήσαντα
δέξεται ἐν μεγάροισι γέρων ἱππηλάτα Πηλεὺς
οὐδὲ Θέτις μήτηρ, ἀλλ᾽ αὐτοῦ γαῖα καθέξει.

Alas, I uttered an empty word that day when I encouraged
the hero Menoetius in his house. I said that I would bring
back his famous son when he had sacked Troy and received
a share of the spoil. But Zeus *does not bring about* for men
all their *intentions*. For both of us have been fated to pour
out our blood on the same ground here in Troy, since I too
will not return home to be received by the aged horseman
Peleus in his house, or to my mother Thetis, but will be held
fast by the earth in this place.

That the two speeches above follow a very similar pattern is
evident. In both passages Achilles refers to a *nóos* (or *nóēma*),
which consists in his own *nóstos*, and which will remain un-
accomplished precisely because he will not "return." Within this
general pattern the details may vary: in one speech Spercheius,
in the other Zeus, fails to accomplish the *nóos*; and in one speech
Peleus, in the other Achilles himself, is the party to whom the
nóos belongs. What does not vary is the negative collocation of
nóos (or *nóēma*) with *néomai* (or *nostéō*); this collocation is
therefore to be regarded as the traditional core within the two
speeches. Once again Homeric traditionally, when isolated and
identified, points to an original connection between *nóos* and
néomai.

In light of the above, it will now be interesting to observe what
Homer does with the first speech in which Achilles declares that
he will not "return." This speech, in fact, occupies a crucial place
in the struggle, which is kept alive throughout the *Iliad*, between
fate and Achilles' own will as the determining factor in his failure
to "return." Homer attempts to have this issue both ways, and

his method of doing so is to have Achilles lose his own "mind" to return.

Before this speech Homer has left the issue of free will and fate in an ambiguous state. Early in the poem Achilles reveals that he knows he is fated to have a short life; cf. ι 352:

μῆτερ, ἐπεί μ' ἔτεκές γε μινυνθάδιόν περ ἐόντα
Mother, since you bore me to be short-lived. . . .

But in *Iliad 9* he is still undecided whether to remain in Troy and achieve *kléos*, "glory," or to forsake *kléos* in return for a *nóstos* (ιχ 412 ff.).

The speech occurs early in *Iliad* 18, and it is here that Achilles appears to "decide" to remain and fight. But his speech follows upon and reflects another speech, that which Thetis delivers to her sister Nereids before going to her son; and from her speech it is clear that fate has already decided Achilles will not return. Let us compare what Thetis says with what Achilles says.

When Achilles learns of his dearest companion's death and cries out in grief, his mother hears him. In her speech to the other Nereids she says the following (xviii 59 ff.):

τὸν δ' οὐχ ὑποδέξομαι αὗτις
οἴκαδε νοστήσαντα δόμον Πηλήϊον εἴσω.
ὄφρα δέ μοι ζώει καὶ ὁρᾷ φάος ἠελίοιο
ἄχνυται.

No more will I receive him coming home to the house of Peleus. But even while he lives and sees the light of the sun he grieves.

One may schematize the sequence of ideas in these lines as follows: (1) Achilles will not return because (2) (implicit) this is his fate; (3) even while he is alive he grieves. In the third part it is well worth noticing the verb *ákhnutai,* "grieves," which has a special relevance to Achilles by virtue of its connection with his name;[2] in the scene to follow, "grief" plays an important role.

In the following lines (XVIII 89ff.) Achilles speaks first and Thetis responds; the passage repeats part of the passage above, but the implicit second point is now made explicit. More importantly, the second point now occurs last, in the response by Thetis to what she hears from her son:

> τὸν οὐχ ὑποδέξεαι αὖτις
> οἴκαδε νοστήσαντ᾽, ἐπεὶ οὐδ᾽ ἐμὲ θυμὸς ἄνωγε
> ζώειν οὐδ᾽ ἄνδρεσσι μετέμμεναι, αἴ κε μὴ Ἕκτωρ
> πρῶτος ἐμῷ ὑπὸ δουρὶ τυπεὶς ἀπὸ θυμὸν ὀλέσσῃ.
> Πατρόκλοιο δ᾽ ἕλωρα Μενοιτιάδεω ἀποτείσῃ."
> τὸν δ᾽ αὖτε προσέειπε Θέτις κατὰ δάκρυ χέουσα·
> "ὠκύμορος δή μοι, τέκος, ἔσσεαι, οἷ᾽ ἀγορεύεις·
> αὐτίκα γάρ τοι ἔπειτα μεθ᾽ Ἕκτορα πότμος ἑτοῖμος.

No more will you receive me coming home, since my heart does not bid me to live and to be among men unless Hector first be smitten by my spear and lose his life, and thus pay back the spoiling of Patroclus, the son of Menoetius." Then Thetis, shedding tears, addressed him: "Your fate will be swift, my child, from what you say; for immediately after Hector's doom your own will be at hand.

For the sake of comparison, one may schematize the sequence of ideas in these lines as follows: (1) Achilles will not return because (2) his heart feels such grief that he no longer wishes to live; (3) Thetis reveals that Achilles is fated to die if he kills Hector. The change in the sequence of ideas makes it appear that Achilles himself has chosen what had already been fated for him.

The same ambiguity continues in the lines following the passage above. In response to his mother's words *autíka . . . pótmos*

2. For the derivation *Akhi-lāwos, where akhi- is related to ákhos, and the whole compound has to do with "grief of the war-folk," see L. R. Palmer, *The Interpretation of Mycenean Greek Texts* (chap. 4, n. 1), p. 79, and, in support of Palmer, Gregory Nagy, *Festschrift L. R. Palmer* (Innsbruck, 1976), pp. 209–34.

hetoîmos, "at once your doom will be at hand," Achilles says *autíka tethnaíēn*, "at once may I die," and again vents his feelings of grief without in the least relating his lack of desire to live to the decrees of fate. Following this second expression of grief, Achilles *seems* to take notice of what his mother has revealed. This is the first impression given by line 101:

νῦν δ᾽ ἐπεὶ οὐ νέομαί γε φίλην ἐς πατρίδα γαῖαν

Now, since I will not return (*ou . . . néomai*) to my dear fatherland . . . .

But the conclusion to this thought, after a long and disjointed passage, is the following (l. 114):

νῦν δ᾽ εἶμ᾽, ὄφρα φίλης κεφαλῆς ὀλετῆρα κιχείω.

Now I shall go that I may find the slayer of that dear head.

Achilles has in effect said, "Since I will not return home, I will now go and slay Hector." From the point of view of fate, the sequence of thoughts would be just the reverse: "Since you are going to go and slay Hector, you will not return home." Only after asserting his own decision to die does Achilles acknowledge—grudgingly—the role of fate (ll. 115–16):

κῆρα δ᾽ ἐγὼ τότε δέξομαι, ὁππότε κεν δὴ
Ζεὺς ἐθέλῃ τελέσαι ἠδ᾽ ἀθάνατοι θεοὶ ἄλλοι.

I will accept my death whenever Zeus and the other immortal gods wish to bring it about.

These observations make the line:

νῦν δ᾽ ἐπεὶ οὐ νέομαί γε φίλην ἐς πατρίδα γαῖαν

Now, since I will not return (*ou . . . néomai*) to my dear fatherland . . .

an expression of Achilles' resolve to die, which he has asserted forcefully in the lines preceding (*autíka tethnaíēn*); from the point of view of tradition, this resolve to die surely represents Achilles' own lack of "mind" to go on living. This is what a comparison with the third speech clearly suggests (XXIII 149–50):

ὣς ἠρᾶθ᾽ ὁ γέρων, σὺ δέ οἱ *νόον* οὐκ ἐτέλεσσας.
νῦν δ᾽ ἐπεὶ οὐ νέομαί γε φίλην ἐς πατρίδα γαῖαν . . .

So the old man prayed, but you have not brought about his *intention*. Now, since I will not return to my dear fatherland. . . .

Homer's handling of the first speech of Achilles is thus a subtle working out of traditional elements, the original intent of which he has been able to approximate closely by abandoning part of the traditional vocabulary (the word *nóos*).[3] It should be noted that the loss of *nóstos* which is at stake in the first speech does not only refer to an eventual death in Troy through the workings of fate; Thetis does represent fate, but Achilles *himself* says, *autíka tethnaíēn*, "may I die immediately." By subordinating the notion that Achilles will not "return home," Homer has closely equated a "loss of mind" with "death."

3. For a similar situation, see chap. 3, sect. 3 on the relation between *mêtis* and *Oûtis* in the Cyclops adventure.

6 *Evidence for the meaning of the Indo-European Root* *nes-

1 INTRODUCTION

THE PURPOSE OF THIS CHAPTER is to explore the background of the Greek root *nes-*. In Greek itself three factors are involved: the meaning of the root, the interpretation of this meaning, and the presence of the root in the word *nóos*. These factors have been considered at length, and the problem now is to determine what in each case was inherited by Greek from Indo-European.

One can approach this problem only by means of the comparative method. In this chapter, therefore, I shall be concerned with attestations of the root *nes-* in languages other than Greek. The evidence to be considered bears, first of all, on the meaning "return to life" of Greek *nes-*; the cardinal evidence for this is provided by Germanic languages, which will therefore be considered first. As for the involvement in sun symbolism of the root *nes-*, the main evidence is provided by Sanskrit, although the meaning "return to light" seems to have been preserved in Germanic as well, and also in Albanian. Attention will therefore be paid to this in section 2, "Germanic," and a brief section 3 will then be devoted to Albanian. In section 4, "Indic," the context of sun symbolism will be explored more fully.

The final factor is the derivation of Greek *nóos* from *nes-*. In the Indic section a case will be made that this root already implied "intelligence" in Indo-European.

2 GERMANIC

The modern German word *genesen*, "get well, recover," contains the Indo-European root *nes-*, and, by its meaning, still bears witness to the original meaning of the root. With only this word in mind one can understand what led Sigmund Feist to reconstruct the earliest Germanic meaning of *nes-* as "zum Leben zurückkehren (return to life)."[1] The correlation between this and what has been found in early Greek leads to the conclusion that the meaning "return to life" goes back to Indo-European times.

The discussion to follow will deal first with the forms from *nes-* in Gothic, secondly with those in West Germanic, and lastly with those in Nordic. In each case the original meaning "zum Leben zurückkehren" can still be seen, or at least inferred. In each case there is also a certain amount of evidence for an original meaning "return to light," although the nature and strength of this evidence vary from dialect to dialect.

In dealing with Gothic one must take account of the problem that our evidence is contained in a translation of the Greek Bible. The context in which words appear is therefore predetermined. The element of choice, however, enters into the translator's use of a particular word in a given context. In the case of the root *nes-*, this point has a kind of general relevance; for the Gothic forms from this root are used to translate such Greek words as *sṓzein* and *sōtēría*, which in the original text have to do with the specifically Christian notion of "salvation." This notion, furthermore, implies a "return from death" to life everlasting. While it does not follow automatically from this that the Gothic forms from *nes-* imply a "return from death," this possibility is at least distinctly present.

The same argument holds for the meaning "return to light." At the center of Christianity there is a *sōtḗr*, "savior," who is

1. S. Feist, *Vergleichendes Wörterbuch der gotischen Sprache*[3] (Leiden, 1939), s.v. *ganisan*.

called not only "the life," but also "the light."[2] The Gothic translation of *sōtḗr* is *nasjands*, and as an example of a significant context in which the word appears, I quote the Greek original of 2 Tim. 1 : 10, which speaks of the "grace" conferred by Christ:

(χάριν) φανερωθεῖσαν
δὲ νῦν διὰ τῆς ἐπιφανείας τοῦ σωτῆρος ἡμῶν
(*nasjandis unsaris*) Ἰησοῦ Χριστοῦ,
καταργήσαντος μὲν τὸν θάνατον, φωτίσαντος
δὲ ζωὴν καὶ ἀφθαρσίαν διὰ τοῦ εὐαγγελίου

But it [grace] is now made manifest by the illumination of our savior Jesus Christ, who has nullified death, and has brought to light life and incorruption through the gospel.[3]

In the following I will give the various Gothic forms and a sample context in which each appears. Most of the total occurrences of each form refer to Christian redemption, for which much is implied, but I will not limit myself to these, for other contexts as well can be revealing.[4]

The verb *ganisan*, which translates Greek *sōzesthai*, "be saved," is intransitive and is composed of the root *nes-* in its Gothic form together with the perfective element *ga-*.[5] The verb demonstrates that the meaning "get well" of its modern German equivalent, *genesen*, is old; cf. Mark 5 : 23: ἵνα σωθῇ καὶ ζήσῃ, *ei ganisai jah libai*, "that she may get well and live."

---

2. Cf., e.g., John 8 : 12: "I am the light of the world: he that followeth me shall not walk in darkness, but shall have the light of life."

3. It may be noted that the image of Christ as *tò phōs*, "the light," completely dominates the fourth Gospel, the one which betrays the greatest Greek influence; cf. *A Dictionary of Christ and the Gospels*, vol. 2, ed. J. Hastings (Edinburgh, 1924), pp. 34–35. A point unrelated to Gothic, but in itself well worth noting, is that in Greek Hermetic writers there are about ten references to a deity called *Noûs* and defined as *phōs*, "light," and *zōḗ*, "life"; for these references, see W. Arndt and F. W. Gingrich, *A Greek-English Lexicon of the New Testament and Other Early Christian Literature* (Chicago, 1957), p. 341.

4. For a list of attestations of the various Gothic forms, see H. C. von der Gabelentz, *Ulfilas*, vol. 2 (Leipzig, 1843), s.vv.

5. For the derivations given here, see S. Feist (n.1), s.vv.

For the context of Christian salvation, cf. 1 Cor. 5 : 5:

παραδοῦναι
τὸν τοιοῦτον τῷ Σατανᾷ εἰς ὄλεθρον τῆς σαρκός, ἵνα τὸ
πνεῦμα σωθῇ *(ei ahma ganisai)* ἐν τῇ ἡμέρᾳ τοῦ κυρίου
Ἰησοῦ

To deliver such a one to Satan for the destruction of the flesh,
that the spirit may be saved in the day of our lord Jesus.

Based on *ganisan* is the feminine noun *ganists,* which is formed
with the abstract suffix *-ti-,* and which translates *sōtēría.*[6]
Christian "salvation" is opposed to death in the following
context, 2 Cor. 7 : 10 :

ἡ γὰρ κατὰ
θεὸν λύπη μετάνοιαν εἰς σωτηρίαν (*du ganistai*)
ἀμεταμέλητον κατεργάζεται, ἡ δὲ τοῦ κόσμου λύπη
θάνατον κατεργάζεται.

For sorrow which is according to God brings about
repentance, steadfast unto salvation; but the sorrow of the
world brings about death.

The verb *nasjan* is a causative formation and therefore has a
transitive sense, translating *sōzein,* "to save." Christian salvation
is again opposed to death in the following phrase, Mark 3:4:
ψυχὴν σῶσαι (*saiwala nasjan*) ἢ ἀποκτεῖναι, "to save a soul
or kill it." The participle from *nasjan* is *nasjands,* "*sōtēr,*" which
was discussed above.

The verb *nasjan* also appears as *ganasjan,* with the perfective
element *ga-.* This verb translates *sōzesthai,* "be saved," in the
following interesting example; in Luke 8 : 50 the context involves
a young girl presumed to be dead, concerning whom Christ says
to her father: μόνον πίστευε, καὶ σωθήσεται (*jah ganasjada*),
"only believe and she will be saved." The verb also translates
iâsthai, "to heal," and thus acts as a causative to *ganisan* in the
sense "get well" of the latter; cf. Luke 6 : 19: καὶ ἰᾶτο πάντας
(*jah ganasida allans*), "and he healed all."

6. Cf. chap. 4, n. 60 for the possibility of a similar Greek formation *néstis.*

Based on the verb *nasjan* is the feminine noun *naseins*, formed with the suffix *-eins* from original *-ī-ni-, and translating *sōtēría* and *sōtérion*; the latter stands in the original of Luke 2 : 30ff.:

> ὅτι εἶδον οἱ ὀφθαλμοί μου τὸ
> σωτήριόν σου (*nasein þeina*), ὃ ἡτοίμασας κατὰ πρόσωπον
> πάντων τῶν λαῶν, φῶς εἰς ἀποκάλυψιν ἐθνῶν

Because my eyes have seen your salvation, which you have prepared before the face of all people, a light for the revelation of the Gentiles.

This completes the list of Gothic forms, the contexts of which must speak for themselves, and their cognates in West Germanic may now be considered. Here the meanings of Gothic *ganisan*, both "be saved" and "get well," are closely reflected in Old English *genesan* (also *nesan*) and Old Saxon *ginesan*, "be saved," and Old High German *genesan*, "be saved, get well"; similarly, Old Saxon and Old High German *ginist* means "salvation" and "recovery."

The cognates of Gothic *nasjan* require more comment, for here there was, in part, a semantic development, reflected in the modern German cognate *nähren*, "nourish." *Nasjan* itself simply means "save," and this meaning was preserved in Old English and Old Saxon *nerian*; similarly, the participles *neriend* and *neriand* mean "savior" in the two respective dialects.

Before proceeding to Old High German, it is worth giving one example of Old English *nerian*, "save," in which the sense "bring back to light" is at least implied by the context. The example occurs in *Beowulf* 569ff., a passage in which the hero tells of the aftermath to his victory over the "nickers nine," the sea-monsters he overcame one night in the ocean depths:

Leoht eástan com,	Light came from the east,
beorht beácen Godes,	God's bright beacon,
brimu sweþrodon,	the seas grew calm,
þæt ic sǽ-næssas	so that the sea-nesses I
geseón mihte,	might see,
windige weallas.	windy walls.

> Wyrd oft *nered*   Fate often *saves*
> unfægne eorl,   an undoomed man,
> þonne his ellen deáh.   when his valor avails.

"Salvation" in these lines, with their emphasis on the sun and the hero's ability to see about him, seems intimately related to a "return to light."[7]

In the Old High German forms *nerian* and *nerren,* the meaning "nourish" developed, as also in Old Frisian *nera;* alongside this new meaning, the old meaning "save" persisted even into modern High German, but today only the developed meaning "nourish" is current.[8] For the development of this new meaning, one might compare the Latin idiom *corpus curare cibo.*

The semantic development in Old High German and Old Frisian is of importance for the Nordic evidence, to which we now come. For it seems likely that the Nordic languages borrowed the German word in its developed meaning, and that this explains the origin of the following forms, all meaning "nourish": Old and Modern Icelandic *næra,* Norwegian *næra,* modern Swedish *nära,* and Danish *nære.*[9]

From these forms, which are found in both East and West Norse, should be distinguished another set of forms, which are limited to West Norse. The latter forms appear to be inherited, and it is the meaning "kindle" of two of them in which we are interested. This is the meaning of Norwegian and Swedish-dialect *nöra.*[10] Beside the meaning "kindle" in Norwegian and Swedish-

7. Rhys Carpenter, *Folktale, Fiction, and Saga in the Homeric Epics* (Berkeley, Calif., 1956), pp. 138–39, compares Beowulf's descent to the ocean depths to Odysseus's descent to the underworld, arguing that both derive from the same ultimate source (the "Bearson" legend); the argument is at least interesting in light of the posited etymological meaning of *nered* as "brings back from death."

8. Cf. J. and W. Grimm, *Deutsches Wörterbuch* IV.1.2.7 (Leipzig, 1878), s.v. *genesen.*

9. See J. De Vries, *Altnordisches etymologisches Wörterbuch* (Leiden, 1962), s.v. *næra,* who further argues that the borrowings were not from Old High German, but rather from a Low German form *neren* (which one must assume had the same meaning).

10. The Swedish dialects in question are those of Bohuslän and Dalsland, both of which are West Norse in origin.

dialect, the meanings "stärken, erfrischen, ernähren (invigorate, refresh, nourish)" are attested in Old Icelandic *næra*, modern Icelandic *næra*, and Norwegian dialect *nöra*. [11]

Thus, West Norse appears to have had a verb with two separate meanings, "revive" and "kindle." The formal evidence suggests by its distribution that the meaning "kindle" developed from a more basic meaning of the verb. But then the problem is to determine precisely what this basic meaning was. I do not agree with the suggestion[12] that the meaning "kindle" developed from the notion of "feeding" or "nourishing" a fire. There are two arguments against this. The first is simply semantic; it is difficult to see how the expression "feed a fire" could come to mean "light a fire." But the second argument is more basic; it is not the set of forms represented by *nöra*, "kindle," that has "nourish" as its primary meaning. This is, rather, the set of forms apparently borrowed from West Germanic. [13]

In order to determine the oldest meaning of the first set, which is native to West Norse, one must consider the evidence of Old Icelandic. It emerges from this that Old Icelandic *næra* did not mean "nourish" at all, but still had the older sense of "revive, bring back to life."

For the sake of comparison, let us first cite an example of Old Icelandic *næra,* "nourish." These occurrences are few and late—thus the phrase *næra sin hibýli,* "to feed his family," in the *Konungs Skugg-sja* (326B), a late translation of the *Speculum Regale.*

The meaning of *næra* is quite distinct from this, as the following examples will show. (In these examples I shall quote the spelling of the texts, which frequently have *næra* for *næra*;

11. For Icelandic, cf. De Vries (n. 9), s.v., and A. Noreen, *Altisländisches Grammatik* (Halle, 1890), p. 90; for Norwegian dialect, cf. I. Aasen, *Norsk Ordbog* (Christiania, 1873), s.v.

12. Made by R. Meringer, *Wörter und Sachen* 1 (1909): 168ff.

13. It should be noted that Faroese *nøra,* "provide with food; breed or raise (livestock)" does not contrast with another form *næra*; has the falling together of two forms thus given *nøra* the meaning "nourish"? Such a coincidence of forms has taken place in the case of Icelandic (see below in text).

the reason for this is that -æ- and -œ- have fallen together in modern Icelandic, thus obscuring the distinction in which we are interested; the meanings, however, will serve to identify the forms as coming from *næra*.) An example that might at first seem to have to do with "feeding" but does not, is found in *Fornaldar Sögur* 3.571: *hón dreypir víni á varrir þeim ok nærdusk þeir skjótt,* "she dripped wine on their lips, and they brought themselves back to life again." The meaning naturally cannot be "and they nourished themselves again."

For *næra* as "bring back to life," one might also consider the following striking example, *Fornmanna Sögur* 6.353: *nærdisk hón svá sem frá leid,* "she brought herself back to life who had *perished* (i.e., swooned)", where the context has nothing at all to do with "nourishing."

These examples serve to show that the meaning "kindle" of Norwegian and Swedish dialect *nöra* has to do, not with "feeding," but with "bringing back to life." The association with fire is important, because it suggests that West Norse could have inherited the meaning "return to light" as well as "return to life" for the root *nes-*. The association with fire, furthermore, is old, to judge by the following Old Icelandic passage, *Fornmanna Sögur* 10.368; this passage concerns a queen who says that she has been so wasted by grief for her husband, *at engi gneisti lífsins má næra mik edr lífga,* "'that no spark (*gneisti*) of life may "kindle" me or bring me back to life.'"[14]

3 ALBANIAN

One of the forms commonly cited as a derivative from Indo-European *nes-* is the Albanian verb *knełem,* "erhole mich, werde

14. It should also be noted that corresponding to the Old English compound *ealdorneru,* "life's salvation, refuge," is the Old Icelandic compound *aldrnari,* which, however, is a designation for "fire" in the context of the Ragnarök—the destruction and recreation of the world (*Völuspa* 57.3).

wieder lebendig (I recover, come back to life)."[15] The derivation was first proposed by N. Jokl,[16] who saw in the meaning of this verb a clear correspondence to the Germanic forms discussed above. The verbal base of *knełem* is to be segmented *k-nel-*, with *k-* a perfectivizing element like Germanic *ga-*. The element *-nel-* would then go back to *nes-l-*, and the verb itself would derive from an adjective built on a formant *-lo-*.

If this derivation is correct, as the meaning of *knełem* would argue, then it provides a useful piece of evidence. For "werde wieder lebendig" is only one of the meanings of the verb. For the total range of the verb, I quote the complete entry contained in a recent Albanian-English historical dictionary.[17] Used intransitively, the verb means: "recover, get well; thrive; (*of light*) *brighten*." Used transitively, it means: "refresh, revive; *make red-hot*."

Jokl was aware of the meaning "brighten" from an Italian dictionary of northern Albanian, which glossed *knełem* with "divenire vivo e splendente, rischiararsi," and he drew attention to Scandinavian *nöra*, "kindle." He assumed that the similar meanings in the two cases resulted from an independent "pregnant" usage.[18] Based on the evidence of Greek, however, it seems more than likely that the Albanian "prägnante Verwendung für das Feuer oder die Sonne (pregnant usage for fire or the sun)" has been inherited from the same Indo-European source as the meaning "kindle" of Scandinavian *nöra*.

---

15. Cf. J. Pokorny, *Indogermanisches etymologisches Wörterbuch* (Bern, 1954), 2:766; M. Mayrhofer, *Kurzgefasstes etymologisches Wörterbuch des Altindischen* (Heidelberg, 1956–74), s.v. *nasate*; H. Frisk (chap. 1, n. 4), s.v. *néomai*. (Frisk, however, adds a caution that the form is ambiguous.)

16. N. Jokl, *Sitzungsberichte der Akademie der Wissenschaften zu Wien* 168: 1, 40.

17. Stuart E. Mann, *An Historical Albanian-English Dictionary* (Cambridge, 1957).

18. Jokl repeats the notion that the basic meaning of Old Icelandic *næra* is "ernähren (nourish)"; but one should note that at least Albanian *knełem* has nothing to do with "feeding."

4 INDIC

Sanskrit *násate* is an exact formal cognate to Greek *néomai*. But the meanings of the Sanskrit verb, "approach, resort to, join," have developed too far to shed light on the meanings of the Indo-European verb.[19]

Both Sanskrit and Avestan have a neuter noun *astam*, "home," which has been reconstructed as **ns-to-*, with zero-grade of the root *nes-*.[20] This reconstruction is probable, and it indicates that the secular meaning "to return home" of Greek *néomai* goes back to Indo-European (cf. p. 23 above).

For the sacred meaning of IE *nes-* the crucial Sanskrit form is the proper name *Násatyā*. This name, which is in the dual, belongs to a pair of twin gods in the Vedic pantheon. The etymology of *Násatyā* has yet to be established with certainty, but the prevailing modern view is to derive the form from the root *nes-*.[21] The Vedic twins have the characteristic functions of "saving" and "healing" distressed mortals, and this has suggested a connection with the Gothic verb *nasjan*, "to save" and "to heal." In the rest of this section I propose to show that *Násatyā* is indeed derived from *nes-*, and that the form contains precious comparative evidence for the sacred meaning of the Indo-European root.

Sanskrit *Násatyā* has equivalents in Avestan and Mitanni, and is thus known to go back to Common Indo-Iranian. Avestan *Nåŋhaiθya*, a singular form, designates a demon in the Zoroastrian system, and Mitanni *Nasattiįa(nna)*, a plural form, apparently designates the same twin gods as Vedic *Násatyā*.[22]

19. Sanskrit also has the reduplicated form *nimsate*, "kiss," to which Greek *nísomai* is thought to correspond; the difficulty with the Greek form is that original *-ns-* should have produced *-n-*, not *-s-*. For a bibliography of proposed solutions, see Frisk (chap. 1, n. 4), s.v. *néomai*.

20. For the derivation, see M. Mayrhofer (n. 15), s.v.

21. See n. 27 below.

22. The Mitanni name occurs on a treaty from the fourteenth century B.C. between the Mitanni king Matiwāza and the Hittite king Suppiluliuma. Mitanni

Since Sanskrit *Nāsatyā* originated at least as early as Common Indo-Iranian, it is probable that even the Vedic poets no longer knew what it meant. Later Indian tradition provides three distinct interpretations of the name, but all are based on folk-etymologies. One of these (*nā = nar + satya,* "true warriors") is clearly impossible;[23] a second, found in Pāṇini (*na-asatya,* "not untrue") has rightly been rejected on both formal and semantic grounds;[24] the third (*nāsā-tya,* "the nose-born"), although it has been defended in modern times by Hermann Lommel, is equally to be rejected.[25]

The first to suggest a derivation from the root *nes-* was Brunnhofer.[26] The difficulty, however, has been to explain the morphology of the form, and for this Hermann Güntert is

equivalents of the Vedic *Mitra, Varuṇa,* and *Indra* occur on the same treaty and thus establish the identity of the *Nasattiia(nna).* For the Mitanni evidence, see M. Mayrhofer, *Die Indo-Arier im alten Vorderasien* (Wiesbaden, 1966), pp. 14–15, with further bibliography; there is a convenient summary of the evidence in T. Burrow, *The Sanskrit Language*[2] (London, 1965), p. 28. The Iranian demon *Nåŋhaiθya* is twice cited in the *Avesta* (*Vīdēvdāt* 10.9 and 9.43).

23. The *Petersburger Wörterbuch* of Böhtlingk and Roth, which cites all three interpretations, does not mention the source for this one.

24. See Hermann Lommel, *Festschrift Walther Schubring* (Hamburg, 1951), p. 29, who points out that *na-* instead of *an-* in such a compound would be highly unusual, and who argues that the name "not untrue" (or "not unreal") would be too abstract and undistinctive to be old.

25. This derivation is given by Yāska (*Nirukta* 6.13) and defended by Lommel (n. 24), pp. 29–31. The story on which the derivation is based is found in the *Brhaddevatā* 6.162–7.7 to *RV* 10.17.1–2: the twins' mother Saraṇyū conceived them when she and her husband Vivasvat, in the form of horses, attempted to mate; the seed of Vivasvat fell on the ground and Saraṇyū breathed it in through her nostrils. This myth, which has a close parallel in the Purāṇas (see Lommel, p. 30), cannot have to do with the original meaning of the name *Nåsatyā.* The decisive objection, which will be argued later in this section, is that *Nåsatyā* was originally singular and designated one twin in opposition to the other. The interpretation "nose-born," which must concern both twins equally, is thus to be rejected.

26. H. Brunnhofer, *Vom Aral bis zur Ganga,* p. 99—unavailable to me but cited by Lommel (n. 24), p. 29, and H. Güntert, *Der arische Weltkönig und Heiland* (Halle, 1923), p. 259.

credited with the best solution.[27] Güntert began with the Indo-Iranian ancestor of Sanskrit *násate,* to which he ascribed the meaning "hasten to safety" on the basis of the Germanic evidence. He then posited a nominal derivative **nasati-,* "salvation through hastening to the rescue," on the parallel of *vasati-,* "dwelling," derived from *vásati,* "to dwell." The name *Násatyā* would then be based on **nasati-* just as the name *Ādityá-* is based on *áditi-.*

Güntert's solution is possible, but the hypothetical abstract noun **nasati-* is weak. One would have expected **nasti-* in view of Gothic *ga-nists,* or even **asti-* on the basis of Indo-Iranian *astam.* Given this weakness, I would propose a different solution.

Gregory Nagy, in a discussion of Old Persian *xšāyaθiya-,* "king," has argued that the underlying form **kšāyatya-* is perhaps a "nominalization (with *vṛddhi*) of an archaic syntagma **kšayati-ya,* 'he who has power.' "[28] Such a combination of third-person verb plus relative pronoun has parallels in Celtic and perhaps Italic, and the syntactic order is well attested in Indo-Iranian.[29] If Nagy is correct about the origins of **kšāyatya-,* I propose that Indo-Iranian *Násatya-* is likewise a nominalization (with *vṛddhi*) of an archaic syntagma **nasati-ya,* "he who brings back to life and light." The verb **nasati* would be an activized

27. H. Güntert (n. 26), p. 259. Güntert's derivation has been accepted by Wackernagel-Debrunner, *Altindische Grammatik,* vol. 2, pt. 2 (Göttingen, 1954), p. 939. M. Mayrhofer (n. 15), s.v. *Násatyā,* regards a derivation from *nes-* as likely and credits Güntert with the best solution.

28. G. Nagy (chap. 4, n. 55), p. 43 n. 121. The Old Persian form is a Median borrowing; for the verb in question, cf. Old Persian *xšay-,* "rule," Avestan *xšāy-,* "have power," and Sanskrit *kṣay-,* "possess."

29. I quote from Nagy's discussion, which also cites Hittite evidence:

For a parallel syntagma in Celtic, cf. Old Irish 3rd plural relative *bertae* "they who bear" < **bheronti-io:* likewise Gaulish *dugiiontiio* "they who serve," discussed by C. Watkins, "Preliminaries to a Historical and Comparative Analysis of the Syntax of the Old Irish Verb," *Celtica* 6 (1962) 24. Such a syntactical order is well-attested in Indo-Iranian: cf. *Rig-Veda* 1.70.5: *dáśad yó asmāi* "he who awaits him," as discussed again by Watkins, *op. cit.* 29. . . . I add here some possible parallels suggested to me by C. Watkins:

form, otherwise unattested, of *násate,* and as such would be parallel to the Homeric verb **nései* that we have reconstructed in *xviii* 265.[30]

A singular verb **nasati* would imply that *Nǻsatyā* was also originally singular. Avestan *Nǻŋhaiθya* provides comparative evidence for such a singular in Common Indo-Iranian, and even the *Rig-Veda* contains one instance of a singular "traversing *Nǻsatya-*" in 4.3.6.[31] For the most part, however, the *Rig-Veda* does not make distinctions between the two twins but treats them as an identical pair. Hence we must begin with the notion of two *Nǻsatyā,* who both "bring back to life and light."

The two twins, as noted above, "save" and "heal" distressed mortals. They perform these functions in a series of archaic myths which the *Rig-Veda* refers to frequently. Three such myths, furthermore, provide explicit evidence that the underlying function of the two "saviors" and "healers" was in fact "to bring back to life." The myths concern the mortals Rebha, Bhujyu, and Śyāva.

Lūcetius, the name of one of the followers of Turnus: Vergil, *Aeneid* IX 590. Servius *ad loc.:* . . . *lingua Osca Lucetius est Iuppiter dictus a luce.* Cf. also Gaulish *Leucetios,* epithet of the god of war. For references and further instances (including a possible occurrence in the *Carmen Saliare*), cf. J. Whatmough, *The Prae-Italic Dialects of Italy* II, 197.

Δουκέτιος, the name of a king of the Sicels: Diodorus Siculus 11.78.7. For references and further instances, cf. again Whatmough, *PID* II 452.

Hence **leuketi-jo* "he who shines" and **deuketi-jo* "he who leads," both nominalized. There is a parallel syntagma in Hittite: e.g. in *Laws* I 25, *paprizzi kuiš* "he who defiles" (a well, in this case); also, in an Akkadian-Hittite vocabulary (*Keilschrifttexte aus Boghazköi* I 42 31), the Akkadian participle ḫābilu "gewalttätig" is glossed as *dammešḫiškizzi kuiš,* literally "welcher schädigt."

30. The fact that a god is the subject of the activized verb in this reconstruction of the divine name *Nǻsatyā* is to be noted; cf. chap. 4, n. 58 above.

31. The epithet *párijman,* "traversing," is also used of the twins as a pair (e.g., *RV* 1.46.14). For the dual form *Nǻsatyā* as originally meaning "*Nǻsatya-* and his brother," cf. J. Wackernagel, *Zeitschrift für vergleichende Sprachforschung* 23 (1877): 302 ff., on the Homeric dual *Aíante* as originally meaning "Ajax and his brother."

Rebha was bound, stabbed, and cast into the waters for nine days and ten nights before being saved by the twins. *RV* 10.39.9 says that he was "dead" (*mamrvā́ṃsam*) when the twins "raised him up" (*úd airayatam*).[32]

Bhujyu was saved after his father or evil companions abandoned him at sea. *RV* 1.119.4 refers to the twins as "bringing (Bhujyu) home from the dead ancestors" (*nivāhantā pitṛ́bhya ā́*).[33]

Little is known about Śyāva, to whom there are only two references in the *Rig-Veda*.[34] But one of these, *RV* 1.117.24, says that he was "split in three" (*trídhā . . . víkastam*) when the twins "raised him up to live" (*új jīvā́sa airayatam*).

Not only do the twins "bring back to life," but they also "bring back to the light." To Bhujyu, who was "cast forth on the unsupporting darkness" (*anārambhaṇé támasi práviddham*, 1.182.6), the twins gave "light-bringing help" (*svàrvatīr . . . ūtír*, 1.119.8). Rebha they "raised up to see the sun" (*úd . . . airayatam svàr dṛśé*, 1.112.5), and likewise Vandana (ibid.). Vandana, who was buried in a pit when he disintegrated with old age, is also the object of a pair of similes which strikingly connect the ideas of "returning from death" and "returning from darkness". *RV* 1.117.5 says that the twins restored Vandana "like one who had fallen asleep in the womb of the death goddess"[35] (*suṣupvā́ṃsam*

---

32. Cf. also *RV* 1.117.4, another reference to the myth of Rebha, which says: "you two, by your miraculous powers, put him back together again when he had come apart" (*sám tám riṇitho víprutaṃ dáṃsobhir*). For other references to this myth, see K. F. Geldner, *Der Rig-Veda*, vols. 1–3 [*Harvard Oriental Series* 33–35] (Cambridge, 1951), on *RV* 1.116.24.

33. Geldner takes *pitṛ́bhya ā́* as "to his parents," but the *Rig-Veda* always uses the dual when the meaning is "parents." See Geldner on *RV* 1.116.3–5 for other references to the myth of Bhujyu.

34. *RV* 1.117.24 and 10.65.12.

35. Vedic *nírṛti-* can be either the goddess or the concept of "destruction" or "dissolution," and it is not in fact clear which is meant in this verse. For a comparison of the goddess with the Roman *Lua Mater*, see G. Dumézil, *Déesses latines et mythes védiques* (Brussels, 1956), pp. 107–15. Related to *nírṛti-* is the verbal adjective *nírṛta-*, which is applied to the same Vandana in 1.119.7: "Vandana, who was decomposed by old age (*nírṛtaṃ jaraṇyáyā*), you miracle-workers put back together again (*sám invathaḥ*) as craftsmen do a chariot."

ná nírṛter upásthe), and "like the sun dwelling in darkness" (*sûryam ná . . . támasi kṣiyántam*).

The twins, who were invoked at dawn, have a close connection with Uṣas, the dawn goddess. She is bidden to awaken them (8.9.17), they follow her in their chariot (8.5.2, etc.), they hitch their steeds when she is born (10.39.12), and their chariot is once said to arrive before her (1.34.10).[36] As their hour of invocation indicates, the twins have to do with a "return from darkness" in cult as well as myth. In three hymns the poet marks the time of invocation with the phrase "we have reached the other shore of this darkness" (*átāriṣma támasas pārám asyá*).[37] In another hymn the poet prays to the twins for "refreshment" (*íṣam*) "which will deliver us across the darkness" (*yá naḥ píparad . . . támas tiráḥ*, 1.46.6). The twins are called "darkness slayers" (*tamohánā*, 3.39.3), and their horses and chariot are described as "uncovering the covered darkness" (*aporṇuvántas táma á párivṛtam*, 4.45.2). One hymn invokes the twins as "you who have made light for mankind" (*yáv . . . jyótir jánāya cakráthuḥ*, 1.92.17).

The Vedic twins, then, clearly have the function of "bringing back to life and light" in a context of solar mythology. Their connection with solar mythology, moreover, is known to go back to Indo-European. The twins are closely associated with a female figure named *Sūryá*, a feminized form of *Sûrya*, the "Sun." The twins are called *Sūryá*'s husbands and wooers, and she is frequently said to mount their chariot at dawn.[38] *Sūryá* is also called *duhitá súryasya*, "the daughter of the Sun,"[39] and this name corresponds exactly to Lithuanian *Saulés dukterys* and

36. For more on the relationship between the twins and the Dawn see n. 66 below; for general remarks on this relationship see Donald Ward, *The Divine Twins* (Berkeley and Los Angeles, 1968), pp. 11 and 15.

37. *RV* 1.183.6, 1.184.6, and 7.73.1; the same phrase occurs in *RV* 1.92.6 to Uṣas.

38. They are called "husbands" (*páti*) in *RV* 4.43.6, "wooers" (*vará*) in *RV* 10.85.8–9; *Sūryá* mounts their chariot in, e.g., *RV* 5.73.5 (*á . . . vām súryá rátham tíṣṭad*).

39. The *duhitá súryasya* mounts the chariot of the twins in *RV* 1.116.17, 1.118.5, and 6.63.5; she "chooses" their chariot in *RV* 1.117.13 and 4.43.2.

closely to Latvian *Saules meita*. These two "daughters of the Sun" are associated with the Baltic counterparts to the Vedic twins, the Lithuanian *Dievo sunéliai* and the Latvian *Dieva déli*. In Vedic the "daughter of the Sun" is the common wife of the two twins, while in Baltic she is their sister. In Indo-European she was probably both wife and sister simultaneously.[40]

Now that I have made a case for the two *Nåsatyā* as "they who bring back to life and light," I return to the question of an originally singular form. I shall begin by considering comparative evidence having to do with the Greek Dioscuri. Like the Vedic twins, the Dioscuri are "saviors" and "healers" of distressed mortals, and their cult title and literary epithet, *sōtêres*, "saviors," has been compared with the Vedic name *Nåsatyā*.[41] Unlike the Vedic twins, however, the Dioscuri have preserved their internal oppositions, and from this perspective, only one of the twins is a "savior." Since Polydeuces is immortal and Castor mortal, Polydeuces actually brings Castor "back to life."

The crucial moment for the Dioscuri is their battle with Idas and Lynceus, when Castor is mortally wounded and Polydeuces gives up half of his immortality in order to save him. Our best source for the episode is Pindar's *Nemean* 10.[42] In his introduction to the narrative, Pindar says that Polydeuces, given the choice of becoming entirely a god, instead "chose the life of Castor who had *perished* in battle" (l. 59):

εἵλετ᾽ αἰῶνα φθιμένου Πολυδεύκης Κάστορος ἐν πολέμῳ.

40. The Latvian *Dieva déli* are actually called their sister's suitors; see Ward (n. 36), pp. 10–11, who also discusses the Greek Dioscuri and their sister Helen; cf. also Gregory Nagy, "Phaethon, Sappho's Phaon, and the White Rock of Leukas," *Harvard Studies in Classical Philology* 77 (1973): 162–77.

41. For the cult title and literary epithet of the Dioscuri, see A. Furtwängler, "Dioskuren," in Roscher's *Lexikon* (chap. 3, n. 12), vol. 1, no. 1, cols. 1163–64. D. Ward (n. 36), pp. 14–15, 18, summarizes the evidence for the Indo-European origins of the twins' functions as "saviors" and "healers."

42. The same episode was narrated in the *Cypria*; fragment 11 (Allen) tells how Lynceus spied the Dioscuri before the battle began. Apollodorus 3.11.2 also narrates the episode.

In the narrative itself, Pindar says that Polydeuces "opened the eye, then the voice" of his fallen brother (l. 90):

ἀνὰ δ᾽ ἔλυσεν μὲν ὀφθαλμόν, ἔπειτα δὲ φωνὰν
χαλκομίτρα Κάστορος.

In Pindar's account, the immortal Polydeuces clearly brings his mortal brother "back to life." [43]

We cannot know for sure whether the immortal/mortal opposition which determines the actions of the Greek twins also characterized the Vedic twins, but this is a likely supposition. The Greek twins are so opposed because they have different fathers,

---

43. In the actual narrative Pindar says that when Polydeuces reached Castor, the latter "was not yet dead, but still gasping" (1.74):

καί νιν οὔπω τεθναότ᾽, ἄσθματι δὲ φρίσσοντα
πνοὰς ἔκιχεν.

Apollodorus 3.11.2, however, says that Idas "killed" (κτείνει) Castor, and that Polydeuces refused immortality from Zeus "while Castor was a corpse" (ὄντος νεκροῦ Κάστορος).

Pindar's word φθιμένου, "perished," expresses the underlying reality of the situation, which is that Castor, as a "mortal," had to "die." Fragment 6 of the *Cypria* (Allen) expresses this reality in terms of Castor's "fate":

Κάστωρ μὲν θνητός, θανάτου δέ οἱ αἶσα πέπρωται,
αὐτὰρ ὅ γ᾽ ἀθάνατος Πολυδεύκης, ὄζος Ἄρηος.

Castor, on the one hand, was mortal, and a fate of death was allotted to him, but Polydeuces, scion of Ares, was immortal.

As a combination of immortal and mortal elements, the Dioscuri, even as a pair, experience a regular alternation between "life" and "death." Such an alternation is precisely what characterizes the twins in our earliest evidence, *Odyssey* 11.302–04:

οἳ καὶ νέρθεν γῆς τιμὴν πρὸς Ζηνὸς ἔχοντες
ἄλλοτε μὲν ζώουσ᾽ ἑτερήμεροι, ἄλλοτε δ᾽ αὖτε
τεθνᾶσιν.

Obtaining honor from Zeus even beneath the earth, now they *live*, on alternate days, and now they *are dead*.

Iliad 3.243–44 is not inconsistent with this passage, although it is briefer, and Pindar *Nemean* 10.55–57 follows a similar tradition.

the immortal Zeus and the mortal Tyndareus.[44] The Vedic twins
also have different fathers, and one of these is *Dyáus*, the exact
cognate of the Greek *Zeús*. This information comes from *RV*
1.181.4, the only Vedic text which explicitly distinguishes one
twin from the other. The same text calls the other father *Súmakha*,
"Good Warrior," a figure who is unknown otherwise but who
was almost certainly mortal like the Greek Tyndareus. The dual
paternity of the Greek and the Vedic twins apparently goes back
to the same Indo-European source, where one of the fathers was
the immortal "Sky God" **Dyēus*, and the other father, in all
likelihood, a mere mortal.[45] If Sumakha was indeed mortal, then
his son must also have been mortal, and it is hard to imagine how
such a "mortal" twin could continue to exist unless his immortal
brother brought him "back to life."

As stated earlier, the Vedic twins are closely connected with
sunrise in the *Rig-Veda*. But in addition to their well-attested
morning ritual, the twins also had an evening ritual. The two
times, evening and morning, are clearly paired and contrasted in
three hymns of the *Rig-Veda*: *doṣá . . . uṣási* in 8.22.14, *doṣâm
uṣásaḥ* in 10.39.1, and *doṣâ vástor* in 10.40.4.[46] The evening/
morning opposition which characterizes the twins' ritual must
also have characterized the twins themselves. A passage quoted
by Yāska (*Nirukta* 12.2) bears this conclusion out by stating that
"one (of the twins) is called the son of night, the other the son of

44. Cf. Zeus's speech to Polydeuces in *Nemean* 10. 80–82:

'Εσσί μοι υἱός· τόνδε δ' ἔπειτα πόσις
σπέρμα θνατὸν ματρὶ τεᾷ πελάσαις
στάξεν ἥρως.

You are my son; but as for this one, a hero afterwards let drip his mortal seed
when he approached your mother as her husband.

45. Cf. D. Ward (n. 36), pp. 4–5 and 12–14, who emphasizes that dual paternity,
frequently involving an opposition between an immortal and a mortal father, is
a common feature in twin mythology the world over.

46. Cf. also *RV* 5.76.3, which bids the twins to come "day and night" (*divā
náktam*), but apparently a third time as well—namely, "midday" (*madhyámdine*).

dawn."[47] Now if only one twin was properly connected with sunrise, then only one twin can properly have had the function of "bringing back to life and light." It is this twin who is to be connected with the name *Nāsatya-*.

To continue this investigation I now shift my attention from pre-Vedic to post-Vedic tradition. The Swedish scholar Stig Wikander has brilliantly shown that Sanskrit epic indirectly preserves old oppositions between the twins which the *Rig-Veda* ignores.[48] Two of the heroes of the *Mahābhārata,* the twins Nakula and Sahadeva, are depicted as sons of the divine twins, and, as Wikander has shown, are characterized in terms of their fathers' archaic attributes.[49] But while Nakula and Sahadeva often act in common like their Vedic fathers, they are not an identical pair: rather, they are opposed to each other as "warrior horseman" to "intelligent cattleman." These oppositions can be shown to be old, and Sahadeva's attributes—both "cattle" and "intelligence"—are of great importance to the name *Nāsatya-*.

47. It is also probable that the Vedic twins were identified with the morning and evening stars; cf. D. Ward (n. 36), pp. 15–18, who cites bibliography and also considers the comparative evidence of other Indo-European twins; cf. also Gregory Nagy, "Phaethon, Sappho's Phaon, and the White Rock of Leukas" (n. 40), pp. 172–73, n. 94.

48. S. Wikander, "Nakula et Sahadeva," *Orientalia Suecana* 6 (1957): 66–96.

49. This is just part of a larger argument that Wikander put forth in "Pāṇḍavasagan och Mahābhāratas mytiska förutsättningar," *Religion och Bibel, Nathan Söderblom-sällskapets Årsbok* 6 (1947): 27–39 (translated into French by Georges Dumézil in his *Jupiter Mars Quirinus* [Paris, 1948], 4: 37–53). In this earlier study, Wikander dealt with the structure of the Pāṇḍavas, the five heroes of the *Mahābhārata,* as a group. All five are the sons of different gods, and Wikander convincingly showed that the fathers represent the old trifunctional scheme which Dumézil has discovered and elaborated. Wikander showed further that the five sons preserve archaic representations of their fathers, and of the three functions with which they are associated. In "Nakula et Sahadeva" (n. 48), Wikander went on to study separately the representatives of the third function, the twins Nakula and Sahadeva, as they preserve old oppositions that are not directly attested for their fathers. Dumézil has summarized and expanded all of Wikander's findings in the first part of his *Mythe et épopée,* vol. 1 (Paris, 1968), which is now the best source to consult; for the structure of the five Pāṇḍavas, see pp. 53–102, and for the twins in particular, pp. 73–89.

Wikander began his study of the epic twins with a survey of their characteristic epithets. What distinguishes Sahadeva absolutely from his brother is his characterization as "intelligent":[50] he is called "wise" (*vidvān,* 17.2.54), "intelligent" (*prājña,* 17.2.56), "endowed with understanding" (*buddhimān,* 14.72.2103), "learned" (*paṇḍita,* 2.63.2155), "clever" (*matimān,* 3.269.15710), "acute" (*nipuṇa,* 5.49.1838), and "clairvoyant" (*cakṣuṣin,* 6.75.3282).

Nakula, on the other hand, is "warlike" and possessed of a warrior's "beauty."[51] He is called "skillful in all forms of war" (*sarvayuddhaviśārada,* 7.165.7364), "good in war" (*kuśalaṃ yuddhe,* 7.98.3976), and, most characteristically, "fighting in a wondrous manner" (*citrayodhin*).[52] He is also called "beautiful" (*darśaniya,* 3.27.1020, 4.3.61, 5.49.1996), "the most beautiful in the world" (*darśaniyatamo loke,* 2.78.2625), and "the most beautiful of heroes" (*darśaniyatamo nṛṇām,* 2.75.2555).

Wikander discussed two scenes in the *Mahābhārata* which underscore the opposition between Nakula's "warrior beauty" and Sahadeva's "intelligence."[53] In the great dice game, Yudhiṣthira, the twins' eldest brother, characterizes both of them

50. Wikander, "Nakula et Sahadeva" (n. 48), pp. 72–73. The author also shows here that Sahadeva is differentially characterized as "modest, correct, obedient," and the like. D. Ward, "The Separate Functions of the Indo-European Divine Twins," in J. Puhvel, ed., *Myth and Law among the Indo-Europeans* (Berkeley, Calif., 1970), pp. 193–202, has shown that this feature of Sahadeva's character is paralleled in other Indo-European twins, and is thus highly traditional. I cannot, however, agree with Ward's main thesis that the "modest" Sahadeva (and the Indo-European twin he represents) is differentially associated with Dumézil's *third* function. Wikander (n. 48), pp. 75–76, in showing that Sahadeva is associated with Yudhiṣthira while Nakula is associated with Bhīma in battles of the *Mahābhārata,* demonstrated that Sahadeva is differentially associated with the *first* function, and Nakula with the second. Dumézil, *Mythe et épopée* (n. 49), 1 : 81–86 devotes a separate section to "Sahadeva et la première fonction": he calls Sahadeva an "auxiliaire de la première fonction" on p. 86. As we shall see below, Sahadeva is to be connected with the son of Dyaus, and one would naturally expect this twin to be ranked above the son of Sumakha.
51. Wikander (n. 48), pp. 71–72.
52. 1.139.5533, 5.47.1832, 5.49.1996, 5.89.3168, 8.76.3814, 9.10.477.
53. Wikander, pp. 73–74.

when he puts them up as stakes: Nakula he calls "dark, young, with eyes of flame, the shoulders of a lion, and huge arms" (2.63.2152), while Sahadeva "teaches justice and has acquired in this world a reputation for being *learned*" (*paṇḍita*, 2.63.2155). Similarly, near the end of the poem, when the twins die, Yudhiṣṭhira interprets their deaths as the result of peculiar moral flaws:[54] Nakula's flaw was to think "there is no one equal to me in beauty" (*rūpeṇa matsamo nāsti kaścid iti*, 17.2.62); Sahadeva, on the other hand, "always thought that no one was as *intelligent* as himself" (*ātmanaḥ sadṛśaṃ prājñaṃ naiṣo 'manyata kañcana*, 17.2.56).[55]

The second great opposition between the epic twins contrasts "horses" with "cattle." Wikander discovered this opposition in the fourth book of the *Mahābhārata*, where the twins and their three older brothers all assume different disguises in order to spend their last year of exile at the court of king Virāṭa. The twins both disguise themselves as *vaiśya*-s—members of the third caste, having to do with agriculture and production. This disguise

54. Draupadī, Bhīma, and Arjuna also die in this scene, and Yudhiṣṭhira also interprets their deaths as the result of peculiar moral flaws; see Dumézil, *Mythe et épopée* (n. 49), 1: 81–82, who shows that essential features of the characters in question have in this scene been turned into flaws.

55. Sahadeva's "intelligence" is also a marked feature in two aberrant traditions of the *Mahābhārata*, as Dumézil (n. 49), pp. 82–85 has shown. The first of these is the Persian account of the "Sons of Pan" (see Dumézil, pp. 82–83). According to this, each of the five sons received a particular talent as a result of his teacher's prayers; Sahadeva, "who looked for wisdom and who did not speak unless spoken to, asked for the science of the stars and a knowledge of hidden matters." The second aberrant version is that of the eighteenth-century Swiss Colonel de Polier, who studied with an Indian teacher and whose extensive notes, including a résumé of the *Mahābhārata*, were published as *La Mythologie des Indous* by his cousin, the Chanoinesse de Polier, in 1809 (see Dumézil, pp. 42–43, for the nature and value of this text). In the *Mahābhārata* of the Colonel de Polier, the five Pāṇḍavas are all characterized at their births, and Sahadeva is called "the most enlightened of mortals, the most perspicacious, and the most learned in the knowledge of past, present, and future" (see Dumézil, p. 84). The fault which causes Sahadeva's death in this version is more particular than it is in the vulgate: Sahadeva did not tell his brothers that their mother Kuntī had had a son (Karṇa) by the god Sūrya before they were born, "although he had penetrated this mystery by means of his great intelligence" (see Dumézil, p. 85).

is a reflection of their fathers' archaic nature, for the divine twins had once been the *vaiśya* gods.[56] The disguise as *vaiśya*-s, however, also reveals an opposition between the twins that would not have been suspected otherwise: while Nakula disguises himself as a groom and takes charge of Virāṭa's "horses," Sahadeva speaks warmly of his preference for "cattle" and becomes Virāṭa's cowherd.[57] This opposition between horses and cattle has been shown by Dumézil to be as old as Indo-European,[58] and it will prove crucial in my further analysis of the Vedic twins.

To correlate the oppositions between Nakula and Sahadeva with the Vedic twins, we begin with *RV* 1.181.4, which calls one twin the son of Dyaus and the other the son of Sumakha. The son of *Súmakha*, "Good Warrior," is also called "conquering" (*jiṣṇú*) and "lordly" (*sūrí*), and, as Wikander has argued,[59] he plainly corresponds to the "warrior" Nakula. Sahadeva, then, corresponds to the son of Dyaus.

The crucial point, however, is to connect Sahadeva, the "intelligent cattleman," with the name *Nåsatyā*. To do this we now take into account the fact that the Vedic twins actually have two names, both in the dual: they are not only the *Nåsatyā,* but also the *Aśvínā,* the "Horse-Possessors." As I will argue below, the Vedic names *Nåsatyā* and *Aśvínā* function like the Greek names *Dióskouroi*, "Sons of Zeus," and *Tundarídai*, "Sons of Tyndareus":[60] each name refers properly to a different twin.

56. See p. 48 in Dumézil's translation of Wikander's 1947 study (n. 49 above).
57. Wikander, "Nakula et Sahadeva" (n. 48), p. 76. Sahadeva expresses his preference for and competence in handling cattle in 4.3.67–72, and 4.10.288–93.
58. Dumézil, *Mythe et épopée* (n. 49), 1: 87–89. The closest parallel is the Iranian female pair Drvāspā, "Mistress of healthy horses," and Gə̄uš Tašan, "Builder of the cow," or Gə̄uš Urvan, "Soul of the cow" (see Dumézil, pp. 88–89). For the Indo-European comparison, Dumézil cites somewhat looser parallels in Scandinavian, Italic, and Greek (pp. 87–88).
59. Wikander, "Nakula et Sahadeva" (n. 48), p. 79.
60. Cf. Homeric Hymn 33.1–2, where both twins are first called "sons of Zeus" and then "sons of Tyndareus":

ἀμφὶ Διὸς κούρους ἑλικώπιδες ἔσπετε Μοῦσαι
Τυνδαρίδας. . . .

Further, the name *Aśvínā*, "Horse-Possessors," corresponds to the "horseman" Nakula, and the name *Nā́satyā* corresponds to Sahadeva, the "intelligent cattleman."

Wikander has also argued that the two dual names were originally singular, but he thought that both names belonged to the same twin, the father of Nakula.[61] Wikander's own methodology, however, supports a different conclusion.

Following a suggestion of Geldner's, Wikander noticed that certain of the twins' dual epithets have a statistical tendency to occur in the same strophe with the dual name *Aśvínā*.[62] Such co-occurrences, he argued, reveal old oppositions between the epithets in question and the name.[63] One of the epithets is *divó nápātā*, "sons of Dyaus," which, like Greek *Dióskouroi*, represents the extension of one twin's title to both twins. In three of the five occurrences of *divó nápātā* in the *Rig-Veda*, the name *Aśvínā* occurs in the same strophe. The ratio 3:5 bears out an opposition between the "son of Dyaus" and the father of the "horseman" Nakula which we have already seen indicated.

Wikander detected two further oppositions by this method. An opposition between *Aśvínā* and *vŕṣaṇā*, "bulls," is indicated by a ratio of 13:28, and an opposition between *Aśvínā* and *dasrá*, "the miracle-workers," is indicated by a ratio of 24:44.[64] Wikander failed to observe, however, that a comparable ratio of 32:100 indicates an opposition between *Aśvínā* and *Nā́satyā*.

More important than the statistical count, however, is the evidence of one strophe which contains the *Nā́satyā/Aśvínā* opposition: in *RV* 2.41.7 this opposition is closely correlated with a further opposition between "cattle" and "horses." The

61. Wikander, "Nakula et Sahadeva" (n. 48), pp. 79 ff. For the evidence that led Wikander to this conclusion, see below in text.

62. Wikander, "Nakula et Sahadeva" (n. 48), pp. 79, 81–82.

63. The origin of such oppositions may have been dual dvandva compounds which split and resulted in two separate dual terms (*ekaśeṣa*-s); see Wikander (n. 48), p. 79.

64. These figures are based on my own count; Wikander (n. 48), pp. 81–82 reports only eight cases of co-occurrence for *vŕṣaṇā*, and only twenty for *dasrá*.

strophe is divided into three segments, the first two of which articulate the two oppositions in question. The first segment begins with the adjective *gómad*, "rich in cattle," and ends with the vocative *Nāsatyā*, while the second segment begins with the adjective *áśvāvad*, "rich in horses," and ends with the vocative *Aśvínā*. The parallelism between these two segments makes it clear beyond doubt that "cattle" are associated with the name *Nā́satyā* and "horses" with the name *Aśvínā*:

> *gómad* ū ṣú *nāsatyā/ áśvāvad* yātam *aśvinā/* vartí rudrā nṛpåyyam
>
> Come quickly (*ū ṣú . . . yātam*) along the path (*vartí*) rich in cattle, you *Nāsatyā*; come quickly along the path rich in horses, you *Aśvínā*; come quickly, you *Rudrā,* along the path which protects men (*nṛpåyyam*).

The evidence of *RV* 2.41.7, decisive in itself,[65] is further confirmed by *RV* 7.72.1. This strophe has two segments, and the adjectives "rich in cattle" (*gómatā*) and "rich in horses" (*áśvāvatā*) are again set in opposition to one another in different segments. Although the name *Aśvínā* is omitted in this strophe, the name *Nā́satyā* is again plainly associated with "cattle" in segment 1:

> ā́ *gómatā nāsatyā* ráthena/áśvāvatā puruścandréṇa yātam
>
> Come here (*ā́ . . . yātam*) on your chariot (*ráthena*) rich in cattle, you *Nāsatyā*; come here on your chariot rich in horses and abundant with gold (*puruścandréṇa*).

The evidence of *RV* 2.41.7, supported by that of 7.72.1, establishes conclusively that the names *Nā́satyā* and *Aśvínā*

---

65. It should be noted that this strophe occurs in a catalogue of gods whom Dumézil has identified as the Indic gods of the three functions; such catalogues are rare in the *Rig-Veda,* and highly traditional. Strophes 1–6 of *RV* 2.41 are devoted to the gods of the first two functions, and strophes 7–9 are devoted to the twins, the representatives of the third function. For Dumézil's analysis of this hymn, see his *Tarpeia* (Paris, 1947), pp. 45–56, and *Mythe et épopée* (n. 49), 1: 51.

originally designated different twins, and that the name *Nāsatyā* is to be correlated with the "cattleman" Sahadeva, while the name *Aśvínā* is to be correlated with the "horseman" Nakula. It is also now certain that the son of Dyaus, the prototype of Sahadeva, had the name *Nāsatya-* in opposition to his brother. There is thus every reason to believe that this *Nāsatya-*, like the Greek son of Zeus, originally brought his brother "back to life and light." The "cattle" and "intelligence" of Sahadeva establish beyond reasonable doubt that the name *Nāsatya-* derives from the root *nes-*, and that it originally signified "he who brings back to life and light."[66]

We return now to take account of Wikander's argument that a singular *Nāsatya-* originally designated the father of Nakula. Wikander based this argument on the dual compound name *Nasatyadasrau*, which is applied to the divine twins in Sanskrit epic, and which names one of the twins *Nāsatya-* and the other *Dasra-*.[67] The name *Dasra-* comes from the twins' dual epithet *dasrá*, "miracle-working," which Wikander's statistical argument showed to be opposed to the name *Aśvínā* (see p. 147 above).

66. Earlier in this section there was a brief discussion of a mythological relationship between the *Nāsatyā* and the dawn goddess *Uṣás*; subsequent remarks on *gómat* and *áśvāvat*, the two adjectives which serve to oppose the twins to each other, permit further remarks on the relationship with Uṣas. The two adjectives in question occur simultaneously in the *Rig-Veda* only in references to the twins and to Uṣas: *RV* 1.92.14 invokes Uṣas with the vocatives *gómati áśvāvati*, "rich in cattle, rich in horses"; in *RV* 1.48.2, 1.123.12, and 7.41.7, *Uṣásas*, "Dawns," in the nominative plural, is modified by *áśvāvatīs gómatīs*, "rich in horses, rich in cattle."

What is an opposition in the case of the twins, however, cannot be so in the case of Uṣas, a solitary figure. As the "Dawn goddess," furthermore, Uṣas has more to do with cattle than with horses. Besides her well-known "ruddy cows," we also have the formal evidence of the adjective *gómat*, which twice modifies "dawns" in the plural, without any accompanying form of *áśvāvat* (*RV* 1.113.8 and 2.28.2); the adjective *áśvāvat*, on the other hand, is never used of Uṣas without an accompanying form of *gómat*. Uṣas is, in fact, characterized by her cattle; one wonders whether *Rā́trī*, "Night," in the old pair *Uṣás-Rā́trī* (see G. Dumézil, *Déesses latines et mythes védiques* [Brussels, 1956]), was once somehow associated with horses. This would correlate well with Yāska's statement (see p. 142 above) that Rātrī and Uṣas were the simultaneous mothers of the twins.

67. Wikander (n. 48) p. 79.

Since the epic compound opposes *dasrá* to the name *Nåsatyā,*
Wikander concluded that the names *Aśvínā* and *Nåsatyā*
originally designated the same twin.

The problem with Wikander's argument is his reliance on the
epic compound, which cannot be old. Wikander himself admitted
that statistics do not bear out an opposition between the duals
Nåsatyā and *dasrá* in the *Rig-Veda.*[68] The two terms, in fact,
have a tendency *not* to occur in the same verse.[69] Once again,
however, specific texts are more conclusive than statistics. There
are three more strophes in the *Rig-Veda* that contain an
opposition between "cattle" and "horses," and in these strophes
dasrá actually takes the place of *Nåsatyā* on the "cattle" side of
the opposition. This shows as clearly as possible that the terms

68. Wikander (n. 48), p. 79, and again on p. 81 as follows: "pour ce qui concerne
les termes *nāsatya* et *dasra,* on n'observe nulle part, dans les textes vediques, une
relation claire entre les deux, ni d'opposition ni d'autre sorte (as far as the terms
nāsatya and *dasra* are concerned, nowhere in the Vedic texts does one observe a
clear relation between the two, either of opposition or of another sort)." With
one reservation (see n. 69 below), I agree with Wikander's statement, but his next
step is misleading. Since there is no phraseological evidence in the *Rig-Veda* for
an opposition between *Nåsatyā* and *dasrá,* Wikander attempts to establish a
Rig-Vedic opposition between *Nåsatyā* and *divó nápātā,* and to infer an opposition
between *Nåsatyā* and *dasrá,* given the equation *dasrā = divó nápātā* (see p. 147
above). The problem with this argument is the supposed opposition between
Nåsatyā and *divó nápātā,* which, like the supposed opposition between *Nåsatya*
and *dasrá,* simply does not exist. Wikander argues its existence on the basis of
RV 1.117.11–12, a two-strophe passage containing the name *Nåsatyā* in strophe
11 and the epithet *divó nápātā* in strophe 12. But the term *Aśvínā* is also present
in each strophe, and there are thus two genuine oppositions in the passage
(*Nåsatyā/Aśvínā* and *divó nápātā/Aśvínā*). Each opposition is articulated within
a single strophe, as is required; the argument that terms in different strophes
(*Nåsatyā* and *divó nápātā*) are opposed to each other seems to me to be a pure
figment.

69. There are only four cases of co-occurence, namely 1.3.3, 1.116.10,
1.116.16, and 1.183.4; in none of the four cases is there any opposition between
the terms in the various contexts, and one context (in 1.116.16 the *Nåsatyā . . .
dasrā* are invoked for having restored a mortal's eyes) suggests that the term *dasrā*
was perhaps used to gloss *Nåsatyā:* the full gloss would have been *dasrā bhiṣajā(u),*
"you two miracle-working doctors" (see n. 70 below). One may argue, therefore,
that 1.116.16, far from opposing the terms *Nåsatyā* and *dasrā,* which would have
been untraditional, actually glosses the old name *Nåsatyā* with the phrase "you
miracle-working doctors."

Nā́satyā and dasrā́, far from being opposed, are in fact isofunctional, and that the compound Nasatyadasrau is secondary.

All three strophes contain the phrase gómad dasrā híraṇyavat, consisting of the vocative dasrā and the neuter adjectives gómad, "rich in cattle," and híraṇyavat, "rich in gold." In RV 8.22.17, the collocation gómad dasrā in the third segment of the strophe is clearly opposed to the collocation áśvāvad aśvinā in the first segment:

> ā́ no áśvāvad aśvinā/vartír yāsiṣṭam madhupātamā narā/ gómad dasrā híraṇyavat

> Come to us (ā́ no . . . yāsiṣṭam) along the path (vartír) rich in horses, you Aśvinā; come, you who most enjoy the sacrificial drink, you heroes (madhupātamā narā); come along the path rich in cattle, you dasrā, rich in gold.

RV 1.30.17 contains the same opposition, but the syntax is varied on the "horse" side of this opposition, and the phrase gómad dasrā híraṇyavat is appended loosely to express the "cattle" side:

> áśvināv áśvavātyā/iṣā́ yātam śávīrayā/gómad dasrā híraṇyavat

> Come here (ā́ . . . yātam) with a surpassing wealth (iṣā́ . . . śávīrayā) rich in horses, you Aśvinā; rich in cattle, you dasrā, rich in gold.

RV 1.92.16 follows the pattern of the two previous strophes but omits the adjective áśvāvad altogether:

> aśvinā vartír asmád ā́/gómad dasrā híraṇyavat/arvā́g rátham sámanasā ní yacchatam

> Being of one mind rein in your chariot in this direction (segment 3), along the path toward us, you Aśvinā (segment 1), which is rich in cattle, you dasrā, and rich in gold (segment 2).

By comparing the three texts just examined with the two that were examined earlier (*RV* 2.41.7 and 7.72.1), we may conclude that the terms *Nåsatyå* and *dasrå* are indeed isofunctional. This conclusion, furthermore, provides a final, important piece of evidence for the etymology of *Nåsatyå*. The epithet *dasrå*, as stated, means "miracle-working," and it relates to the twins' function as "magic healers."[70] Since the epithet is isofunctional with the name *Nåsatyå*, there is now every reason to connect this name with the root *nes-*, and with the "miraculous" function of "bringing back to life and light."

The epithet *dasrå* also confirms that the name *Nåsatyå* has to do with "intelligence." The epithet has an exact cognate in Avestan *daŋrō*, which means "clever, skillful," and the Indo-Iranian forms are in turn related to the family of Greek *daênai*, "to learn." Sanskrit *dasrá* must also have implied "intelligence,"[71] and this quality, which is so essential to the epic Sahadeva, is thus confirmed for his Vedic prototype as well.

It is at least highly probable that the name *Nåsatyå*, as derived from the root *nes-*, implied "intelligence" directly. The name is thus a precious comparison for Greek *nóos*, indicating that the root *nes-* had to do with "intelligence" already in Indo-European.[72]

70. Note the collocation *dasrā bhiṣajā(u)*, "miracle-working physicians," in *RV* 1.116.16 and 8.86.1.

71. Note the collocation *dasra mantumaḥ*, "you miracle-working wise one," which is twice applied to the god Pūṣan: *RV* 1.42.5 and 6.56.4; for the Indo-Iranian origins of this collocation, see R. Schmitt, *Dichtung und Dichtersprache in indogermanischer Zeit* (chap. 2, n. 28), pp. 160–61, on Avestan *dangrā mantū*, "by wise resolution," in *Yasna* 46.17.

72. I will simply note here a comparison between Vedic *Nåsatyå* and Greek *Néstōr*, which I intend to pursue in a separate study. The comparison also involves Nestor's regular Homeric epithet *hippóta*, "the horseman," which corresponds to the twins' second name, *Aśvínā*. The double comparison between *hippóta Néstōr* and the *Nåsatyå/Aśvínā* raises the question of whether Nestor's origins have to do with Indo-European twin mythology. Has the Greek Nestor, like the Avestan *Nåŋhaiθya*, become separated from a twin brother? (For *Nåŋhaiθya*, see n. 22 above and end note 4.)

7 *Epilogue*

NOW THAT A CONNECTION has been established between Greek
nóos and the Indo-European root *nes-*, it will be interesting to
consider a few further instances in Greek tradition where the
notion of "mind" suggests a latent connection with the notion
of "return." I shall begin with two Homeric episodes which have
not figured in the discussion so far—the ransom of Hector in
Iliad 24 and the night raid in *Iliad* 10.

It is well recognized that Priam's ransom of Hector in *Iliad* 24
is represented as a journey to the underworld and a consequent
"return to life." [1] Priam is led into and back from this underworld
by Hermes, who takes with him for this twofold mission his
"ambivalent" staff, which can both put mortals to sleep and
reawaken them. [2] The place where Hermes meets Priam, furthermore, is the tomb of Ilus, and the time of day is sunset (XXIV
350 ff.); thus Priam and the psychopomp Hermes seem to follow
the setting sun as they venture into the "oltretomba." When
Priam returns with the body of Hector, on the other hand, he
reaches the tomb of Ilus just as the sun is rising, and at this point
Hermes leaves him (XXIV 694 ff.).

The ransom of Hector is thus a journey into "darkness and
death" and a "return to life and light." In such a context it would

---

1. As Priam sets forth, his people follow him (XXIV 328):

πόλλ' ὀλοφυρόμενοι ὡς εἰ θάνατόνδε κιόντα.
Lamenting for him much, as if he were going to death.

2. XXIV 343 ff.; see chap. 3, sect. 4 above for the same lines in connection with
Hermes' mission to free Odysseus from Calypso.

be natural to find the root *nes-*, and this is in fact the case. The root is present in the word *nóos*, which is used repeatedly in the passage describing the initial encounter between Priam and Hermes. From a traditional standpoint, the entrance into the underworld would have been characterized by a loss of *nóos*, and the return to life by a regaining of *nóos*. Both of these phases, however, seem to have been compressed within the initial encounter; at first Priam and his charioteer, surprised by Hermes' approach, feel threatened, but when they realize that Hermes intends no harm, this feeling gives way to a sense of "salvation."

In the space of twenty-odd lines the word *nóos* occurs four times. When the charioteer notices Hermes lurking nearby, he says to Priam (354):

> φράζεο, Δαρδανίδη· φραδέος νόου ἔργα τέτυκται
>
> Observe, descendant of Dardanus; this is a matter for an observant *mind*.

Priam, realizing that "real" death may be close at hand, is described as follows (358):

> . . . σὺν δέ γέροντι νόος χύτο, δείδιε δ' αἰνῶς.
>
> The *mind* of the old man collapsed, and he feared terribly.

In this line one sees Priam's initial loss of *nóos*. When Hermes reveals his friendly intentions, he reinforces the idea that to venture forth without an adequate guide will involve a loss of *nóos*; so, from a traditional standpoint, one may interpret his question to Priam (366–67):

> τῶν εἴ τίς σε ἴδοιτο θοὴν διὰ νύκτα μέλαιναν
> τοσσάδ' ὀνείατ' ἄγοντα, τίς ἂν δή τοι νόος εἴη;
>
> If someone (of the Greeks) should see you bringing so many goods through the swift black night, what *mind* would you have then?

When Priam realizes that Hermes will guide him to "salvation," he himself uses the word *nóos*, this time in a compliment to his guide (374ff.):

ἀλλ' ἔτι τις καὶ ἐμεῖο θεῶν ὑπερέσχεθε χεῖρα,
ὅς μοι τοιόνδ᾽ ἧκεν ὁδοιπόρον ἀντιβολῆσαι,
αἴσιον, οἷος δὴ σὺ δέμας καὶ εἶδος ἀγητός,
πέπνυσαί τε νόῳ.

But some god was still holding his protective hand over me when he sent to meet me a courteous guide like you, who are marvelous in build and appearance and prudent in your *mind*.

The frequency and the nature of the use of the word *nóos* can hardly be accidental in this episode.

A second famous night-adventure in Homer is found in *Iliad* 10, the "Doloneia," or "Nuktegersia." In this episode Diomedes and Odysseus volunteer to venture into the Trojan camp by night to spy on their enemies and learn their plans. They do not do this, however, but instead slay the Thracian king Rhesus in his sleep and drive off his horses. This outcome is highly interesting in view of the fact that Rhesus, according to tradition, was a cave *daimon* in his native Thrace.[3] When Diomedes and Odysseus drive off his horses, therefore, one is tempted to think of the Cyclops, his cave, and the animals Odysseus "frees." Furthermore, when Diomedes and Odysseus, toward dawn, return with their capture, Nestor, in greeting them, says that their new white horses "are terribly like the rays of the sun" (547):

αἰνῶς ἀκτίνεσσιν ἐοικότες ἠελίοιο.

Another detail worth mentioning is the importance given to "returning" in this adventure. In lines 281–82, Odysseus prays to Athena for a glorious return to the Achaean ships, and in line

---

3. Cf. Euripides, *Rhesus* 962ff.

509 Athena herself appears to "remind" Diomedes of his "return," with the words *nóstou dè mnêsai*.[4]

Given this overall context, it becomes significant that the words *nóos* and *noéō* play a prominent part in the passage in which Diomedes first volunteers for the adventure. After offering himself, he asks for a companion, giving the following explanation for his request (224 ff.):

σύν τε δύ᾽ ἐρχομένω, καί τε πρὸ ὃ τοῦ ἐνόησεν
ὅππως κέρδος ἔῃ· μοῦνος δ᾽ εἴ πέρ τε νοήσῃ
ἀλλά τέ οἱ βράσσων τε νόος, λεπτὴ δέ τε μῆτις.

When two go together one *looks* before the other to see what is best; but a man by himself, even if he *perceive closely*, has less *mind* in him than two, and his wits have less weight.

Diomedes then chooses Odysseus as his companion; in commenting on the value of Odysseus's intelligence, Diomedes provides us with a collocation of the verbs *nostéō* and *noéō* (246–47):

τούτου γ᾽ ἑσπομένοιο καὶ ἐκ πυρὸς αἰθομένοιο
ἄμφω νοστήσαιμεν, ἐπεὶ περίοιδε νοῆσαι.

If this man followed me we would both *return* even from blazing fire, for he knows best how to *use his mind*.

In this episode once again, the choice of language must have something to do with a traditional connection between the words *nóos* and *néomai*.

With this discussion of *Iliad* 10 and 24 we may now leave Homer, in order to consider briefly how the same etymological connection may have survived even after Homer's time. A natural place to begin is with the cults to Helios; unfortunately, however, these cults are for the most part as prehistoric as the connection

---

4. For the significance of this expression, see chap. 3, sect. 1 above.

to be investigated. Nevertheless, one such cult survived on the island of Rhodes, and, although little is known about it, a legend has been preserved by Pindar which concerns the origins of the special honor paid to Helios on this island. Pindar gives the legend in *Olympian* 7. He says that the legend is old (ll. 54–55), and the main points of his account are as follows. When Zeus and the other gods first divided the earth among themselves, Helios, being absent, did not receive a lot. But when Zeus offered to re-apportion the earth, Helios refused, for he had seen an island—Rhodes—rising out of the sea, and he wanted this to be his share. Thus Helios obtained Rhodes, made love to her, and sired seven sons, one of whom was to sire, in turn, the eponymous heroes of the three Rhodian cities.

With this hierarchy of generations, the legend indicates its own antiquity. What is significant for our purposes is that the word *nóēma*, "mind," appears in connection with the oldest phase, the seven sons of Helios himself. Pindar says that these seven sons "inherited" from Helios "the wisest *noēmata* among former men." The passage (ll. 71 ff.) reads as follows:

> ἔνθα 'Ρόδῳ ποτὲ μειχθεὶς τέκεν
> ἑπτὰ σοφώτατα *νοήματ'* ἐπὶ προτέρων ἀν-
>   δρῶν *παραδεξαμένους*
> παῖδας.

There (Helios) once made love to the nymph Rhodes and fathered seven sons who *inherited* from him the wisest *minds* among former men.

Through the derivative form *nóēma*, the word *nóos* is thus indirectly attested in the context of a Greek cult of the sun. It also seems possible to read the meaning "return to light" of the root *nes-* into Pindar's account. The very emergence of Rhodes from the sea is described as a "return from darkness to light": at first the island lay "hidden in the depths" (*en bénthesin . . . kekrúphthai*, 1.57), and it was then "sent into the radiant ether" (*phaennòn es aithéra . . . pemphtheîsan*, 1. 67). This "return to light" provides the context in which to understand the reputation for *nóos* of the island's first children.

Such is the scanty—but significant—evidence provided by Greek sun worship, which for the most part was quicker to die than the epic tradition. Where the influence of both, insofar as *nóos* is concerned, might be expected to have survived is in the Greek philosophical tradition. It would require another study, of another kind, to investigate the importance of sun symbolism in Greek philosophical thought. Here, therefore, I wish to draw attention to only two contexts where a precise connection between *nóos* and *néomai*, both signifying "return to life and light," is suggested.

The first is the famous and mysterious "proem" of Parmenides, which describes the philosopher's own "return to light." Two influences on this proem are distinctly noticeable: that of Greek epic, especially the *Odyssey*,[5] and that of sun mythology. In the opening lines Parmenides speaks of the road (*hodós*) he has travelled; this road "carries the wise man through all cities" (l. 3):

... ἣ κατὰ πάντ' ἄστη φέρει εἰδότα φῶτα.

This line has a clear relation to the third line of the *Odyssey*:[6]

πολλῶν δ' ἀνθρώπων ἴδεν ἄστεα καὶ νόον ἔγνω.

He saw the cities of many men and learned their minds.

The same line, however, also has to do with sun mythology, to judge from the following Orphic fragment:[7]

5. See E. Havelock, "Parmenides and Odysseus," *Harvard Studies in Classical Philology* 63 (1958): 133ff. (discussed in end note 5; cf. also n. 9 below).
6. So also Havelock, p. 136: "The 'man who knows' who is conveyed on a 'famous journey' 'through all towns' is that Odysseus who is introduced at the opening of the *Odyssey*."
7. Diels-Kranz. 1B 21.3.

Ἥλιε Πῦρ, διὰ πάντ' ἄστη νίσεαι.

Helios, Fire, you go through all cities.

More significant is the extent to which sun symbolism is involved in the rest of the proem. The journey "to light" begins at the "gates of the paths of day and night" (l. 11):[8]

ἔνθα πύλαι Νυκτός τε καὶ Ἤματός εἰσι κελεύθων.

The goddesses who conduct the philosopher from these gates along his subsequent road are the "daughters of the Sun" (ll. 8 ff.):

ὅτε σπερχοίατο πέμπειν
Ἡλιάδες κοῦραι, προλιποῦσαι δώματα Νυκτός,
εἰς φάος, ὠσάμεναι κράτων ἄπο χερσὶ καλύπτρας.

. . . when the *daughters of Helios* hastened to convey (me) into the light, leaving the house of Night, and pushing the veils from their heads.

In view of this sun symbolism, it is significant that the verb used to designate the philosopher's "journey to light" is *néomai,* a verb which appears nowhere else in the pre-Socratic corpus. At the gates of day and night the philosopher is greeted by the goddess *Díkē,* "Justice," who says that "it is not an evil destiny that sends you forth to *return* along this road which lies apart from the beaten track of men" (ll. 26–27):

χαῖρ', ἐπεὶ οὔτι σε μοῖρα κακὴ προὔπεμπε *νέεσθαι*
τήνδ' ὁδόν (ἡ γὰρ ἀπ' ἀνθρώπων ἐκτὸς πάτου ἐστίν).

The word *nóos* does not occur in the proem, but since the "return" is that of a philosopher, this hardly matters. Attention may be drawn to Parmenides' use of the word "road" throughout the proem, because in subsequent fragments *hodós* is collocated

8. See pp. 60ff. above for the discussion of this line in relation to the Laestrygonian adventure in the *Odyssey.*

with both the verb *noéō* and the noun *nóēma*. Fragment 2 begins
as follows:

> εἰ δ' ἄγ' ἐγὼν ἐρέω, κόμισαι δὲ σὺ μῦθον ἀκούσας,
> αἵπερ ὁδοὶ μοῦναι διζήσιός εἰσι *νοῆσαι*
>
> Come now and I will tell you—and you must listen and take
> my word—what are the only *roads* of enquiry that exist for
> *thinking*,

and fragment 7 as follows:

> οὐ γὰρ μήποτε τοῦτο δαμῇ εἶναι μὴ ἐόντα·
> ἀλλὰ σὺ τῆσδ' ἀφ' ὁδοῦ διζήσιος εἶργε *νόημα*.
>
> For this will never win out, that things which are not are; but
> you must restrain your *mind* from this *road* of enquiry.

There could be no clearer testimony for the importance of sun
symbolism in understanding the relationship between *nóos* and
néomai than the proem of Parmenides. While Parmenides, as a
philosopher, is part of the "rationalization" of this symbolism,
he still plainly reveals the primitive source of the word for the
rational faculty itself.[9]

A second famous "return to light" in Greek philosophy is
provided by Plato's *Republic,* specifically, in the myth of the cave.
What happens in this myth is well known; we are asked to imagine
the joy of a man, previously chained to the wall of a cave where
he could see only shadows cast in firelight, when he emerges from
the cave and contemplates the light of the sun. His emergence is
like a return from death. Plato does not say this explicitly, but he
does say that the man involved would rather "be the serf of a poor

---

9. E. Havelock (n. 5), pp. 138–40, has argued that the sun symbolism in
Parmenides is a direct borrowing, with modifications, from the *Odyssey*; while
I do not doubt Parmenides' use of literary reminiscence, I also believe that his sun
symbolism has a deeper origin than this; see end note 5 for discussion.

man on earth" than return to the cave. This is a direct quotation of Achilles' statement to Odysseus in the underworld, which concludes, however, "than rule over all the dead." Since it is thus equated with death, Plato's cave cannot help but remind us of—among others—the cave of the Cyclops.[10]

The association with death becomes very significant in understanding the role of *nóos* in Plato's myth. The ascent from the cave to the light of the sun is, in fact, a metaphor for the intellectual ascent from the realm of *doxastá*, "matters of opinion," to the realm of *noētá*, "intelligible matters." This is clear from Socrates' statement in *Republic* 7.517b:

> τὴν δὲ ἄνω ἀνάβασιν καὶ θέαν
> τῶν ἄνω τὴν εἰς τὸν νοητὸν τόπον τῆς ψυχῆς ἄνοδον τιθεὶς
> οὐχ ἁμαρτήσει τῆς γ᾽ ἐμῆς ἐλπίδος
>
> And if you assume that the ascent and the contemplation of the things above is the soul's ascension to the intelligible region, you will not miss my surmise.

The word *ánodos*, "ascent," strongly reinforces the idea that the "ascent" from the cave is a "return from death";[11] the fact that the *ánodos* is *eis tòn noētòn tópon*, "to the intelligible region," shows plainly that the "return from death" is an acquiring of *nóos*.

Plato must have drawn on authentic tradition in connecting *nóos* with the return from the cave. But it is worth noticing the understated way in which Socrates permits the equation: *oukh hamartḗsei tês g᾽ emês elpídos*, "you will not miss my surmise." This suggests to me that the equation may in some sense be real, but it also draws attention to the fact that the myth of the cave was introduced only as a comparison to the ascent of the spirit.

10. Note also that those in the cave can only see *skiaí*, "shadows," and that this word suggests the "shades" of the underworld.
11. Cf. the *ánodos* of Persephone.

The gap between comparison and actual equation, which Plato to some extent blurs, nevertheless remains; I believe this gap is the gap between the classical Greek *noûs* and its primitive origins.

Notes

As argued in chapter 2, section 1, the context of the form *neîai* in *xi* 114—a prophecy among the dead—indicates that this form originally meant "you will return from death." If the form's original meaning is in fact dependent upon the context, then the context itself must be highly traditional. Since the Nekyia as a whole has often been judged to be a late addition to the *Odyssey,* further comment is required.

Denys Page, *The Homeric Odyssey* (Oxford, 1955), pp. 21 ff., follows the analyst tradition in arguing that the Nekyia was once a separate poem which was later inserted into the *Odyssey.* I do not wish to go into the merits of this argument, but only to point out that Page considers the role of Teiresias to have been an essential part of an original Nekyia (pp. 24 ff., 40). With this I would agree, but the important question then becomes what the original role of Teiresias was. Page's argument seems to me to be weak at this point. He refers to the "dismal science of necromancy" (p. 24) as practiced by the Greeks, especially in Teiresias's native Boeotia, but his explanation of Teiresias's original role has little to do with this "dismal science," at least in any real sense. He thinks that Teiresias merely served as a link between Odysseus and his dead acquaintances, whom he had come to the underworld to visit: "For if he [Teiresias] is summoned in the customary manner by blood-sacrifice, will not the feeble ghosts of the Homeric Underworld come to drink the blood, and then will they not also revive and speak?"

This explanation seems very dubious to me. Surely the only role for a prophet is to prophesy, and this must be what Teiresias always did in the Nekyia. But the substance of his prophecy need not have remained unchanged. Here another of Page's arguments, that many details in the Nekyia have secondarily been made to fit the context of the *Odyssey,* is to the point. The prophecy of

Teiresias may well have been adapted to take account of what occurs after *Odyssey* 11—namely, the slaughter of the cattle of Helios. My only claim is that the line with *neîai* formed part of an original *Nekuomanteía* ("Oracle from the Dead"), and that the original context of the line would have made it clear that *neîai* referred to "returning from death." Homer, in adapting the prophecy, has made *neîai* mean "you will return home"; but by leaving the word in the mouth of Teiresias, in the underworld, he has still allowed us to see its original meaning.

This discussion should also make it clear why Homer has Circe repeat and expand the prophecy of Teiresias (including the line with *neîai, xii* 141); Circe has more to do with the events to follow than Teiresias does, at least as far as the cattle of Helios are concerned, for she is herself the daughter of Helios.

NOTE 2

One is tempted to speculate about the peculiar word *boulūtónde* which occurs twice in Homer, in the same formulaic line (*ix* 58 = xvi 779: see chap. 3 n. 38): *êmos d' ēélios metenís(s)eto boulūtónde*, "but when the sun began to go *boulūtónde*." The line refers to the sun's setting, and the word *boulūtónde* has traditionally been taken to mean "to [the time for] the unyoking of oxen," with a verbal adjective from *lúō*, "loosen," forming the second part of the compound. But the long vowel quantity is surprising; elsewhere in Greek only *lŭtós*, with the expected short vowel, is found. The comparison with Latin *soluo, solūtus* does not avail, since the latter is the result of vowel lengthening before an accented secondary suffix, as discussed by J. Kuryłowicz, *L' apophonie en indo-européen* (1956), pp. 125–26. It is also odd that the particle *-de* should have to express "to the time of." Finally, if the word is old, as the compound formation with verbal adjective suggests, then it is odd that it does not allow the normal dactylic rhythm in the fifth foot of the hexameter.

These peculiarities are removed by supposing a different underlying form, with a verbal adjective from *loúō*, "bathe," as the second element. One might reconstruct either **boulowetónde* or *boulewotónde* (the latter in accord with the vocalism of Mycenean *lewotreios,* "for bathing"). Both forms would have contracted to give long close *o,* which one must then suppose was changed to long *u* as the result of reinterpretation.

What would the meaning be? I suggest that the word once referred to the cattle of the sun, whose coming and going accompanied sunrise and sunset. The sun is often said to return to the streams of Oceanus, and the stars are specifically said to set in the *loetrà Ōkeanoîo,* "baths of Oceanus" (cf. *v* 275); in v 6 the expression *lelouménos Ōkeanoîo,* "bathed in Oceanus," is used of the autumn star to which Diomedes is compared for his brilliance.

Admittedly, however, the idea of a "cattle-bathing" is odd, and one would like to see other examples. There is an overt example in Euripides' *Iphigenia among the Taurians,* where cowherds are bathing cattle in the sea when they capture Orestes and Pylades; cf. line 255, where the episode is reported:

βοῦς ἤλθομεν νίψοντες ἐναλίᾳ δρόσῳ.

We had come to bathe our cattle in the water of the sea.

There may also be a latent example in the following lines from the Hymn to Hermes (115–16):

ὄφρα δὲ πῦρ ἀνέκαιε βίη κλυτοῦ Ἡφαίστοιο,
τόφρα δ᾽ ὑποβρύχιας ἕλικας βοῦς ἕλκε θύραζε.

While the force of famed Hephaestus was kindling the fire (Hermes) dragged the curve-horned *hupobrúkhias* cattle outside.

Elsewhere in Greek (Herodotus, Plato, etc.), the adjective *hupobrúkhios* always means "underwater." Particular attention is drawn to the following lines from Homeric Hymn 33, to the Dioscuri, in which distressed sailors call on the two *sōtêras . . . anthrṓpōn . . . neôn te,* "saviors of men and ships" (ll. 6–7). The sailors are represented as sacrificing white sheep on the ship's stern, which the wind and waves have meanwhile "submerged" (11–12): *tḕn d᾽ ánemós te mégas kaì kûma thalássēs/thêkan hupobrukhíēn.* At this point the Dioscuri come to the rescue.

Two things are important in this passage. First, the context is a "rescue," and secondly, the word *hupobrukhíēn* in line 12 occupies the same metrical slot as *hupobrukhías* in the Hymn to Hermes. One also notices the context and the metrical position of the adverbial form *hupóbrukha* in v 319, which describes Odysseus as he struggles to "return" (cf. *nóstou* in v 344) to Phaeacia:

τὸν δ' ἄρ' ὑπόβρυχα θῆκε πολὺν χρόνον, οὐδ' ἐδυνάσθη
αἶψα μάλ' ἀνσχεθέειν μεγάλου ὑπὸ κύματος ὁρμῆς.

It submerged him for a long time, and he was unable to reach the surface quickly because of the rush of the great wave.

The word *hupobrŭkhías*, as applied to the cattle of Hermes, has been connected with the verb *brūkháomai*, "bellow," but the vowel quantity is wrong for this, unless the reading is emended to yield an unattested *hupobrŭkhous*, "softly bellowing."

But the text may be defended by making certain assumptions about the underlying myth. Since the stolen cattle belong to Apollo, they may once have been related to the cattle of Helios. The fact that Hermes drives the cattle westward to a hiding place near Pylos points to such a relation. Hence one wonders whether in an older version of the myth Hermes did not drive the cattle *boulūtónde* in the sense suggested above. Since Hermes not only conceals the cattle but also brings them back, perhaps the latter action was originally described by the words *hupobrukhías . . . boûs hélke thúraze*, "he dragged the submerged cows outside." In the present version of the story the discovery of fire accompanies the action described by these words; the discovery of fire fits well with a latent "sunrise" motif.

NOTE 3

It is striking in how many points Homer's description of Calypso resembles Hesiod's description of Styx (*Theogony* 775ff.). Both goddesses live apart from the other gods; compare the reference to Calypso in v 80: *apóprothi dōmata naíei*, "she inhabits a dwelling far away," with the reference to Styx in *Theogony* 777: *nósphin dè theōn klutà dōmata naíei*, "she inhabits her famed dwelling apart from the gods." Both goddesses are visited only rarely by the messengers of the gods. In the case of Styx, it is Iris who seldom comes (*Theogony* 780–81):

παῦρα δὲ Θαύμαντος θυγάτηρ πόδας ὠκέα Ἴρις
ἀγγελίην πωλεῖται ἐπ᾽ εὐρέα νῶτα θαλάσσης.

Swift-footed Iris, the daughter of Thaumas, seldom comes with a message over the wide back of the sea.

In the case of Calypso, Hermes is the infrequent visitor, as her own greeting to him makes clear (*v* 87–88):

τίπτε μοι, Ἑρμεία χρυσόρραπι, εἰλήλουθας
αἰδοῖός τε φίλος τε; πάρος γε μὲν οὔ τι θαμίζεις.

Hermes of the golden staff, honored and dear that you are, why have you come? Before now you have not been a frequent visitor.

Both goddesses are reached by crossing the sea; compare *Theogony* 781, with reference to the rare visits of Iris, with *v* 50ff., where Hermes flies across the sea as if he were a bird. Both goddesses live in caves; this is well known in the case of Calypso, and seems to be true of Styx as well—her house is described in *Theogony* 778 as *makrêisin pétrēisi katērephé'*, "covered over by great rocks." There is a further, more indirect comparison in the fact that the house of Styx is surrounded by columns which stretch to the sky (*Theogony* 778–79):

ἀμφὶ δὲ πάντη
κίοσιν ἀργυρέοισι πρὸς οὐρανὸν ἐστήρικται.

All the way round it is supported by silver columns reaching to the sky.

As M. L. West, *Hesiod: Theogony* (Oxford, 1966), p. 372, has pointed out, Hesiod probably imagines these columns to be at the edge of the world, where the river Styx is said to be connected with the river Oceanus (*Theogony* 789); West goes on to conjecture that the columns may have something to do with the common notion of pillars which support the sky, and this, I believe, is the case. If so, the columns associated with Styx bring to mind the titan Atlas, who also is located at the edge of the world, where he supports the sky (*Theogony* 517ff.). This apparent relationship between Styx and Atlas in Hesiod is paralleled by an explicit relationship between Calypso and Atlas in Homer—she is his daughter. One wonders whether it is co-incidence that Homer, when he calls Calypso the daughter of Atlas, also mentions the columns of the latter (*i* 52ff.):

Ἄτλαντος θυγάτηρ ὀλοόφρονος, ὅς τε θαλάσσης
πάσης βένθεα οἶδεν, ἔχει δέ τε κίονας αὐτὸς
μακράς, αἳ γαῖάν τε καὶ οὐρανὸν ἀμφὶς ἔχουσι.

The daughter of malevolent Atlas, who knows the depths of the entire sea, and himself holds the great columns which keep heaven and earth apart.

To return to more overt parallels, both goddesses detain exiled beings in their domains; Styx detains gods who have forsworn their oaths (*Theogony* 793ff.) and Calypso detains Odysseus. When Hermes comes to set Odysseus free, he brings his staff with which he "awakens the sleeping" (cf. chap. 3, sect. 4, for discussion); with this should be compared the "evil sleep" which, according to *Theogony* 798, "covers" a god who has forsworn himself: *kakòn dé he kôma kalúptei*. The verb *kalúptei*, "covers," in this context suggests a very real connection with *Kalupsó* and the virtual sleep from which Odysseus must be awakened. Still more suggestive is the epithet *ōgúgion*, "primeval," which Hesiod uses of the water of the Styx in *Theogony* 805–06: *toîon ár' hórkon éthento theoì Stugòs áphthiton húdōr/ōgúgion*, "such an oath did the gods make of the undying, primeval water of the Styx." For *Ōgugíē* is the name (or, more probably, epithet) which Homer gives to Calypso's island.

Calypso offers to make Odysseus immortal (cf. *v* 135–36); in connection with this it is worth noting that the water of the Styx was thought to be an elixir of life, as in the story of the immersion of Achilles (cf. West, *Hesiod*, p. 378, for references to this story).

On the basis of these correspondences it may be suggested that the figure of Calypso, who exists solely for the story of the *Odyssey*, was created by epic tradition on the model of the goddess Styx. The fact that Hesiod makes both of them Oceanids, and therefore sisters (cf. *Theogony* 359 and 361), indicates that he saw a certain kinship between the two. Calypso is, of course, no carbon copy of Styx (note, for example, that a god would "delight" in Calypso's pleasant surroundings, according to *v* 73–74, and contrast this with the gods' experience in Styx's domain according to Hesiod). Calypso is at most a rather free imitation of Styx; it is somehow agreeable, even though highly speculative, to imagine that Homer still knew of Calypso's Stygian origins when he had her swear by the water of the Styx not to harm Odysseus (*v* 185 ff.).

NOTE 4

Chapter 6, section 4, above, presents the Indic evidence which establishes a correlation between the two Vedic names, *Nǎsatyā* and *Aśvínā*, and the two epic twins, Sahadeva and Nakula, respectively; the same section criticizes Wikander's arguments in favor of a partially different conclusion, namely, that the name *Nǎsatyā*, as well as *Aśvínā*, is to be correlated with the "horseman" Nakula. Still to be discussed is Wikander's use of Iranian evidence, having to do with the demon *Nǎŋhaiθya* (cf. chap. 6, n. 22), to support his conclusion.

Wikander contends that *Nǎŋhaiθya* (whom he considers the descendant of the Indo-Iranian "horseman" twin) was demonized precisely because of his association with the horse ("Nakula et Sahadeva," pp. 81 and 85); he argues further that the "cattleman" twin has also survived in Iranian in the form of Ātar, the fire god and son of Ahura Mazdāh (pp. 85–96). This second argument is judged by Ward, "The Separate Functions of the Indo-European Divine Twins" (chap. 6, n. 50), p. 195, to be "not as convincing" as the remainder of Wikander's study. I would now add that Wikander's interpretation of *Nǎŋhaiθya* is also to be rejected.

While it is true that the Zoroastrian pandaemonium absorbed mainly old "second function" gods (cognate with the war god *Indra* is the Avestan demon *Indara*), another explanation must be sought for the demonization of *Nǎŋhaiθya*. I suggest that the key to the status of this figure is the fact that he has become separated from his twin brother. When twins remain together, they often become proverbial for undying friendship; this is the case for the Greek Dioscuri, as is suggested, for example, by Theognis 1087ff.:

> Κάστορ καὶ Πολύδευκες, οἳ ἐν Λακεδαίμονι δίῃ
> ναίετ᾽ ἐπ᾽ Εὐρώτᾳ καλλιρόῳ ποταμῷ,
> εἴ ποτε βουλεύσαιμι φίλῳ κακόν, αὐτὸς ἔχοιμι·
> εἰ δέ τι κεῖνος ἐμοί, δὶς τόσον αὐτὸς ἔχοι.

O Castor and Polydeuces, who dwell in shining Lacedaemon by the beautifully flowing Eurotas river, if ever I should devise evil against a *friend*, may I get that evil myself; if my friend, on the other hand, should devise some evil against me, may he get twice as much himself.

When twins abandon one another, on the other hand, they do so out of hositility; see Ward, *The Divine Twins* (chap. 6, n. 36), pp. 6–7, who cites the examples of the biblical Jacob and Esau, the Greek Acrisius and Proetus, and the Roman Romulus and Remus. Now the little that is known above *Nåŋhaiθya* characterizes him precisely as a cause of hostility between superiors and inferiors. According to the Persian source which is translated by E. E. K. Antia, *Cama Memorial Volume* (Bombay, 1900), p. 163, and is also quoted by G. Dumézil, *Naissance d'archanges* (Paris, 1945), p. 167, *Nåŋhaiθya* creates discord between men and God, parents and children, teachers and pupils, husbands and wives, masters and servants. This demonic function may well derive from a tradition that *Nåŋhaiθya* quarreled with and abandoned his twin brother.

NOTE 5

Eric Havelock, ''Parmenides and Odysseus'' (chap. 7, n. 5), pp. 138–40, has pointed out several striking parallels between Parmenides and the *Odyssey*. Parmenides' frequent use of the noun *dízēsis* and of the verb *dízēmai* in relation to his philosophic ''quest,'' for example, is illuminated by the line in which Teiresias correctly identifies Odysseus's reason for coming to the underworld (*xi* 100):

> νόστον δίζηαι μελιηδέα, φαίδιμ᾽ Ὀδυσσεῦ

You are striving for (*dízēai*) a honey-sweet homecoming, shining Odysseus,

and by a similar line in the account of himself which Odysseus gives to Penelope (*xxiii* 253):

νόστον ἑταίροισιν διζήμενος ἠδ' ἐμοὶ αὐτῷ

Striving for (*dizếmenos*) a homecoming for my companions and myself.

A fascinating parallel is that between Odysseus's command to his steersman to "ward off the ship" from both Scylla and Charybdis (*ěerge nễa* in *xii* 219–20) and Parmenides' admonition in Frag. 6.3–4:

πρώτης γάρ σ' ἀφ' ὁδοῦ ταύτης διζήσιος ‹εἴργω›,
αὐτὰρ ἔπειτ' ἀπὸ τῆς . . .

First I ward you off (*eírgō*) from this road of enquiry, but then also from this one . . .

and his command in Frag. 7.2–3:

ἀλλὰ σὺ τῆσδ' ἀφ' ὁδοῦ διζήσιος *εἶργε* νόημα
μηδέ σ' ἔθος πολύπειρον ὁδὸν κατὰ τήνδε βιάσθω . . .

But ward off (*eírge*) your mind (*nóēma*) from this road of enquiry, and do not let custom, born of much experience, force you along this road. . . .

Havelock nicely comments (p. 138) that "the object to be controlled is no longer a ship but a mental process," and draws attention to Frag. 6.5–6, where there is a more concrete instance of the ship metaphor:

πλάττονται δίκρανοι· ἀμηχανίη γὰρ ἐν αὐτῶν
στήθεσιν ἰθύνει πλακτὸν νόον· οἱ δὲ φοροῦνται . . .

They wander about two-headed; for helplessness *steers the wandering mind* (*nóos*) in their breast; they are carried along. . . .

Where I would like to modify Havelock's argument is in the explanation for the parallels he has discovered. The author (p.

139) notes that Odysseus, in voyaging to Laestrygonia, Aeaea, and Thrinacia, has gone "beyond normal human latitudes," and concludes that in the imagination of Parmenides, whose "own journey is also an excursion beyond the bounds of accepted experience," these adventures "are all correctly remembered as allegories of the world's end, a mysterious bourne far off the beaten track, a region of mystery and peril but also of revelation." The author, in other words, regards his discoveries as purely a matter of literary reminiscence; I find this too narrow. My point is illustrated by a lapse on Havelock's part, who, in mentioning the Laestrygonians, renders *x* 86:

ἐγγὺς γὰρ νυκτός τε καὶ ἤματός εἰσι κέλευθοι

as "the gates of the paths of day and night." The author has inadvertently translated Parmenides, Frag. 1.11:

ἔνθα πύλαι Νυκτός τε καὶ Ἤματός εἰσι κελεύθων,

and has thus overlooked the crucial difference between the two lines in question. I have argued earlier that Parmenides, far from being the imitator in this case, has preserved the genuine form of a line which Homer has modified (see p. 60 above). I have further tried to show that Hesiod, in the *Theogony,* was dealing independently with the same mythic material as Homer and Parmenides (see pp. 60–63 above); this at once suggests that more is involved in Parmenides than particular literary reminiscences.

I need not belabor my major argument: that Parmenides has preserved in his proem another, more important, element which is likewise older than Homer—namely, the connection between *nóos* and *néomai.* Havelock is on the right track when he explains "the central affinity which Parmenides feels for his prototype" (p. 139) in terms of Odysseus's motivation for going to the underworld, namely, "to gain knowledge from Teiresias" (the phrase *prìn Teiresíao puthésthai* is formulaic, occurring in *x* 537, and *xi* 50 and 89). But Parmenides has done more than recognize and remember "a slight overtone of allegory" in the *Odyssey*. For what appears as such in Homer actually reflects a deep and important etymological connection, and when Parmenides recaptures this connection so fully, we cannot believe that he has been entirely dependent on Homer.

My adjustment of other points in Havelock's study follows the same lines. There is certainly a parallel between Parmenides' view of the mental helplessness of the "tribes uncounted and uncritical" (Frag. 6.7):

κωφοὶ ὁμῶς τυφλοί τε τεθηπότες ἄκριτα φῦλα

Deaf and blind at once, dazed, uncounted [uncritical] tribes,

and the foolish companions of Odysseus, as well as the ghosts in Hades whom these companions soon join. But the notion of an "amorphous mass of common men" from whom an "elite" is distinguished is basic both to the *Odyssey* and to the development of a philosophic tradition; and in both cases, as I have argued earlier, sun mythology seems largely responsible for this notion (see pp. 20–23 on the *Odyssey* and pp. 31–33 on the Greek philosophic tradition). Given this, I cannot believe with Havelock (p. 140) that Parmenides, in conceiving of his *Hēliádes,* has seized upon the daughers of Helios who guard their father's cattle in the *Odyssey,* and "converted (them) from herdsmen into outriders." The entire situation in Parmenides' proem speaks too strongly for the independent influence of sun mythology.

Havelock draws particular attention to the cattle of Helios, which are not born and do not die (*xii* 130–31):

γόνος δ᾽ οὐ γίγνεται αὐτῶν
οὐδέ ποτε φθινύθουσι

They do not have any birthgiving, and they never die,

and suggests that this detail, more than anything else, led Parmenides to "link the daughters of the sun with the marvels of a mental journey which had taken the traveller into an absolute, where there is no coming to be and no passing away"; the author here refers to the cornerstone of Parmenides' thought, which is articulated in Frag. 8.21 by the words:

τὼς γένεσις μὲν ἀπέσβεσται καὶ ἄπυστος ὄλεθρος

So coming into being is extinguished and perishing is unimaginable.

Once again Havelock's observation seems to me to be full of insight, but once again I prefer to reverse the argument. Is it because Parmenides' thought excludes "coming to be" and "passing away" that he introduces, by way of literary reminiscence, the daughters of the sun? Or is it, rather, that the tradition of sun mythology has influenced his thought? In Parmenides' realm of Truth, there is only Being; Non-Being is impossible, and "perishing is unimaginable" (*ápustos ólethros*). Only in the realm of Opinion does there seem to be such a thing as Non-Being. I suggest that these distinctions are very similar to those with which the primitive root *nes-* is involved. In the line:

ásmenoi ek thanátoio, phílous olésantes hetaírous
Having returned from death, having lost our dear companions,

common men are lost (compare *olésantes* with *ólethros* in Parmenides), but the elite "return from death;" in other words, are immortal. Does the root *nes-* ("return from death") not erase the distinction between Being and Non-Being, and in so doing stand in opposition to "destruction"? The history of this root, it seems to me, should be taken into account in attempting to understand the thought of a philosopher who, by his possession of *nóos* and his awareness that Non-Being does not exist, considers himself to be elite, and who relegates the idea of "destruction" to the "tribes uncounted and uncritical."

In a profound sense, therefore, the "journey" of Parmenides is the same as that of Odysseus. I do not doubt that Parmenides himself was aware of the similarity, and that he was influenced by Homer's account. I only suggest that the parallels between Homer and Parmenides should be viewed in a larger context, which to a great extent (and this cannot be determined precisely) included both authors.

Index

Achilles: name of, 121–22
Aeolus, 63, 73*n*
Agamede, 88–89
Agent suffix -*tōr* in personal names, 82, 97–99, 111, 114
Alcinoos: name of, 79–80
aldrnari: Old Icelandic, 132*n*
Alternative question markers in Homer, 110*n*
Apollonia, 43–44
Arete: name of, 79*n*
ásmenos: Greek: original meaning of, 6–11; Homeric interpretation of, 15–18, 53–54; semantic development of, 24–27
—collocated with *ek thanátoio* in Homer: 9–11, 16, 17, 18–19, 23, 55, 64, 72–73, 102–03, 109–10
—collocated with forms of *pheúgein:* 16, 18–19, 26, 27–28
—collocated with forms of *horân:* 26–27
aspásios: Greek, 17–18, 64
astam: Indo-Iranian, 134, 136
Aśvínā: Vedic, 146–52 passim
Athena, x, 15, 76–78, 94
Atlas, 168
Augeias, 88–90

Bechtel, Friedrich: on meaning of Homeric *ásmenos,* 18–19
Benveniste, Émile: on meaning of IE root **nes-,* 23; on lack of a Greek form **peku,* 69*n*; on force of the agent suffix -*tōr,* 111*n*, 114
boulutónde: Greek, 56*n*–57*n*, 164–66
Bouprasion, 95

Calypso, 21, 73–74, 166–69
Cantieni, Räto: on Nestor's story in *Iliad 11,* 86*n*, 95
Castor: name of, 114. *See also* Dioscuri
Cattle: of Helios, 20, 38–47 passim, 50–51, 55–56, 57*n*, 63, 69, 87–90 passim, 164–66, 173; of Uṣas, 44*n*, 45, 149*n*; of the Paṇis, 45–46, 68–69; of Nestor, 87–90, 92; of Neleus, 90–92; of Virāṭa, 145–46; vs. horses in Indic

twin mythology, 145–46, 147–52; associated with name *Nāsatyā,* 147–52
Ciconians, 54–56
Cimmerians, 48–50, 62
Circe, 10*n*, 13*n*, 37–40 passim, 47–53, 62, 164
Companions of Odysseus: lost during return, 19–23, 39, 40–41, 55–56, 57, 63, 64, 173, 174; characterized as "foolish," "mindless," 20, 33, 39, 55–56, 73*n*, 173, 174
Cyclops, 14, 44*n*, 47, 57, 59, 63–73, 76, 155, 161

dasrá: Vedic, 147, 149–52
Diachronic: vs. synchronic, xi–xii
Dieva dēli: Latvian, 140
Dievo sunêliai: Lithuanian, 140
Dioscuri, 114, 140–42, 146, 147, 165–66, 170–71
divó nápātā: Vedic, 147, 150*n*
duhitā sūryasya: Vedic, 139–40
Durante, Marcello: on name *Nēleús,* 96–97; on names *Nēleús* and *Néstōr,* 97–98
Dyaus, 142, 146, 147, 149

Eliade, Mircea: on features of primitive sun worship, 21–23, 32, 41*n*, 50, 67*n*
Elpenor, 39
érebos: Greek, 21*n*
Euenius, 43–44, 46

Fränkel, Hermann: on the threshold of day and night in Hesiod, 62*n*
Frei, P.: on the etymology of Greek *nóos,* 4*n*, 33*n*

ganisan: Gothic, 7, 8, 23, 127, 128, 129
ganists: Gothic, 128, 136
Gates of day and night, 60, 61, 62, 92–93
genesen: German, 109*n*, 126, 127
Geryon, 46, 90*n*
Güntert, Hermann: on the etymology of Vedic *Nāsatyā,* 135–36

hairéō: Greek, in meaning "kill," 107–08

halískomai: Greek, in meaning "die," 103–09 passim

Havelock, Eric: on Parmenides and the *Odyssey,* 158*n*, 160*n*, 170–74

Helios: and companions of Odysseus, 20–23, 33, 38–39, 40–41; called *sōtḗr,* "savior," in Arcadia, 23*n*; characterized as seeing all, hearing all in Homer, 31; episode considered late in *Odyssey,* 37–38; episode analyzed, compared with non-Homeric traditions, 40–47; cults to, 43, 156–58. *See also* Cattle; Sheep; Sun mythology

Hermes, 51–53, 74, 153–55

Hermetic writers: on a divinized *Noûs,* 127*n*

Heubeck, Alfred: on the etymology of Greek *nóos,* 4; on the agent suffix *-tōr* in personal names, 98*n*; on a transitive force of the Greek root **nes-,* 112*n*

Horses: vs. cattle in Indic twin mythology, 145–52 passim

Húpnos: Greek, 39*n. See also* Sleep

hupobrúkhios: Greek, 165–66

Iphínoos: Greek, 2, 4, 79. See also *Wiphínoos*

Jokl, N.: on the etymology of Albanian *knétem,* 133

khráō: Greek, 112*n*

khráomai: Greek, 112*n*

knétem: Albanian, 132–33

Kretschmer, Paul: on the agent suffix *-tōr* in personal names, 98

Kuhn, Adalbert: on the etymology of Greek *Kúklōps,* 66–67, 68, 69

Laestrygonians, 17–18, 57–63

lanthánomai: Greek, 35, 36, 37, 51, 75

lḗthē: Greek, 36, 75

Lommel, Herman: on the etymology of Vedic *Nā́satyā,* 135

Lotus-eaters, 35–36, 37, 63

McKenzie, R.: on a comparison of Greek *nóos* with Sanskrit *nayaḥ,* 3; on

smooth-breathing of Greek *ásmenos,* 7*n*

Macurdy, Grace: on the agent suffix *-tōr* in Greek names, 98

Mahābhārata, 143–46

maraínesthai: Greek: active form of, 112*n*

Medea, 50, 89

médomai: Greek, 35

Melampus, 91–92

Mentor: name of, 114

mêtis: Greek, 71, 72, 73, 85, 124*n*

mimnḗskomai: Greek, 35, 51

Monro, D. B.: on the Homeric form *anései,* 101–02

Mühlestein, Hugo: on the etymology of Greek *nóos,* 4; on the name *Iphínoos,* 4; on the name *Alkínoos,* 79–80; on Pylian associations with Hades, 93; on the names *Nēleús* and *Néstōr,* 97–98; on a possible Mycenean name *Philonéstas,* 112*n*

Nagy, Gregory: on an active form of Greek *maraínesthai,* 112*n*; on the name of Achilles, 122*n*; on Old Persian *xšāyaθiya-,* 136; on IE twin gods, 140*n*, 143*n*

Nakula, 145–52 passim, 169

Nā́ŋhaiθya: Avestan, 134, 135*n*, 137, 152*n*, 169–70

násate: Sanskrit, 23–24, 134

Nasattiianna: Mitanni, 134

Nā́satyā: Vedic: 134–52 passim; etymology of, 135–37, 149; originally singular, 135*n*, 137, 140–52 passim

Nāsatyadasrau: Sanskrit, 149–52 passim

nasjan: Gothic, 7, 8, 30*n*, 127, 128, 129, 134

nayaḥ: Sanskrit, 3

Neaira: name of, 41–42

Nehelāwos: Mycenean, 82–83, 86, 96–99, 112

Neíleōs: Greek, 82–83, 96–97

Nēleús: Greek, 83, 96–97

nḗpios: Greek, 33, 56

Nestiánōr: Mycenean, 112*n*

néstis: Greek (hypothetical), 112*n*, 128*n*

nímsate: Sanskrit, 134*n*

nísomai: Greek, 134*n*

noéō: Greek: formation and semantics of, 29–31

Noeús: Mycenean, 2*n*

nöra: West Norse, 130–32, 133

ōgúgios: Greek, 168

Oûtis: Greek, 65, 71, 124*n*

Page, Denys: on Helios, Circe in the *Odyssey,* 37*n*; on Elpenor, 39*n*; on the Nekyia, 163–64

Palmer, L. R.: on the names *Nēleús* and *Néstōr,* 83, 86, 97–98; on the name of Achilles, 122*n*

Panis, 45–46, 68–69

Parmenides, 60, 62, 158–60, 170–74

Periclymenus, 93

Phaeacians, 74, 76, 78–80, 115

pháos: Greek, 24–27, 127*n*

pheúgein: Greek: collocated with *ásmenos,* 16, 18–19, 26, 27–28; collocated with *aspásios* in Homer, 17–18, 64; collocated with *thánaton* in Homer, 55, 64, 72, 73, 92, 102–03, 105, 106–07

Philonéstas: Mycenean, 112*n*

Plato, 160–62

polútropos: Greek, ix, xi

Polydeuces. *See* Dioscuri

Priam, 153–55

Prophecy: and the return of Odysseus, 11, 13, 14, 15, 39–40, 51, 163–64; in story of Euenius, 44; in story of Melampus, 92; and the return of Telemachus, 109

Pylos, 81, 92*n*, 166

Rhesus, 155

Rhodes, 157–58

Risch, Ernst: on the etymology of Greek *nóos,* 4

Rjrāśva, 44*n*

Ruijgh, C. J.: on the etymology of Greek *nóos,* 4*n*, 30*n*

Sahadeva, 143–52 passim, 169

Saulés dukterys: Lithuanian, 139

Saules meita: Latvian, 140

Schmitt, Rüdiger: on the etymology of Greek *Kúklōps,* 66*n*, 67–68

Schwyzer, Eduard: on the etymology of Greek *nóos,* 1*n*, 2

Secular contexts of the IE root **nes-,* 23, 112, 134

Sheep: of Helios, 42, 43–44, 46–47, 92; of the Laestrygonians, 59, 63; of the Cyclops, 63, 68–69

Sisyphus, 36–37, 118

Sleep: of Odysseus in Thrinacia, 38–39, 75; of Odysseus on return to Ithaca, 39*n*, 74–75; associated with Calypso's name, 73*n*, 168

Snell, Bruno: on the semantics of Greek *nóos, noéō,* 30, 31

snutrs: Gothic, 2

sōtér: Greek: epithet of Helios, 23*n*

—*sōtêres:* epithet of Dioscuri, 140, 165

Stanford, W. B.: on Homeric *Néaira,* 42*n*; on the Laestrygonians, 59

stugéō: Greek, 58

Styx, 58*n*, 74*n*, 166–69

Sumakha, 142, 146

Sun mythology: primitive ambivalence of, 21–23, 32, 39, 40–41, 47–48, 50–51, 67*n*, 93, 173, 174; and the etymology of *nóos,* 31–33; theme of blinding in, 44*n*; cave as a feature of, 45–46, 47, 57–58, 63, 65–66, 68–69, 70–72, 90, 92, 161–62; in the Ciconian episode, 56; in Odysseus's return to Ithaca, 78; in Nestor's story in *Iliad 11,* 87–90; and Gothic derivatives from IE **nes-,* 127, 128, 129; and *Beowulf,* 130; and Albanian *knefem,* 133; and the Vedic *Nåsatyå,* 138–40, 142–43; and Parmenides, 158–60, 170–74 passim; and Plato, 161. *See also* Cattle; Helios; Sheep

Süryå: Vedic, 139–40

Synchronic: vs. diachronic, xi–xii

Taenarum, 46–47, 92

Teiresias, 11, 39–40, 163–64

Tēlépulos: Greek, 60, 62

Thánatos: Greek, 39*n*, 105*n*

Theoclymenus, 109
Thieme, Paul: on the etymology of Greek
    Kúklōps, 68–69
Transitive force of the IE root **nes-*: in
    Greek, 4, 29*n*, 79, 82–83, 99–113
    passim, 137; in Indo-Iranian, 136–37
Tyndareus, 114, 141–42

Uṣas, 44*n*, 139, 142–43, 149*n*. *See also*
    Cattle

Virāṭa, 145–46

Wackernagel, Jacob: on the etymology of

Greek *ásmenos*, 7, 8, 9; on the Homeric
    dual *Aíante*, 137*n*
Ward, Donald: on Vedic twin gods, 139*n*,
    143*n*; on IE twin gods, 140*n*, 142*n*,
    143*n*, 144*n*; on features of universal
    twin mythology, 142*n*, 170
Wikander, Stig: on the Sanskrit epic twins
    Nakula and Sahadeva, 143–46; on the
    Vedic names *Nấsatyā* and *Aśvínā*,
    149–52, 169; on Avestan *Nẫŋhaiθya*,
    169
Wiphínoos: Mycenean, 2. See also
    Iphínoos

Zeus: Polydeuces the son of, 114, 141–42